TALK YOU TO DEATH

OTHER BOOKS BY DANNY DRAVEN

The Filmmaker's Book of the Dead: A Mortal's Guide to Making Horror Movies

Genre Filmmaking: A Visual Guide to Shots and Style

TALK YOU TO DEATH:

Filmmaking Advice From the Mavericks of the Horror Genre

DANNY DRAVEN

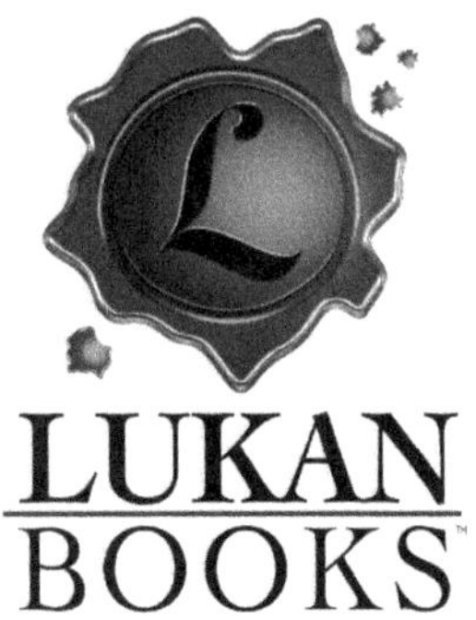

LUKAN BOOKS

LOS ANGELES / LAS VEGAS

ISBN-10: 0692869514
ISBN-13: 978-0692869512

ABOUT THE AUTHOR

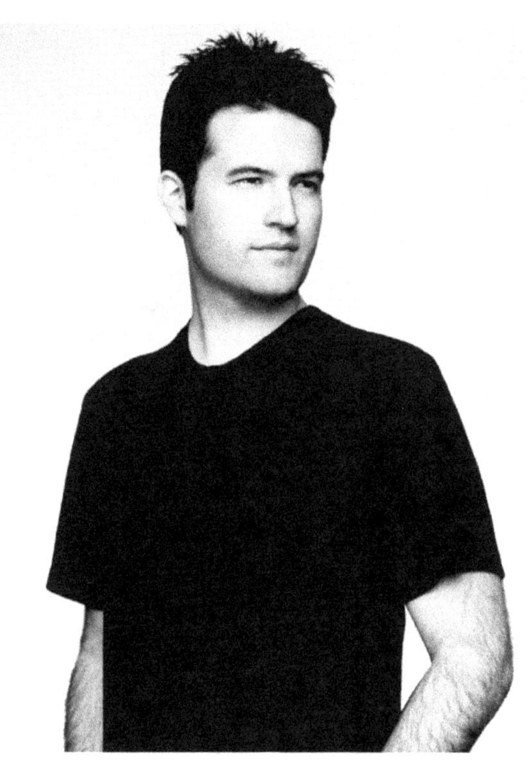
Danny Draven

Danny Draven is a award-winning writer, director and producer of genre films. After receiving his film degree from Emerson College, he moved to Hollywood and worked his way up through the ranks until he began producing and directing sci-fi/horror films for genre studio Full Moon Pictures (Puppet Master series, Trancers) where he cut his teeth before starting his own production company, Lukan Pictures. He has edited over 80 feature films, including films for Lionsgate, NBC Universal's Chiller TV and the SyFy Channel. He has worked with and been mentored by Hollywood veterans such as Master of Horror Stuart Gordon (Re-Animator) and legendary cinematographer Mac Ahlberg (Beverly Hills Cop 3, House), and executive producer Mark Ordesky (Lord of the Rings Trilogy). He is also the author of three published books on genre filmmaking, a member of the Producers Guild of America, a martial artist, and a dog aficionado. His most recent film PATIENT SEVEN stars genre icon Michael Ironside (Total Recall).

TWITTER: @DannyDraven
INSTAGRAM: @DannyDravenOfficial
FACEBOOK: https://www.facebook.com/DannyDravenOfficial/
WEBSITE: www.dannydraven.com

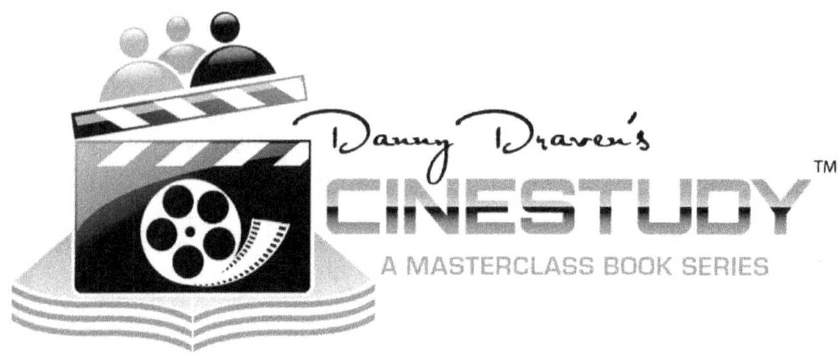
Danny Draven's
CINESTUDY™
A MASTERCLASS BOOK SERIES

FOR MARLENE (A.K.A. MOM)
WHO “TALKED ME TO DEATH” FOR YEARS,
BUT NOW I’M GLAD I LISTENED.

TABLE OF CONTENTS
(IN ALPHABETICAL ORDER)

ACKNOWLEDGMENTS & SPECIAL THANKS

Jordan von Netzer & Jana Davidoff of CW3PR
Cynthia Brown & Roger Corman of New Horizons Picture Corp.
Dark Delicacies in Burbank, California – Del and Sue Howison

CHRIS ALEXANDER

EDITOR / WRITER / FILMMAKER

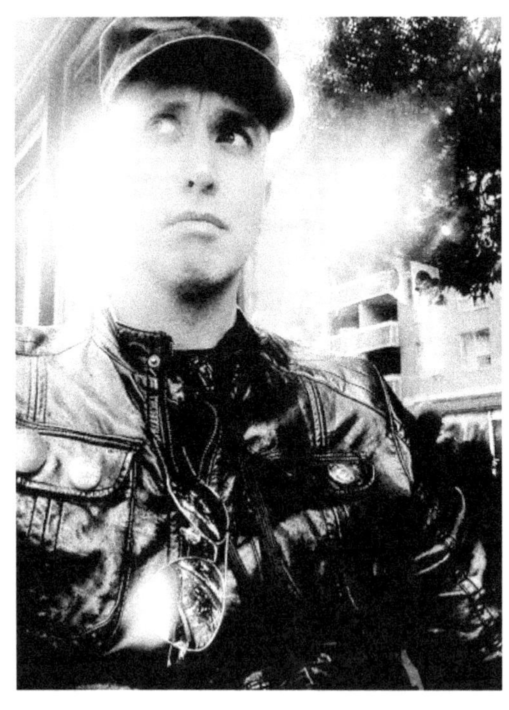

CHRIS ALEXANDER

Chris Alexander is a Canadian-based, internationally published writer, editor, composer and filmmaker. From 2009 – 2015 he served as the editor-in-chief of legendary horror film magazine FANGORIA and its sister periodical GOREZONE as well as the specialty line of FANGORIA Legends magazines. He is the editor and co-founder of Full Moon Entertainment's cult film magazine DELIRIUM, the editor of KISS: The Official Magazine (the licensed periodical for the iconic rock band KISS) and an editor at film news website www.ComingSoon.net. Prior to this, he was a critic and columnist for RUE MORGUE magazine and a writer and critic for The Toronto Star's METRO newspaper, which he still contributes to frequently. As a filmmaker he is the writer, director and composer of the award winning vampire film BLOOD FOR IRINA, its follow-up/sequels QUEEN OF BLOOD and BLOOD DYNASTY and the erotic surrealist drama FEMALE WEREWOLF.

What is the current state of the horror genre? Is horror dead, or in a revival phase and why?

Noooo…it's not dead! On the contrary, it's thriving. Look at the small screen. Television is bursting with endless horror content and it's gory, provocative stuff. It's like the golden age of Dan Curtis in the 1970's but a steroidal, explicit and sophisticated version. And as far as cinema goes, there is SO much great genre product being produced all over the world that is there if you seek it. And with the advent of technology, it's really not hard to find it. That said, because now anyone can produce and distribute their own films, a lot of tone deaf would-be artists are pumping out junk. But that's been happening for half a century. It's just a bit easier to do today!

No one on earth sees more independent horror films than staff at Fangoria. In your experience at the magazine, what are the biggest pitfalls you see when reviewing horror films, both ultra low budget and studio films? Is it production quality, script, character, gore or something else, and why?

I mentioned the phrase "tone deaf" above. I mean that. Filmmaking is music. As is writing. Acting. Painting. You need a sense of rhythm and music. It has to be in you or else you, as a filmmaker, are doomed to fail. I could care less how much anyone spends on a picture. If I don't feel the music , if that sensuality is just not there, then the film is a failure. But we're not mean. Plenty of wonderful, passionate people make terrible films and what we do at FANGORIA, is ignore the indie stuff we dislike and instead champion the stuff we love. Why kick the little guy? It's hard to make a film and I'm not in the business of deflating anyone's dreams…

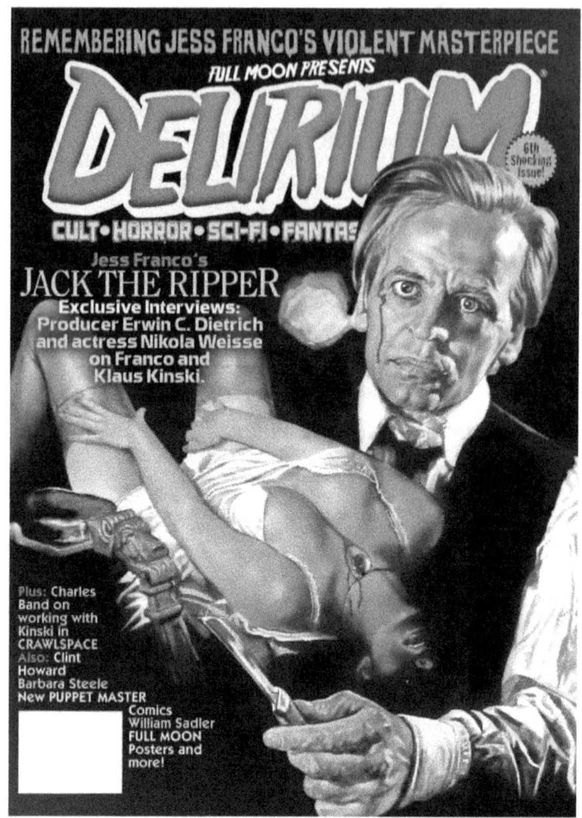

DELIRIUM MAGAZINE

It seems to me that a lot of independent horror films and distributors are using B to Z level actors with a "name" value, even if that person is only in the film for a few minutes. Do you think this recycling of actors approach helps a movie in terms of fan response and sales, or is hurting the genre, and why?

Good question and no, I don't. It's easy enough to see these indie guys for what they are, when the blast out every D level star they find and give them nothing to do. They just breeze through their local horror convention, pay the celeb a days guarantee and throw them in the flick. Awful. You need to DO something with them, to make their presence matter. Otherwise it's a transparent and ineffective move and half the time, having a "star" in your film is detrimental. Some of these guys bring massive baggage as they are often forever associated with other films.

As the former editor-in-chief of Fangoria Magazine and an author, filmmaker and horror scholar, what is it about the genre you love so much, and where do you think the future of horror will take us?

Listen, I have loved the bizarre, fantastic, gothic and creatively perverse since I was a child. I love things that are larger than life, earthy, bloody, exciting. I get off on feeling dread, of immersing myself in other worlds. I am obsessed with the human condition, of the mind, of the "big questions" and I believe no other entertainment can investigate these things better than a horror film does. I love all film, of course, but the horror film is my life. It really is. The future of horror is in altering perception of what a horror film can be. Of redefining genre. Of not regurgitating what has been done to death, but to push those tropes and concepts. We need fresh, innovative artists and visionaries to put their own stamps on the genre and trust that we, the audience will follow. Studios need to spend less money and give these new visionaries long leashes to experiment.

What is your favorite horror film and why does the film work for you?

George A. Romero's DAWN OF THE DEAD is my absolute favorite horror film because it's a great film, period. It's a brilliant action film, tragedy, drama, bloodbath, horrorshow and it is bristling with an indie spirit, with innovation and eccentricity. I watch it once a month. Argento's PHENOMENA is another obsession. One of the greatest weird movies ever made. Charles Laughton's NIGHT OF THE HUNTER is a film like no other. ANGEL HEART has stayed with me since I saw it as a child and really pushed the concept of music and sound design to affect the viewer on me. Ken Russell's THE DEVILS. BLACULA. Lars von Trier's ANTICHRIST is a film that has a towering power as does his kinky NYMPHOMANIAC. I love von Trier. Nicolas Refn's VALHALLA RISING and DRIVE and ONLY GOD FORGIVES are horror films to me. As is Jonathan Glazer's blistering UNDER THE SKIN. I live to watch Hammer Horror movies and Roger Corman Poe films. So many movies…

What are some things you see in indie horror films that beginners should watch out for when making their own films?

Don't make product. Make art. Fuck being commercial. When you're in the indie ghetto, starting out, it is the ONLY time you will be able to be free to be dangerous and make whatever the fuck you want. So make whatever the fuck you want. If you build it they might not come, but if they DO come…they'll likely stay.

Who do you think would win if Pinhead, Freddy, Jason and Pumpkinhead got into a street fight?

Pinhead is a ponce and would be a drag to hang with. Jason is a big dumbass. Freddy is a nickel and dime pervert. Pumpkinhead is like the honey badger, he doesn't give a fuck. He's programmed to fuck you up. He'd deep six 'em all.

CHARLES BAND

PRODUCER / DIRECTOR

FULL MOON FEATURES

www.fullmoonstreaming.com

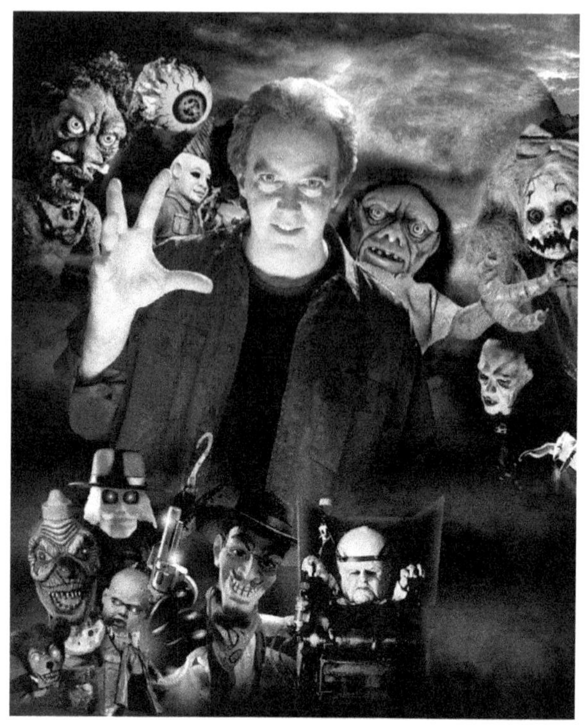

CHARLES BAND
Full Moon Features

Charles Band is a leading producer of home video movies, with nearly 300 films under his belt and over 30 years in the business.

Charles learned how "the fantasies were put together" on the movie sets of his father, veteran director Albert Band. He produced his first film, MANSION OF THE DOOMED at age 21. In 1977, Band paved the way for the colossal home video boom by founding Media Home Entertainment, one of the first independent video distributors. In the 1980s, he directed two 3-D features: METALSTORM (1983) and PARASITE (1982), which featured a young Demi Moore and special effects by future Oscar winner Stan Winston. His films—including the popular PUPPETMASTER, TRANCERS, and SUBSPECIES horror series—have been shown across the globe. In the decade since he founded Full Moon, Band's sci-fi/horror empire remains a mainstay in video stores and online across the United States.

Full Moon is now ready to explode with new franchise stories and characters like Kill-joy, The Gingerdead Man, Doll Graveyard, and Evil Bong . More crossovers are coming, and infinite ideas and adventures abound in his never-ending Full Moon Universe!

In 1977, you helped pave the way for the home video market by founding Media Home Entertainment, one of the first indie video distributors. Over the years, how has the business changed for you and the way you sell your movies?

Today we are in a transition period. DVDs will be somewhat of an antique someday, like the VHS format. We live in digital times, and the distribution outlets are becoming more digital download oriented, with things like video on demand [VOD] and pay per view [PPV]. The days of renting videos at stores and getting charged late fees are almost over, and with that, it's the artwork and title that will be the big ingredient for capturing people's attention.

In today's world, the title is becoming one of the most important elements for capturing your imagination. On most digital services today, your choice usually starts with the title first. There is no artwork attached unless you choose the title first, then you can choose the trailer, etc. On a movie selection list, all the choices will be by title, and there is a very long list, all in alphabetical order. With this scenario, you must have a unique and strong title to pop out. The closer it is to the letter A, the better, due to the attention span of someone zipping thru the menu.

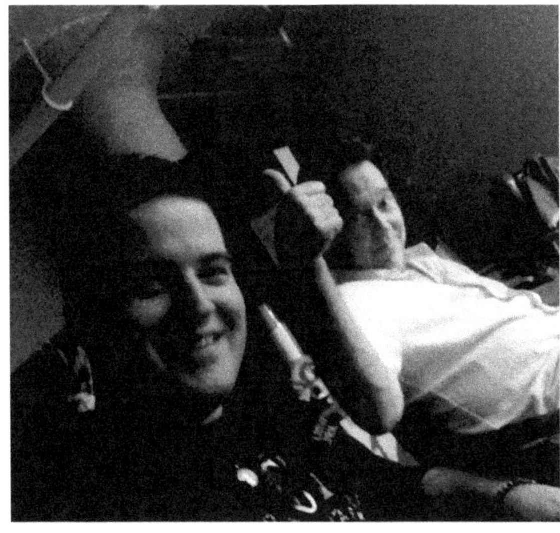

Danny Draven & Charles Band on set in 2013. Draven and Band have a long history of working together as a filmmaking team in various capacities.

In today's world, pay more attention to the title, artwork, marketing campaigns, and your first impressions. That is key.

As an indie producer, what is a day in your life like during a production?

The day changes shape and color every 60 minutes. You have to break it down and be responsible to your budget. Everything in every category has a tendency of going over. People are always asking for more gear or money, and every one item that is added is death by a thousand blows. You just keep agreeing to things because you want to do the right thing. The day becomes a roller-coaster ride. There are hours when you say, Oh my God, how are we going to get thru this; how are we going to finish this; or this was the stupidest idea ever!

As the producer, you have different mood swings. You must always be making sure people are doing a good job and dealing with all the little problems that come up daily. A good producer always keeps a calm demeanor because freaking out doesn't help anyone or solve the problem. You need to keep your director, actors, and crew happy at all times. On some days, I sit back and feel like Cecil B. DeMille and think everything is awesome. On other days, it's back to thinking about the money, marketing, release dates, and other issues. You're not just building a house—you're marketing the house, too. It's a whole crazy experience.

Full Moon has always had fantastic artwork. How important is the artwork and trailer when selling a film?

Things are way different these days than 10, 20, or 30 years ago. Today, you can't really presell a movie. You need to actually make it first and then come up with the most clever campaign that may only rely on a title.

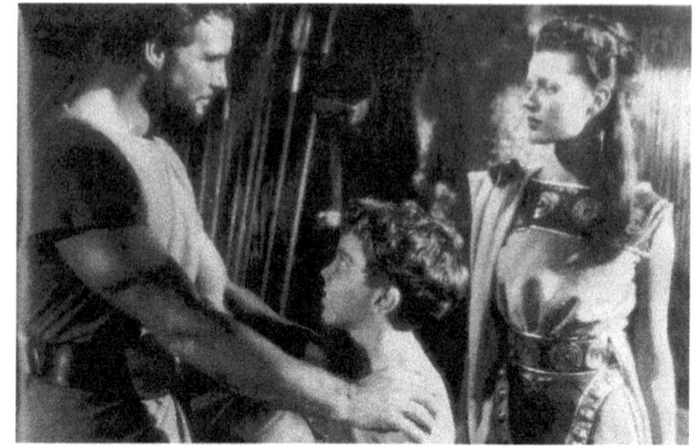

Hooked on the movies at an early age, a young Charles Band appears in a scene with Steve Reeves as an extra with Hercules in THE AVENGER (1962), a film directed by father Albert Band in Italy under the alias Alfredo Antonini.

Today is different than in the early 80s when the video market was exploding. In my career, especially in the 80s and 90s when we were making 18–20 movies per year, many of those films at that time were exploding because we had a lot of creditability, because our films were doing well commercially. I could presell a movie with nothing more than some art and a synopsis, which is a pretty heavy stretch to be able to do that. That doesn't exist anymore as far as I know.

The market conditions have changed. I think that in the digital market, with outlets like pay per view and video on demand, they will be so hot in a few years that a great title for a low-budget movie could be presold again.

From BLADE and PINHEAD to MARVIN and EVIL BONG, Full Moon consistently gives the fans strange and bizarre characters. What is your creative process for dreaming up such bizarre characters and catchy titles?

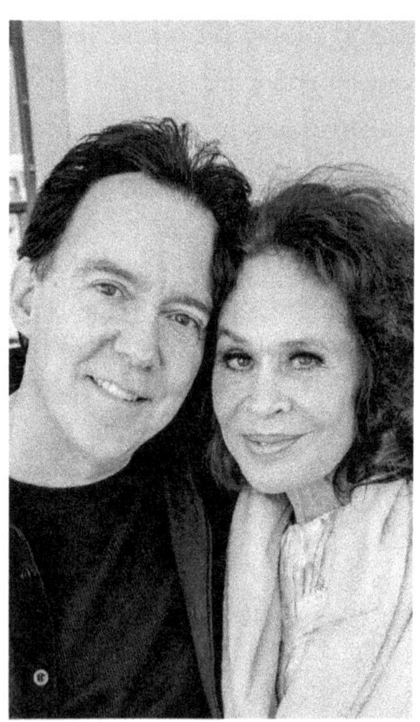

Charles Band & Karen Black on set.

When it comes to creativity, whether you are writing a song, novel, or coming up with ideas for a movie, it's difficult to give a recipe. For me, ideas come in all shapes and forms.

I have a lot of artwork and scrap material I've put together through the years. I surround myself with this material and get inspired from it. It usually starts with what sort of genre or subgenre I'm working in, whether it's a killer doll movie—which I'm known for—or something new. I have a material bank of thousands of titles and images that I've had for many years. Sometimes, I'll just go through that and see what comes out and makes sense. Many times I will play around with words. Simply say the right word at dinner and I will go, "Oh my God, that's a perfect movie title!" Then the title idea will spawn the movie concept and story.

A big film that has the luxury of a $150 million ad budget will certainly educate the public as to what the title means or what kind of film it is. But when you have no money and you're at a video store or scrolling down the menu on iTunes or Apple TV, the title has to be understandable so people get it. If you can tell a story without even a log line, you've got a killer title. "Evil Bong" does it. No one has to wonder what that movie is about. The greatest title of all is the shortest title and one that absolutely tells the story.

As someone who pioneered early 3-D films like PARASITE and METALSTORM, what are your thoughts on seeing it reemerging in today's world with films like MY BLOODY VALENTINE 3-D? Do you think this is the future of the genre?

From my experience, and having seen a lot of 3-D films and directed a few, it's a very different mindset. It's like a special effect that is there from start to finish, layered on to the story that you are trying to tell. Telling that story with your actors through a 3-D window is a gimmick. It depends on how it's used.

Would every horror movie benefit by being 3-D? I don't know. You have to think of the classic ones and wonder if they would have been better off done in 3-D, or if 3-D effects distract you from the storytelling. I like it for some films and look forward to doing some again in the future.

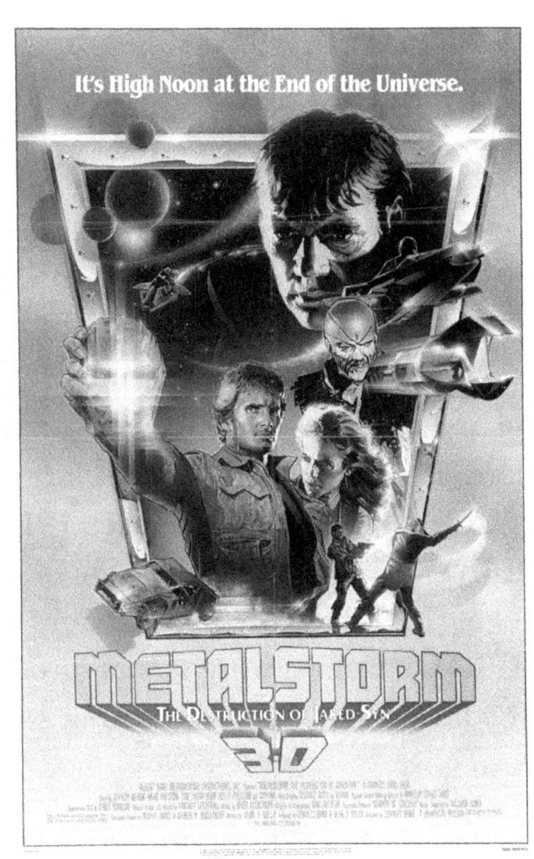

METALSTORM (1983).

The PUPPETMASTER franchise is the most successful straight-to-video horror series ever. From a producer's perspective, what is it about these films that made them successful and spawn so many sequels?

The first PUPPETMASTER film was shot in 1989 and released in 1990, and we were at the height of the exploding video market. At that time, a lot of money was spent at the video store to promote films.

With the first PUPPETMASTER films, we did our job well enough in the marketing campaigns to shape the way people perceived these movie before they were released. We would tease the video stores with media and run some ads. Some people would look at these ads and ask themselves, "Maybe I missed this movie when it was out in the theater." I think shaping their perception and thinking it was a theatrical release and something they might have missed was part of the success of PUPPETMASTER series.

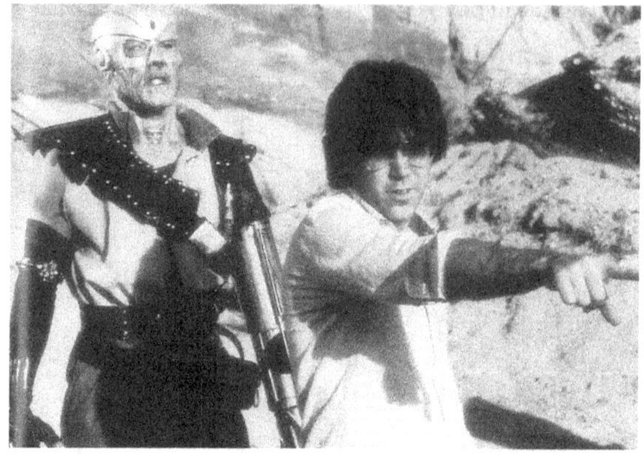

Like father, like son: twenty-one years later, Charles Band directs David Smith in 3-D as the half-man, half-machine Baal of METALSTORM (1983).

First and foremost, it's the title that says it all, and the cool-looking evil puppets coming out of the case, which was pretty unique. A whole case of puppets, a theatrical-looking ad, with a great title and a lot of marketing made it a huge success. Not the #1 or #2 of the year, but people fell in love with the characters. The originality of the piece made all the sequels do well.

In your career, you've started out actors like Helen Hunt (TRANCERS), Demi Moore (PARASITE), Mariska Hargitay (GHOULIES), Julia Louis-Dreyfus (TROLL) and Viggo Mortensen (PRISON) to writers like David S. Goyer (DEMONIC TOYS) to directors like John Carl Buechler (TROLL), Scott Spiegel (INTRUDER), Stuart Gordon (RE-ANIMATOR) and Renny Harlin (PRISON). For aspiring actors, producers, and directors who want to break in to the film business, do you think starting out making a horror film is the right way to go?

There are so many misconceptions of what people say that are actually opposite of the truth. You think, "I'm going to start my career and make a low budget horror movie." Or a director, who has no feature film experience but has done some documentaries and works in theater, says, "The only way I can get going is make a low-budget movie."

The trouble is, ironically, the people that are best suited to make a low-budget movie are the more experienced. The perfect director for doing this is the guy who's made 50 of them. He has tons of experience and knows how to get in there in 4–6 days and get the job done. That is the best director for a low-budget movie, not the beginners with all the good intentions in the world who has no experience and makes all the mistakes that everyone makes. Then again, how else can you begin? I would say, you should start on an inexpensive product and make those mistakes either on your dime or someone else's.

Then there are those first-time directors like Stuart Gordon, who directed RE- ANIMATOR (1985)

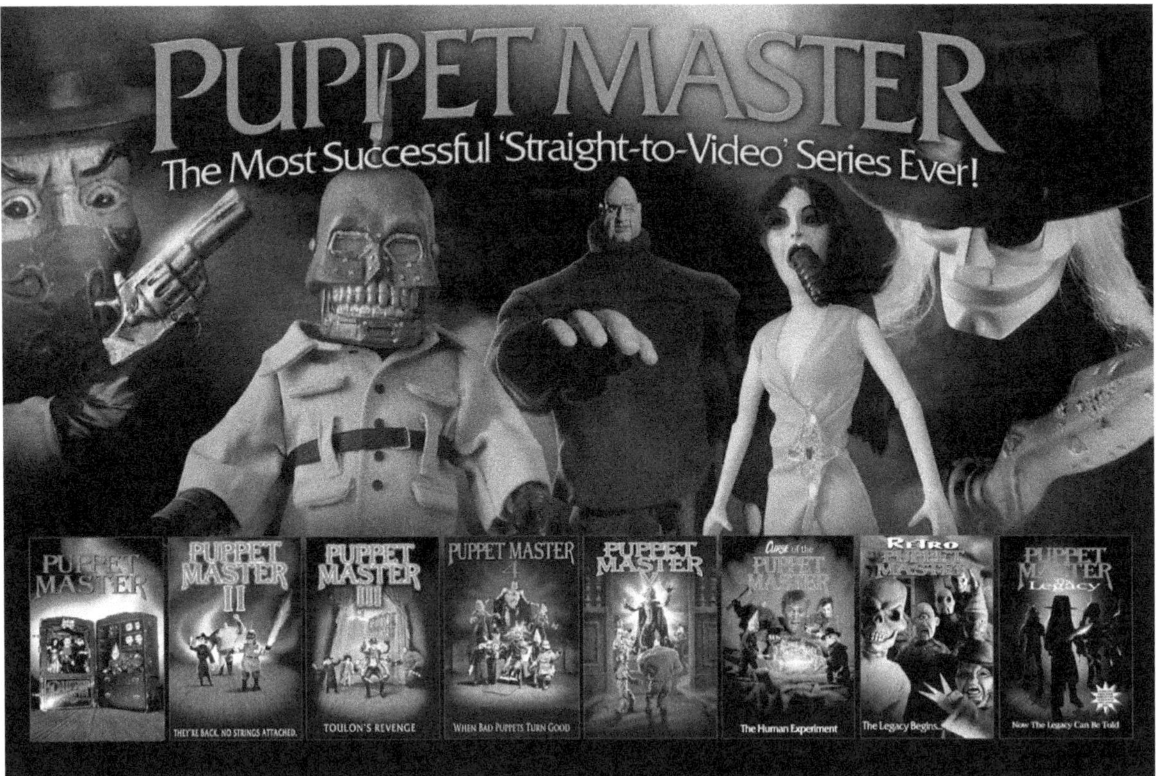

The Puppet Master Franchise!

for me at Empire Pictures, who did an amazing job. He had my help, my father's, and a lot of others' who were pros. He is a very confident guy. Then you'd ask, what did he have that other people didn't have that made Stuart so good? Well, he had 20 years of experience in the theater and knew how to direct and tell a story.

Today, some people are too caught up in the technical side, but in my opinion it is almost meaningless. Of the thousands of people who can shoot a show well, edit well, and are good craftsmen, few know how to really tell a story with a camera and direct actors. Once you have that down, the rest is, well, you know...

I am much more interested in a movie that is shot straight up and a story that has wonderful acting because that's what you care about. No one walks away and says, "That acting really sucked, but what great camera work!"

Is horror dead?

I think the horror genre will never be dead; it's completely evergreen. Some people think that every one of these movies has been so beat up. Every other month there is another horror film being released at the box office. Hundreds are made and dozens are released every week. Just when you think it's over, you have the remake of FRIDAY THE 13TH (2009) come out grossing 30 million in one weekend, the biggest gross in theatrical history of any horror film. So, there is an appetite there for the right thing. Yes, it is oversaturated. So you have to judge that. People love horror films; they love a good roller-coaster ride. I think nothing can drive that home like successful theatrical horror films that have done really well.

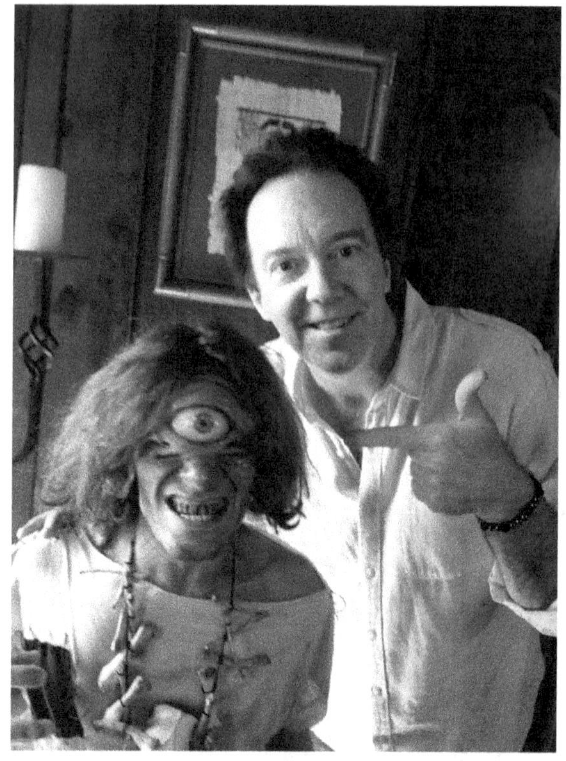

Charles Band and Cyclops on the set of UNLUCKY CHARMS (2013)

Horror is evergreen. It's true that no matter what, people love horror films. If you have material that you are really close to, a story you want to tell, and you have a real affinity or passion for, than that's the movie to make—horror or not.

LISTEN TO THIS FULL UN-EDITED AUDIO INTERVIEW ON MY YOUTUBE CHANNEL FREE AT:

https://www.youtube.com/c/DannyDraven

REGGIE BANNISTER

ACTOR, MUSICIAN, PRODUCER

www.ReggieBannister.com

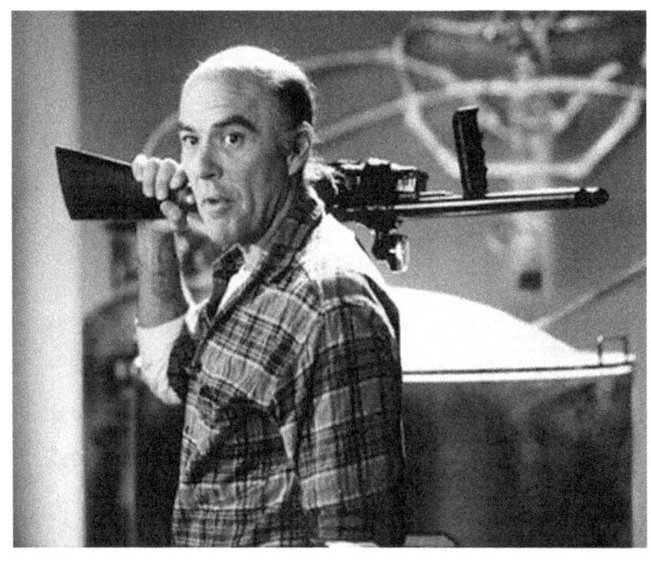
REGGIE BANNISTER in PHANTASM 2 (1988)

REGGIE BANNISTER's film career began in the early 1970's through a chance meeting with Don Coscarelli, who asked Bannister to play a character in his first feature film, JIM THE WORLD'S GREATEST. A lasting friendship and working relationship was born, and Bannister went on to perform in 9 of the 12 productions Coscarelli has directed as of this writing. Bannister has appeared in more than 40 feature films, performed musically on television and film, has two solo albums, and owns and operates a production company with his wife, Gigi Fast Elk, in Southern California. His new film is PHANTASM: RAVAGER (2016).

What is it that actors really want from their director?

I believe that every actor should want to know that they are moving in the right direction with their character. One begins to develop their character from the very first time they read the very first dialog line their character speaks in the script. As the character grows, the actor needs to have creative conversations with the director to make sure that they share the same vision. Once in production, the actor simply needs the director's guidance through creative collaboration.

The original PHANTASM (1979) is one of the great low-budget horror films and was directed by a young Don Coscarelli. It's horror film lore that Don Coscarelli rented all the film equipment on Fridays, shot all weekend, and returned it Monday and only paid a 1-day rental rate for the entire shoot. During the production, in what other ways did the production cut costs?

Well for one thing, they didn't pay the actors! Just kidding...sort of. They did "defer" actors' pay, and perhaps pay for a few others (though I do not recommend actors—or anyone else—agreeing to that since many times the deferment never comes). I must say, however, that some of the same solutions to cutting costs then are certainly true today—only on steroids. For example, Coscarelli didn't have a hard and fast shooting schedule, he took his time and shot as budget and actor availability would permit. I think that allowed him the opportunity to show his footage around to potential investors and grow his budget. Remember that he had two fairly successful films under his belt by 1976; both JIM THE WORLD'S GREATEST and KENNY & COMPANY had enjoyed theatrical releases. The biggest budget drawback for us, in those days, was that we had no option but to shoot on 35mm film. It's incredibly expensive between the cost of the film stock and then getting it processed. Today, we have all these wonderful HD cameras and software to give our footage that 35mm look, a film noir look, or even a comic book look. We can have it pretty much any way we want it now and it's cheap.

In PHANTASM (1979), what low-budget tricks did they use for the silver ball FX?

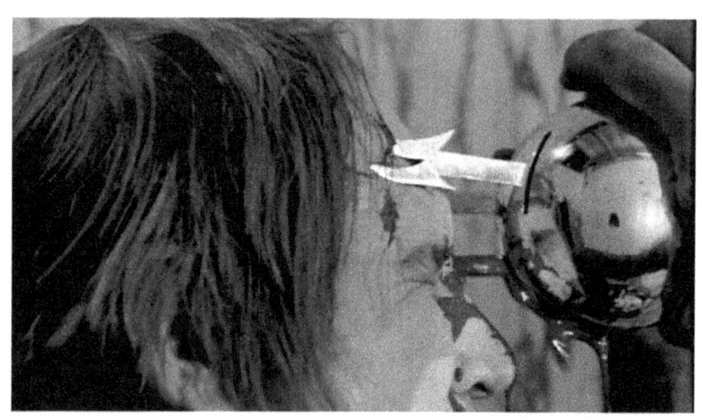

The Silver Ball.

All the organic (in camera) tricks or sphere FX gags we used in the first picture we were still employing in the fourth picture with more finesse. As we moved from one film to the next, amazingly creative organic gags were used to make the spheres fly, wobble crazily, rotate, and kill. For example, to make the sphere fly into camera and hover menacingly in an actor's face we simply attached a sphere to a fishing pole with black line. The puppeteer works from a ladder off camera and swings the sphere into frame and stops in front of the actor's face.

Another simple gag to emulate the sphere flying at an actor from the actor's POV is to take a silver painted rubber ball and throw it down a mausoleum hall or other location while standing next to the camera. If it's a 35mm camera the DP overcranks the speed at which the film goes through the camera, then the shot is processed in reverse so that the ball looks as if it's screaming down on the actor at lightning speed. If you were to use an HD camera it's simply a matter of setting your frame speed higher and reversing the shot in editing. This reverse shot effect can be used for stabbing gags, beating gags as with a bat or some other instrument of death or any number of on-camera killings.

When you are discussing a new character with a director, what questions do you usually ask and why are they important to you?

A character must be three-dimensional to be believable, so the actor must build the framework on which the character will exist. The actor needs to know why the character is behaving the way they are written in the script, so unless there are flashbacks of the character written in the script one must start from scratch to create a past that explains the behavior of the present. I always insist on reading the entire script, so I won't have a conversation with the director about my character until I have a pretty good idea of who I am and what my character means to the story. At that point, I will pitch the character to my director as I see it and ask if we're in agreement as to the direction I'm taking. I will ask questions regarding the foundation of my belief about why this character behaves and reacts the way they do. If we agree I begin detailing the character and the end result is what goes on the screen.

A warning to actors and actresses: The only time I didn't follow the protocol above I got blindsided on the first day of shooting by a director who had an absolutely different vision of my character than I presented...not good! I really had to scramble to give him what he wanted on the spot.

From an actor's perspective, what are the pros and cons of making low-budget horror films?

When you think about low-budget projects, you have to be aware that perhaps the cast, crew, producers, and the director may not have much experience at making a film—regardless of the remarkable talent they may possess. The negatives for an actor might be producers who don't understand the need to hire a professional stunt coordinator, in which case that actor could be injured performing a stunt. They might, for example, hire a makeup artist who has no experience with special effects makeup and actually use a product on the actor's face that causes a chemical burn. (This actually happened on a film I worked on.) An actor should resolve these kinds of issues with the producer/director before agreeing to participate in the project.

The actor must keep in mind that little money brings little or no amenities, such as no actors' trailers, low-budget dinner breaks (read pizza for every meal) or no dinner break at all. They may have to provide their own wardrobe and even find themselves outside shooting scenes in the middle of a blizzard...brrr!

The upside of indie film is the incredibly free and creative atmosphere of the film experience. There is a feeling of ownership shared by everyone on the project that's hard to beat and, might I add, that shooting in the middle of a blizzard adds a production value that would otherwise cost a large part of the budget.

What do you think are the three most important elements for a low-budget horror film to have to be sellable in the horror market?

First is the story. It has to be something that grabs you at the most primal essence of your human being.

Second is well-written characters acted in a three-dimensional fashion on the screen. The actor has to make the audience value them whether they like them or hate them or no one will care if the character's life is in jeopardy or they are killed.

Third is production quality. It's difficult to sit through a picture—any picture—that is poorly shot, lit, or has a terrible soundtrack and Foley. No film will get picked up for theatrical distribution without decent production quality. I'm firmly convinced that at least 15 percent of a filmmaker's budget should be dedicated to postproduction.

For a low-budget producer, what are the advantages and disadvantages of using SAG (Screen Actors Guild) actors for their film?

SAG actors are professionals. This means they will deliver the performance you need to make your picture honest. There can be no drawback in hiring SAG actors.

With the new SAG low and ultralow budget agreements, a low-budget producer has the flexibility to hire SAG actors of various experience to fit their budget. They are constrained to pay the actors a certain minimum amount per day; however, that doesn't prevent them from making separate deals with actors whose names will help get distribution for the picture after postproduction.

Also, a growing number of SAG members have made the decision to take Financial Core with the union. Financial Core status allows a SAG actor to work union and nonunion films, which has greatly broadened the ability of the low-budget horror film industry to hire experienced name actors for their projects.

NATHAN BARR

COMPOSER

www.NathanBarr.com

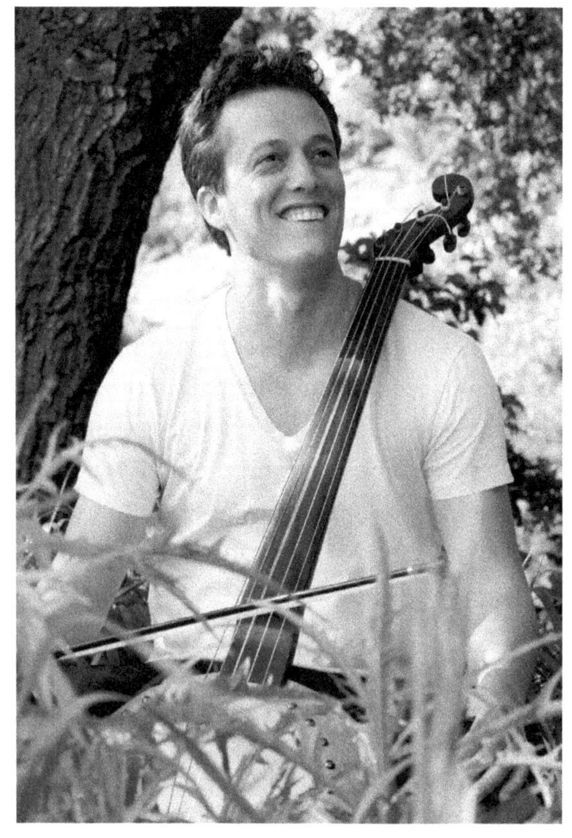

NATHAN BARR

Nathan Barr is a unique breed of composer. In addition to writing scores, he also performs all of the instruments in many of his compositions. Skilled in many styles and genres ranging from orchestral to rock, Barr is known for his collection and inclusion of rare and unusual instruments from around the world, such as human bone trumpets from Tibet, dismantled pianos, a rare glass armonica, and gourd cellos, among many others.

Barr began studying music in Tokyo, Japan at the age of four. He grew up surrounded by eclectic music ranging from Kabuki theater to the sounds of his mother performing on the koto and piano and his father playing the banjo, guitar, and shakuhachi. His interest in the art form was further influenced by extensive travels around the world, where he experienced music ranging from Bali's Kecak Orchestras to China's Beijing Opera. Barr went on to study at Skidmore College, and during the summer of 1993 he toured Italy and Switzerland with the Juilliard Cello Ensemble.

In 1996, Barr moved to Los Angeles to pursue a career composing for film. Shortly thereafter, he joined Media Ventures (now Remote Control Productions) and worked as assistant to world-renowned composer Hans Zimmer on films such as AS GOOD AS IT GETS (1997) and THE PRINCE OF EGYPT (1998). After just 8 months, Barr landed an agent and his first feature film (Lions Gate's romantic comedy TOO SMOOTH) and set out on his own.

Since then, Barr has scored more than 24 feature films, including Warner Bros.'s theatrical remake of the southern comedy series THE DUKES OF HAZZARD, the unconventional Broken Lizard comedies BEERFEST and CLUB DREAD, New Regency's hit supernatural thriller SHUTTER, Lions Gate's horrifying thriller HOSTEL and HOSTEL PART II directed by Eli Roth, and Universal Pictures's critically acclaimed documentary BEYOND THE MAT, among many others. Barr's most ambitious solo project to date has been scoring and performing all episodes of Alan

Ball's award-winning HBO series True Blood. Barr is currently scoring the second season of True Blood and Strike Entertainment's film COTTON, produced by Eli Roth and Eric Newman.

What is your creative process in arriving at the concept for a horror film score?

I'm not sure my creative process for a horror film is any different from my creative process in other genres. Generally speaking, my process first starts with digesting the film, figuring out who the characters are, what the ultimate point of the story is, where it's strengths and weaknesses lie, and what ultimately the vision of the director is for the film and its musical score. Once these elements have been established, then I sit down in my studio and begin plucking instruments off the wall, improvising to picture, and gradually (sometimes painfully) piecing together a palate of sounds and themes that seem to fit comfortably into the world of that particular film. Once the director reviews my work and we agree I am on the right track, then it becomes largely a technical exercise of placing themes in their appropriate scenes, creating tension or romance or drama wherever required, and hoping for those bits of inspiration or happy accidents that take the score from average to spectacular.

In the horror genre, what are the biggest mistakes you see in film scores in both low-budget and major studio films?

The first problem I see with the horror genre in general is a lack of imagination on the part of many of the writers and directors working in the genre. The film industry seems to be inundated with the same old stories, the same old techniques, with only sporadic moments of inspiration which push the genre a bit further and into new and exciting places. Having said that, I love the genre enough to continue to go and see most horror films that are theatrically released, so maybe I'm a part of the problem since I'm still paying my 10 bucks for the same old song and dance!

Musically the problem is very much the same. It's very hard for composers to think outside the box and really go for something totally original and unique when the film doesn't achieve that end. This means that oftentimes the score is as dreary and boring and predictable as the film it accompanies. Composers tend to (and don't get me wrong—I consider myself a guilty party at times!) lean on drones and the same old orchestral effects that have been used for half a century now.

There is often way too much music, and this is more often than not because the film needs the help. The really good horror films don't need to overscore because they are well directed, acted, edited, etc.

What is the best way for a director to communicate with the composer musically?

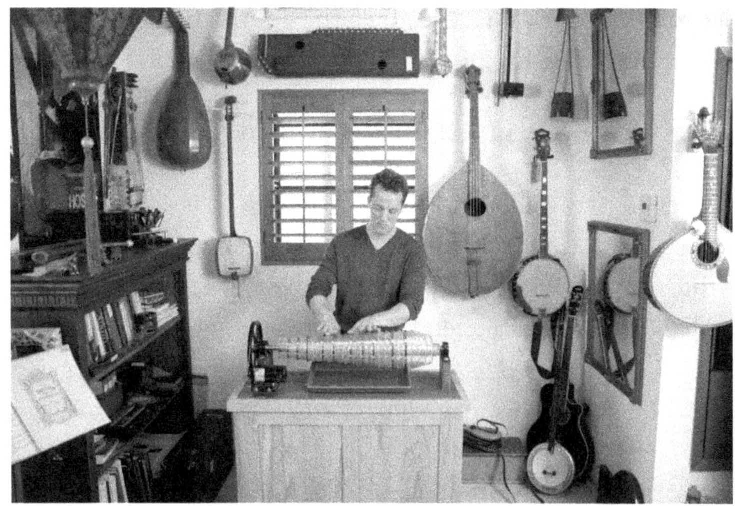

Barr playing the glass armonica in his studio.

Great question. Music can be such a difficult thing to discuss using words. Imagine a director with little or no musical experience trying to speak about music! I find that the most successful communication I have with directors is working with those who are willing to admit that they do not know how to speak about music. We can talk in a general sense about what it is we hope to accomplish with the music in the film. Perhaps the director dislikes certain instruments or a particular composer's body of work, and this sort of information is very helpful to know at the outset. One director I worked with said "I don't like that flute part," but there was no flute part in the cue! Instead of making him feel like an idiot and telling him there was no flute part, I asked him to tell me what about the flute part he didn't like, and as he began to talk about what wasn't working for him, I was able to narrow down the real issue, which was that the cue reminded him of something else which he wasn't a fan of which did have a prominent flute part. I made some minor adjustments, he stopped hearing "the flute," and we were back on track.

In horror films, how do you determine a cue's dramatic function (e.g., fear, dread, suspense) and then execute your idea musically? Also, how do you know what to leave silent?

A cue's dramatic function is very much determined by the director's intention in the way he shoots and directs any given scene. Sometimes the director is inexperienced or perhaps short on talent, and the intentions become muddled or confusing. At this point, I speak with the director and get them to explain to me what they are hoping for in the scene, and this gives me some guidance as to what direction to take. Once the direction has been determined, then I sit down and dig into my tool chest and begin to put together the music for the scene.

One of my greatest fears is overusing the tools in my toolbox or writing the same score over and over again—a problem that plagues some of the greatest composers in our business. So oftentimes I spend the first couple days or weeks coming up with stuff that works great but might sound too similar to other work I have done, or be a little too generic, and then I throw all that out and look for something more exciting.

Do you write on paper, or do you use software packages?

I use Logic to write all my film scores. These days since directors expect to hear mock-ups that are very close to what the ultimate sound of the score will be once recorded, it is overkill to write everything out in pencil and paper and then go to the synths and mock everything up. I know of only a handful of older generation composers who still work with pencil and paper, and honestly I can't think of a single one of my peers today who works outside of some sort of sequencing program. The programs make life so much easier... particularly with our nasty deadlines!

In terms of style and technology, has the music for horror films evolved since you first started? If so, how and why?

In terms of style I don't believe I have heard any real change in the music for horror films since I started in the business about 10 years ago. There have been a handful of really solid horror films made, but as they haven't necessarily initiated great change in the genre, so the music hasn't really either. In the past 30 years, a director like Dario Argento has really experimented with the genre and its music and pushed the limits of what is possible in horror. Using the bluesy, bell-infused music of Goblin in films like DEEP RED (1975) and SUSPERIA (1977) is super innovative and interesting. He really went for something totally different, and instead of high, eerie string parts as someone creeps down a hallway or approaches a house, he has a bluesy rock riff accompanying the scene.

In the low-budget horror films these days, there seems to be an epidemic of filmmakers using library music and recycling the same tired cues over and over again. I believe every film is unique and therefore the music should be original. What are your thoughts on filmmakers who try to save money by bypassing the composer and looking to libraries for their score?

It's regrettable to see directors and producers recycling library cues in their original films. It's almost always about budget, so to some extent it's understandable, but still very regrettable. There are some exceptions though. Stanley Kubrick used previously recorded classical music to great effect in most if not all of his films. The famously terrifying score to THE SHINING (1980) is almost entirely assembled from previously existing modern classical music, and man does it work!

What do you think are the three most important musical elements for a score to have in the horror genre?

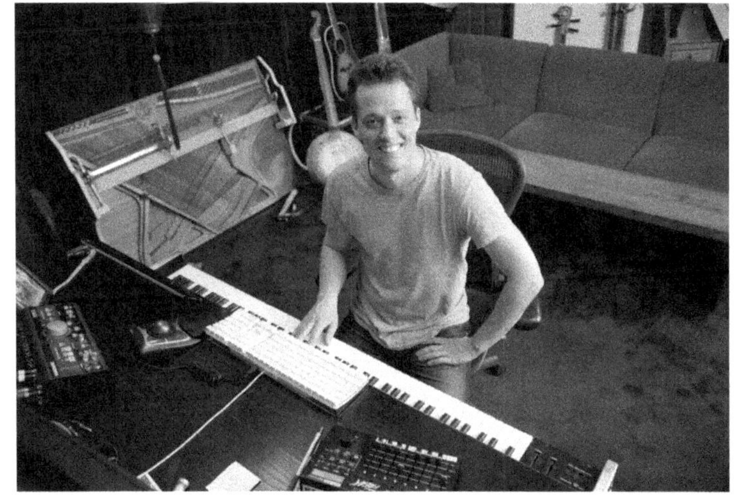

Barr in his studio.

From a story standpoint, horror movies are successful largely based on how well they create and release tension. How many times have we seen the knife-wielding teenager creeping down a hallway, tension building with every step they take, only to have one of their friends (or the killer) jump out from behind the refrigerator, releasing all the tension, giving the audience a false sense of security before the next big scare. So musically I would have to say the first important element is the score's ability to use tension and release in an effective way. Secondly, I think the score needs to establish the overall mood of the film through melody and texture. This instantly sets the tone for the journey the audience will be taking—we know it's going to be a scary or bizarre journey because we've paid our 10 bucks for a horror film, but what kind of scary journey? The very opening notes of the score should establish that. And thirdly, theme is generally very important, though there are exceptions, THE SHINING being one. I think having some sort of motif or melody or even texture that attaches to the audience's psyche when they leave the theater will help with the success of the film in its ability to really scare people. John Carpenter's theme in HALLOWEEN (1978) left the theater with every person that saw it and has since become a part of most everyone's sense of what horror film music is! PSYCHO (1960) would be another example. It is perhaps these two musical scores that people would hum before any others in the genre, and I think that shows how important theme can be.

In the horror genre, what are your favorite scores, and why?

One of my very favorite horror scores is Wojciech Kilar's score to Francis Ford Coppola's DRACULA (1992) film. It's traditional orchestral in style, but the melodies and textures are first rate, thoroughly adding to the film's intensity, romanticism, and style. I do love Goblin's scores to DEEP RED and SUSPIRIA because the style of music was so unexpected at the time for the genre and they create such great mood for those films. And then of course I love John Carpenter's theme for HALLOWEEN, Bernard Herrmann's staccato strings in PSYCHO, Krzysztof Komeda's bizarre and beautiful score to ROSEMARY'S BABY (1968)—to name just a few.

ANDREA BEESLEY-BROWN

FESTIVAL DIRECTOR

INTERNATIONAL HORROR & SCI-FI FILM FESTIVAL

www.horrorscifi.com

Founded in 2004 by Brian Pulido and the Phoenix Film Foundation, the International Horror & Sci-Fi Film Festival is Arizona's premier genre film festival highlighting new and classic horror and sci-fi films from around the globe. Produced mostly by volunteer staff, it runs in October annually and awards filmmakers who excel in the genres of horror and sci-fi as well as celebrating cult classics and new releases.

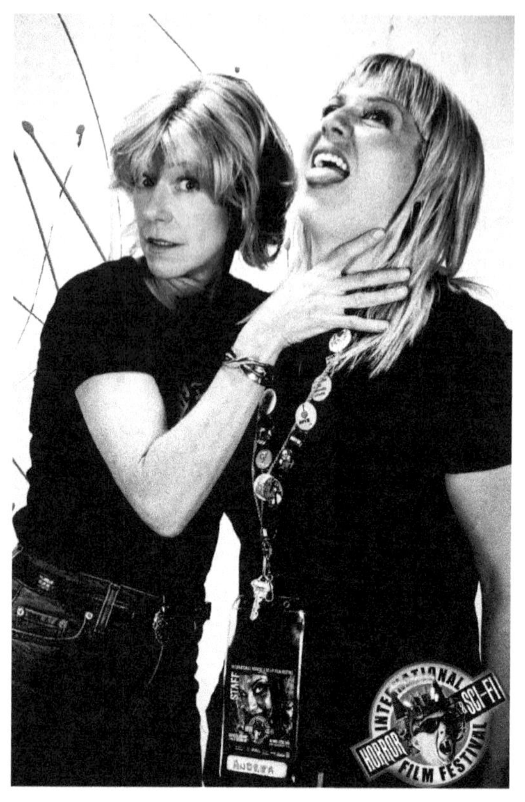

Actress Adrienne King (FRIDAYTHE 13TH) and festival director Andrea Beesley-Brown. Photo Credit: Bradley Thornber (2008)

What are the common mistakes you see filmmakers make when submitting to a film festival?

Presentation. It's not necessarily the thing that we take into consideration the most, but we do like to look at the whole package of the film, the press kit, how thorough the submission is and its overall presentation.

Once accepted to the festival, what should all filmmakers have ready and why?

Filmmakers should have their media materials ready. For our festival we are able to promote the films heavily in advance through print media (posters, postcards) on display at the venue and also should have a trailer available to upload online to our web site and begin the online promotion engine.

What does the festival look for in a horror film in order to be accepted to the festival?

Originality and ingenuity in the script. We look for innovative storytelling and a strong horror narrative. Films that will thrill, scare, and haunt the viewer in a way that they haven't seen before.

Can you give us a glimpse of how the judging process works, and what criteria may be used to determine the winners?

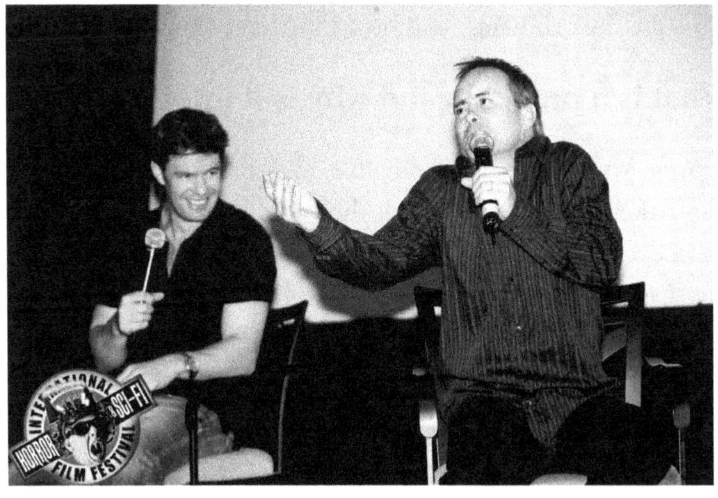

Film critic Craig Outhier and actor Jeffrey Combs (RE-ANIMATOR) doing a Q&A. Photo Credit: Bradley Thornber (2008).

Each film is reviewed in full twice by members of our viewing committee. After that, the top films are forwarded to the program directors of each genre to consider and make the final choices. Every film submitted is watched at least twice, and many others are viewed three or four times.

Do film acquisitions executives lurk in the audiences at your festival, or is it mainly horror and sci-fi fans?

With our festival, I would say a strong majority of the audience are horror and sci-fi fans; however, on occasions we will have acquisition executives from various distribution companies, not lurk but openly network with filmmakers.

Do the winners of awards from festivals like yours, who then display "Best Picture" or "Best Actor" on the box art usually help the film in terms of sales or finding distribution?

We hope so! As our festival grows and gains notoriety each year, our hope is that award winners can use their accolades to further their film's sales and distribution chances.

There seems to be a never-ending list of genre film festivals emerging every year. A low-budget filmmaker can spend thousands in expensive submission fess and press kits just trying to get accepted. What criteria can filmmakers use to judge the quality of a film festival and make sure it's not a backyard operation?

I would suggest filmmakers do their research on the founders and organizers of the event. Do they have legitimate and ample experience? What guests have they worked with (as far as talent)? Communicate with previous filmmakers who have attended and get their feedback. What studio films are they showing, and how long have they been in operation?

What is a press kit, and why is it important for a film festival?

A press kit is a visual and tangible advertisement of the film, and it is very important. Since the filmmaker isn't able to submit their film in person, they need to make an impact on the judge immediately. With snappy graphics, a solid letter, trailer DVD and professional photos, a press kit can instantly grasp the attention of a judge who has hundreds of submissions to review.

What is your advice for a filmmaker who wants to network at the festival?

Bring business cards and a smile! Take all the opportunities that you can to mix and mingle at parties, Q&A sessions, with fans and festival organizers. What better way to promote your product than to be an active part of the festival?

Does a film with a star or a higher production budget get priority over micro-budget productions?

We program the best films, period. We want to provide our audiences with the best quality out there disregarding the filmmaker's budget. Many times, the big-budget movies will get blown away by a small film with a great story. Therefore, lower budget films with more powerful acting and narrative will often prevail.

JAMIE BERNADETTE

ACTRESS / PRODUCER / WRITER

jamiebernadette.com

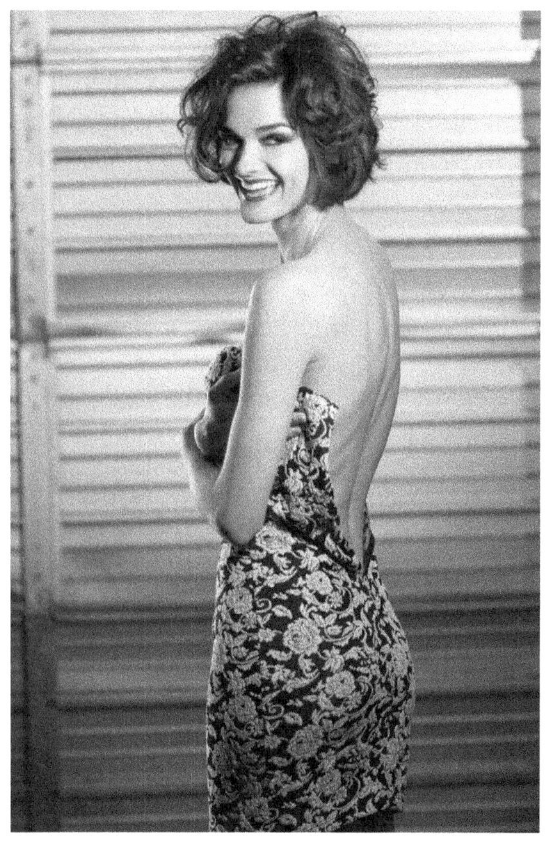

JAMIE BERNADETTE
Photo By Gabriel Parra Photography

Jamie Bernadette grew up in Kankakee, Illinois, a small town 70 miles south of Chicago. She was born the youngest of nine children. Jamie has four sisters and four brothers. At four months of age, Jamie's father passed away, leaving her mother to single-handedly raise nine children—the oldest child only thirteen years old. Jamie attributes her and her siblings' strengths—very responsible, industrious and self-sufficient—to this hardship.

Jamie began as a theatre actress before she ventured out to Los Angeles. Since moving to LA, Jamie has since acted in thirty-five feature films, twelve short films, seven television shows, five internet web series, five commercials, and performed as the lead in two music videos. Jamie's early credits include features by cult classic director Ulli Lommel, including "Absolute Evil" starring David Carradine. Jamie gained notoriety and a large fanbase from her role as "Alex" in the globally-released teen comedy "Milf", which is often compared to the popular "American Pie".

Jamie's recent works include "I Spit on Your Grave: Deja Vu", the sequel to the original horror cult classic film "I Spit on Your Grave", in which Jamie plays the lead as "Christy Hills", the daughter of "Jennifer Hills", played by Camille Keaton who was the star in the original film. The film is expected to release in late 2016. Also coming out in 2016, is "The 6th Friend", a feature-length horror film that Jamie wrote and produced. Jamie stars alongside Dominique Swain (Lolita, Alpha Dog). We should also see "Smothered by Mothers" in 2016 in which Jamie played a supporting role as "Lola", starring alongside such greats as Heather Matarazzo (Welcome to the Dollhouse; The Princess Diaries), Burt Young (Rocky) and Jim O'Heir (Parks and Recreation). Jamie just finished filming in "State of Desolation", starring alongside Craig Stark (Hateful 8, Django Unchained) and acting with a strong supporting cast including Dominique Swain, Daniel Buran (True Blood), Jessica Morris (One Life to Live) and Maria Olsen (Paranormal Activity 3). In April 2016, "All Girls Weekend", a horror feature film that Jamie stars in, comes out, and we should expect to see "Elder Island", another horror feature Jamie stars in come out in later 2016. In the year of 2014 alone, Jamie had a long list of films that came out including FOX's "The Secret Children", which stars

Elyse Cole of "Divergent", horror film "The Bunnyman Massacre", the long-awaited sequel to "Bunnyman", and horror film "Axeman". In 2015, Jamie made an appearance next to Johnny Depp in "Mortdecai" and again, had a long list of films that came out including comedy feature film "What Now" with music stars Ice-T, Bone Thugs and Harmony, Steven Adler of Guns and Roses, Asking Alexandria and Jeffrey Star.

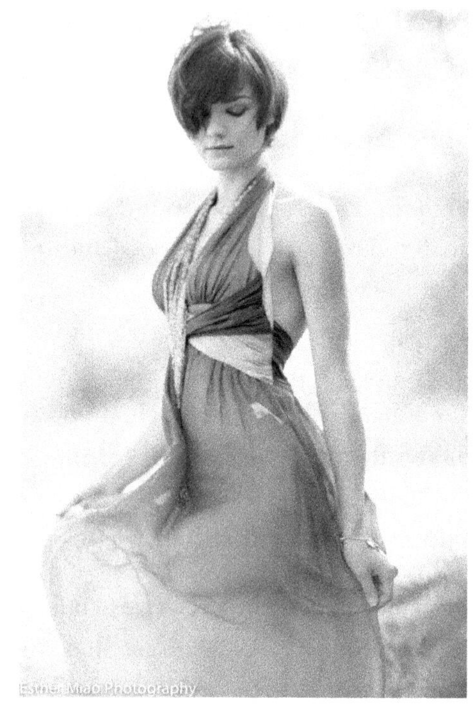

JAMIE BERNADETTE
Photo By Esther Miao Photography

Jamie enjoys writing poetry and is in the process of compiling a book for publication. She also loves camping, hiking, hanging out with her dog "Walter" and visits home to her big family in Illinois.

What do you think makes a strong female protagonist in a horror film? What about an unforgettable female antagonist?

A strong female protagonist is an intelligent, independent, and brave woman. She creates her own path in life and doesn't look to others to save her; she saves herself.

An unforgettable female antagonist I think is one who the audience will have dichotomic feelings about. They will hate her, and, at the same time, there is something about her that they will love.

As an actress, what do you look for in a director? How do you like to be directed on set?

I love directors who are calm, pleasant and positive. This kind of director creates a safe space in which the actors can work comfortably. This is very important for an actor's creative process. A director who is kind and lifts people up will bring out the best work in an actor. This may not be true for every actor, but I feel it is true for me. I like when a director communicates that the work is good. Letting an actor know after each take that they liked the work, even if it's just a "good", goes a long way. If we never hear anything about the work, take after take, pretty soon we start to wonder if the director is happy or if the work is coming across ok. Then our attention is on that when it should be on the present time of the scene. A communicative director, I believe, brings out the best work in an actor, rather than one who says nothing. For dramatic work that is dark or emotional, I like the director to come over and talk to me quietly when he has a suggestion. I think that a quiet set should be maintained for this kind of work.

What is the best direction you've ever received on set?

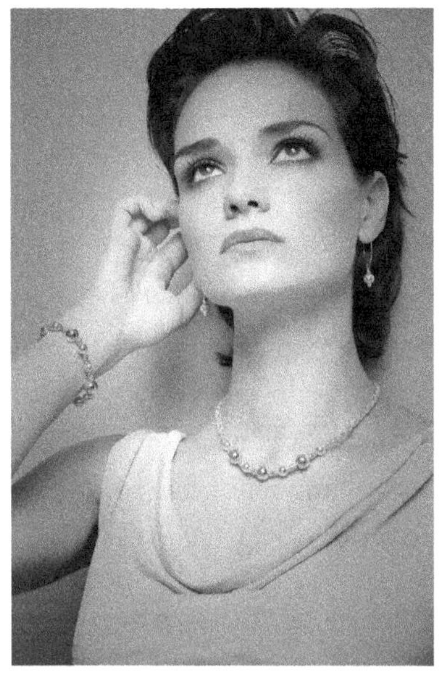

JAMIE BERNADETTE
Photo By Jason Christopher Photography

One of my favorite directions I've ever received was by director Letia Clouston on the set of "Broken Toy" when she said, "Now do this take for you. Do whatever you want." I just love that because it allows an actor the freedom to create outside of what the script says and what they were directed to do before. It gives the actor the permission to play. I think that doing some carefree, fun takes like this could possibly result in some interesting, new ways that the scene could be cut together that had never been visualized before.

You starred in I SPIT ON YOUR GRAVE: Deja Vu (2016) in which you play the daughter of the lead character played by Camille Keaton in the original cult classic. What is your preparation process like for a role of this nature?

I prepared for months. I watched so many videos about rape crimes that I became scared when I was going to bed at night or walking to my car. I read statistics about rape across the world, including what percentage of victims reports the crime to the authorities and if they decide to keep quiet, what is the psychological reasoning that they come to this decision. I read about how women were treated in the 1970s, which was when the original film was made, when they reported such a crime, and I learned that they were often the ones who were questioned and blamed. I studied what penalties a rapist faces and found that the penalties are usually not very grave at all, which could make the victim take justice into his/her own hands. What I discovered was very sad, actually, and it definitely darkened my days during that time of research, but it was all worth it and had to be done. And of course I fully researched the film itself. I had seen the film before I ever auditioned or even knew anything about a sequel. People kept recommending it to me and then I was about to film in "State of Desolation" and the director Jim Towns told me to see it before we starting shooting and that was the first time I watched it. I fell in love with the raw truth in which the story is told. I thought it was brilliant. When I booked the role, I went back

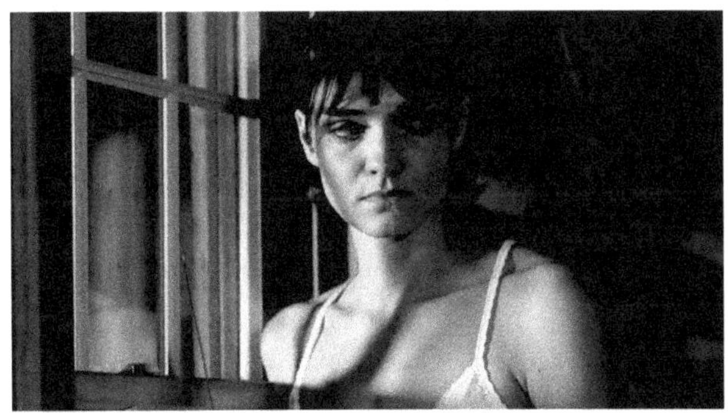

JAMIE BERNADETTE starring in THE 6TH FRIEND.

and watched it a few more times and also watched the 2010 remake and then the second film, which came out in 2012. And of course there is the backstory of the character that I developed, which wasn't too hard since I knew so much about her mom from the first film so I could imagine her life with Jennifer Hills pretty easily. The preparation of the script itself also began months in advance. I couldn't even tell you how many times I read that script. I lost count somewhere. One particular scene that was perhaps about 5-7 pages long with dialogue between me and Camille Keaton, I actually videotaped myself doing that scene over and over. Because of the heavy dialogue—it was just enormous paragraphs— I wanted to visually see what was working and what wasn't working on camera. I don't do this very often at all; in fact, this was only the second time in my career that I did this, but I felt it was necessary. I know some actors like to work in the moment and not think too much beforehand and I like to do that as well sometimes, but, other times, like in this case, for me it helped to work on it on camera.

What are your thoughts on extreme violence in horror films?

I really don't have any strong thoughts or reactions to extreme violence in horror films, or any film of any genre for that matter. A movie is a movie. A story is being told and sometimes that story will have violence.

Your film THE 6TH FRIEND (2016) was a horror project you wrote, produced and star in alongside Dominique Swain (Lolita). As the writer, what inspired you, and what advice can you give others brave enough to write their own horror script?

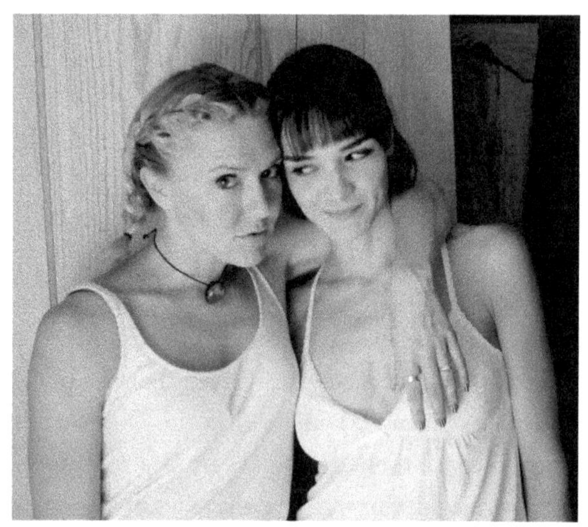

DOMINIQUE SWAIN & JAMIE BERNADETTE on the set of THE 6TH FRIEND.
Photo By Natacha Barbieri

I saw the film "The Descent" and was inspired to write a script with an all-female main cast. I wanted the women to be independent, strong and intelligent and save themselves, rather than looking to a man to save them, as is so often the cliché in horror. I wrote each character with the intention to stay away from women stereotypes such as "the blond, dumb one", "the promiscuous one", "the lesbian". We see this over and over not just in horror films, but in films spanning the different genres. I wanted "The 6th Friend" to break away from that. The director I hired, Letia Clouston, came on the film and wrote a second draft and then she and I bounced the script back and forth several times. Letia really made the script phenomenal. She brought in some wonderful ideas and I was open to the collaboration and the script became so much better. So, for other writers, I would say to have an open mind. Be able to listen to other viewpoints, especially of those who are working on the film with you, about the script without getting offended. As the writer, you can take their suggestions or you can leave them, but too often than I would like, I have seen writers just shut down suggestions from others and get instantly defensive. It isn't necessary to defend your ideas or your writing. Making a film does become very much a collaborative process when you get on set. I remember one time Dominique Swain and Letia didn't understand the line I had written and we were about to film the scene. If both of them didn't understand it, then I felt it should come out, and it did. That is an example of what I mean when I say be open to collaboration when it comes to writing a script and making it into a film. Don't get too attached to anything in a script because it's also possible that it will change in the editing room. Entire scenes may come out. As writers we tend to become very attached to what we write. So I would just be prepared for change when it comes to your screenplay becoming a film.

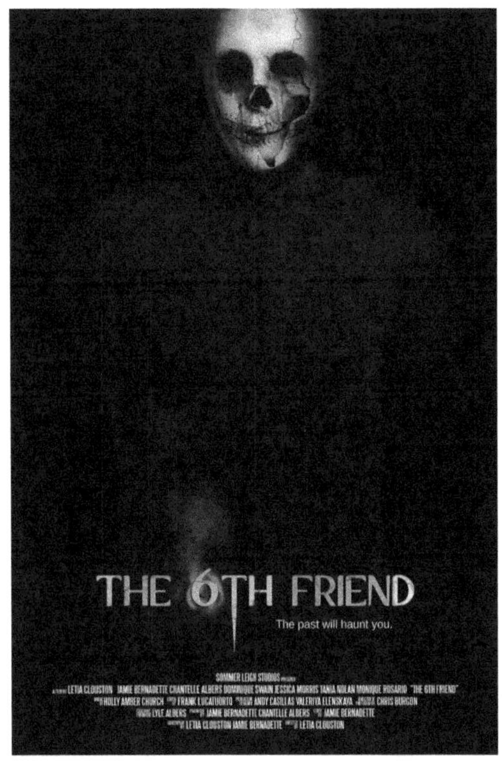

THE 6TH FRIEND

As an actress, you've auditioned and been through the casting process many times. As a producer, what did you notice about the process from the other side of the table? Any advice you can give actors auditioning for a horror film?

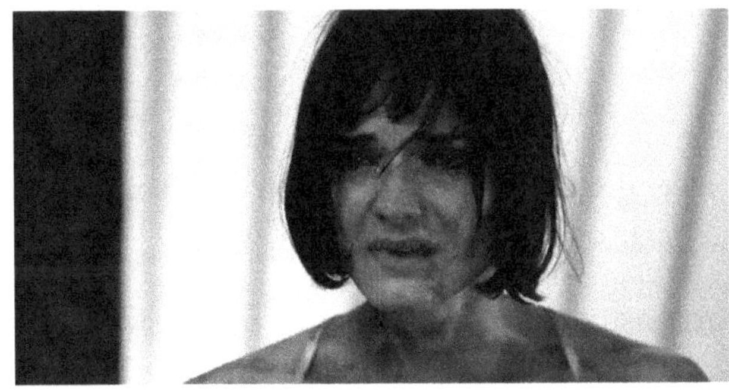

JAMIE BERNADETTE starring in THE 6TH FRIEND.

I noticed that actors were really prepared for the auditions. I was very impressed. One girl came in acting a bit moody and we couldn't figure out if she was being the character, who was a depressed, slightly antagonistic character, or if she was really that way in real life. It made us a bit afraid to cast her. I have heard of people saying to come into the audition room being the character, and maybe that is the way it should be. However, having sat on the other side and observed that, I don't recommend it.

You want to show the production that you are a warm, kind person to work with. No one wants to be around a negative person all day on set. When you start the scene, be in character then. When the scene ends, go back to speaking to them as you. Show them who you are and who they will be working with.

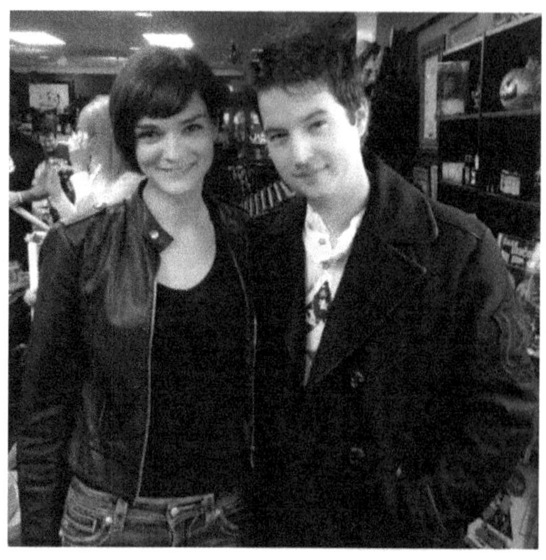

Jamie Bernadette and Danny Draven at the DVD signing for REEL EVIL (2013). Jamie had a small part in the film.

Another thing that I noticed is that a lot of actors do fine with small lines of dialogue but when they would hit a large paragraph, it wouldn't sound natural. It would either sound like over-acting or it would sound too rehearsed, as if they were reading it. If I ever cast a film again, I will always include a large paragraph in the sides for this reason. Really work on those paragraphs would be my suggestion. Get them to sound as natural as possible.

For your freshman producing effort THE 6TH FRIEND (2016), what challenges did you face? What did you learn from your experience?

This would require a large novel to answer this question. I have learned every step of the way and I am still learning. My recommendation is that when you find good crew members, including your post-production team, hang onto them.

Be very upfront about the requirements of the crew or cast position. Most upsets stem from no-communication or miscommunication. Get your contracts done with your entire team and stick to them. Agreements should be in writing to maintain happy, healthy group relations.

When you don't know something, admit it. Be upfront and honest. Because there will be a lot of thing you don't know when you produce a film for the first time and that is to be expected and it's totally ok.

Finally, when things go wrong, don't be too hard on yourself. Producing a film is a huge undertaking. It is the most challenging thing I have ever done. The fact that you even attempted to do it is something to be proud of. Always remember that.

If you could choose one horror film performance in the history of horror cinema that influenced you as an actress, what would it be and why?

Jessica Biel in "The Texas Chainsaw Massacre". Jessica's portrayal of the different ranges of emotion is this film is stellar. She is in sheer terror at a level I don't think I have ever seen in any other horror film. I know it must've been very strenuous for her to reach these emotional heights—just absolutely physically and mentally draining. She just trembles and is confused and in grief and in stark terror all at the same time with such believability. I have huge respect for her for what she accomplished in this role.

What is your favorite gross out moment on set (that happened to you)?

I don't know if I would define this as "favorite", but rather the "worst". I was playing an anorexic drug addict in this feature film called "Scarf" and I had to take lasagna into my hands and spread it on my face around my mouth. Honestly, anything with food I have a hard time with. I will never complain on set ever and would never tell anyone, but nothing grosses me out more than dealing with food and I have no idea why. I eat just fine so I don't know what it is. I had to mix grape soda and I think it was peanut butter in "State of Desolation" and put it in my mouth and then spit it out like I was throwing up and it really disgusted me. It makes me completely uncomfortable. I don't like my food to touch other food on the same plate. It has to all be nicely separated, so maybe I just have some strange hang-up with food.

What does your adorable dog Walter think about you being in horror movies?

He thinks it's awesome and he wants to be in the movies just like me! He is so very intelligent and knows all kinds of tricks. I hope he joins me one day.

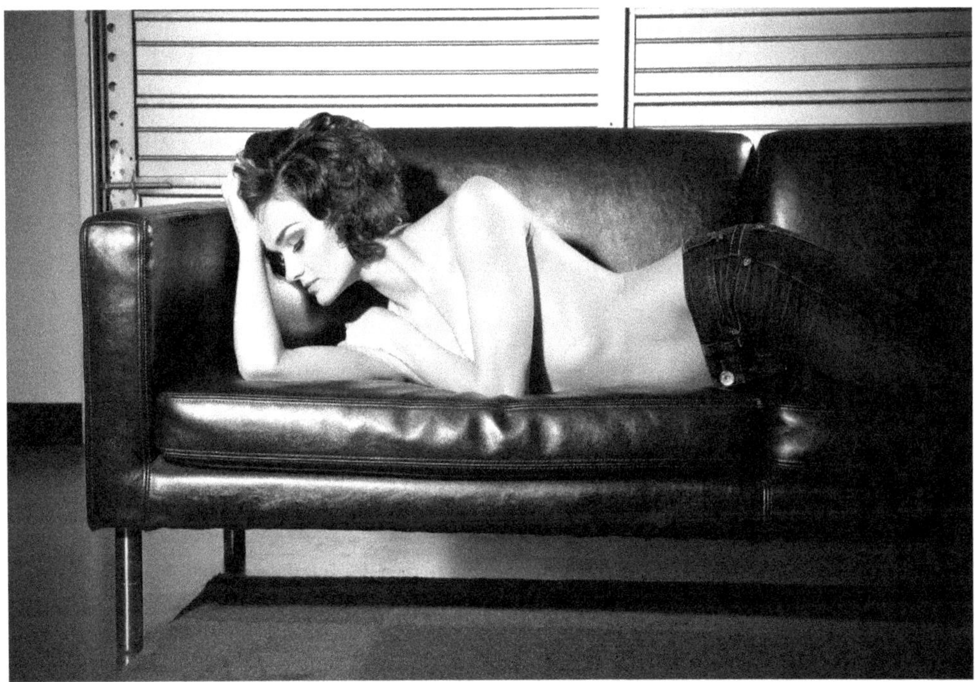

JAMIE BERNADETTE
Photo By Gabriel Parra Photography

MICHAEL BERRYMAN

ACTOR

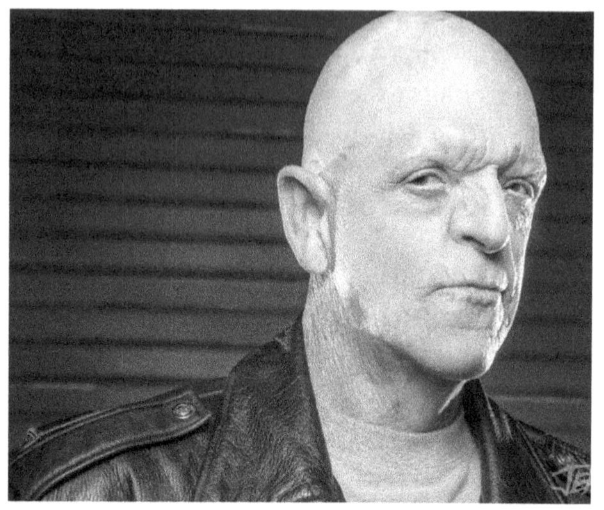

Acting veteran and horror genre icon Michael Berryman was born in Los Angeles, California. He was born prematurely with Hydrochrotic Ectodermal Dysplasia, a rare condition leaving him with no sweat glands, hair, fingernails or teeth. Michael's father was renowned neurosurgeon Sloan Berryman and his mother, Barbara, was a Registered Nurse. Michael as a young child had extensive cranial reconstruction at the Children's Hospital in Los Angeles. Michael took all these challenges and turned them into a golden career in film and television, thanks to legendary film director George Pal discovering Michael, who at the time owned and worked at a gift shop/art gallery in Venice, California.

George Pal cast Michael in the Western DOC SAVAGE, then shortly after that Milos Forman discovered and cast Michael in ONE FLEW OVER THE CUCKOO'S NEST.

Berryman went on to star as PLUTO in Wes Craven's cult classic THE HILL'S HAVE EYES. Additionally, Berryman has appeared in such films as WEIRD SCIENCE, STAR TREK IV, ARMED RESPONSE, CUT AND RUN, SOLAR CRISIS, THE DEVIL'S REJECTS, etc. He also has appeared in more main-stream roles such as the comedy SPY HARD and family favorite SCOOBY DOO. Michael's many television credits include TALES FROM THE CRYPT and X FILES. Michael Berryman portrays a gamut of characters, ranging from evil, dangerous and creepy to wise, gentle, sage, mystical, whimsical, comedic and even angels. Michael is an adored favorite of horror and sci-fi movie fans worldwide.

Michael and his wife Patty own and run a farm in Northern California where he and his wife have walnut, apple, pear, cherry and plum orchards and raise their beloved horses. Michael loves to bake pies.

Most recently, Michael stars with Edward Furlong in the feature film BELOW ZERO, as well as horror/ thrillers EREBUS, SELF STORAGE, starring opposite Eric Roberts, RED AND YELLA KILL A FELLA and ARMY OF THE DAMNED. Michael will also star in the television series HELL HUNTERS (based on the popular comic boo) as well as the series HELL'S KITTY.

Your character Pluto from The Hills Have Eyes (1977) is one of my favorite

roles in your career. What are the mechanics underneath that made Pluto such an unforgettable character that any one of us could possibly encounter if our car broke down in the middle of nowhere?

What I brought to set for Pluto was the ability he possessed; that is, adaptation. Pluto was cunning. He could effectively change in an instant. His skill set included the ability to use anything at his disposal to prevail. Pluto trusted his natural instincts and nothing evaded his observation. Wit and focus made him very dangerous.

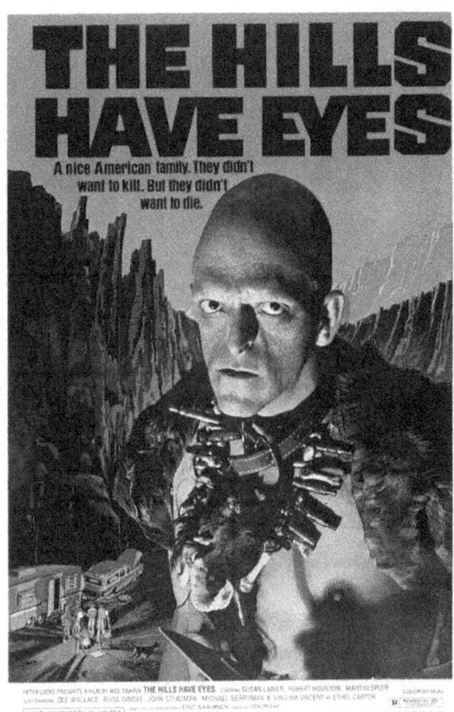

Michael Berryman as Pluto in Wes Craven's THE HILLS HAVE EYES (1977).

As an actor, what qualities do you look for in a director?

A director with the ability to communicate is key. For me, I understand camera, and every cut is an important piece of the whole. I look for a director that has trust in the cinematographer. Very often, a good script falls flat as a motion picture because the editing is choppy or distracting to the flow of the emotional performance by the actors. A good director can bring all of the artistic elements of the filming process together, and this blending is the skill that makes it work.

If you could chose one horror film or performance in the history of horror cinema that influenced you as an actor, what would it be and why?

The 'Hitcher', and Rutger Hauer's performance, remains my all time favorite. The presence and mood are smothering. The danger and intensity are visceral and get under your skin. As in 'Hills'...there is the moment when Bobby asks 'they killed Big Bob, Beauty and Mom...they will be back, what are we going to do?' In these moments, the audience is in the seat of the rollercoaster and is committed to see it through. I have always appreciated a strong antagonist.

On a film set, what is the worst direction you have ever received from a director?

Well, there has been more than one. Here we go. I had a film in Wisconsin and arrived on the set to meet the director and cast, having just flown in. The director wanted to shoot right then, but I reminded him that my work day started the next day, but we could rehearse a scene. The director wanted me to bare my ass in a rape scene and say to the girl, 'come to Daddy' and pull her toward me. The scene had been changed before I arrived via a 3-way phone call, and the decision was a less repulsive image. But he thought he could get away with the old version. I refused and suggested the better choice would make for a stronger scene. I had wanted the camera behind me, pants on, I buckle my belt, I step aside, the camera is on her face, close-up and she could emote all of the obvious foul deed in a moment of vulnerability. As an artist, I believe graphic becomes numbing and emotionally sterile in storytelling. You can loose your audience in such a manner and you wind up with no emotional content...instead you just 'shock the monkey', so to speak.

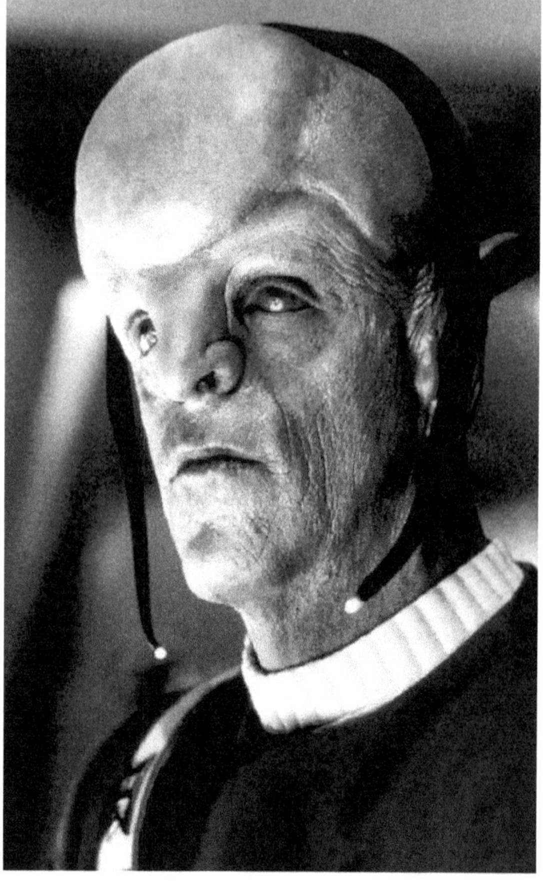

Michael Berryman in STAR TREK IV.

What do you think are the key elements to making a scene scary?

Fear is primal and so are our senses. So, for me, the visual media in which we create must be respected. The sets and the designs, the music, the colors, the wardrobe choices, the editing cuts and how they flow; all of the non-acting/performance elements are the support structure for the actors. Mood is huge! All of the mentioned elements are blended by the director to bring the story to life! When I work on a well-prepared set, I can tap into those energies. I cannot stress enough how important storyboards can assist in keeping the direction on track. Always refer to them, they help.

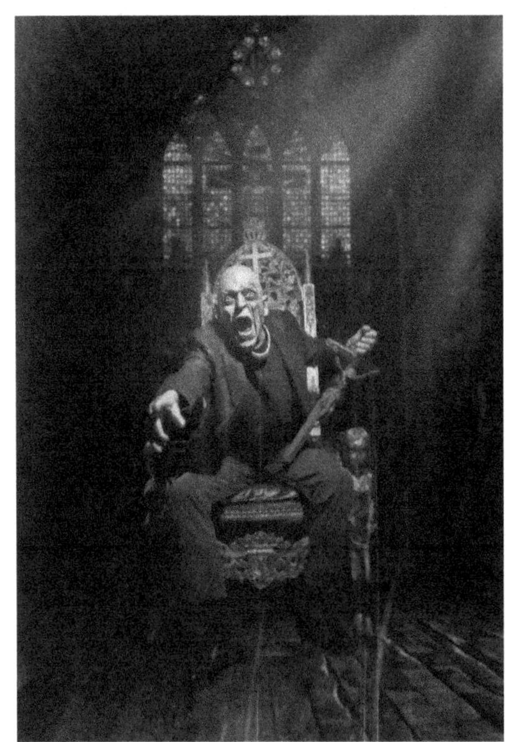

What is the best advice you have ever received in the film business and why was it meaningful to you and your career success?

On the set of 'One Flew Over The Cuckoo's Nest', I asked Milos Forman for advice. He took me over to the Panavision camera and said 'Look at the glass, I want you to have a love affair with the lens'. Remember, the camera captures everything. Expression and nuance on an actor's face comes from deep within. I have spent many hours just looking in the mirror and practicing this skill. It helps a lot to know your lenses and how they work in formatting a shot.

If Pluto and Leatherface were to meet unexpectedly and fight over a possible victim, who would win?

Pluto vs. Leatherface? Well Pluto would win. He would throw something into the saw to jam the chain. His fast reactions and cunning would obviously prevail!

STEVEN M. BLASINI

VFX SUPERVISOR

www.bfximageworks.com

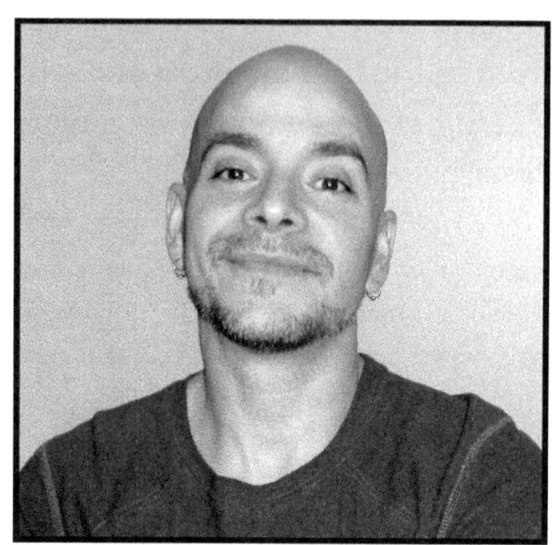

STEVEN M. BLASINI

BFX IMAGEWORKS, located in Los Angeles, California and founded in 2001, has produced high-end visual effects for independent studios throughout the United States and Europe. Our strength lies in our core business engine and strategies. By keeping our overhead low, we can provide very high-end work that is obtainable even within the modest budgets afforded independent film productions. Our work can be seen on Sci Fi Channel, ABC Family, HBO, Starz, MTZ, VH1, and more.

What does a VFX supervisor do? Can you describe your work flow and responsibilities during a film production?

I believe that can vary from shop to shop, but I can tell you what I do. Generally (if the process is done correctly) I'll get early copies of the script, perhaps even just the three- or four-page treatment, and I let the producers know if there are any VFX items that may cause difficulties or be too costly. Once the script is locked, I then produce a VFX Breakdown that isolates all the scenes in the film that will be either completely VFX or VFX enhanced. I then create a budget based on those shots so that the total cost of the VFX can be known. Once principle photography starts (and if the production has enough money to cover the costs) I go on set and work closely with the director on all the shots requiring VFX. It is not uncommon that I then take on the role of second unit director for the shots that will require VFX, taking a small crew out and shooting background plates or specific talent performances that will involve VFX.

If the production doesn't have enough money to cover the costs of my being there, we usually keep phone contact with the director. This, however, is almost always dangerous, since shooting schedules don't always allow for calm phone interaction. I've seen many shots ruined using this method...but if that's all you can afford then we accommodate you.

Once the film is shot I am involved in the editing process, making sure that any shots/performances that are selected are indeed the best ones for the post job ahead. A lot of times a director/editor will just select a shot based on performance, but there may be a glitch in the setup of the shot that will make the VFX difficult, if not impossible, to complete.

Once the film is locked, we then order all the background plates from the lab and begin work at our studio creating all required elements and completing shots. We go through an approval process with the director then the producers until everyone is happy with the work. After approval, all shots are rendered in their final resolutions (usually Film 2K or HD) and delivered to the postproduction lab where it is usually color corrected, then sound/Foley/music are added.

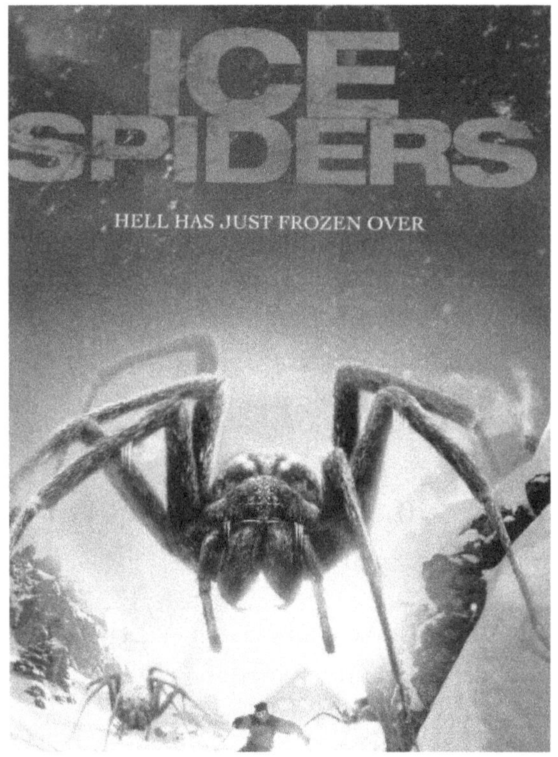

ICE SPIDERS (2007)

What is the best way for a director to communicate his vision to the VFX artist?

In our experience, the best way for a director to communicate his vision is via storyboards. However, it is unfortunate that usually at the budgets afforded to the average independent feature, there is not enough money for this. So it comes down to having as many preproduction meetings with the director and crew prior to principle photography as possible. Then location surprises or script rewrites have to be taken into consideration. For that reason, easy communication between the director and the VFX supervisor for on-the-spot decisions is a must.

Do you think CGI characters such as spiders, snakes, etc., are out of reach for independent filmmakers? Or can it be done on a low budget?

It is definitely within reach of the independent filmmaker. The core of our very business has helped to establish that. Our design was structured so that most of the costs associated with having a VFX studio are low so we don't have to recover the many operating costs. The result is an obvious and immediate savings to the producers. The bulk of all our clients are independent filmmakers.

What types of CGI techniques are available to filmmakers in the horror genre (e.g., digital gore, digital makeup, etc.)?

With us, the entire gamut of CGI techniques is available. This includes digital gore and digital makeup as well as set extensions, matte paintings, wire and rig removal, and mood establishers (fog, smoke, fire). We've even had to do a shot where the dead victim flickered his shut eyes and we had to add steady digital eyelids!

Do you do a lot of digital gore FX, and how can a filmmaker prepare for this during production?

The most important factor when shooting something that will need digital enhancement or replacement is the use of some kind of tracking marks that can then facilitate the frame-by-frame task ahead. Contrary to popular belief, it doesn't always have to be something specifically painted on for the process. As an example, we were called upon to create a digital eye morph on moving actors. Their eyes were to change from normal human to reptilian eyes. So I asked the director to make sure that he lit the talent in such a way that would produce a specular light reflection on the surface of the eyes that we could then use to track the motion. It worked flawlessly and didn't require anything on the person directly.

What are the biggest mistakes you see new filmmakers make when doing VFX on low-budget films?

They underestimate how complex a shot can really be. It's amazing how many directors and producers think that something can be just painted out or painted in. They forget that in order for a VFX artist to paint something out, there has to be some sort of palette to draw from that contains what is behind the item that has to be painted out. The less film shooters think ahead and provide to the VFX artist, the more expensive the shot becomes.

For filmmakers who can't afford a VFX artist, what tools/software do you suggest for them to do it themselves, and why?

There are many VFX software packages out there that are accessible to anybody. The real way to answer this question is: go out and try them all yourself. What works for me doesn't necessarily work for you and vice versa. Before we established that we would use NewTek LightWave 3D as our main 3-D software and Adobe After Effects for our 2-D and compositing software, we spent many hours with all the packages available and decided which ones we felt comfortable with, not only in learning curve but ease of use and cost.

J.R. BOOKWALTER

PRODUCER / DIRECTOR

J.R. BOOKWALTER began his career at in 1985 at age 19 with THE DEAD NEXT DOOR, an ambitious zombie epic financed by a now-legendary Hollywood director. After learning the ropes with a series of work-for-hire features, Bookwalter founded Tempe as an outlet to make & self-distribute such films as OZONE and POLYMORPH. In 1997, Bookwalter relocated to Hollywood, where he produced 12 features for Full Moon Pictures in just 3 years as well as directing two popular WITCHOUSE sequels.

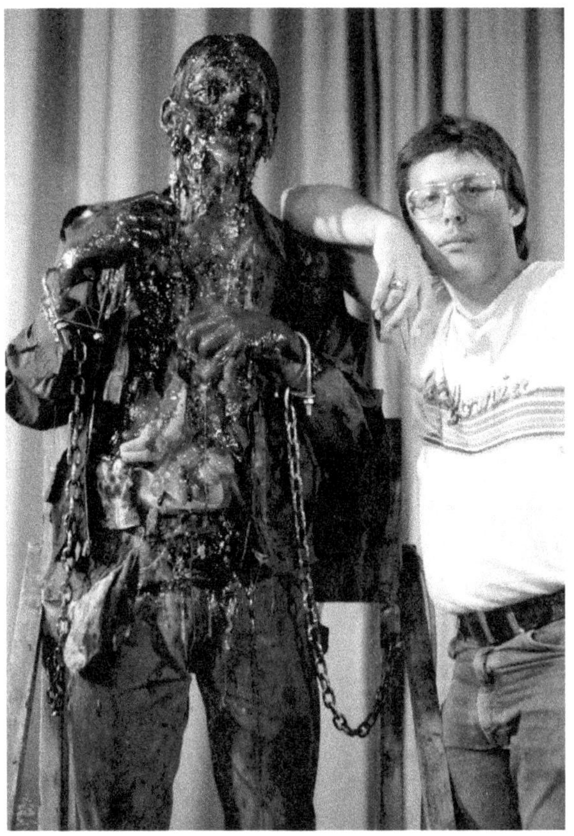

J.R. BOOKWALTER and a zombie pal.

The Akron, Ohio native went back on his own in 2003 with Tempe DVD, releasing deluxe Special Editions of his past work as well as creating a new home for some "not-so-classics" with the comedy series BAD MOVIE POLICE. Considered by many to be a "pioneer" in the wildly popular shot-on-video movement, in 2005 Bookwalter celebrated his 20th year in the business, marked by Anchor Bay's release of THE DEAD NEXT DOOR Special Edition DVD, bringing his career full circle.

What were the most important things you learned making THE DEAD NEXT DOOR (1989) and what advice do you have for others who want to make their debut in the horror genre?

The business was in a very different place when I started that film back in 1985… there was no Internet, no YouTube and few places for budding filmmakers to collaborate! It was amazing to me that people found the movie at all, especially considering how long it took to make and get released. But, I think the movie had an interesting take on the zombie genre, and it certainly had a unique behind-the-scenes story as far as how it got made, and those two things helped create enough interest for people to seek it out. And they still are… every year, the movie seems to get more popular, instead of disappearing as I've often wished it would. (laughs) So, I would say the first piece of advice would be, try to bring something unique to the table… that's easier said than done, but believe me, I'm not the most talented guy in the world. Sometimes, with a lot of patience and persistence, you can be resourceful enough to overcome your own limitations. And you better have patience, because you'll need it in this business.

As far as what I learned… I was barely 19 years old when I started THE DEAD NEXT DOOR, and by the time it was released I was almost 25 and married for the first time! So I did a lot of growing up over those years. I can't say that I learned as much from the movie itself, mostly because I had the luxury of time and an ever-evolving budget to play with, so there wasn't a lot of discipline there. But during the downtime, when nothing was happening with the movie, I shot weddings and music videos and even recorded & mixed a lot of music for myself and others — so I learned how to be resourceful and find other ways to survive. (laughs)

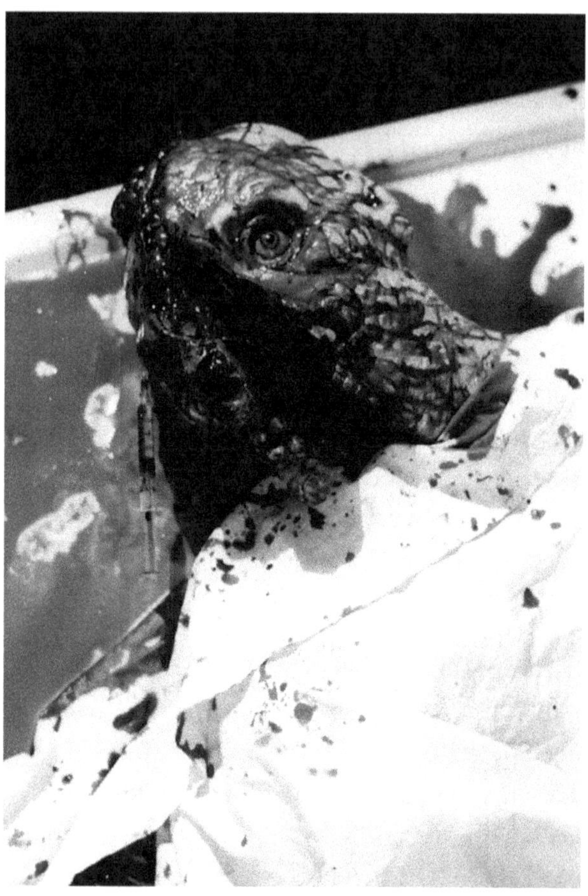

An experiment in Dr. Moulsson's lab, affectionately dubbed by its creators as the "Spazo" zombie in THE DEAD NEXT DOOR (1990).

What are the five most important things for an indie producer to do during production to save money?

It sounds terrible, but the real secret to making low-budget movies is simple: Don't pay for anything! And if you have to pay for something, pay as little as possible. (laughs) Seriously, it's not rocket science, folks. Spend your money wisely, and make sure every dime of it is on the screen… and then some! You have to be somewhat of a dictator with the dollars that you do have, and not squander it on things that don't make a better production. That said, you want to treat your cast & crew right… feeding them a decent meal goes a long way toward keeping them happy, and if they're happy, they'll work those long, grueling hours and perform better for you.

The biggest thing is to stay connected to people, places and things, or know reliable people who are well connected. You'd be amazed what you can get from asking the right person, and remember, the worst thing that can happen is that somebody might say "no," so why not give it a try?

When scheduling an indie horror film, what are some tricks you learned and how has it helped the production be more efficient?

Man, when I started on THE DEAD NEXT DOOR, we used those old-school, expensive production boards with the cardboard strips. It was a nightmare, especially because the schedule changed so frequently! Now they have great software to do the same thing, but filmmakers shouldn't feel pressured into spending the dough on that stuff. Some of the better schedules I've done over the years were on tiny projects like OZONE, where I just printed out some calendars from my computer (for free!) and scribbled on them until things made sense. To me, the scheduling is much easier if you have a production-ready, production-friendly script to start with. That means, write what you can pull off efficiently, yet effectively. I've seen too many writers scribble all these big ideas on paper, and more often than not, that stuff gets whittled down to a shadow of its former self on location. Get the script in tip-top shape for shooting and the schedule will fall into place easily.

What is the key to shooting quickly during a production?

A lot of filmmakers think that pages of dialogue will help them speed through a shoot, but in my experience, that's rarely the case. Sure, if your actors have their lines memorized and you know what you want them to do (and they can actually do it), it can be done. But let's face it, with low-budget movies, you're often dealing with actors of questionable talent, and many times they might have no other on-set experience!

More than anything else, it falls on the shoulder of the director (and almost as equally on the cinematographer)… have the shooting day mapped out in your head, know what you want and have some good ideas how to get it, and for God's sake, be prepared for things to not work out the way you planned, because they seldom do.

What are the advantages and disadvantages to guerilla-style filmmaking, and why?

The biggest advantage is the freedom to do whatever you want, within your means. On a movie like OZONE, we had a great home base that doubled as our main location… it was an abandoned building on this large property belonging to the adjoining rehabilitation center. I was able to store all of the gear there and shoot probably 75% of the movie in and around that building. It was really like a studio playground for such a small movie! I think we were holed up there for almost a year until they said, "You guys have to get out now." (laughs)

That said, the biggest disadvantage is you wear too many hats and you'll burn yourself out quickly. Trust me on that, I've done it time and time again! When I started out, I wanted to be writer, director, producer, camera operator, editor, cameo actor, squib guy, makeup effects guy… you name it. After awhile, it gets to be too much, so I gradually scaled back to mostly producing, directing and editing. And be very careful what projects you pick… I've said "yes" to way too many movies that I later wish I had never been involved with. (laughs)

Tempe Video is your indie distribution company and has been in business since 1991. When you release a film, what are the most important things you look for in a film for it to be sellable in the marketplace?

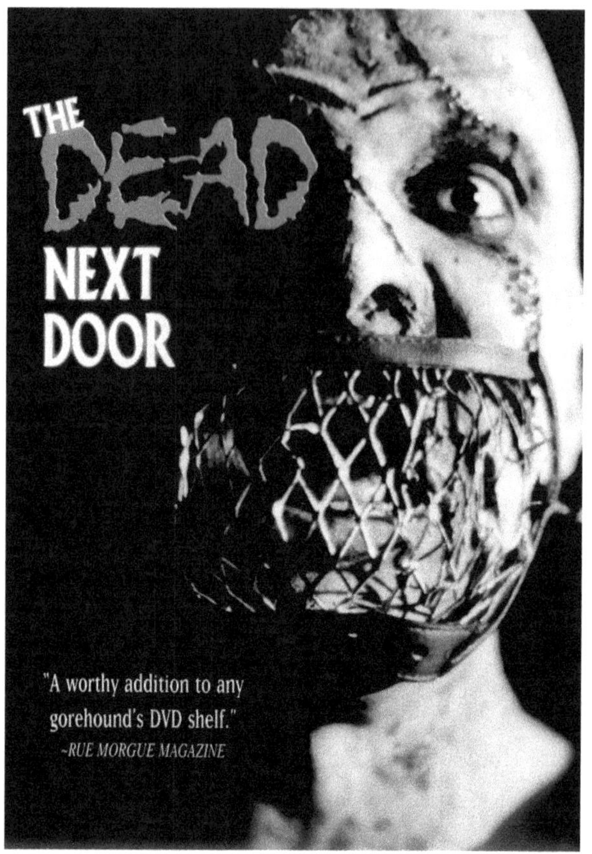

THE DEAD NEXT DOOR on DVD & Blu-ray from Tempe Video.

I get asked that question a lot by producers: "What kind of movies are you looking for?" And I always tell them the same thing: "Make whatever you want!" My reason for that is simple… you're stuck with these things for life! They're your children, even if sometimes they're of the red-headed stepchild variety. (laughs) Better to make something that you want to see, rather than make something you think will appeal to a distributor. If you make what you think the market wants, very often that trend will have shifted by the time you're ready to sell the movie, and then you're stuck with something that nobody wants to see. Today there are plenty of ways to get your movie seen, and even with a distributor, there's no guarantee you'll see any money, let alone recoup on what the thing cost you to begin with.

Now the flip side of that advice is, try to put stuff in the movie that will appeal to an audience! While it's true that there's an audience for everything, you'll probably have a better shot at seeing a profit making a ballsy, gory zombie flick than some costume drama that's a hard sell. You have to decide up front what your intentions are, and have the fortitude to stick to your convictions when all of the distributors pass or you can only sell 10 copies at some convention.

During production, how do you deal with day-to-day problems that arise on set?

The movie business is a veritable cess pool of insecure, neurotic "artist" types. I've seen more ego on display making $5,000 movies back here in Ohio than I have doing much larger movies in Los Angeles! So, it's a good idea to stay grounded and even-tempered. Go in knowing that things can go wrong, and take them with a grain of salt. I've often compared being on set to a military operation, because no matter how well you plan it, you can't always control the outcome… you've gotta be prepared to follow another course of action, rather than throw up your hands, pitch a fit and give up just because your "vision" isn't being realized. I'd venture to say that few films ever turn out 100% the way their creators intended, regardless of budget, and your odds go down dramatically if you don't keep a cool head.

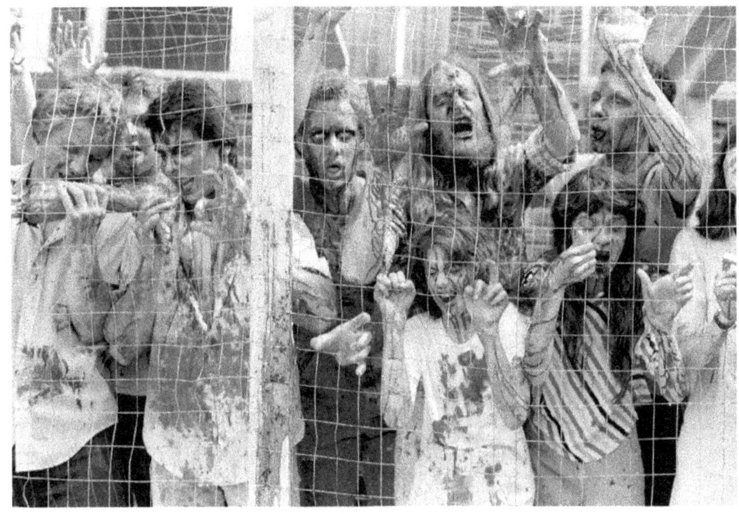

DEAD NEXT DOOR Zombies in cage.tif** Caption: A whopping 1,500 area locals came out to play zombie extras in J.R. Bookwalter's THE DEAD NEXT DOOR (1990).

If you could pick one tip to give an aspiring horror filmmaker, what would it be and why is it important?

That's an easy one: Don't be an ass! (laughs) Seriously, so much of this so-called business revolves around pandering to egos and dealing with a lot of B.S., and people can make the crappiest movies and still have a swelled head about it. I'm not saying don't be proud of your accomplishments, I'm just saying to temper it with a dose of humility. Yeah, I know, we've all seen bad behavior rewarded in our society, but trust me, people are more likely to want to work with you if you leave the chip on your shoulder at home. And don't believe everything you read in reviews, especially the good stuff — the higher you fly, the further you have to fall. (laughs)

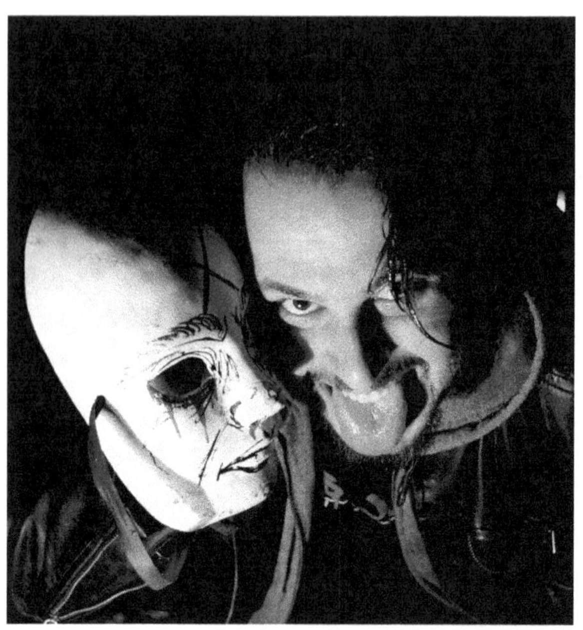

JAMES CULLEN BRESSAK
PHOTO BY SYDNEY CASSATTA

JAMES CULLEN BRESSAK

WRITER / DIRECTOR / PRODUCER
www.jamescullenbressak.com
Twitter: @Jamescullenb

Bursting upon the indie horror scene at the age of eighteen with his first feature My Pure Joy, James Cullen Bressack has been called "horror's new hope" (Studio City Patch - Mike Szymanski) and "a talent to watch out for." (H.S.T.- Ben John Smith) as well as garnering rave reviews on almost every horror web site. Released by Media Blasters on their Fresh Meat Shriek Show label in 2012, the film quickly rose to the top of the best sellers list on Amazon.com in the horror category. His second feature, a real shocker, Hate Crime, was a festival favorite and garnered many awards and became one of 3 films in the past 10 years to be Banned by the BBFC. Bressack then made history with his next feature, To Jennifer, which was the first feature film shot entirely on an iPhone 5. The prolific filmmaker then made Pernicious, filmed in Thailand. His film, 13-13-13 followed and his most recent feature, Blood Lake, which aired on Animal Planet, was a top ratings getter. Recently, he wrote and directed a film for LIFETIME among other projects due out soon. A winner of multiple Best Picture and Best Director awards on the film festival circuit, James is very active on social media and interacts with fans daily.

What are some of the mistakes you see younger filmmakers make when directing for the first time?

Honestly, it's the same mistake I made when I first got started. It's hard to kill babies. In my mind I would be like, I wrote, directed, shot and edited the scene, I put all this work into it. There is no way I'm cutting it out of the movie. And my first film really suffered from a lot of that. Looking back on it, I cringe every time. I seriously should have cut 30 minutes out of that film I mean it's 2 hours long. I realize that it's so hard to kill your babies on a film, especially the first one because you want everything you did to be in the film because it could be the only film you ever make. I know I felt it was going to be the only film I ever made, I mean I thought I would make more, but deep down I had this fear it would be. I think as a filmmaker, killing babies and overcoming internal fear is the way to really triumph.

You shot TO JENNIFER (2013) entirely on a iPhone 5. What were some of you challenges doing so and could the newer smart phones be a new resource for filmmakers to shoot indie films with?

Shooting on the iPhone 5 was actually one of the most freeing and exhilarating things I ever did as a filmmaker. I was able to bend the rules to a degree I never had before. It was 100% gorilla. I mean we even shot a scene on a real airplane, we just shot it while we were on a flight. No one ever though it was weird seeing someone pointing their phone at another person. We got away with anything with that phone. Shooting "To Jennifer" reminded me making movies could be fun again. I had just left a project I was shooting on the east coast, due to production issues and creative differences, and I was feeling really down as a filmmaker. I had a movie in me, but no means to get it made. But then I remembered the advice I always said as a filmmaker to people looking to break in, "just go out there and do it". It was time to practice what I preach. So I took the camera that was most acceptable to myself and other people and got to work.

I had done low budget before, but nothing as low budget as this. So I took out my phone and just pointed it at my friend Chuck, who was the DP on the project we had just left, and I said "Talk" and that's what he did. The first scene was entirely improve and only 1 take. After seeing that my mind started racing and I wrote out the script and we started shooting. I took the little money I had in my pocket, literally a couple hundred bucks, and we made a movie. This is why I continue to say to a lot of filmmakers looking to break in, go out there and do it! There are now 3 films in the JENNIFER franchise, the latest starring Tony Todd and Derek Mears and Directed by Frank Merle.

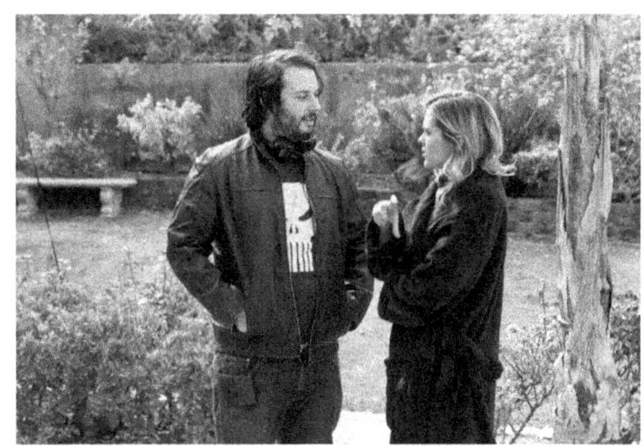

On the set of BLOOD LAKE talking with actress Susie Abromeit. Photo by Temma Hankin. © Global Asylum

What is the worst thing an actor can do on set while working with a director? The best?

The best thing an actor can do on set would be to know their lines, know how to take direction, and know how to work well with others. I love collaborating with my actors. I am a firm believer of the fact that film is a living breathing thing, it's a collaborative medium. This is why you have so many intelligent people working in one place. I look at every character in my films as a blank canvas, I take my ideas about the character as informed by the script, and the actor takes their ideas about the character as informed by the script. We both throw our ideas at the canvas, and whatever sticks for both of us is what we use to paint the picture of who this person is. The idea is to look past the page, past what's there, to find who the person really is. Some amazing things I never even dreamed of about one of my characters have come out of this process. So for actors I feel be open minded and able to bend and work with your director and vice versa for directors with your actors.

As a indie producer, what is a day in your life like during a production?

Literally anything and everything. You name it. Recently I produced a movie and it was an art beast.

Literally, like 20 different sets had to be built on the stage, and art was behind. So every day after filming for 12 hours I would stay and work on getting the sets ready for the next day with the production designer. Eventually, he started joking around asking if I was really a producer or if I was art department. But that's the job. As a producer you have to get your hands dirty and do everything you can to support your director. I want the film to be great, and I do everything in my power to make sure it can be. Even if sometimes its running out to get coffee because all the PA's are busy. There's no ego in that job, I just keep my head down and work.

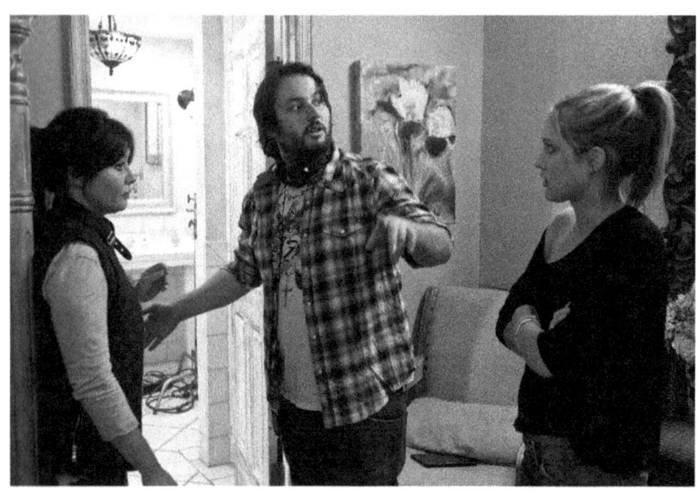

On the set of BLOOD LAKE working with actresses Shannen Doherty and Ciara Hanna. Photo by Temma Hankin. © Global Asylum

What are your thoughts on extreme violence & gore in horror films? Is the audience de-sensitized to it now? Do you think it's impacting our society or is the horror story something we need as a culture?

I'm a huge fan of extreme violence and gore in films. It's fun and exciting. I think audiences are seeming to shy away from ultra gore now, but I've always been a massive practical FX fan. I don't think horror films are causing people in real life to be violent. If someone is disturbed and wants to cause physical harm to another person in real life, a horror movie didn't do that to them. They had that in themself all along. I think they are just looking for a reason, and they could find it anywhere. More comedies are made every year than horror movies, and I don't see the world getting any funnier.

Do you think aspiring filmmakers should go to film school or not? If not, what is the best way to learn the craft?

I wasn't in film school. So having not gone I cant really answer this. I don't really quite know. Personally, I think it's better to take the money you would spend and make your first film, but that's just me. What made me decide to not go to film school is when I was making my first film for $7,000 and I posted on Craigslist looking for free PA's. I was getting resumes from USC and UCLA film school graduates, wanting to volunteer on my movie. I didn't want to go to film school to volunteer to be a PA on some random guys movie. I wanted to be the random guy making the movie. I didn't go to film school. I spent every cent I had buying DVDs of amazing and obscure films. I studied them my own way. I didn't have many friends growing up, I had films. I guess that really meant I had the best friends a kid could ask for, James Bond, Indiana Jones, Freddy Kruger and Princess Mononoke!

As a little boy, I dreamed of making movies, though I never thought I actually would. I pretended to think it, but I never really believed it. I dreamed of making films every time I would see a movie, thinking one day I would finally watch my own. Films took me places. I went to different worlds, saw different things, went on different adventures, fought different monsters. Film has always been the only constant in my life. The only thing I've ever had.

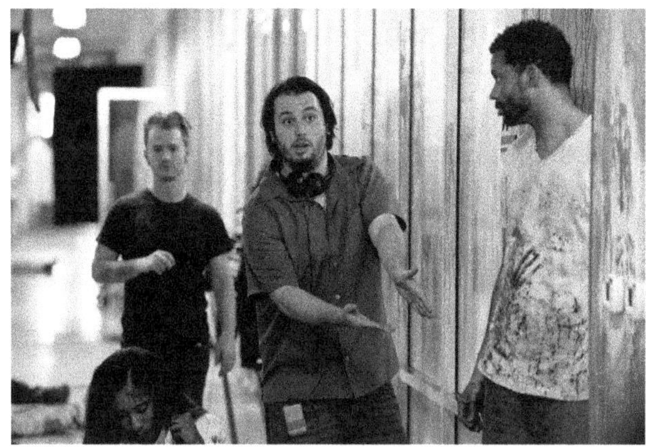

James working on the set of 13/13/13. Photo by Temma Hankin. © Global Asylum

What really pushed me to become a film maker, was when my dad got very ill when I was in the 5th grade. He was bed ridden for years so all we did together was watch movies. It was our escape. Sick as he was, he could still discuss movies better then anyone else. I would come home every day from school and go to his room and we would watch a movie. It's how we spent our time together. Before that we use to play baseball and go bowling and stuff, but once he got sick all we could really share was film. Thankfully he got better but This experience inspired to want to make movies. I wanted to give someone, in the off chance that they were in my same situation that I was in when I was little, and they happened to see one of my films, it would be one extra movie they can watch and talk about with a loved one. A collection of 4,000 DVDs later I felt I was ready to start making them. Film had influenced my life so much, it only made sense. I never saw myself doing anything else. Everyone thought I was crazy but at 18 years old, with no money and a dream, I made a movie.

What I've learned is that the odds are always against us, not everyone will like what you do, you can't make everyone happy, but you can tell your stories. You can pour your heart and soul into them and hope for the best. If that doesn't sound appealing, being a filmmaker probably isn't for you, but if it does, maybe you are a little crazy too.

I never made films to be rich, I never made films to be liked by people, or to be popular, or to have friends or to get girls or win awards or anything like that. I made films because it's all I've ever had. It's all I ever knew, and it's all I ever cared about. I made films because I had to, because I needed to. Because I had stories I had to tell that ate me up inside until I told them.

Before anyone goes thinking because I came from a showbiz family, that's how I broke into film, obviously doesn't know about me. Yes, my parents were supportive emotionally about my dreams. My father also taught me a lot about writing and story structure. But I would have had to have been crazy to want to follow in their footsteps. I didn't grow up rich, or well off. I didn't have a silver spoon. I saw my parents live paycheck to paycheck. My mom left the business to become a teacher. My dad still works as a writer, but it's never constant work, it's always been feast or famine. They never gave me money towards making films, I never used their connections to get films made. Not once. I say this not to strengthen my own accomplishments, but to inspire those reading this thinking they can't do it because they didn't come from the same background I did. I have been blessed enough to be able to live my dream. I've directed 13 feature films by the age of 24, written and produced even more than that. But I'm not where I want to be, not even close. I have a long road ahead. I'm still going to keep pushing forward. I'm still going to keep fighting for my dream.

Tell us a bit about your new film BETHANY (2017) and what your preparation process is like when making a new film?

BETHANY is by far my best film. I really worked hard on it. Every single page of the script is full with my notes. I drew overhead maps for blocking for every scene, shot-listed the entire film. I had color coded notes on every page for every department. I literally directed the entire thing in notes before I ever stepped foot on set. I also Cast it and Co-wrote it with Zack Ward. I lived with it in post for a year. My grandma was one of my biggest inspirations in life and one of my biggest supporters as a filmmaker. She passed away the first day of filming my movie HATE CRIME. I've made many movies since then and only ever thanked her on the films. I waited till this film to dedicate it to her. I really feel this is my best work and my most personal project.

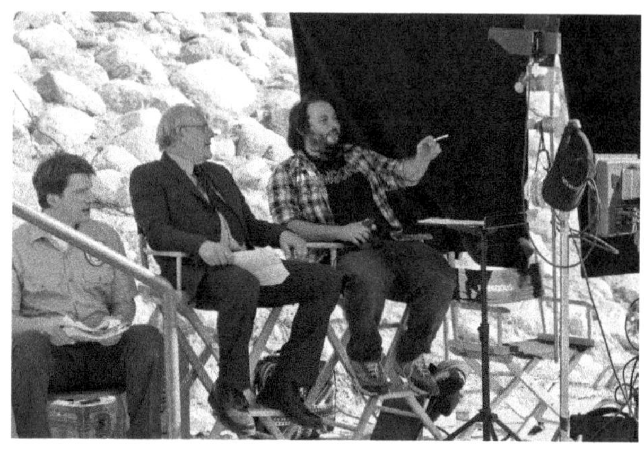

James watching the monitor with Christopher Lloyd and Jason Brooks on the set of BLOOD LAKE. Photo by Temma Hankin. © Global Asylum

As a director BETHANY was my last horror film. Since then I have directed 5 features, none of which are horror. I won't be back in the horror genre as a director for a while. All my planned projects as a director in the future aren't horror. I miss the genre, but I'll be back eventually. For many reasons Bethany means a lot to me, but one big one is that it was my last Hoorah in my favorite genre. I promise I put everything into it.

Do you use storyboards and how useful are they when directing on set?

I always like to board out my kill scenes. It's the best way to go and most efficient. Visually, it's like seeing the edit. I'm currently directing an animated film and for that we are of course boarding out the whole movie. It's a great tool to have and any extra work always makes the final product that much better.

If you could choose one horror film director in the history of horror cinema that influenced you as a filmmaker, who would it be and why?

I would have to say probably Wes Craven. Wes actually gave me some filmmaking advice that really stuck with me. "Those that persevere and stick with it, succeed. Those that give up, give up." I really try to live by that now. He went on to explain that even he at times thought maybe he should go back to teaching instead of this. Knowing that everyone has these same thoughts from time to time made it feel okay.

Is horror dead, or do you think it's in a revival now?

Just look at the current Box Office. Horror is KILLING it. I think that speaks volumes on if it's dead or not.

How important is networking in the film business and why?

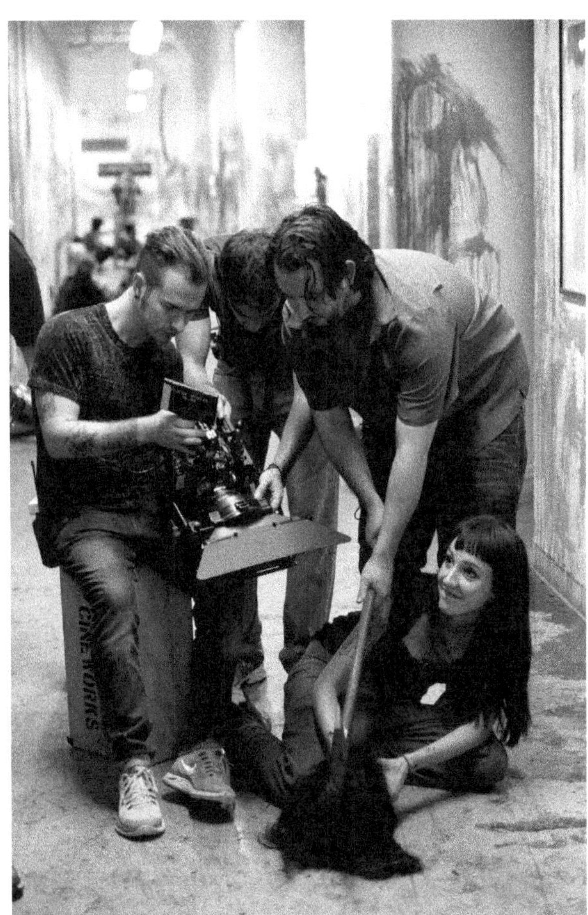

James working on the set of 13/13/13. Photo by Temma Hankin. © Global Asylum

Networking is very important in this business. Success will not find you, you have to get yourself out there. Think of yourself as a spider, if you have a small web, you will only catch one fly, the bigger the web the more flies you catch. You are also able to trade favors with other filmmakers, always look at them as your allies, not your competition.

I'm not in a competition against any filmmaker ever. I have my own distinct style. People either want to hire me or don't. Other filmmakers don't threaten me, if they are good at what they do and make good films, I admire them and enjoy their work. I will gladly champion any film I love. I am a film lover first and foremost. If they don't make films I connect with in my opinion, I get excited to see something different on future films. I always have respect for anyone who finishes a feature film. Going through the trenches I know how hard it is. I have nothing against other filmmakers and I don't feel anyone is ever in competition with me for a job, or has taken a job away from me because ultimately I direct the films I'm meant to direct, I tell the stories I'm meant to tell. I wish all filmmakers had this outlook.

About a year ago, I did a interview series for Film Courage and I've had an overwhelming amount of filmmakers reach out to me for advice. I have also done quite a bit of panels on the topics as well. I don't know all the answers, but I do know what works for me. I'm no where near where I would like to be in my career, but I am always happy to help fellow filmmakers and to make myself available to them. Any filmmaker that wants to talk films can ALWAYS reach out to me. I'll always make time.

Any tips to first time writers?

Playing with action figures is one of a child's first steps towards storytelling. It's amazing how they create such unique and interesting storylines so easily when they don't realize they are. I know I use to do that. It's amazing how uninhibited we become while being preoccupied. Sometimes when I'm trying to think, I still play with my old action figures, it makes me think without realizing I am, and shuts off the part of my mind that blocks me because the most important thing is having fun in that moment and not getting caught up in overthinking the details. You can always go back and add the details after. Just get stuff on the page. Once you aren't facing the blank page, it's a lot less intimidating. I always like to come up with something that really excites me about the movie, which is usually the ending. That way I build up to that the whole time.

JEFF BURR
DIRECTOR

Jeff Burr is a filmmaker who has written, produced or directed 25+ feature films and television shows. His work has played in film festivals such as South By Southwest, Sitges, Milan and Tokyo, and he has been honored with 4 screenings at the American Cinematheque. His independent film EDDIE PRESLEY was one of the first feature films bought by the Sundance Channel, and he has worked with such actors as Viggo Mortensen, Vincent Price, Terry O'Quinn, Roscoe Lee Browne and Quentin Tarantino. He is currently developing several films and television shows through his company Clan Cameron Cinema.

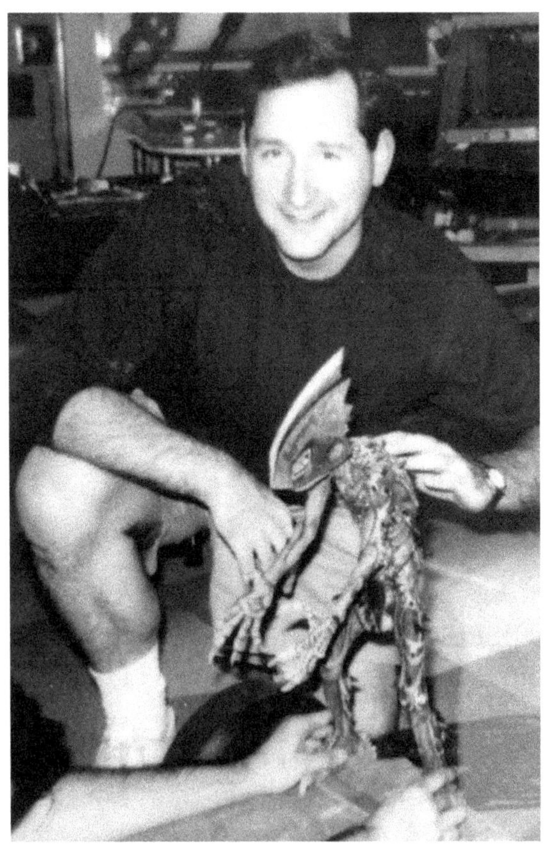

JEFF BURR
On the set of Puppet Master 5

What made you want to become a director? Why the horror genre?

Many things made me want to be a filmmaker...as a kid, I had a big interest in storytelling and entertaining. My parents were involved in community theater, and seeing them onstage and seeing sets constructed, being backstage for rehearsals sometimes, etc. contributed to the magic of performance, even if it was a small stage in Dalton, Georgia. I was also always intrigued by movies. Movies had a bigger cultural relevance and impact in the pre-internet days. If you didn't see a movie in the theater, who knows when you could see it? So it was much more "special" to go to the movies than now. I was involved in theater in junior high and high school, and I started making little super 8 movies around junior high. I really got more and more obsessed with it, and the movies became more and more elaborate. My brother, who was a few years older than me, was a big influence too. He would help me with the super 8 movies, and would turn me on to certain films and music. As for the horror genre, I was definitely captivated by the Universal horror cycle of the 30's and 40's, which I saw on TV, and by early David Cronenberg, Carpenter, etc etc. Too many to mention. But I always had a love for horror, sci-fi, cult, outre' films. The disreputable genres! But let me make it clear, I also was in love with many other different types of films. And it is a total cliché, but I saw Citizen Kane for the first time in a pristine 35mm print at the Tivoli theater in Chattanooga TN in the spring of 1979 and that had as big an impact on me as any other film I ever saw. That was the kind of film that made you want to run out and make a film after you saw it. Totally inspirational and totally mesmerizing. The other film to have that immediate and strong an impact on me was 2001:A Space Odyssey.

Your first film THE OFFSPRING (1987), you cast Susan Tyrrel, Clu Gulager and Vincent Price! How did that casting come about and what did making that movie and directing a legend like Vincent Price teach you about making movies and working with top actors?

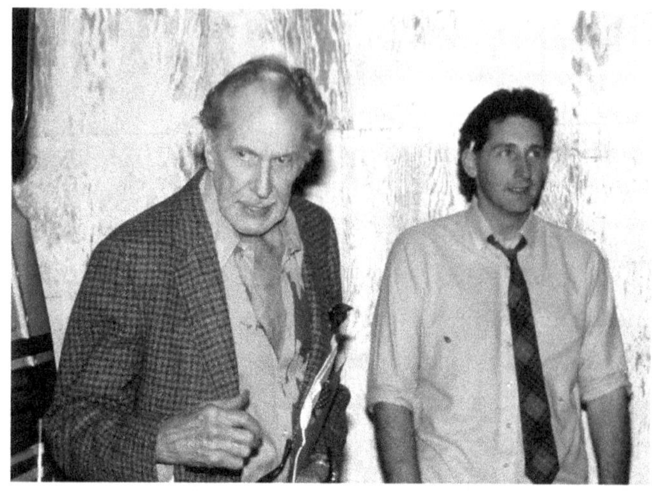

The legendary Vincent Price and Jeff Burr on set.

The casting of my first film FROM A WHISPER TO A SCREAM was done by me. We did not have a casting director. Of course it was a different time, a different era, and I don't know if it would be possible to do it today the same way with the same results. The saga of getting Vincent Price in the film was a textbook example of "never give up, never take no for an answer". Aim high and see what happens. The thing about wanting these actors in my film was simply this: I was sincere about my admiration of their talent, and I knew a lot about their work in the past. What I learned from that film was that actors are everything. It is amazing what genuinely good actors can bring to a film. That is not to say that I served all the actors in the best way, in particular Susan Tyrrell, who was an amazing talent and presence, in that case I may have imposed a performance onto her that wasn't the best road to take. I made it a point however, to cast a lot of the actors against type, or to give them roles that they hadn't had the opportunity to explore before. I learned a heck of a lot from each and every actor in that movie. Directing Vincent Price was not directing a legend, it was directing an actor who wanted direction. He made it easy for me to work with him in the short time we had, and was nothing short of totally professional and totally engaged and totally entertaining on and off of the set. I am very lucky to have been able to work with him, and it is something I will never forget and will always appreciate. Forgive the shameless plug, but anyone remotely interested in this film, please get the Scream Factory Blu Ray, which has two amazing documentaries from Daniel Griffith's Ballyhoo Productions.

In 1990, you directed LEATHERFACE: Texas Chainsaw Massacre III with R.A. Mihailoff as Leatherface, which by the way, I snuck into the theater when I was 12 to see it and it scared the hell out of me for weeks! It was the first Chainsaw film I ever saw and made me go check out the first two and see what I had been missing. I'm glad I did, so thanks Jeff! What was it like for you

stepping up to the plate to direct a sequel of a beloved classic? What were some of the challenges you had during the making of the film and what did you learn from the experience as a director for a studio produced film (as opposed to an indie with more control)?

That film was a strange experience for me for many reasons. I took over the film from another director with little prep time, it was the first film that I made that I didn't have a personal connection to the producers on the set, and it was the first film which I had to totally exhaustively justify every creative decision I made to a studio. It really was a clash of personalities all the way around, as I never bonded with Bob Shaye, Mike Deluca, Sara Rischer, or especially Bob Engleman. That is not to say that I was right and they were wrong, etc. It was probably that we all had different sensibilities. But on this particular film, I feel that if I was left alone to make the film I had in my head, it would have been a better film (at least before the MPAA got involved). But any director worth his salt would say that. What I did learn from the experience, although it took me a while to learn it, is that the only solution to a bad film experience is to make another film. You have to move forward, like the proverbial shark, or you die. You cant beat yourself up over a bad experience, even though it does take a psychic toll. You have to jump on the cinematic horse again as soon as possible and ride. And forgive another shameless plug, but if you are remotely interested in this movie, check out the New Line DVD put out over a decade ago which has some good revealing documentaries made by Jeffrey Schwartz.

What is the best way for a new director to communicate with an actor on set? Any shorthand tips?

The best way a new director should communicate with an actor is from a position of mutual respect and especially mutual trust. A director has to create an environment for the actor to be confident enough to fail, to try things that may not work but will lead to some amazing discoveries along the way. I know it is often impossible, but try to spend as much time with the cast BEFORE shooting starts. This will actually save time in shooting because the "feeling out" period has already happened. It doesn't have to involve formal rehearsal, although that can be wonderful too. It could involve talking about everything BUT the character and the movie. There is no shorthand to a really good performance. That said, you can sculpt a performance in the editing room. That is one of the most imperative things for a director to do, a filmmaker to do. You have to be right with the actors on the set, and you have to be just as close to them in the editing room. Every day. YOU (the filmmaker) have to pick the takes that are used. YOU the filmmaker have to determine which moments are used. A performance is a mosaic made up of many tiles and you have to put them together.

When casting, what is the number one quality you look for in an actor? How

do you distinguish good acting from bad?

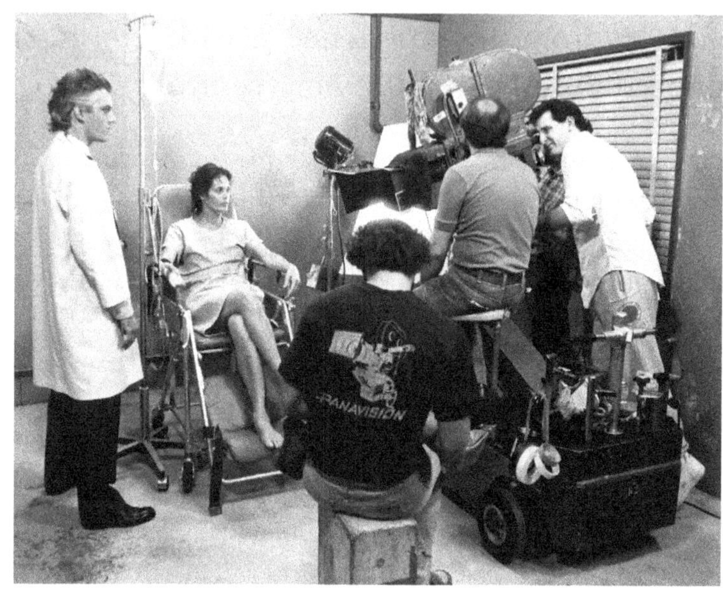

Burr behind the camera on set.

Casting is an amazing process, and it can be exhausting too. One thing that I look for is a "spark", some kind of intelligence, charisma, talent, humor, whatever. I try to make the uncomfortable situation as comfortable as possible. I don't look for a performance in the room, that will take place on the set between "action" and "cut". You just want to see a spark, some creative ideas and choices, that may be totally "wrong" at the moment, but hints at greater things underneath. And so often, your preconceived notions about the character are blown out of your mind by an actor who brings something totally different. Also, you might learn more about an actor's approach to the work by just talking with them, as opposed to making them read one or two pages with little or no context. Delay the final decision as long as is possible for the film, as keeping your options open until the last possible moment can yield huge dividends. In a professional situation, you also have to have a good rapport with your casting director, and if it is humanly possible, cast the casting director yourself. He or she has to know the film you have in your head to make, and you have to be on the same page. And make sure there is no agendas with the casting directors. I've had bad experiences with some in-house casting directors that had their own "favorite" actors, and would bring them in even after I said no to show the producers. Distinguishing good acting from bad? Well, often that is in the eye of the beholder, a matter of taste. Ultimately it is the director who is going to be working closely with the actors, so it should ALWAYS be his or her call as to who is in the movie. Unfortunately, in a professional context, it doesn't always work that way, especially with the leads. One last thing about the casting process...trust your gut, intuition, whatever you want to call it. If you feel it, and continue to feel it, there is something there. And one last last thing about the casting process...whenever possible, see the damn actors in person, don't rely on a tape/upload. There is a NIGHT AND DAY difference between seeing someone in the room and relating as fellow artists, and seeing an image on the computer.

In your experience, what are the mechanics needed for a successful scare in a

horror movie? Is it hard today to make things "scary"? Do you think audiences are being desensitized to violence in today's world and is that having an effect on the modern horror films being made?

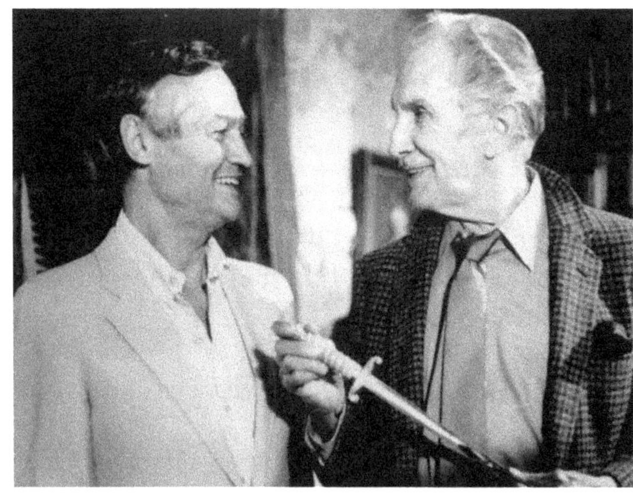

Roger Corman and Vincent Price on set.

The sheer volume of horror films made are one of the main reasons it is hard to make something "scary". Audiences feel they have seen it all, and they have, so it is up to the filmmaker to make them see something they haven't seen before. Easy to say, darn near impossible to do, because we have such collective influences, etc. Horror films have been around now for about 120 years, so that is an awful lot of iconic images in our unconscious. And yes, the world as we know it and see it every day in a variety of ways impacts what really is scary. I think people are more desensitized to images in general. So the filmmaker truly has to work harder, a lot harder, to come up with genuinely unsettling things for their horror movies. I think the only way to do it is to really delve into what makes you scared, what is totally creepy to you, what experiences do you have that were tense/panic-inducing/pants-shitting terrifying? It is the specific that becomes the universal.

What is the worst thing an actor can do on set while working with a director? The best?

The worst thing an actor can do on set while working with a director is not know his lines, be totally unprepared, immersed in social media right before the director says "action" and right after the director says "cut", etc. This has actually happened to me. What the actor has to realize, as does the director (and if they haven't realized it, they shouldn't be on a set) is that the time between the words "action" and "cut" are sacred. Everyone on the crew is totally focused on bringing exactly what is needed for the performers to do their thing, and magic, real magic, real alchemy, real history, can happen. So the actor has to be so ready to bring every ounce of their talent and magic too. Concentration, total concentration is vital. And another obvious thing that is disastrous to the process is substance abuse. I have worked with more than one actor who has had a problem, and needless to say, it brought nothing to the work other than misery. The best thing an actor can do is come to the set totally prepared, with a point of view, and a willingness to alter his preparation in search of another idea. You could say the same thing about a director!

If you could pick one tip to give yourself when you were making LEATHERFACE: Texas Chainsaw Massacre III (1990), what would that be and why?

To have more joy in the process if not the result. Because in that situation, as a so-called "director for hire" (A term I despise) the result was so often out of my hands, as it is in any corporate filmmaking gig. Take the joy in the process, not the result, is one of the more cogent pieces of advice I can offer.

What are the biggest mistakes you see new directors make?

Probably the biggest mistake I see new directors making is being too easily satisfied. Too easily satisfied with the idea, with the script, with the cast, with the editing, with the movie!! Another thing I see is the filmmakers being more excited about the gear they are using (we've got an awesome drone! We're shooting on the RED, etc.) than what's being put in front of that amazing equipment. I (and the rest of the world) would rather see a fascinating movie with interesting actors that doesn't have ten drone shots in 8k than the reverse. The script and the actors cannot be totally fixed in post-production. They can certainly be improved, but the lipstick on a pig saying is applicable.

What are two of the biggest pitfalls you have encountered in making independent films, for yourself and others, and what is your advice to help others avoid similar things happening to them?

In all honesty, in my independent films, one of the biggest problems is that I have been so eager to show my independence that the films invariably become self-indulgent. You have to be hard-headed and have a vision to get any independent film off the ground, but I feel I have been looser as a director on some of my "corporate" films than my indie ones. I don't make any distinction between them, however, I give my all to each and every movie I make. There is no A job and B job, there is just to try and make the best film possible given the variables you have to work with and around. But self-indulgence is a trap and I don't have an answer to what it actually means. Because every personal film is an indulgence, and every film you make personal is one too. David Lynch is one of the most self-indulgent filmmakers around, as was Fellini, but damn if you cant take your eyes off their work! You just have to make the film in your head, get the film that is in your head onto whatever capture medium you are working with! But in the end, if ten people you totally trust say you are creatively drunk, you might want to sit down and have an espresso.

Who is your favorite horror movie monster and why does this monster work for you as a director and lover of the genre?

I would say Frankenstein's monster is probably my favorite horror movie monster because of the pathos and the implications of the themes in those films. Any movie monster that can make you question "what is human" and scare you to boot is okay in my book. Also I have a real soft spot for aquatic monsters, because I love the water. Of course the Creature from the Black Lagoon heads that list.

What was it about Leatherface's character that made him so terrifying and how did you use those elements in your film and to terrify the audience?

Leatherface in Tobe Hooper's 1974 movie was terrifying because he was physically imposing and seemingly without a traditional moral center, just like the rest of the family. No amount of logic, pleading, crying, would ever help your case if you were trapped in their house. And Leatherface seemingly regarded outside humans as just another source of sustenance. The Texas Chainsaw Massacre is one of the most intense films ever made, it is grueling, and yes, there are some laughs but those laughs come out of fear and disbelief. It is a true masterpiece of independent, regional filmmaking, and deserves every ounce of recognition it has received. The New Line film LEATHERFACE was an entirely different construction, much more corporate and safe. What I did try to do with Leatherface and the whole family was to give them an organic dynamic, and to me the most interesting parts of that movie are the family's interaction.

What are the top elements you look for in a horror script as a director?

What I look for in a horror script as a filmmaker is a solid original idea, and an ever-building sense of dread. Of course, every director says the same thing too: characters you can relate to, or at least one character that is an audience surrogate, dramatic reversals, twists as the story progresses, etc. One main thing I would look for is an actual STORY worth telling, not just cardboard characters waiting to be cut up. But of course any director who has made his share of horror films have made films that fall into that category!

What is your approach to working with a film crew? Is there a routine? Could you tell us the process in which you work with a crew & DP on set?

The main thing about working with a DP and a crew is that YOU ALL HAVE TO BE MAKING THE SAME MOVIE. And in order for that to happen, you as a director have to have a vision of the movie and be able to communicate that vision to everyone. That is why pre-production time is essential. You as the director have to have "dream time" with the script, enough time to think about what the movie is really about, and to make it your own. Then you have to cast the technical team just like you cast the actors. Take your time, aim high, and LISTEN. Everyone on the crew can contribute amazing things, if they know what you are going after, if they know the game plan, then they can riff off that plan. It is the director's job to see the big picture, and to know how each set-up will integrate into the next. Working with the DP in pre-production always involves talks of look, style, etc. It is good to show examples of ideas to them, but not just clips from other movies. Look for paintings, sculpture, a line from a poem, that may help articulate what you are going for. Don't be afraid to be a little obtuse. You never know what will make something click in someone else's mind. And it is very important to develop a mutual respect and trust with your DP, just like your actors. And, another tip: the more involved your crew is the better the experience will be. Make your script available to everyone on the crew and insist they read it. That way they will know context, which will help in the non-linear scheduling of most movies. On the other side of the coin, if there is a disruptive influence on the crew, take them aside and voice your concerns. If it still persists, don't be afraid to get rid of them. As a famous director used to say on the first day of filming to his gathered crew: "I know you are all great at what you do, but I also know there is always one asshole. And I will find him."

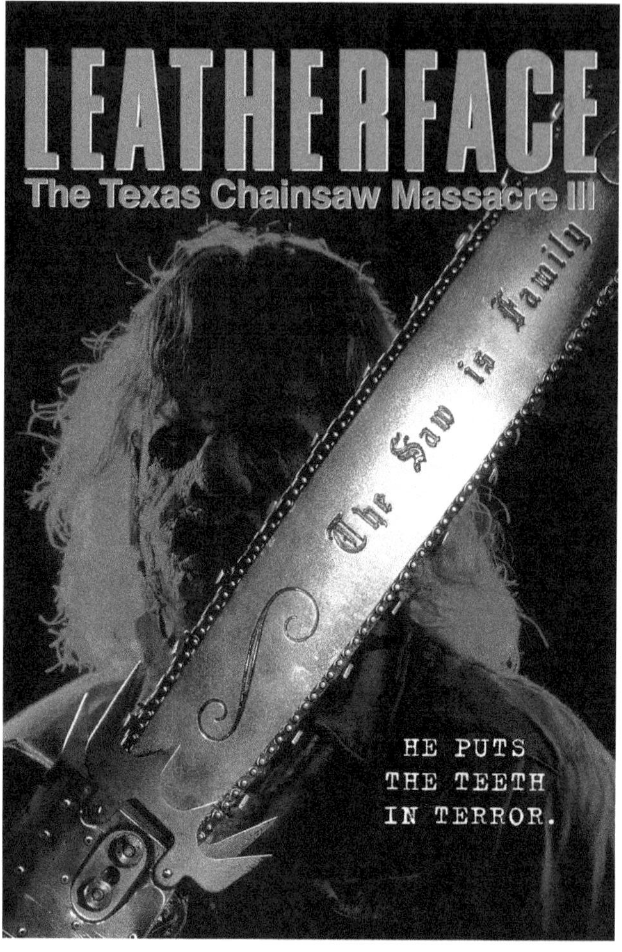

LEATHERFACE: Texas Chainsaw Massacre III (1990)
Directed by JEFF BURR

If you could choose one horror film director in the history of horror cinema that influenced you as a filmmaker, who would it be and why?

I would have to say George Romero, he's more of an inspiration than anything. The way he makes movies is the way I would always like to make movies, such as working with a small batch of close collaborators, totally independently, in a region far from Hollywood that he knows so well. And I would have to put David Cronenberg and John Carpenter in there too, for their independent spirit and intelligence and craft.

What was the biggest production challenge you've ever faced, how did you deal with it and were you happy with the outcome?

As a filmmaker, I am never happy with the outcome. In your mind, it can always be better, different, whatever. Being a filmmaker dooms you to a lifetime of "what ifs, I shouldas, if onlys," etc. I have had my share of production challenges, and they are all different but all the same. They have to be solved with a combination of knowing what battles are worth really fighting, dealing with a variety of people in a variety of different ways, not giving up, and knowing when to move on. You have to be able to think on your feet, and also to think like a chess player, several or many moves ahead, especially on low budget films. That only comes with experience, so the best way to learn is by doing. And of course you are going to make a ton of mistakes, but on every film, and I really mean this, on every film you learn more and more and more. That is the beauty of filmmaking, or any art form...you can never learn it all. There will always be a new way of doing things, new techniques that are available, new actors with new points of view, etc. You have to keep an active mind and body for any kind of longevity in this field.

If you could pick 5 horror films that would be required viewing for a new filmmaker about to make their first horror film, what would those be and what can they learn from watching them?

Picking any five films for anyone to watch is so difficult. But I would say to expand the definitions of the genre by these picks:

PEEPING TOM and PSYCHO...both 1959/60.

EYES WITHOUT A FACE (1959)

THE THING 1951/1982 (both versions)

INVASION OF THE BODY SNATCHERS 1956/1978 (both versions)

THE VANISHING (1988)

What was the best advice you've ever received in this crazy business and why did it help you?

The best piece of advice I got from anyone in this business sounded somewhat depressing. It was from the editor/director Peter Hunt, who had done huge movies (all of the early Sean Connery James Bond films, etc), and worked with big stars such as Lee Marvin, David Niven, etc. He told me "Hollywood will be through with you before you are through with Hollywood." And I was 21 at the time! But what he meant of course is that our love for making movies will never leave us, even if the gatekeepers have closed and locked the studio gates. In this era, though, filmmakers don't need the Hollywood system or a lot of money to make films. It has never been easier to create something that lasts 90 minutes or so that looks and sounds like a movie. Getting someone to watch your 90 minutes of movie has never been harder, however! So it is really the truly dedicated, the ones that have a nagging vision, that have a special film in their heads that is eating its way out, the ones that never give up and keep creating beyond all odds, they will get their work out there to be seen and experienced by the viewing public.

AND THOSE ARE THE MOVIES I WANT TO SEE.

WILLIAM BUTLER

ACTOR / WRITER / DIRECTOR / PRODUCER

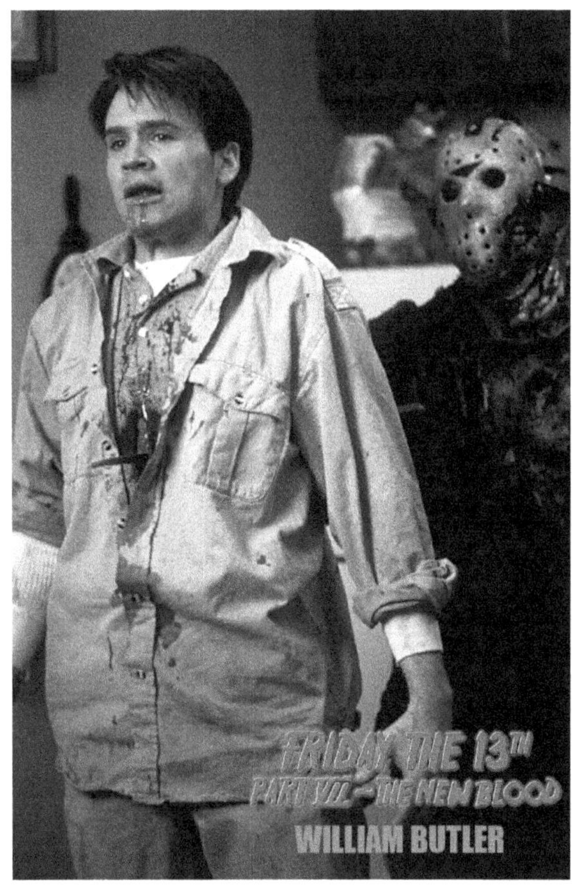

Both Butler and Kane Hodder's first shot in Friday the 13th VII where Butler was Kane Hodder's first kill.

After getting his start as the lead special effects coordinator for Empire pictures, a company responsible for producing over a hundred genre related productions, Butler became horror's boy-next-door, appearing in many films including FRIDAY THE 13th PART VII, LEATHERFACE and the remake of George Romero's classic zombie epic NIGHT OF THE LIVING DEAD (1990) Butler continued acting throughout the 80's and 90's appearing in many other film and television projects such as ARENA, FREDDY'S NIGHTMARES and GHOULIES 2.

Since then he has transitioned to a busy writing and directing career where he has written directed and produced for the Walt Disney Company along with hit genre films such as MADHOUSE, FURNACE, RETURN OF THE LIVING DEAD 4, DEMONIC TOYS 2 and he created the GINGERDEAD MAN franchise which has spawned five sequels, a successful comic book series and toys.

What is the best way for a new director to communicate with an actor on set? How did your background as an actor help you as a director and writer?

It's incredibly important, but it's not just communication as you need to be a bit of a mind reader. Two of my favorite times on set are the first couple of days where you as the director need to quickly figure out how the actor works and what his or her process is to get to where they need to be. Some actors simply rip their pages out of the script and have no real idea what the movie is about, some need to build and entire history for their character, some need tons of rehearsal and others don't want any at all.

The truth is there is no correct way for them to get there as long as they get there. Everybody has a different way of working. My background as an actor helped me tremendously as I had gotten a lot of experience in front of the camera on a variety of projects and budgets.

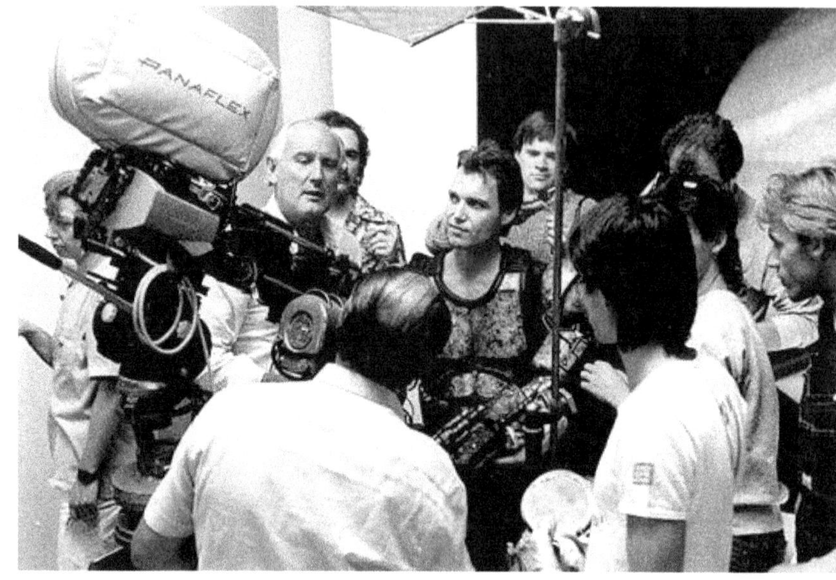

Butler on the set of Empire Picture's ELIMINATORS with actor Patrick Renoylds, Mitch Devane and legendary Director of Photography Mac Ahlberg.

In your experience, what are the mechanics needed for a successful scare in a horror movie? Is it hard today to make things "scary"?

I think in some ways it is growing more difficult to pull off scares due to the massive waves of trend and style that occur in Hollywood. Audiences seem to know all of the tricks we pull and often times anticipate them.

I think the best thing a director can do is dig deep and draw from what truly scares himself in life and draw from that. Every time I have tried to execute a gag that I have already seen or was inspired to do by someone else, it came off as too divisive or manufactured. I think the old trick of letting the audience know ahead of time that something terrible is about to happen and then make them wait for it is often the best course.

What is the worst thing an actor can do on set while working with a director? The best?

Well, in my case the worst thing I ever had happen was when an Oscar nominated actor was smoking crack in his dressing room and then followed me to set (naked) screaming at me followed by throwing a lit butane heater at me. For the average actor, the absolute worst things you can do on my set is:

1. Call cut when you don't like the way they scene is going.

2. Stay in the make-up chair too long.

3. Complain about your hotel room.

4. Don't come to work drunk or on drugs.

5. Sleep with your co-stars (even though they are going to ignore this one)

6. Be late to any part of the production.

7. Change too much of your dialogue without discussing it before hand.

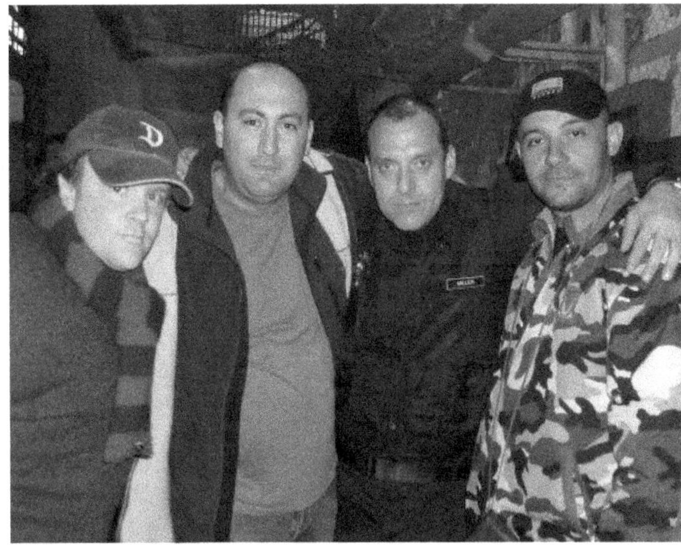

On location in Nashville on the feature FURNACE with Director of Photography Viorel Sergovici and lighting designer Lucian Diaconu and a very intoxicated Tom Sizemore.

8. Ignore my direction.

9. Get drunk every night after wrap.

10. Cut or dye your hair differently after you are cast and before we get to set.

The one thing that performers need to understand is that while you can mess up a directors program on set with bad behavior – we always have the last laugh in the editing room. I have seen a lot of performers close-ups and coverage end up on the cutting room floor for bad behavior on set. The other thing to keep in mind is that I hear, on average, from 3-4 other directors or casting people for a report on your behavior. Once we are free from your antics we do not hold back when it comes to warning our friends.

If you could pick one tip to give yourself when you were making your first feature film, what would that be and why?

DO NOT TRY TO BE EVERYONE IN THE PRODUCTION'S FRIEND. It blew up in my face in so many ways. Once they think you are a pushover everyone on set will try to manipulate you to get their way – from the Executive Producer to the Line Producer. The fact is you are in charge and some people are not going to agree with all of your choices. You have to keep to yourself from day one. Otherwise if you try to be too nice during prep, they will all hate you when you have to put your foot down to make the movie you want. The bottom line is – at the end of the day it's your name that says "directed by" and you will be blamed if you let too much bad input infect your vision.

As an actor, what qualities do you admire and look for in your director?

For me personally, I need a director who is into rehearsal and encouragement. I do not do well with mean directors who think berating you is going to get you there. Back in the day I would give a horrible performance if the director was hard on me as I would become a trembling sweaty mess.

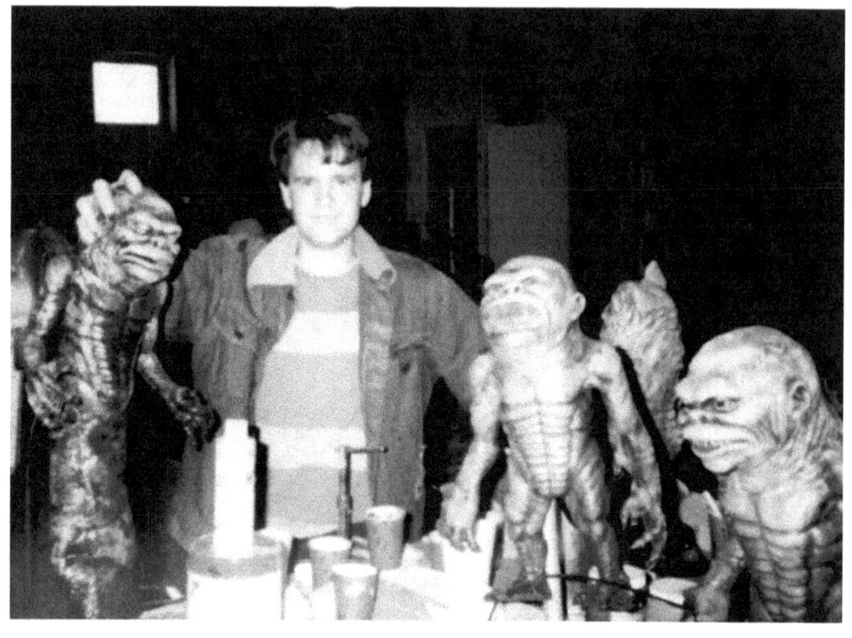

Butler at John Carl Beuchler's MMI where they designed and painted the Ghoulies color scheme.

Who is your favorite horror movie monster and why does this monster work for you as a actor and director?

Hard question, I am into them all. I suppose Jason Voorhees gets my vote as his lore and endurance seems to have worked for so long. Plus it helps that I was one of Jason's many victims!

In the past you worked in special makeup FX. What is that process like in terms of working with a director on set?

In order for the relationship to work, the effects team has to be highly organized and very aware of the director's vision. It is imperative that the FX crew be ready for anything, and that includes the gag or makeups failing or breaking on set. Secret plan B and plan C for the effects guys is very important – and NEVER let anyone in production see you panic or break a sweat.

What's a great low-budget recipe for making fake blood? How about guts and brains?

Corn Syrup Fake Blood:

1 cup corn syrup (commonly sold as Karo Syrup).

3 tablespoons water.

2 tablespoons of red food coloring.

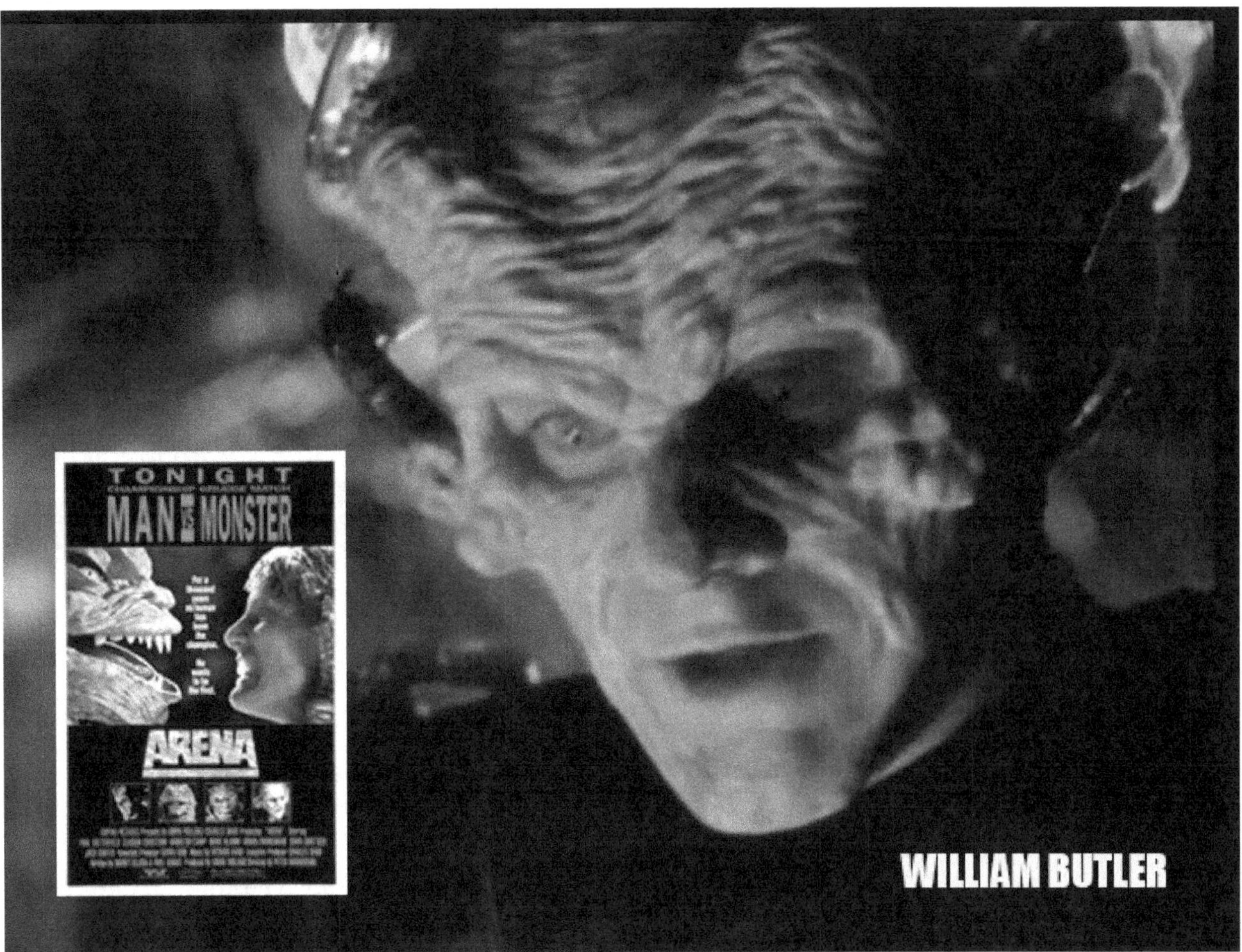

Butler on the set in Italy for Empire Pictures ARENA, make-up designed by artist Jeff Farley. Butler sat in the chair for three hours a day in order for the make-up to be complete.

A few drops of green food coloring.

If you put two table spoons of liquid soap in the mix it will not stain clothes, but you can't put it in your mouth.

Also shaving cream instantly removes fake blood stains from your skin.

When casting, what is the number one quality you look for in an actor?

Connection with the material as well as willingness to listen as much as speak.

What is your approach to working with actors on set? Is there a routine? Could you tell us the process in which you like to work on set?

I prefer the actors show up at least three days prior to shooting for table reads and rehearsal. I also like to work with the performer in advance to make sure they are 100% comfortable with all of the vernacular of the dialogue. For the first few days, I play music in between takes that reflects the tone of what I am trying to pull off to help make sure we all stay on the same page. I do a couple of takes where we strictly stay on book and then with time permitting I let the performers improvise the scene.

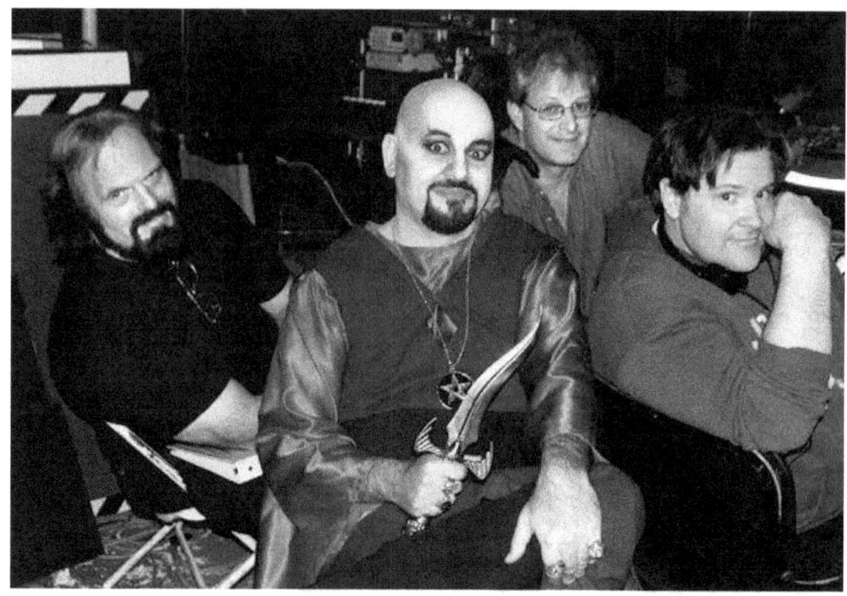

Butler on the set of GINGERDEAD MAN 2, the successful franchise that he created for Charles Band's Full Moon. Along with him are longtime friends and colleague's John Carl Buechler, Kenneth J. Hall and Michael S. Deak.

If you could choose one horror film director in the history of horror cinema that influenced you as a filmmaker, who would it be and why?

I'm a Spielberg boy myself but there are many: Stuart Gordon, Hitchcock and even John Waters.

What was the biggest production challenge you've ever faced, how did you deal with it and were you happy with the outcome?

Being forced to cast Tom Sizemore in a movie while he was in the depths of serious addiction was the most difficult obstacle. I handled the situation, because I wasn't afraid of him. I don't know how someone not strong enough to stand up for themselves could navigate a person like that otherwise. Having had addiction issues of my own in the past, I was very aware of every single childish move he would try to make with me and it frustrated him that I refused to react. In the end, despite him literally falling asleep during half the scenes he was in, we managed to cut him together into a decent performance. Aside from his despicable behavior, he still is a terrific actor. They way I look at it is, whatever gets you there is okay with me.

How important is networking in the film business and why?

It's really important and really gross and irritating. You have to want it very hard but not to appear so. Your behavior while networking is of the utmost importance. No more than a drink and a half while at show business events or parties. Hollywood is a very small town and they love to eat their own so keep it cool and clean.

If Pinhead and Jason had a cage fight with two Gremlins and two Critters, who would win this epic battle?

The referee, because he is secretly Leatherface.

JESSICA CAMERON

DIRECTOR / ACTRESS

www.JessicaCameron.com

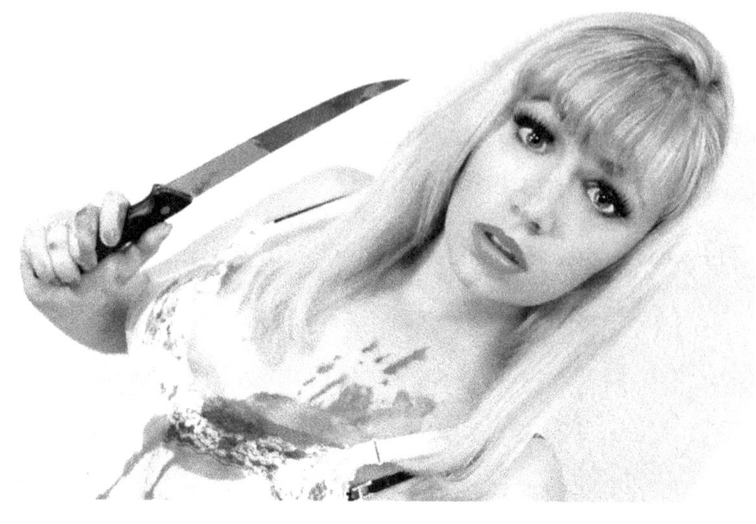

JESSICA CAMERON

Jessica Cameron was born and raised in Owen Sound, Ontario in Canada and moved to Toronto to study fashion at Ryerson University. After finishing her degree she moved to Ohio to work as a fashion designer and in her spare time she decided to try an acting class. The acting bug bit, and Jessica decided to make acting her full time career. In the last few years she has been cast in more then 50 projects including music videos, TV shows and feature films. In 2010 she won an industry award for being a Rising Movie Star. Some of her favorite recent performances include: playing Princess Areola in the film "Potpourri" directed by Elliot Diviney and she starred with horror icon Steven Geoffrey's in the film "Mr. Hush". She also had the chance to work with legendary director Jim Wynorski on the syfy channel film "Camel Spiders" and the established horror director Jeff Burr on "Resurection". She was thrilled to play screen legend Marilyn Monroe in "The Black Dahlia Haunting", having been a fan of hers for many years.

She has starred in 4 web series including the syfy, film noir "Aidan 5" which was nominated for too many awards to list including winning Best Web Series at Gen Con 2012. She played a new age hair dresser Summer Perkins in the comedy series "2 Doors Down",tough as nails Naria Dixon in the action packed series "Caught!" and a horrible mother in the horror series "Funny Man". In 2011 she started her comic book modeling while appearing in Brian Shirley's "Crocaloctopus" and Dennis Willman's "Ginger-Stein". In 2012 she is featured in Dennis Willman's comic book series "The Vengeance of Sleepy Hollow" as well as many more film and TV projects.

On your first directing effort TRUTH OR DARE, what did you learn the most and what do you wish you would have done different in retrospect?

I learned so much about the production side. In retrospect I would never have let my first editor use Final Cut Pro X, which would end up doing a forced up date on itself and un-linking, renaming and triplicating all the files. It was a mess and we basically had to start over from scratch. Then we had to convert everything over to Final Cut Pro 7 and re-edit the film entirely. We did it, and we made some improvements, but it is absolutely terrifying to loose everything like that! Thank goodness my dear friend Aaron M Lane was there to guide me through the process, otherwise I might have gone mad!

What's your approach to working with actors on set?

Honestly it depends on the actor. Different actors work in different ways. On Truth Or Dare my group of actors would run their lines the night before with me in the master suite where we were staying. We would work on intention/inflection/and any changes as a group and then if needed I would work directly with whomever needed more one on one attention. I like to talk with actors about their characters before they get to set so that they can develop the characters completely. I try to hire talented actors that you can trust with developing the material into their own vision which works with mine to make it even stronger.

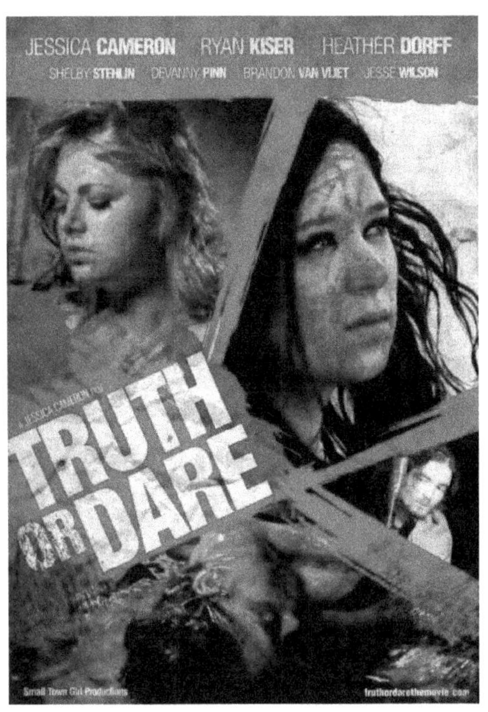

Jessica Cameron's TRUTH OR DARE (2013)

As a female director, what are some of the challenges you faced making your first film in a primarily male dominated genre like horror?

It was a struggle to get anyone to take me seriously at first, people were surprised that I wanted to make a film and many did not know how to react. Many were shocked when they learned that the film I felt so passionate about directing was in fact a graphic, vicious torture flick and some doubted if I could pull it off. The sad reality is there are still some rooms that I find myself in to which I first have to prove that as a woman I deserve to be there. It's not ok, but it is the reality. Luckily for me, I love a challenge. And the more women rise above these difficulties the less these difficulties will occur.

When casting, what is the number one quality you look for in an actor?

The most important thing that I look for is that the actor has the ability to listen and make adjustments well. I would rather have an ok audition from an actor that I can help guide then a great audition from an actor who won't/can't alter their performance upon request. I also check references a lot. I want to know what the actor is like on a real set before they ever get to my set. Some people are just not cut out for it at all, they can't handle the long hours and process.

What do you think about using excessive violence and gore in horror films? What about nudity?

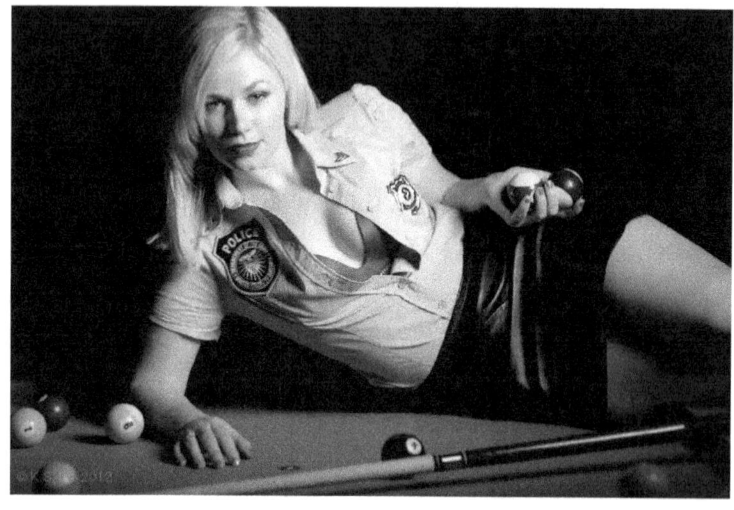

JESSICA CAMERON

If its necessary to the story then I don't have a problem with it at all. If it's done for filler, adding time, or because the film maker is trying to hide some problem then I personally don't like as it usually feels like a distraction. For me as a film fan if its not adding to the story then it is taking away from it. For my latest directing endeavor, MANIA, there is a lot of nudity but its all crucial to the plot. We worked through each of those scenes and during pre-production discussed whether we in fact needed to show everything, and made adjustments based on the best way to bring the story and characters to life. I suspect some will say that the nudity in MANIA is excessive, but I can happily explain why each and every little bit is necessary to the story.

What are some of your pet peeves when acting in lower budgeted movies?

A big pet peeve of mine is when safety concerns are glossed over with little regard. I have been on sets where film makers have tried to get actors to dive off a 35 foot cliff into water, jump off a 9 foot ledge directly onto concrete, fall into patches of poison oak, use live weapons without a proper weapons tech and the list could continue. I understand the nature of low budget film making, but I believe that there are safe ways to do everything without putting anyone at risk.

As an actress, what qualities do you look for in a great director?

I look for directors who have a strong vision that is within reality of what they are able to achieve with the budget that they have. I look for directors who I personally really like as people since if all goes well I know that I will be in regular communication with them for years throughout the life of the project - from pre-production to promoting the finished film. I am a huge supporter of self promotion and of actors promoting their films, and it's stronger for the film when its a collaboration between everyone involved with the project.

What was your biggest production challenge on TRUTH OR DARE and what did you do to overcome it?

The lack of time. As with most films, there's just never as much time as the director would want. We shot Truth Or Dare in 9 days over 11 days. It was hectic, the hours were long and exhausting and everyday we worked our asses off to get all the footage we needed. Luckily we had decided that we would rent out a house that the cast and crew would stay in for most of filming. In retrospect if we had to add in travel time I honestly don't know if we would have been able to get everything that we needed. I am also very honest when hiring cast and crew with what working on a quality indie film will entail - including warning them that this may in fact be the hardest that they ever will work in their life, but it could also be the most rewarding. The pay and hours suck, so its important to find other like minded people whose passion is telling stories like the one that you want to tell, we found the right people on Truth or Dare.

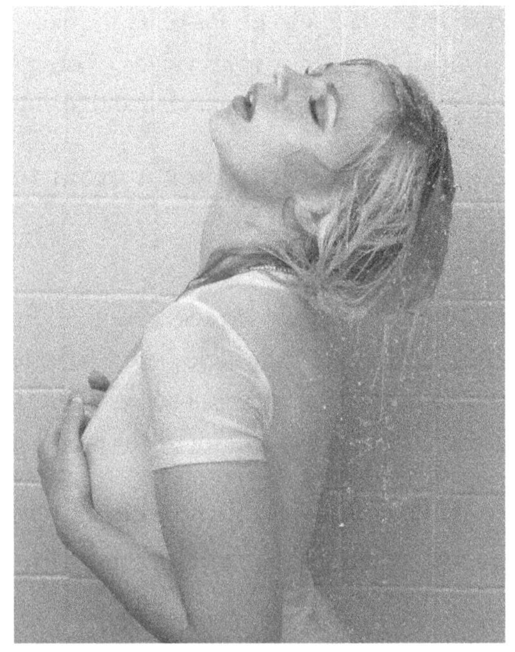

JESSICA CAMERON

The horror genre has a reputation for exploiting and objectifying women, usually to cater to the young male audience. What are your thoughts on this issue?

I personally believe it's the woman's choice whether she wants to put herself in that position (as long as those involved with the film were honest and upfront about their intentions and their story). I have gotten those scripts and met with those type of filmmakers and you know what you're getting yourself into, more often then not. If you don't want to do it then just don't do it. Now I as an actress and filmmaker don't have any interest in being involved in these types of projects, for me it always starts with a great story and progresses from there. I have found that those films which really objectify women typically lack much of a story and have little or no interesting characters. Those are not the types of films I typically watch either, but to each their own.

For our young female readers who want to direct and act, what words of wisdom can you offer to help them stay inspired and avoid some of the pitfalls?

I always say that if you could do anything else with your life and be fulfilled, then do that. Because this industry is a constant fight and constant struggle to which we are all poorly financially compensated for our troubles and rarely if ever do you receive accolades. That said if you cannot imagine your life not in the business, then pursue it with every single moment that you can. Work 18 hours a day, 7 days a week for years to make your dreams a reality. Be early to set, stay late, never complain and go out of your way to learn and help others. The sooner you realize how replaceable we all are, the sooner you will realize that the early bird indeed catches the worm.

What do you think makes a great female antagonist in a horror film? Who is your favorite?

One of my favorites is Amanda Young in the Saw films (played brilliantly by Shawnee Smith). I love her character arc over the series and I have to admit that I did not see many of those twists and turns coming. For me a crucial requirement for a great female antagonist is intellect. Intelligence is dangerous, and sexy so its crucial for modern horror films.

Do you feel that female director works differently than a male one, and if so, what are some of the differences in vision?

Honestly in my opinion every director works differently then every other director regardless of their sex. Directing is really a matter of personal preferences, there is always more then one way to do anything in the film world. Now what works best, well that's a different question.

CHARLIE CLOUSER

FILM COMPOSER

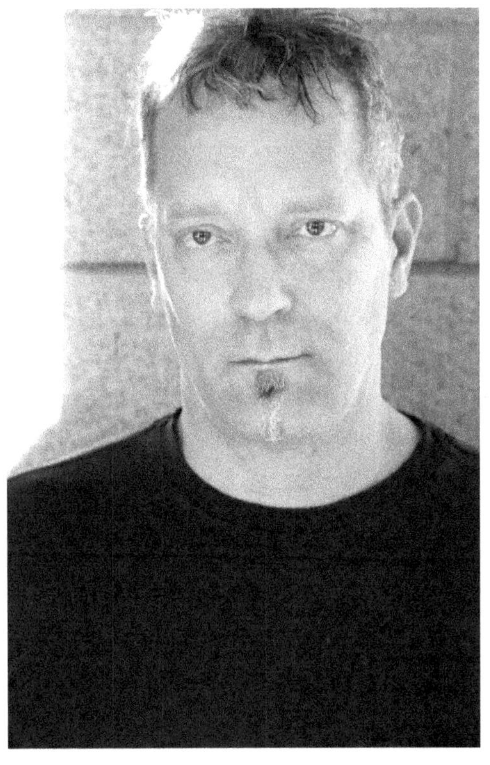

Charlie Clouser
Photo by Zoe Wiseman

Charlie Clouser is a multi-instrumentalist and composer for film, television, and games who lives in Los Angeles. The recipient of ten BMI Film & TV Music awards, Charlie has also received ten platinum and gold record awards for his work with Nine Inch Nails, White Zombie, and others.

His scores for all seven films in the "SAW" series combined brutal electronics and homemade bowed metal instruments with tortured orchestral washes and became landmarks in industrial-strength horror. His scores for "Dead Silence", "Death Sentence", "The Stepfather", "Resident Evil:Extinction", "The Collection" and other films expanded upon these ideas and produced dozens of memorable themes, terrifying ambiences, and tension-filled rhythmic climaxes.

With over two hundred hours of television underscore to his credit, Charlie's scores to the CBS series "Numb3rs" and the NBC series "Las Vegas" spanned a wide range of styles, from ticking-clock hostage dramas and high-energy car chases to comedic casino capers and delicate heartbreak.

Formerly the keyboardist in the band Nine Inch Nails, he has remixed and collaborated with artists as varied as David Bowie, Jamiroquai, Killing Joke, Atari Teenage Riot, and Rob Zombie.

What made you want to become a film composer? What was the transition like for you from playing in live bands to composing scores for Film & TV?

I've always been interested in odd sounds, dark moods, and scary textures more than I was interested in constructing the perfect rock song, and scoring work has a lot of opportunities to pursue those areas of creativity. I seem to associate sounds and chord structures with moods and emotions very strongly, and I guess I have some kind of internal filing system that lets my mind keep track of these associations, so it's never been a struggle for me to decide if a certain instrument or chord structure is right in a given situation. This type of ability is probably more applicable in scoring situations than it is in the world of making albums, although I'm sure it helped me as I made my way in the record industry.

Transitioning from working in the studio and playing live with Nine Inch Nails to scoring was not as big a jump for me as it might be for other recording artists for two main reasons. First off, NIN songs always dealt with dark emotions expressed very strongly, both through Trent's lyrics and vocal performances, but also through the texture and tone of the instrument sounds and heavily processed nature of the whole production. It was these aspects of his music that attracted me to working with Trent in the first place, and my experience and abilities with synthesizers, samplers, and manipulating sound made for a good fit. A second factor that made my transition easier was the years I had spent working in a scoring team before ever becoming involved with NIN. Throughout the late eighties and early nineties I worked as the synth and drum programmer for an Australian composer named Cameron Allan, and together we scored the original "The Equalizer" television series on CBS as well as a few TV movies. Cameron and I shared many of the same musical influences and tastes, artists like Brian Eno, Roxy Music, and Pink Floyd, and it was during those years that I learned how the sausage gets made in the scoring world. Because we had so many of the same musical instincts, this collaboration helped us find ways to create compelling scores that were influenced by the art rock and ambient music genres more than the world of conventional orchestral scoring. After working with Cameron for a decade or so, I then veered off into making records with NIN and doing programming and remixing for other artists in the rock and industrial genres. When I left NIN in 2001 and returned to the scoring world I wasn't just starting from scratch, I already had many years of working as the co-pilot on many scores under my belt. The combination of that earlier scoring experience along with the techniques I honed during the decade of making records made for an interesting mix of skills and influences to bring to the world of scoring, and I'd like to think that combining elements from both of those musical worlds has helped shape my sound and approach a little differently than many other composers.

When you collaborate with a director what is ideal way in which they can communicate their ideas to you in musical terms?

It's rare that I would ever talk with a director in actual musical terms, it's much more likely that we'd talk in emotional terms. So, rather than talking about whether a scene needs major or minor chords, we'd talk about whether a scene needs to feel somber, desperate, or hopeful. That's a simplified description of what actually takes place; we'd usually have a conversation that goes something like, "We need to feel that the situation is not hopeless and that there might be a light at the end of the tunnel, while still feeling a sense of loss for those who died, and a layer of respect for their sacrifice. But not military-style respect and honor… they weren't soldiers after all, so we need to avoid anything that sounds noble in a 'fallen soldier' way. As we move through this thirty-second scene, try to encompass all of those elements while still keeping the tone light and the density low." One of the most important skills to have when working with directors is the ability to discuss emotions in non-musical terms, and to be able to translate between emotion-speak and music-speak in your mind. If the director has a piece of music they've used as a temp track, it's important to find out why they like it and feel that it works with the scene in question, and ideally they might say something like, "I like this piece of temp music because it feels urgent but not big, and it's not conclusive - it doesn't feel like we're at the end of something, it feels more like we're about to find out the 'how' but not the 'why' of the situation. We need to leave the conclusive, resolving, 'discovery of the why' part for later in the story." Being able to internally translate why a piece of music makes someone feel this way, and then express that in musical form without getting bogged down in discussion about the technical or compositional elements in use is a crucial skill. It's rare that a director would really want to talk about the nuts and bolts like tempo, key, or chord structures; it's easier and often more efficient to talk about HOW the music makes them feel rather than WHY it makes them feel that way.

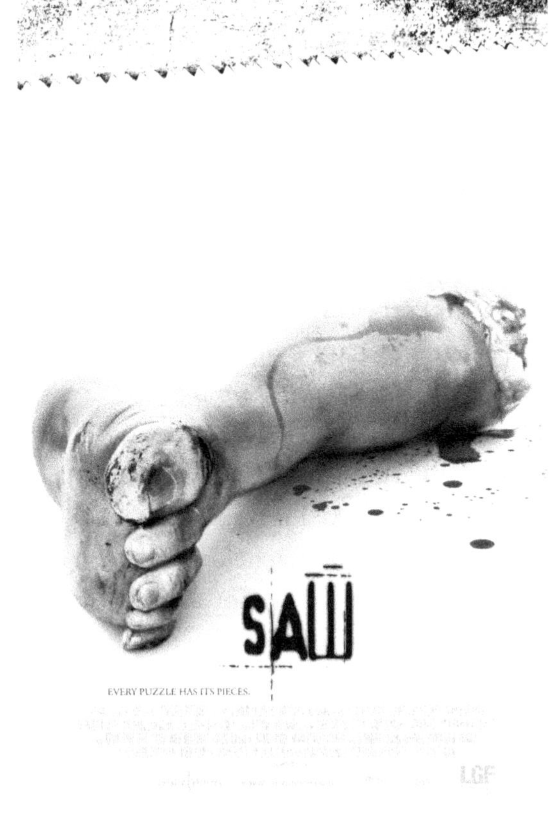

SAW (2004)

When you score, how do you determine when you may have too much music and when it's best to leave it silent?

In some cases the density and intensity of the music needs to be almost the opposite of what's going on in the story at any given moment. If there's lots of action and chaos on screen and in the sound design, such as a big fight scene, it can often be better to have the music take a back seat at that moment. Conversely, it is often the case that a slow, contemplative scene is one where the music can lead a little more, and contain more musical information to help reinforce what the character might be thinking. It's often a juggling act that takes a bit of discussion with the director to determine where the music should follow and where it should lead the story. Sometimes you don't want to let the score foreshadow the story and hint at what's to come, and sometimes the score does need to be "in front of the story" and lead or pull the viewer towards what's going to happen next. Most of the time I rely on my instinct for this, but I always defer to the judgment of the director and always discuss these moments in some detail to make sure that the story is best served by these decisions. Usually, by the time a film is edited and assembled and ready for the scoring process to begin, the writers, director, and editors have already done battle with many of these decisions, and hopefully many of these questions can be marked as "asked and answered" and I can use their decisions as a starting point for my road map of the score. If, during the process of composing the score, I discover an alternative approach for some part of the film, I'll do two versions - one that conforms to the road map that was originally discussed, as well as the alternate approach I may have stumbled upon. At that point, when the director can compare the two ideas side-by-side, it usually makes it easier to decide which approach best serves the story.

What is your personal favorite horror scores and why do you love them so much?

My all-time favorite horror film, and score, is Stanley Kubrick's "The Shining". The dissonant, atonal, clattering nature of the Penderecki pieces that make up much of that score are, to me, utterly unnerving and really conjure up a sense of supernatural events, as though these are the sounds of the spirit world leaking into our dimension. For me that score always sounded as if it was the voices inside Jack Torrance's head, speaking in a language the neither he nor us could comprehend. Those pieces by Penderecki, Ligeti, and Bartok, combined with the ominous and sparse synthesizer pieces by Wendy Carlos and Rachel Elkind, really add up to create a fantastic sense of dread and horror and that film still holds up for me. While not strictly a horror film, I have similar feelings about Kubrick's "2001: A Space Odyssey". There are a lot of Ligeti's compositions used in that film as well, and the atonal, dissonant sound of his choral arrangements really makes me feel as though I'm hearing the voices of the cosmos, and much like in "The Shining", they're speaking in a language I'll never understand.

Is there a bag of tricks you use musically when creating a horror score? Such as certain instrumentation, metallic and grudge sound banks from your library, etc. What is your favorite to use and why?

I do like to use acoustic sounds much more than synthesizer sounds in my scores, and I tend to gravitate towards sounds made by bowing metal instruments and sculptures. I have a nice collection of these instruments, from the well-known Waterphone, which is a fairly common tool in horror sound design, to more elaborate and exotic one-of-a-kind instruments created by the musician, sculptor, and metal fabricator Chas Smith. Many of his instruments have something in common with the Waterphone in that they use metal rods attached to some kind of resonating body, and when the rods are bowed with a normal bow that you'd use with a cello or violin, haunting, sustained, eerie tones are produced. As its name implies, the Waterphone is intended to be filled with water, and when the water sloshes around as the instrument is tilted while bowing, strange pitch effects are the result. However, I prefer to use the Waterphone "dry", which eliminates these wobbly pitch effects and lets me create steady, repeatable pitches and allows me to actually use these sounds more as pitched instruments that can actually play a discernible melody as opposed to just creating wild, wobbly, "horror effects". Chas Smith's instruments do not use water, but create more subtle pitch effects by rotating or flexing the resonant body. As the metal surfaces are bent and stressed, slight variations in pitch and tone are created, and it's these moments that I try to capture to add tension and subtle elements of atonality and dissonance. Recording these instruments can be a challenge from a technical standpoint, but the results are well worth the effort.

I also tend to use a lot of very heavily processed guitar textures, created by playing guitar with a cello bow or an E-Bow electronic bowing device and then manipulated with lots of pitch shifters and echo units. I've been collecting strange guitars and odd effects units for many years, and there are some truly weird instruments in my studio, like the Moog Guitar, some modified lap steel guitars, and other non-traditional guitars that let me create dark drones and strange textures that I rely on quite a bit. The combination of the bowed metal family of sounds along with the processed guitar world allows me to create sounds which have the shape, but not the color, of conventional orchestral instruments. I generally seem to have a mix of about one-third processed guitar, one-third bowed metals, and fill out the remainder with more conventional orchestral sounds like strings and brass. I certainly don't want the music to call too much attention to itself and distract from the story, and using these sounds which are just a little bit left-of-center but still have a familiar tonal shape seems to be a combination I can make work for a wide variety of emotional scenarios.

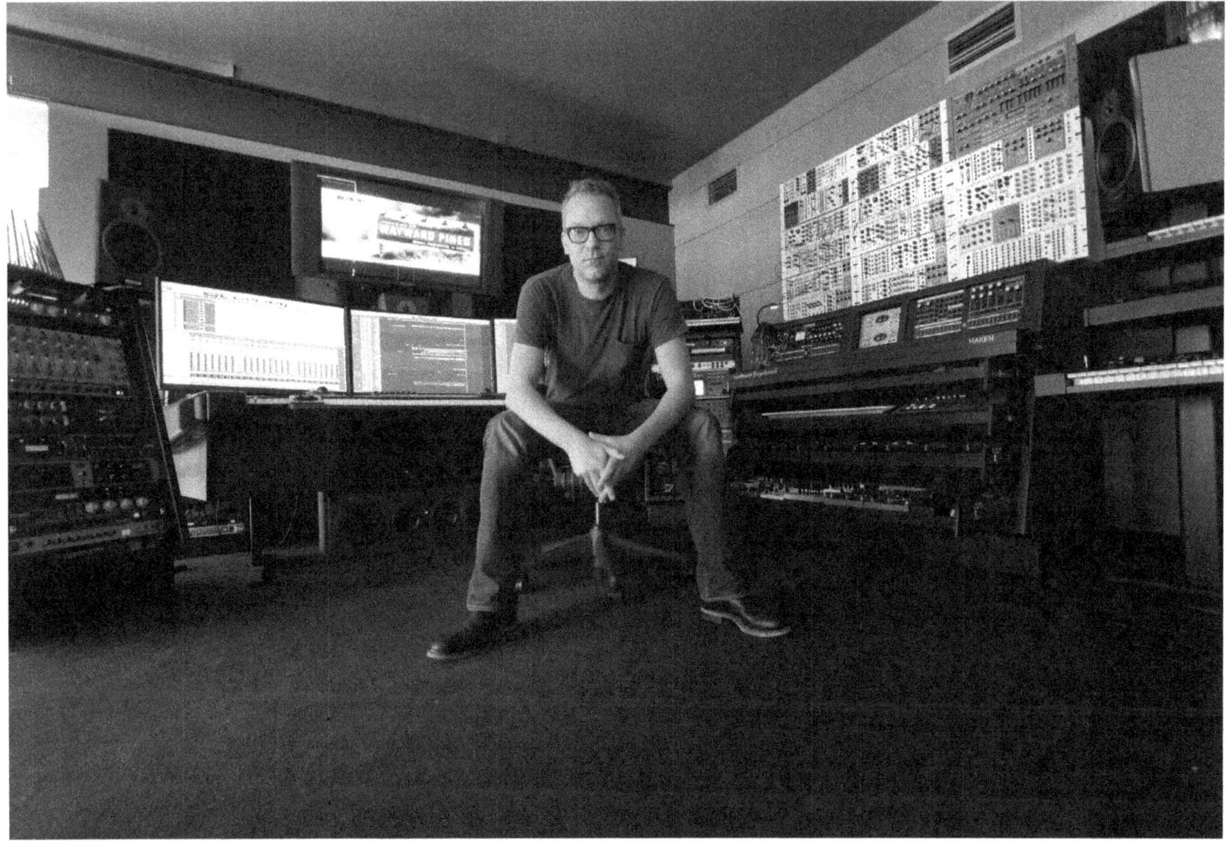

Charlie Clouser in his studio.
Photo by Zoe Wiseman

You can accommodate a lot of emotional shifts by emphasizing or de-emphasizing one sector of that three-way combination. If a scene needs to be totally scary, play down the orchestral stuff and bring up more of the bowed metals. If it needs to be less scary and more warm, eliminate the metal family and use more lush, gentle string sections. I do find that I'm drawn to the types of sounds which can evoke emotion by only playing a couple of notes, and this helps me create a lot of emotional impact while still keeping the compositions very minimal. I don't like energetic flurries of notes and a hailstorm of information flying at the listener; my favorite pieces are usually the most simple and minimal.

What do you think are the three most important musical elements for a score to have in the horror genre?

Dissonance, chaos, and a sense of dread. Dissonance is the easiest aspect to achieve at first but strangely becomes harder to do as you get better at it. The choral arrangements in the Ligeti pieces in "2001" are a perfect example. To me they are a work of pure genius; they're not just a bunch of "wrong notes" smashed together. There's a core that IS harmonious and "tuneful" but other elements work alongside and against the core to create the edge, the sharpness, the sense of endlessly rising or falling that works so well.

Chaos might seem easy at first but can quickly become a mess, and it can take a lot of tinkering to find the right combination of elements that will sound chaotic while still being legible. Those Penderecki pieces in "The Shining" are a great example here - they almost make it sound like Jack Torrance's head is full of insects, or a flock of birds frantically flapping their wings and pecking at his skull, but you can still hear "in between" the sounds and it's not just a solid brick of noisy chaos.

Creating a sense of dread is the perhaps most traditionally musical, and relies a bit less on crazy sound design than creating dissonance and chaos might. This can be accomplished as simply as by using two or three well-picked notes, paced in such a way to evoke a sense of plodding, trudging, limping toward your inevitable doom. John Williams' famous theme from "Jaws" is a great example. There is very little actual musical information contained in the piece, but the instrumentation, the gradually increasing tempo, and the eventual introduction of the higher counterpoint melody really drives the scenes and nobody who hears it will fail to sense the dread it embodies.

What is the scariest scene you've ever scored and what were the elements (visual, musical, etc.) that made it so scary?

The scene that still sends chills down my spine is the ending of the first "SAW" film. [SPOILER ALERT] When the Jigsaw character slowly gets up from the floor, and it's revealed that he's not just the corpse of an earlier victim but is in fact the central figure and mastermind behind the entire plot, it's such a great twist ending. Just when you thought you had the whole thing figured out, this whole new dimension to the story is revealed, and his slow, casual, almost unconcerned performance as he rises and delivers the monologue over the ending montage of flashbacks is one of my favorite scenes to have scored. As Jigsaw trudges slowly toward the door, and the music gradually rises in intensity while maintaining that plodding, "slow but rapid" feel, seems to have become memorable and really helps to wrap up the story in drive home the sense of conclusion. Even though that scene doesn't have much in the way of actual violence or action, the sense of horror at the realization of what Jigsaw's scheme was all about is what makes it so scary for me. Definitely one of my favorite film moments and I'm so glad that I could be a part of it.

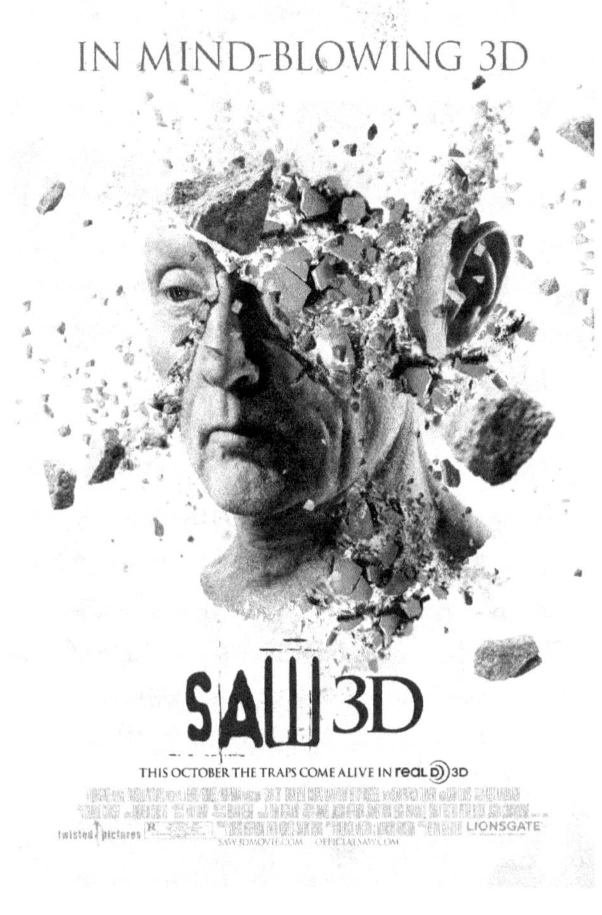

SAW 3D (2010)

In the horror genre, what are the biggest mistakes you see in film scores in both low to mid sized budgets to major studio films?

I think one of the biggest mistakes, and one I'm frequently guilty of, is doing too much, trying too hard to beat the audience over the head with mayhem and noise in an attempt to get them amped up about what's on the screen. Some of my favorite scores, and the ones I'm most envious of, are the most minimal and stripped-down. The score to "Sicario" has some of these moments, where the score is so simple and minimal and yet so effective. Those pieces with the low strings bending downward, which almost evoke the "Jaws" theme, work so well in that film and I think they make the whole thing sound more "important" and "grown-up" somehow. In many of the sequels in the "SAW" franchise, we had to keep upping the ante and raising the stakes, and each trap scene had to be bigger and more extreme than the one before, and in many cases I found myself almost painted into a corner. In many cases I just had to keep jacking everything up and adding more and more layers of extreme sonic mayhem in an effort to avoid the sensation that we'd "taken our foot off the gas" and let the energy level drop instead of endlessly rising toward the film's end. I'm sometimes envious of scores that don't need to do this, and to be fair it's not surprising that this was the case as we worked our way through seven films, one every year, each one more insane than the last. Now that the franchise has had some time to rest, when we start fresh with the next installment we have the opportunity to reset the insanity meter and take a more measured approach and bring things to a boil more slowly, and I'm looking forward to that process.

Who are your musical influences, both in film & TV in in live music? Why are they so influential to you and how did they help shape your musical style and who you are?

In the world of albums, my earliest influences were David Bowie, Brain Eno, Pink Floyd, and Kraftwerk, in about equal measure. I still listen to their records all the time and I think these are the most important artists to me in terms of exposing me to the type of sounds and moods that I find interesting. As my record collection grew and the post-punk movement started in the early eighties, artists like Talking Heads, Joy Division, Killing Joke, Gang of Four, and Public Image Ltd became influential as I searched for darker, more heavily processed textures and more aggressive sounds. Much of the work of these artists has a "cinematic" quality, and I think that's part of the reason I was attracted to them, and also has a lot in common with some of the influences that shaped Trent Reznor's musical approaches, so it wasn't too surprising to find that we shared some of the same ideas about music and sound. One of my favorite albums of all time is a collaboration between David Byrne of Talking Heads and Brian Eno called "My Life In The Bush Of Ghosts". This album was groundbreaking in so many ways, encompassing early sample-collage techniques and odd juxtaposition of elements, and is almost abstract in form while still feeling like it has a strong, propulsive rhythm driving it forward. Another collaboration between Byrne and Eno from that same time period is the album "The Catherine Wheel" which has some of the most amazing musical sound design and strange instrumentation I've ever heard, and I still revisit both of these records frequently to remind myself of what is possible.

In the scoring world, my biggest influences would have to be Ligeti, Penderecki, Bartok, and anyone who's working outside the lines of "normal" orchestral composition, as well as slightly more conventional film composers like Cliff Martinez, Johann Johannsson, and the stuff that Trent Reznor and Atticus Ross have been doing lately, which I quite like. While I recognize the talent, skill, and herculean effort that goes into a big "epic" score like you'd hear in a Marvel movie or other blockbuster film, that stuff doesn't usually make me prick up my ears - it often feels too familiar. I'm usually more interested in hearing something that I've never heard before, a score that will make a film sound totally unique, memorable, and instantly recognizable.

What was the best scoring advice you ever received and how has it helped you as a composer?

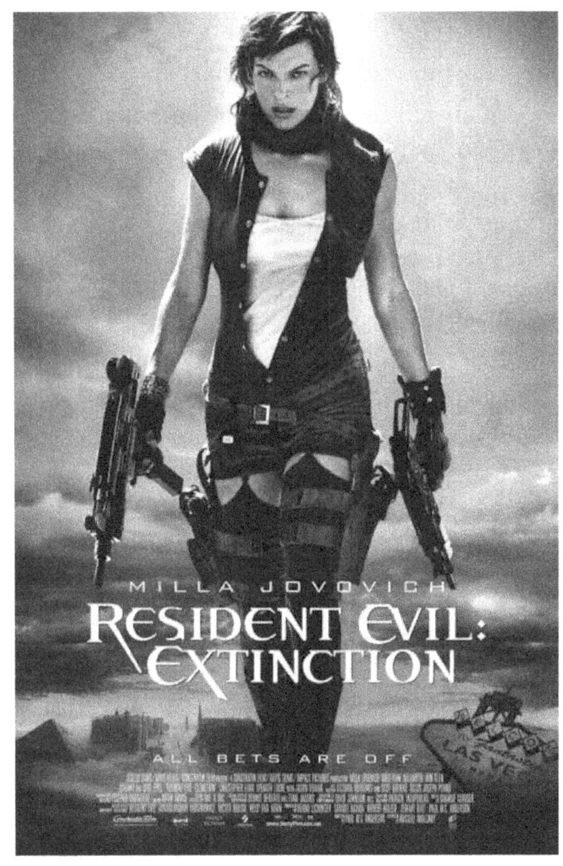

RESIDENT EVIL: Extiction (2007)

Play fewer notes. Use the smallest amount of musical information that can still achieve the desired emotional response. This was the most common advice or criticism given to me by Cameron Allan, the only composer I've ever really worked under. He'd often doze off on the couch while I was working on a piece, but he'd always seem to wake up as soon as I started playing something too "busy", and he'd usually say something like, "LESS. You don't need to do so much. Leave space, fewer notes, play less." While I'm rarely successful at obeying or even remembering this advice, when I do manage to keep it in the front of my mind and let this thought shape my compositions, I'm usually happiest with the result. It's this theory which has helped drive my search for sounds which convey and contain the most emotional information in a single note, like the bowed metal sounds I mentioned earlier. When the sounds themselves embody the emotion, fewer notes are needed to convey that emotion, and the result can be simpler, stronger, and have maximum effect.

How long does it take you to score a scene?

One thing I can say is that it's often surprising how unpredictable is the amount of time and effort that is needed to compose for one scene versus another. For instance, the final theme in the "SAW" films (the "Hello Zepp" theme) was written in an hour or two, and arranged for live strings, recorded and mixed over the next couple of days. Even though it's one of the more important pieces of music in the score, it actually took less time from start to finish than some other pieces of music which were shorter, less complicated, and in the end, were less "important" in the scheme of things. Some of the simple, dark, little ambient pieces that some might consider "filler" material actually wind up taking more time and effort to get them sounding innocuous enough to just sit there without calling too much attention to the score than some of the bigger, bolder pieces. Sometimes the big, strong pieces just fall together very quickly and make musical "sense" without needing to be fiddled with and tinkered with for days on end, while smaller pieces that only need a drone and some scary noises wind up taking days of creating sounds, adding and then removing elements, searching for the right combination that feels right. I haven't yet perfected how to accurately predict this, which is why there are often a lot of late nights in the studio as the score comes together!

ROGER CORMAN

PRODUCER / DIRECTOR
CONCORDE-NEW HORIZONS

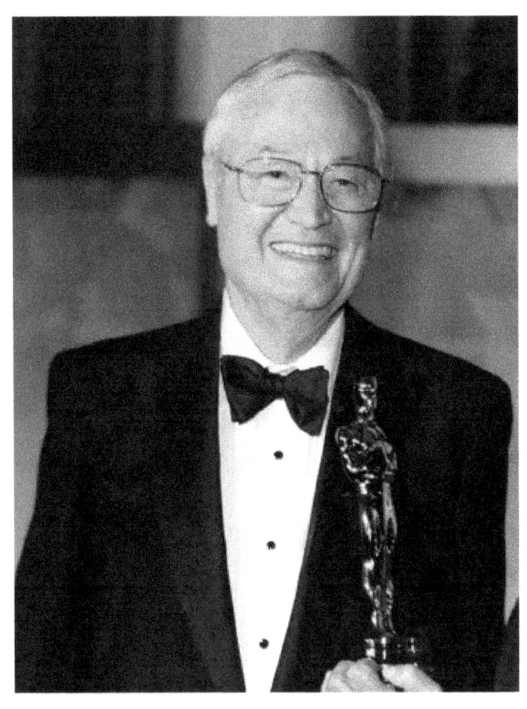

ROGER CORMAN

The saga of independent filmmaker Roger Corman ranks as one of the most amazing motion picture success stories. Having produced more than 550 films and directed fifty others, his influence on American film goes far beyond his own energetic, creative low-budget movies. He is arguably one of Hollywood's most gifted and masterful film makers.

Noted for his keen ability to spot young talents, his most lasting legacy will undoubtedly be the legion of producers, directors, writers, and actors he has fostered, among them: Jack Nicholson, Francis Ford Coppola, Peter Fonda, Bruce Dern, Diane Ladd, Talia Shire, Peter Bogdanovich, Robert DeNiro, Martin Scorsese, Sally Kirkland, Ron Howard, Charles Bronson, Joe Dante, Jonathan Demme, Gale Ann Hurd, and James Cameron.

Born in Detroit in 1926, Corman graduated from Beverly Hills High School. In 1947, he received a bachelor's degree in Engineering from Stanford University. After a stint in the Navy, he took a job at 20th Century Fox and by 1949 was a story analyst at the studio. Disenchanted with a studio protocol, he left Fox for England, where he did post-graduate work in modern English literature at Oxford's Balliol College. Upon his return to Hollywood, Corman worked briefly as a literary agent.

In 1953, Roger Corman sold his first screenplay, entitled HIGHWAY DRAGNET, to Allied Artists and served as associate producer on the film. With the proceeds of the sale he made THE MONSTER FROM THE OCEAN FLOOR the following year, his first film as an independent producer, on the remarkable budget of $18,000.

The triumph of his initial endeavor proved that a high quality film can be made with very little money. As a result, Corman began producing a wide array of low-budget features for American International Pictures; all were extremely successful. He tackled a variety of genres, from Westerns and gangster films to sci-fi, teen-age hot rod and rock'n'roll movies. In 1957 alone Corman turned out nine films - some of which were completed in two or three days.

With this string of box office hits to his credit, Corman began to procure larger budgets. Throughout the 1960s, Corman's cycle of Vincent Price/Edgar Allan Poe horror films earned him international acclaim. When the French Film Institute honored him with a retrospective in 1964,

Roger Corman became the youngest producer/director ever to receive such an accolade.

Always a trendsetter, Corman made the first "biker" movie with WILD ANGELS. Starring Peter Fonda and Nancy Sinatra, the film opned the 1966 Venice Film Festival to great acclaim. Corman also began the late 60's "psychedelic" film craze in 1967 with THE TRIP, written by and starring Jack Nicholson.

As American International Pictures' primary director, Corman's success built the company into a major force in Hollywood. Appalled by the intrinsic waste of time and money, as well as executive interference, Corman opted out of the major studio system. In 1970s, he founded his own production and distribution company, New World Pictures. New World's first year in operation astonished even Corman, as all eleven pictures distributed showed substantial profits.

New World rapidly grew into the largest independent motion picture distribution company in the United States. In addition to providing the public with such fast- paced entertainment as BIG BAD MAMA and EAT MY DUST, or cult films such as ROCK AND ROLL HIGH SCHOOL, New World soon became the independent leader in presenting high-quality foreign films to the American public. New World releases included Academy Award-winning films by Ingmar Bergman, Francois Truffaut, Federico Fellini, Akira Kurosawa, and Werner Herzog.

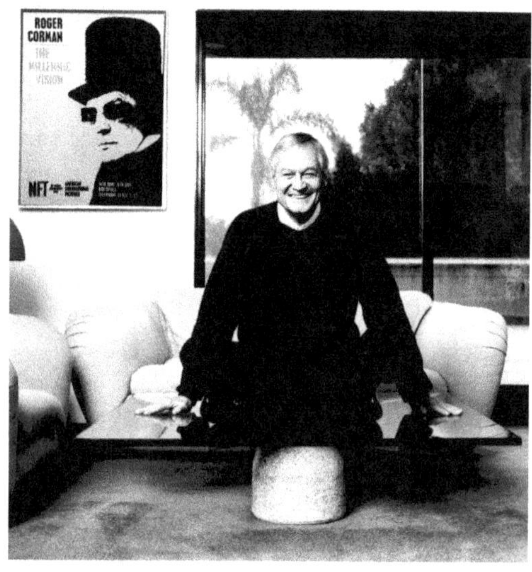

ROGER CORMAN

In January of 1983, Roger Corman decided to sell New World Pictures. The sale allowed him to continue producing films without simultaneously managing a gigantic distribution company. It also enabled him to produce more movies with larger budgets. The day after he sold New World, Corman announced the formation of his new company, Concorde-New Horizons. In the year that followed, he released five new films: the teen comedy SCREWBALLS, the sci-fi adventure SPACE RAIDERS, the sword and sorcery epic DEATHSTALKER, the punk teen drama SUBURBIA, directed by Penelope Spheeris, and LOVE LETTERS starring Jamie Lee Curtis.

Concorde's releases include the critically acclaimed REFLECTIONS IN THE DARK, starring Mimi Rogers and Billy Zane and Paul Anderson's SHOPPING. For Showtime's "Roger Corman Presents", he showcased such films as ALIEN AVENGERS starring George Wendt, BLACK SCORPION II starring Joan Severence, HUMANOIDS FROM THE DEEP starring Robert Carradine and VAMPIRELLA starring Roger Daltry.

In 1990, Roger Corman wrote (with Jim Jerome) his autobiography "How I Made a Hundred Movies in Hollywood and Never Lost a Dime", published by Random House.

More than 50 years after his first foray into filmmaking, Roger Corman shows no signs of stopping. He continues to produce films and gain recognition for his vast array of accomplishments. In 2009, Corman received an Honorary Oscar of Lifetime Achievement from the Academy of Motion Picture Arts and Sciences "for his rich engendering of films and filmmakers."

Roger Corman lives in Santa Monica with his wife, producer Julie Corman, and four children.

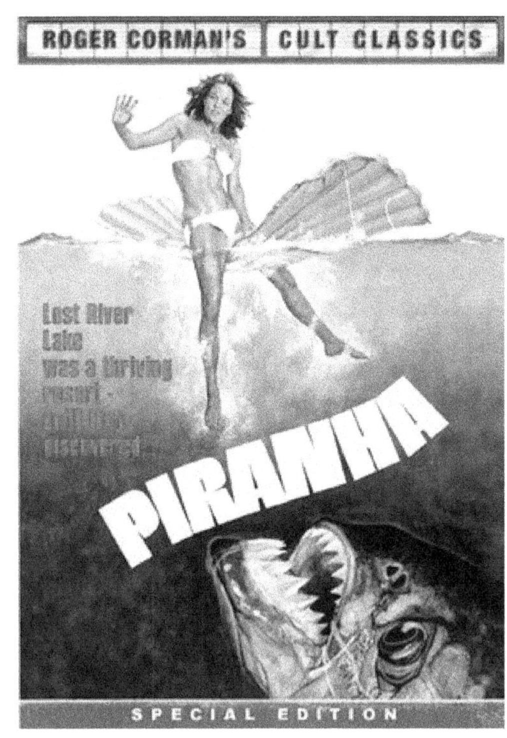

ROGER CORMAN was executive producer on Joe Dante's PIRANHA (1978).

What are the biggest mistakes you see new young directors make?

Too little preparation. You need great preparations.

What is the best way for a new director to communicate with an actor on set? Any shorthand tips?

Work out basics before shooting so little on set is needed and you and the actor are in agreement.

How important are stars in today's world of indie cinema? Are they a must for getting an indie film financed and distributed?

Important, but not always necessary.

Is film school necessary these days to breaking into the movie business? If not, what is the best way?

Get a job on an indie and then look around and learn.

If you could pick one tip to give yourself when you were making your first feature film, what would that be and why?

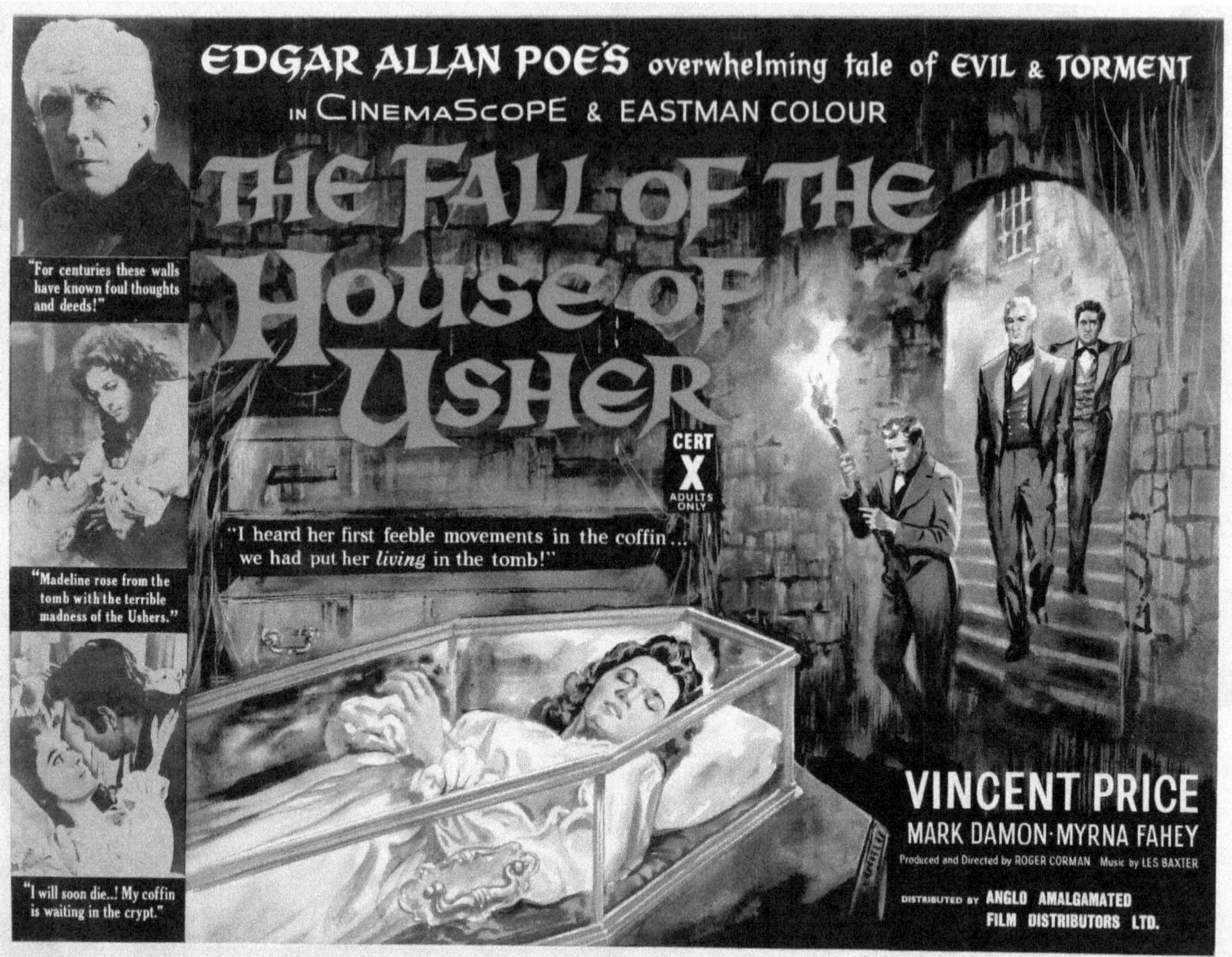

ROGER CORMAN'S THE FALL OF THE HOUSE OF USHER (1960).

Be in charge, but willing to learn. Listen to veterans and take suggestions if you agree.

What are two of the biggest pitfalls you have encountered in producing independent films, for yourself and others, and what is your advice to help others avoid similar things happening to them?

Establish yourself in charge, but you don't want to look overly aggressive. Script and expenses not fitting the budget. Have a little money over the budget, always save a little more.

What are the top elements you look for in a genre script?

Logical, exciting plot and fully developed characters.

What is your advice for a first time filmmaker who has a new feature film looking for distribution? What is the best course of action in today's world of digital distribution?

Film festival exposure. Experienced agent or lawyer.

What was the best advice you've ever received in the movie business and why did it help you?

Screen the film before an audience at least twice:

1. Before final cut

2. Finished film

Audience reaction helps.

If you could pick 5 or more horror films that would be required viewing for a new filmmaker about to make their first horror or sci-fi-fi film, what would those be and what can they learn from watching them?

ROGER CORMAN'S TOP HORROR/SCI-FI FILMS OF ALL TIME

John Carpenter's The Thing is a masterpiece of sci-fi horror. While many scenes thrive off of its shocking gore and disgusting practical effects, the most terrifying aspect of the film is that it exposes how easily us humans can turn on each other once paranoia sets in. Any up and coming filmmaker should watch The Thing to see how to scare audience both through implication and overt terror in a limited setting. The creature of The Thing does not have much screen time, but its presence looms over the entire film, as you never know which character it is currently impersonating. It is a perfect blend between the mystery and unknown of science fiction combined and the bloody carnage of horror. Lastly, it also shows how to do an ambiguous ending right.

Black Christmas thrives off of the terror of implication as one of the first slasher films of the 70s. The film oozes with atmosphere and since the audience never gets a full view of the killer, whenever we even get a glimpse of him, the visual is shocking. In many ways this is both very similar and completely different to The Thing. Black Christmas thrives off of paranoia, as the besieged sorority girls do not know whom among themselves and their friends could be the killer, however most of the violence is completely off screen. Any filmmaker could learn from this how to scare audiences without relying on over the top gore and how not revealing the killer's motive can be just as effective as a chilling confession.

On the opposite end of the spectrum, **Tobe Hooper's The Texas Chainsaw Massacre** succeeds

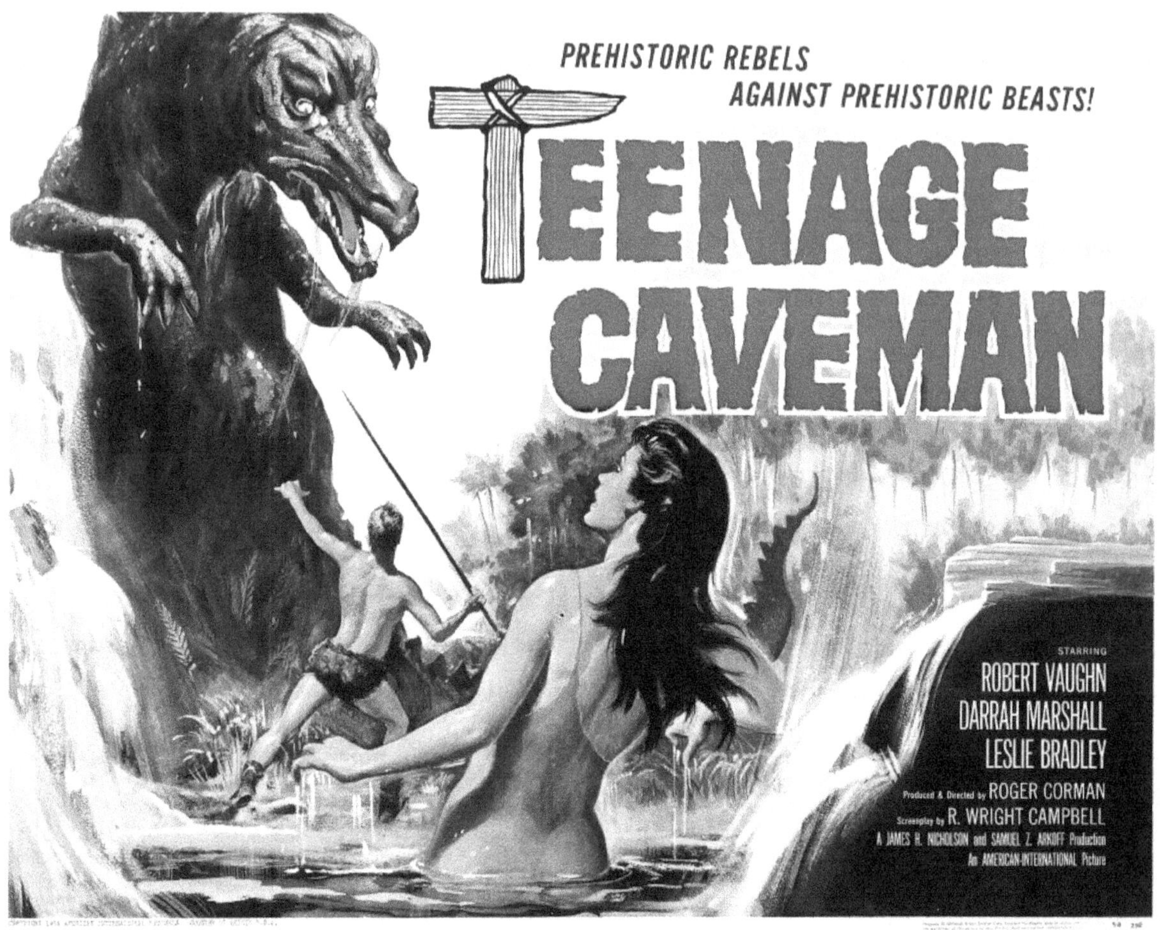

ROGER CORMAN'S TEENAGE CAVEMAN (1958).

primarily due to its lack of subtlety and not allowing the audience to shy away from the carnage on screen. The last thirty or so minutes of the film are an endurance test as our last remaining character endures torture at the hands of Leatherface and his sadistic family. The sheer visceral and gritty quality to the filmmaking that does not waver in the face of brutality displays that while implication can be terrifying, a giant man with a chainsaw running straight for you can as well. Any filmmaker should learn from the film's unique editing, especially during the climatic dinner scene, how to portray chaos without ever losing control of the picture. The chase scene where Sally runs away from Leatherface through the nearby woods is another highlight that should be studied.

Just like any genre, occasionally the formula grows stale and a shake up is needed. That is exactly what **Wes Craven's Scream** did for the slasher genre. Scream managed to critique and poke fun at genre conventions while still managing to be an effective slasher film in its own right. The opening prologue with a lone teenage girl getting increasingly threatening phone calls from the killer is one of the best scenes in horror movie history. Just like the best horror films, the scares start off subtle as the killer's phone calls start off as flirty, albeit strange. Then by the end of the sequence, the killer plays sadistic games with the girl and ultimately guts and hangs her from a tree. Scream is often hilarious, but at its core it remains a brutal slasher, which is key to it being a horror classic. Even though it does something new, Scream knows that being scary remains king.

David Cronenberg's The Dead Zone is a good example of how to create a sci-fi horror hybrid without relying on an alien creature for carnage. The film manages to balance many different tones masterfully as it swings from a hunt for a savage serial killer to a political thriller where the fate of the world hangs in the balance. This is high concept filmmaking at its finest. The film is not scared of changing tones to fit the appropriate scenes and manages to nail an ending that is equal parts tragic and uplifting.

Lastly, **The Changeling** with George C. Scott is one of the best haunted house films of all time. Any good ghost story needs a tragic backstory to accompany the haunting and this is where the film succeeds best. Just watch the séance scene to see how to put together a truly intense scene, which consists mostly of people sitting at a table and talking.

JOHN DEBNEY

COMPOSER

www.johndebney.com

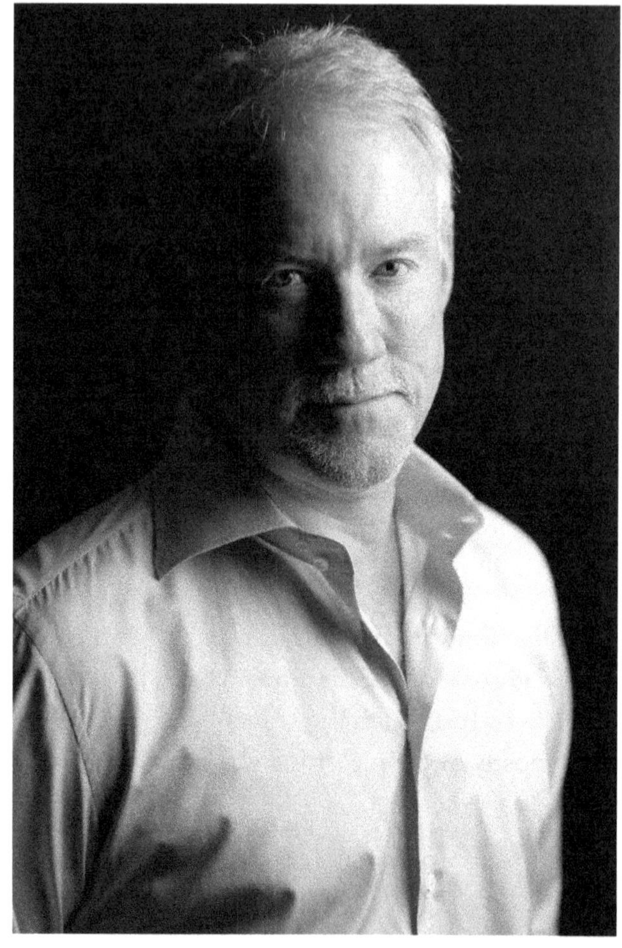

JOHN DEBNEY

Academy award nominated John Debney is considered one of the most prolific and successful composers in Hollywood. His unique ability to create memorable work across a variety of genres, as well as his reputation for being remarkably collaborative, have made him the first choice of top level producers and directors. Debney combines his classical training and a strong knowledge of contemporary sounds to easily adapt to any assignment.

Debney's career seemed almost destined for Hollywood. The son of Disney Studios producer Louis Debney (Zorro, The Mickey Mouse Club), John grew up in nearby Glendale, Calif. where he began guitar lessons at age six and played in rock bands in college. Debney earned his B.A. degree in Music Composition from the California Institute of Arts (1979). After college, Debney's professional entry into the business came from television composing legend Mike Post (Magnum P.I., The Rockford Files, Law and Order) who gave the young composer his start. Debney furthered his hands-on training by working with Hanna-Barbera composer Hoyt Curtin. With this experience under his belt, Debney went on to score television projects as diverse as Star Trek: The Next Generation, A Pup Named Scooby-Doo, and Sea Quest DSV, for which he won an Emmy for Best Main Title. With the Disney comedy Hocus Pocus starring Bette Midler, he secured his first feature film.

Debney has proven his versatility with films ranging from blockbuster comedies such as Elf, Liar Liar and Bruce Almighty, to action adventures like Iron Man 2 and Spy Kids (1 & 2) to dark thrillers including I Know What You Did Last Summer and Sin City. Although Debney had built an industry reputation as a talented composer, it was with his next project that the rest of the world discovered him. Blending symphonic orchestra, a wide range of world instruments and the beauty of the human voice, Debney composed the landmark score for The Passion of the Christ. Strong in his faith, Debney was enticed by the idea of working on a project that held deep, spiritual meaning for him.

Debney's emotional score for the film connected with viewers and listeners and debuted on Billboard's charts at #1 on the Soundtrack and Christian Album charts and #19 on the Billboard Top 200, The record was certified gold by the RIAA and won the Dove award for Best Instrumental Album, as well as garnering Debney an Oscar nomination. Fresh off his success with The Passion of the Christ, he premiered "The Passion of the Christ Symphony" in Rome, Italy. The performance featured an 83-person choir and a 96-piece orchestra, and included special guest vocalist Lisbeth Scott and woodwind soloist Pedro Eustache, plus solo musicians from both the film and the classical worlds. The symphony was a success with the audience erupting into a 15-minute standing ovation catapulting Debney's success not just in Hollywood but worldwide.

John Debney recently scored Draft Day, Stoneheart Asylum and HISTORY's Emmy nominated Hatfields & McCoys as well as the HISTORY's most recent mini-series Houdini. He also scored last year's A&E mini-series Bonnie & Clyde. Debney's upcoming projects include the reimagining of The Jungle Book and The SpongeBob Movie: Sponge Out of Water, both in theaters 2015. In the tradition of classical composers, John Debney enjoys conducting his own work. "A big part of the joy in what I do is that I consider it an honor to stand in front of live musicians and have the opportunity to hear my music played by these talented people." In addition to conducting some of the world's greatest orchestras performing his original works, Debney also conducted the Royal Scottish National Orchestra on a series of classic film scores for Varése Sarabande Records. He has been celebrated for incorporating a myriad of musical styles and techniques into his work, from contemporary beats to ancient instrumentation.

Debney is the youngest recipient of ASCAP's prestigious Henry Mancini Lifetime Achievement Award. As director Robert Rodriguez perfectly described it, "It's not the years, it's the mileage."

As a composer, what is your creative approach when preparing to score a horror film? Is your approach any different from other genres you work in?

My approach isn't necessarily different, but it does depend on the genre, really. Every film is unique, and therefore I like to try and find the signature sound for each one. For a horror film or thriller, I try to find a series of notes that kind of crawl under your skin and take hold so that they can become a very haunting motif of sorts.

What is the director, producer and composer collaboration like for you during post-production?

It's a very close relationship. I work very closely with the director and the producer to create music that will be, again, unique to their film. I try to come up with music that enhances it, and hopefully creates an air of individuality to each film that I score so that the music and remind the listener of the film.

Do you record live orchestra or do you use software packages for your scores (e.g. Logic Pro X, Digital Performer)?

I write my scores in Digital Performer, but most of the time I replace much of my synth orchestral sounds with real orchestral sounds. Even if it is a "synth" score, I like to bring in live soloists as sort of specialty musicians that again, can give the score a very unique and one of a kind flavor, which is what is strive for.

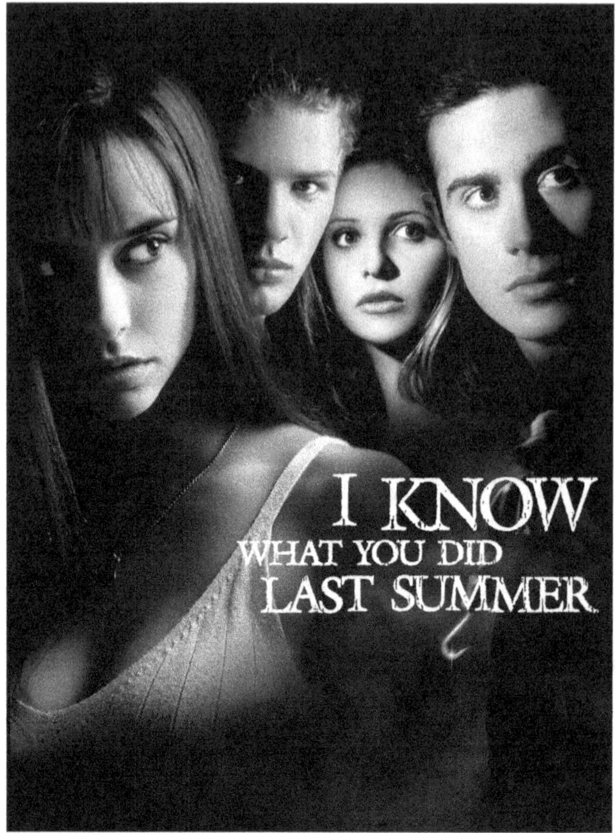

I KNOW WHAT YOU DID LAST SUMMER (1997)

What do you think are the most important musical elements for a theatrical score to have present?

There are a lot of things that are important to a theatrical score. It does depend on the genre mostly. Let's say it's a score like "Iron Man 2" or any big action score nowadays, the music really has to play a role and it has to be able to compete with the sound effects. Sometimes composers are more successful than other times, but it always has to be collaboration between sound and music. Also, one of the most important things for a score to do is create a melody or a motif that people might remember that would hopefully remind them of the film.

I see more and more indie filmmakers turning to library music to track their films, which I think is a shame. What would your advice be to a new filmmaker who may be considering bypassing an original score in place of stock music?

Sometimes, due to budget, they have to use canned music and that's the reality of the situation. But an original score, many times, can highlight all of those crucial moments, whether they be dramatic, aggressive, etc. that a film desperately needs to be highlighted. Many times, library music is generic and doesn't necessarily create a unique sound for the film, and I think that's a shame. A live score that's created for a certain film is infinitely better than library music.

When you collaborate with a director what is the ideal way in which he or she

can communicate his ideas to you musically?

I think the best kind of communication between a director and composer is when a director can try to express an emotion that he/she is going for. I think it's a mistake for directors to get too musically specific, and it's better that they talk about what he scene is about, what he emotion is, what a character is about and what drives them. Those are all dramatic clues as to what the music should be in any one scene.

How is scoring episodic television different from scoring feature films? Do you have a favorite?

They're much different animals. If you're doing a television series, like I'm doing a couple right this moment, it's most important to create a certain sound for a series that you can develop over the course of 13 or, say, 20 episodes. With a film, it's a much shorter amount of time to develop a sound and themes. One or the other are both equally challenging and equally exciting, but they're both just very different. But with a series, as I said, you have the ability to explore musical ideas over a much larger period of time.

Do you spot the film with the director? What is that process like for those of us who may not know?

Yes. I always spot with the director. The process is, basically, we sit in a screening room and we watch the film. We talk about what scenes or parts the director wants to have some score. The spotting is one of the most important parts of the process, because it allows us to talk about the flavor of the music, and how much energy the director wants in scenes. It's crucial to get the directors innermost thoughts during that time. Sometimes spotting sessions go on for hours and hours, but there's always great insight that a composer gleans from a good spotting session.

When you score, how do you determine when you may have too much music and when to just have silence?

Sometimes you don't find that out until you're on the stage recording with an orchestra, really. You have to feel it, and sometimes when were watching a completed reel with sound effects and music, etc. and at that point if there may be too much music, we usually have a discussion about whether or not to have a piece of music in there. It happens all the time really. Usually during the dubbing process is when much of it happens.

In scores, what are some of the biggest mistakes you see musically speaking in low budget, indie or even Hollywood films? Any pet peeves you can share with us?

I think one of the biggest mistakes tends to be that if a score is not suited for a certain type of movie, especially if it's working too hard at drawing attention to itself. That's not a good thing, in my opinion. I think it should always enhance the film that it accompanies and not take the viewer out of the movie-going experience.

What are your personal favorite horror scores and why do you love them so much?

The Omen and Poltergeist by Jerry Goldsmith are two of my favorites. I'm admittedly a big Jerry Goldsmith fan, and I think that both of those scores are wonderful and iconic. Of the more modern scores, I love Chris Young's scores in the horror genre very much. I'd also have to say The Shining was very cool as well, because it was something unique at the time of its release. Even though they used a lot of classical music I think it worked very well and helped enhance that world that Stanley Kubrick created. I'm just a big fan of many horror scores and films in general.

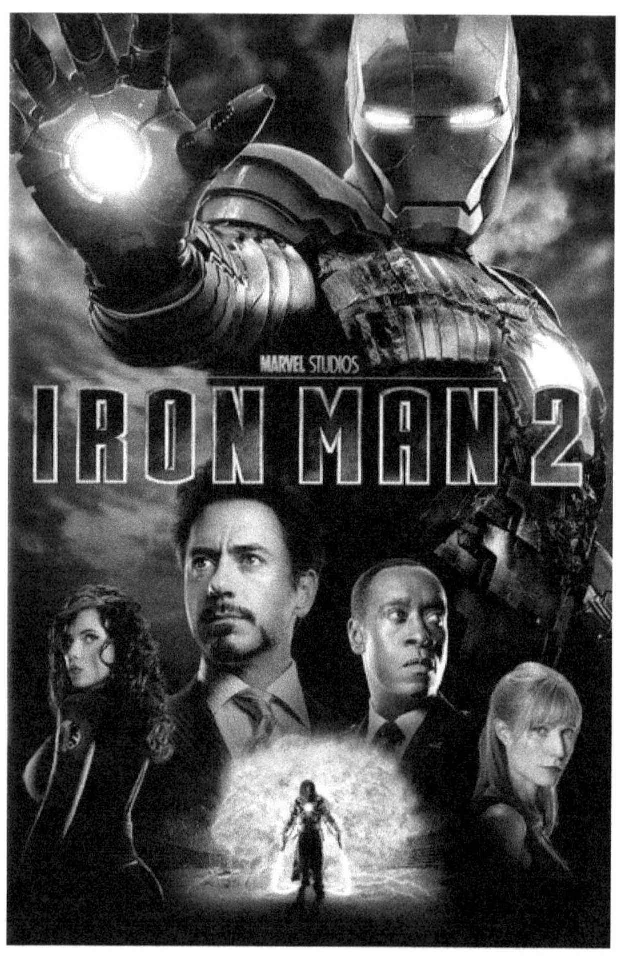

IRON MAN 2 (2010)

Are there certain musical instruments that you would normally use for horror score instrumentation?

Yes, definitely! I find that you need strings to really do much of anything in the horror genre. They're great for effects and melody lines and they're very versatile to do all sorts of things with. So starting out with the strings is always a good idea.

In your experience, what is the darkest musical key for a horror-inspired score and what is it about his key that makes us feel this way?

I think D minor in general is a great key. Especially with strings, D minor gets you a lot of sound from the instruments that makes them really shine in horror scores.

What was the best scoring advice you ever received and how has it helped your as a composer?

The best advice I've ever gotten was to really try to find the heart of a scene and play that. Sometimes you can over score something and I think when the music starts to draw too much attention to itself, as I mentioned earlier, it sort of defeats the purpose of what underscore is. I would say the best advice is to be as subtle and as smart as you can be when writing the music for any one scene, or film as a whole.

DAVID DECOTEAU

PRODUCER / DIRECTOR
RAPID HEART PICTURES

www.RapidHeart.tv

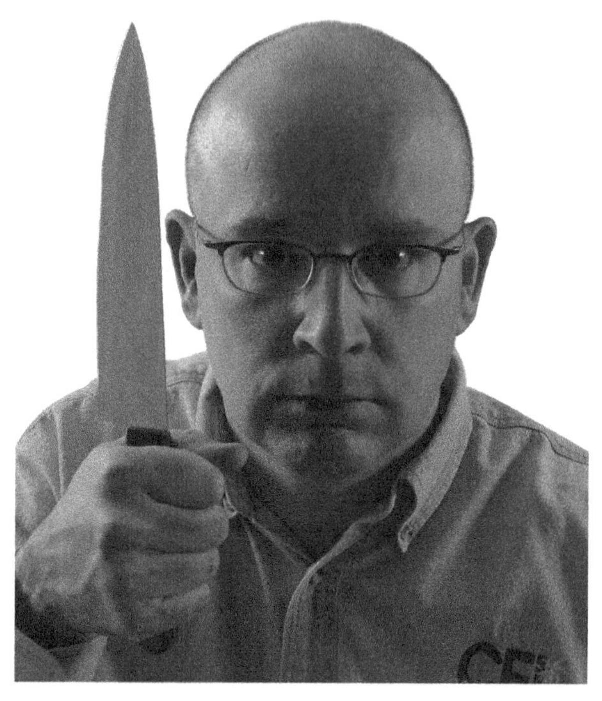

DAVID DeCOTEAU

DAVID DECOTEAU has produced and directed more than 100 motion pictures over the past 30 years. His passion lies in the creation of popular genre programming made for world consumption. DeCoteau's experience in creating content in countries all over the world makes him a proven choice for exceptionally challenging movie projects. His movies are currently in distribution by Paramount Home Video, 20th Century Fox, Showtime, Blockbuster, HBO, Regent Entertainment, Here!TV, OutTV Canada, Syfy, Full Moon Pictures, and many others. He has worked with and learned from the likes of movie legends James Cameron, Roger Corman, Wim Wenders, Ken Russell, Charles Band, Gale Anne Hurd, Paul Colichman, and Robert Halmi, Sr.

Some of his many credits include DREAMANIAC (1986), NIGHTMARE SISTERS (1987), CREEPOZOIDS (1987), SORORITY BABES IN THE SLIMEBALL BOWL-O-RAMA (1988), PUPPET MASTER II (1991), PUPPET MASTER III: TOULON's REVENGE (1991), SHRIEKER (1998), WITCHOUSE (1999), THE BROTHERHOOD (2001), THE RAVEN (2007), GRIZZLY RAGE (2007), HOUSE OF USHER (2008), STEM CELL (2009), PUPPET MASTER 9: AXIS OF EVIL (2009), HANSEL & GRETEL: WARRIORS OF WITCHCRAFT (2013), KNOCK 'EM DEAD (2014), 90210 SHARK ATTACK (2014), DOC HOLIDAY'S REVENGE (2014), SORORITY SLAUGHTERHOUSE (2015), 666: TEEN WARLOCK (2016), BLOODY BLACKSMITH (2016) and A HUSBAND FOR CHRISTMAS (2017).

In your prolific career as a producer and director, you have been known to be a very fast director, sometimes shooting entire feature films in just 4 days. What is the key to being a speedy director on a film set?

I'm really not that fast—just efficient. I was trained at Roger Corman's New World Pictures. Roger is an extremely efficient movie producer. I learned from him. I also worked as a craft-service person during those early years and watched a director take hours just to figure out where to put the camera. I thought to myself, this is ridiculous! We would work 18-hour days! One day I watched the sun come up twice and I said "Screw this! I'm going to start directing." My father was a gravel plant foreman. He was also a welder and mechanic. I come from a working-class family, and my work ethic is similar to my dad's. Work hard and get your hands dirty if necessary to get the job done. I believe working efficiently actually makes better movies. The cast is happier that they don't have to wait around, and the crew can go home earlier. I remember watching Ken Russell direct CRIMES OF PASSION (1984). He was so fast, so precise in his direction, and he would only shoot one or two takes and move on. He also edited in the camera so he was able to deliver his director's cut only a few days after we wrapped. Spielberg shot DUEL (1971) in only 10 days, and it's one of his best movies. Sidney Lumet came in 3 weeks ahead of schedule on SERPICO (1973). My belief is that if you have a vision you can move fast and efficiently and get your movie done for a price. I shoot movies on all types of schedules. The 4-day wonder formula is not new. This is how tiny studios like Monogram made movies in the 1940s. My budgets dictate the shooting schedule pure and simple.

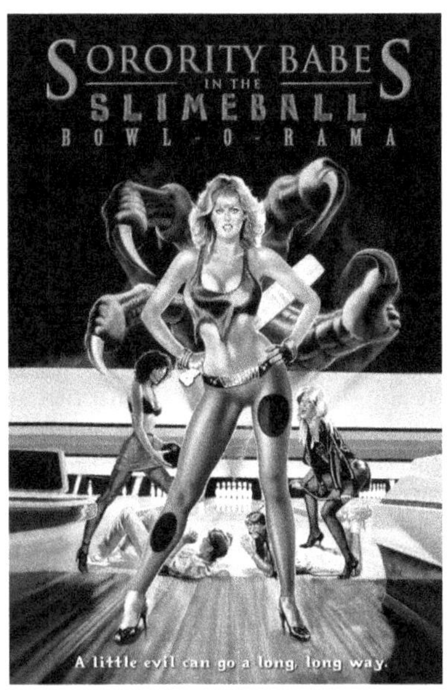

SORORITY BABES IN THE SLIMEBALL BOWL-O-RAMA (1988)

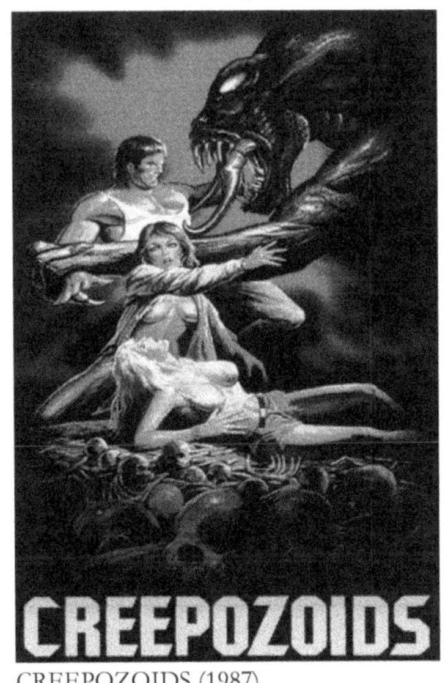

CREEPOZOIDS (1987)

What is the key to scheduling a low-budget film?

The AD [assistant director] usually schedules my movies to maximize lighting setups. I like to shoot story in order on any given day. I like to "ease into" a movie. I don't like shooting the tough stuff first. I like to work into the complicated scenes. I can then get a feel for the movie and also see where its weaknesses are and try to fix those. I never do a shot list. I never storyboard unless the producer needs to see specifically how I want to shoot a VFX scene and he needs to get a bid from an VFX vendor. I play it by ear and shoot the money.

What are the advantages and disadvantages of shooting with SAG actors versus non-union actors?

Depends. I shoot both union and nonunion movies. Signing with the guild allows you to use name actors, which in some cases helps foreign sales. I have had situations where "names" have been a negative. One distributor asked me if he could not use the name actor on the DVD cover because that particular actor was overexposed in the marketplace. I've been very lucky that I have discovered young actors who have gone on to great success by doing non-union movies.

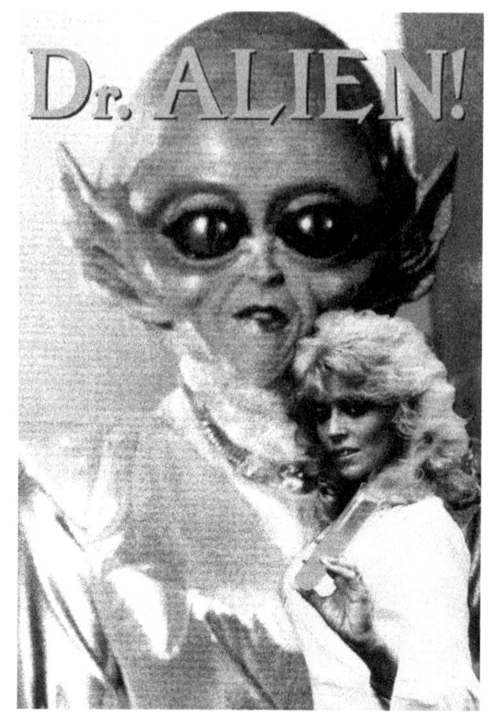

DR. ALIEN (1989)

In today's world, how important is having a star in your film to ensure sales, and why?

Depends on the star. Depends on the movie. Don't think there is an exact science here. If you look at TWILIGHT (2008) as an example, there were no stars in it, but the film was a big success. Success really does rely on the movie itself most of the time.

Do you think shooting two or three cameras saves time during a shoot, or adds more problems?

When I work in Canada, two-camera is usually mandatory. On GRIZZLY RAGE (2007) I shot four cameras even on dialog. I prefer to use a minimum of two cameras. It's helpful as you get more coverage and you may capture a one-ofa-kind performance and you've got two cameras going. When I shoot 35mm it is usually one camera. Whenever I shoot in Los Angeles, I usually only get one camera because you end up spending all your budget on locations—like a state-owned high school costing $4,000 per day to shoot in.

What do you think are the most important elements for a low-budget horror film to have to be sellable in the horror market?

Originality. Timing. All the planets aligning. Luck. I wish there was a rule book to success in this business. It's a crap shoot. Make the best movie you can make. Harry Novak once said that there is a market for everything; you just have to find it. Help your distributor get the word out. Promote the movie. "You gotta tell 'em to sell 'em."

With determination and hard work, you are a person who carved his own way into making movies. For aspiring filmmakers, what do you think is the best way to break in to the film business?

You really have to think outside of the box. I don't think I ever got a directing job from a résumé. It's usually from references and from my terrific agent who has made things happen for me. In most cases, though, I have created my own directing job by developing my own scripts and raising my own finances.

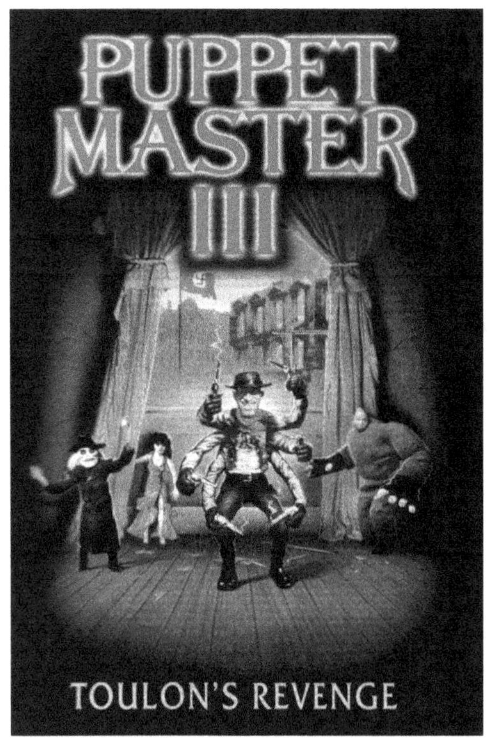

PUPPET MASTER 3: Toulon's Revenge (1991)

How have the new technologies available to filmmakers and new distribution methods changed the way you make and deliver films?

In a way it has become more difficult. A third of my budget is spent on deliveries. My delivery list is longer that my contract. I used to deliver an answer print and that was it. Now the list is a mile long.

Digital cameras, digital post, and Internet distribution has democratized filmmaking. When I got into the business back in the 80s it was a hermetically sealed business. Now everyone has access. This is a blessing and a curse. Seven thousand feature films were submitted to Sundance last year [2008]. The cream doesn't always rise to the surface. You have to be more than brilliant. You have to be an expert sales person, too. Luck comes in handy as well!

THE BROTHERHOOD (2001) marked a new stage of your career. Can you tell us what this new subgenre is, how you became involved, and techniques you use in your films that define your work?

Voodoo Academy was the movie where I realized there might be a larger market for these types of films than I thought. I always knew that gay men and teenage girls love great-looking guys, so I just cast the best-looking and most talented actors I could find. My films are also much less violent and sexual than my 80s/90s films. Foreign sales became crucial, and I didn't want any export/import issue with regard to censorship. Now the films are clean enough to be exported into any country without any cuts. Coarse language was also eliminated so the films can play on basic cable without cuts. I like to consider my films crossover. One of my films, LEECHES!, not only played on Sci Fi Channel, here! TV, and MTV's Logo channel, but it was also available in both Blockbuster and Wal-Mart. If that's not crossover, I don't know what is.

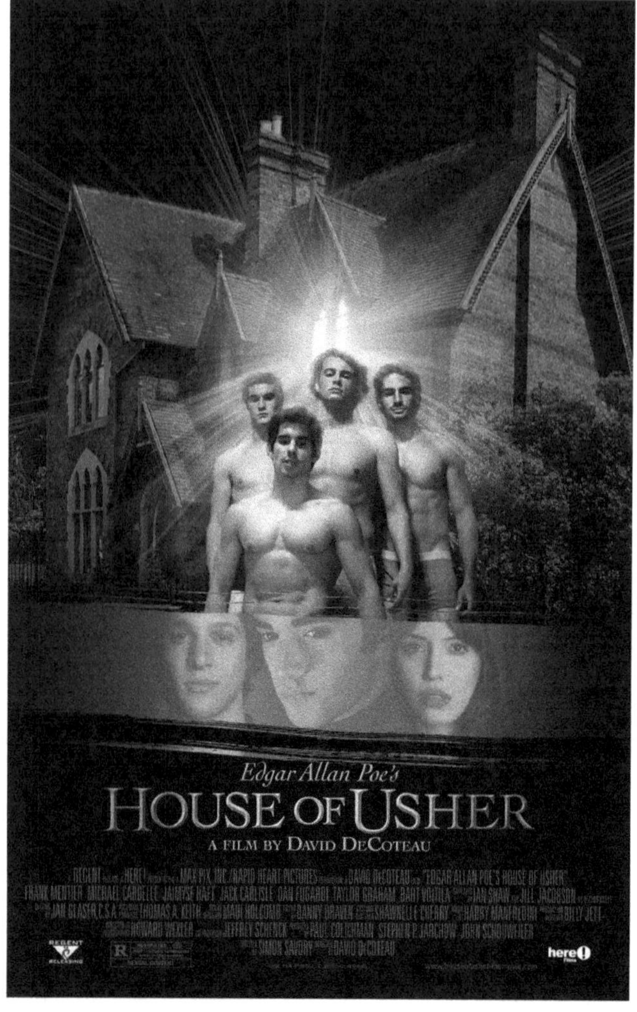

HOUSE OF USHER (2008)
Courtesy of Regent Releasing/Here! Media.

What is the best advice you ever received for how to make movies quickly and cheaply?

The best advice I ever got from anyone in this business is by watching filmmakers work. I was earning while I was learning. I have young filmmakers approaching me asking me to finance their $3,000 movies all the time. I don't finance other filmmakers anymore with the exception of documentary filmmakers who need a little help in completing their films. But even that is rare.

I know you are a lover of shooting on film, especially in the CinemaScope format. In today's digital world, do you think there is still a place for indie filmmakers who want to shoot on film, or is film slowly phasing out to extinction? Is there a sales advantage to shooting on film instead of digital?

When I started shooting exclusively in 2.35:1 35mm CinemaScope it was out of necessity. Digital had just come into the business and so many filmmakers were making films for 20 bucks and I just couldn't compete at that level—and honestly didn't want to. I decided to aim higher and go for something no one else was doing. Shooting in 35mm was just one more way to make the films special and give the perception it was bigger and better. It's all about perception in this or any business. Being able to screen a 35mm Scope print in stereo sound at a film market gave buyers the chance to see the movie in the most ideal way. It's so much better than just dropping off a screener and hoping they watch it on a small TV. The screening made it an event and so much more important. Now digital cameras and projection have gotten so good I have made the switch to HD—but high-end HD. I still need to deliver these movies to European broadcasters whose QC specs are extremely high.

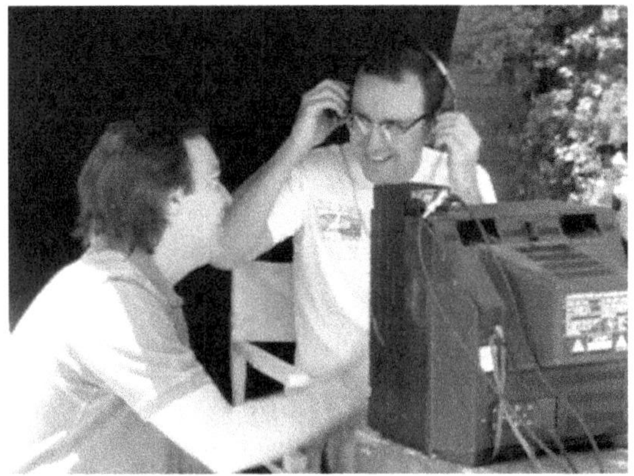

Producer Charles Band and David DeCoteau on the set of BEACH BABES FROM BEYOND (1993)

JIM DOOLEY
COMPOSER

www.JimDooley.com

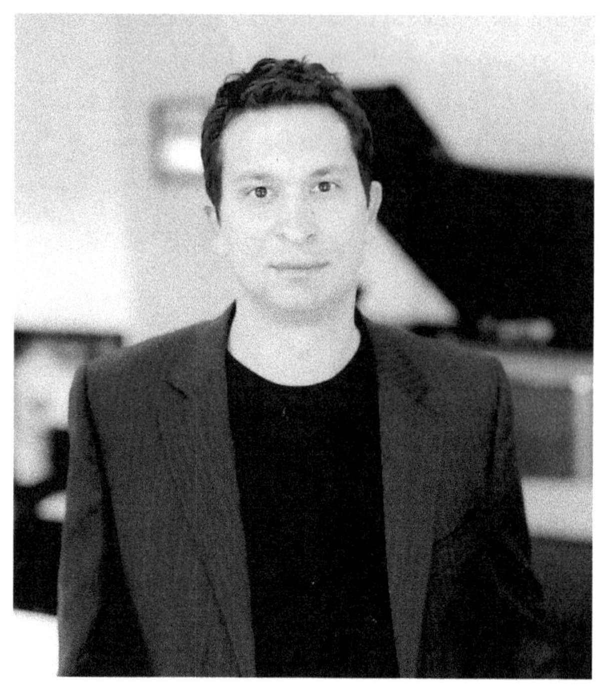

JIM DOOLEY

Jim Dooley, an Emmy Award–winning composer, is a graduate of New York University. Upon completion of his degree, he moved to Los Angeles to study the art of film composing with such prolific scoring legends as Christopher Young, Elmer Bernstein, and Leonard Rosenman. He joined Media Ventures (now Remote Control Productions) in 1999 and began collaboration with the world-renowned Hans Zimmer both as his chief technical engineer on GLADIATOR and as an additional composer, arranger and orchestrator on such notable features as THE DA VINCI CODE, PIRATES OF THE CARIBBEAN: THE CURSE OF THE BLACK PEARL, THE RING, TEARS OF THE SUN, KING ARTHUR, and Ridley Scott's HANNIBAL and BLACK HAWK DOWN. Dooley also worked on several animated feature scores such as SPIRIT: STALLION OF THE CIMARRON, MADAGASCAR and MADAGASCAR 2, its spin-off short A CHRISTMAS CAPER, and the Academy Award– winning WALLACE & GROMIT IN THE CURSE OF THE WERE-RABBIT.

In terms of solo ventures, Dooley's most ambitious projects to date have been scoring all episodes of the critically-acclaimed ABC series Pushing Daisies, for which he received his first Emmy Award in 2008 for Best Original Music Composition for a Series. Dooley also recently completed the score for the upcoming film OBSESSED starring Beyoncé Knowles, and his first solo hit was the original score to Simon West's remake of the cult-classic thriller WHEN A STRANGER CALLS. Dooley's expertise in other mediums can be found in the complex, interactive scores for best-selling video game titles such as SOCOM 3: U.S. Navy Seals, U.S. Navy Seals: Combined Assault, and the upcoming anticipated game Infamous. He also fully scored the German animated release URMEL AUS DEM EIS (IMPY'S ISLAND), DreamWorks Animation's musically acclaimed short FIRST FLIGHT, and worked closely with director Fred Savage on the theatrical sequel DADDY DAY CAMP. Jim has also recently provided scores for episodes of the ABC television series What About Brian, Disney's video hit LITTLE MERMAID 3: ARIEL'S BEGINNING, a sequel to Urmel aus dem, and his first amusement park attraction score for the Simpsons ride at Universal Studios.

Dooley's music can be heard in the theatrical trailers for ELF, MAN ON FIRE, THE DA VINCI CODE, HARRY POTTER AND THE GOBLET OF FIRE, and SPIDER-MAN 3. Known for his interest and expertise in many mediums and genres, other projects include many well-known commercial spots, sports programming ventures, and the ground-breaking documentary THE MARS UNDERGROUND for which he donated proceeds to the Red Cross Disaster Relief Services. Dooley currently resides in Santa Monica, California.

From the time you are hired to the final delivery of your music, what is your technical and creative work flow like?

Horror films typically don't have prerecorded songs or dance sequences, so normally composers are brought on fairly late. It was just like this when I did WHEN A STRANGER CALLS. The film was essentially done, with the exception of the score, when I was brought on.

On the technical side of scoring, just after being hired, the directors and producers will typically have a spotting session with the music editor. They will look at the music choices that have been made and see what I bring to the table. Then we all work together to blend the different ideas and tell the story. The scoring process normally takes between 4 and 8 weeks. Then I send the music and approved cues to the orchestrator. Then, about 2 weeks out, we are completing a reel a day plus fixes and playbacks. All in all, it probably takes close to 2.5 months, if not 3 months to complete.

The creative side really begins in the spotting session. The director and producers that you are working with are responsible for guiding you through the scoring process. They inform you about their ideas and what types of music they used for the temp. Then you discuss your ideas with them and you find a common ground. The next set is to start executing the new idea. You start playing with themes during the early stages of scoring and save your car chases and fights for the end because they hurt your ears the most!

What is the best way for a director to communicate with the composer musically?

Use the tools you have! A director and a composer shouldn't be talking musically. That can be dangerous. For instance, I'm not a writer so I can't talk on that level about story structure. It's the same with directors; they can't speak music because it's almost medical. It's as if you were a doctor—except the difference between a doctor and a musician is the musician has had more training. Doctors start training much later in life. I started training in music when I was 5 years old. It's my job as a film composer to interpret the musical aspect of the film. If a director can speak that language they really don't need me!

In horror films, how do you determine a cue's dramatic function (e.g., fear,

dread, suspense) and then execute your idea musically? Also, how do you know what to leave silent?

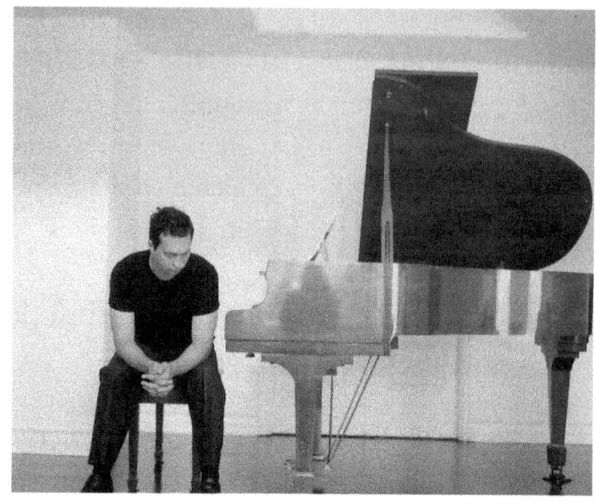

Dooley and his piano.

A cue's dramatic function is usually clear based on the script and story. You're not going to score a chase scene as a love scene.

Many horror films these days are chaotic. Knowing when to leave things silent is a great thing. Music can sometimes let you know what's going to happen. If there's no music it can sometimes be more effective than having a score. There's the story of Hitchcock and Bernard Herrmann. Hitchcock was getting upset that the music was playing such a big part in his movies so he ripped a part of the score out of the picture and let it play totally dry. THE BIRDS, for example, has basically no score. It's one of the scariest movies I've seen. If you have a vision and an approach you can do whatever you want.

What is your creative process in arriving at the concept for a horror film score?

The creative process really depends on the film. Sometimes the movie tells you the approach. For instance, when I worked on THE RING (2002) with Hans Zimmer, we tapped into the music box that plays in her bedroom and that defined the theme. A lot of musical ideas come from the story. It's the best place to go for the theme, not somewhere outside. In THE RING (2002), I scored the horse chase on the ferry. I wrote the cue with sounds from the theme so it would be a constant through the movie.

In the horror genre, what are the biggest mistakes you see in film scores in both low-budget and major studio films?

I have a grudge against composers that make great sounds that cost a lot of money. If you care a lot, you can make great sounds cost-effectively. If you want the sound of a train, go and record a train. Go out and bang on some garbage cans, make a mess of things. Your limitations are your own—no one cares how much you spend. You can hear it in the music when a composer cares. Sometimes there is too much music in film. For studio films, I understand it, you need to create something to help people buy into a fantasy world. But for others...

Do you write on paper, or do you use software packages?

I write on a cue-based rig, but I keep staff paper in my drafting table at work. I've got staff paper in my bedroom, on my piano, and in most of the rooms in my house just in case I have to jot something down. Inspiration can happen anywhere, so I need to be able to express myself. I like writing things out by hand. It's an easy reference. I jot down what I need to know. It's like little keys into what I'm doing without being so elaborate.

In terms of style and technology, has the music for horror films evolved since you first started?

Music technology in film and television has changed incredibly. The majority of people's reactions to change is, "Oh my god. How is this new technology going to affect the community?" I say, in the same way it affects any other part of the industry.

As a composer these days you are as much a technician as a musician. You have to be able to produce the soundtrack using all the fancy programs. The technology for film editors used to be cutting and splicing. Now you have an Avid and you have to know imports and everything else. Technology has changed. We can put abstract things together because of it. We no longer have to do things that are linear-time based. Like with WHEN A STRANGER CALLS, the opening of the movie is a 50 case string drones playing at different speeds. I couldn't record that with a real orchestra. It's like a Picasso collage where you take macros and then put them next to each other. The juxtaposition creates the interest. I suppose technology has made things more easy but also more difficult. There's simply more to choose from.

What are your thoughts on filmmakers who try to save money by bypassing the composer and looking to stock music libraries for their score?

Horror movies can be done very low budget because they sell very well, traditionally, better than any genre of film. The best way to make money! If they skimped on the composer, they skimped on everything else, the acting, design, script, etc. At that point the film is inherently not great. I think it's rare when someone says, "Oh my god, everything in this film is great except for the score!"

If you give your heart to a project, you'll find a composer who will give it his all as well. There's no excuse. But if you're making sandwiches, you can make them elegantly or not, they might sell just as well.

How much time are you usually given to create a score?

Usually, 2 months is the standard amount of time to create a score. For Pushing Daisies I scored about 8.5 minutes of music per day. For PIRATES OF THE CARIBBEAN, we had a team of 10 people working and had 2 weeks to complete it. It really depends on the film.

In the horror genre, what are your favorite scores, and why?

No one does it better than Bernard Herrmann. I don't think it's possible to beat him. I did my thesis paper at USC on the scores to VERTIGO and PSYCHO. But there's also the original Twilight Zone series! Unbeatable. But I also love CITIZEN KANE.

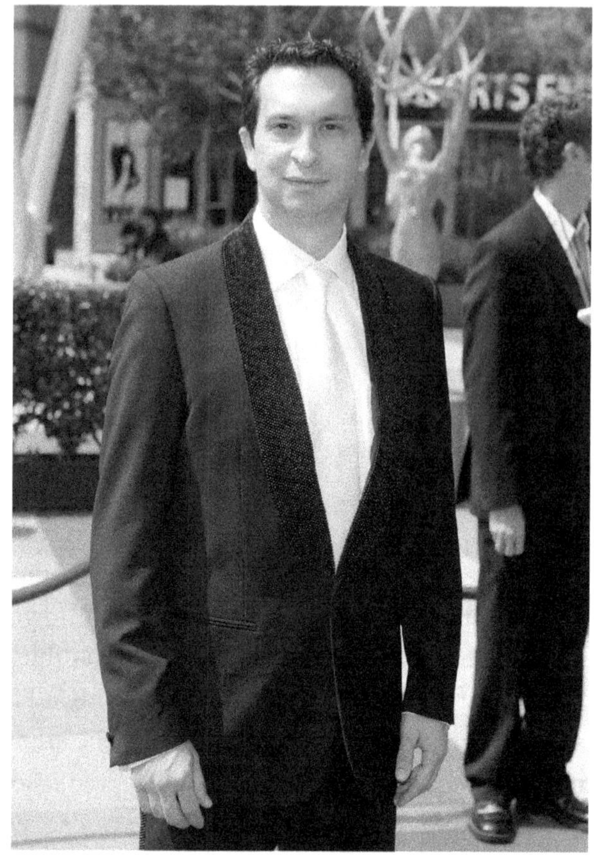

Dooley at the 2008 Emmys! He received his first Emmy for Outstanding Music Composition for a Series for Pushing Daisies.

My paper about PSYCHO described how the film's music reflected the movement of the birds in the film rather than the knife. If you remember, there are many taxidermy birds in the scenes with Anthony Perkins.

The music of VERTIGO was all based around Spanish dance rhythms. All of these rhythms were slowed down, putting tension into the film, but also keeping it organic. In the plot of the film one of the main characters thinks she is the reincarnation of a Spanish woman who was murdered. This is where you find the great decisions; you find something organic and tell the story musically. That's how you do it.

JOJO DRAVEN
COMPOSER

www.jojodraven.com

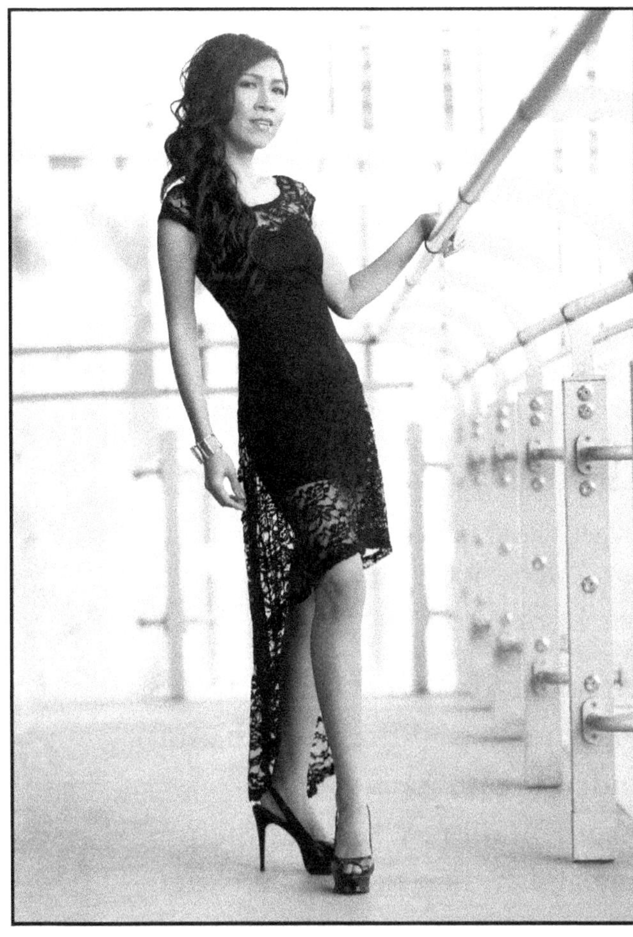

JOJO DRAVEN

Java-born composer Jojo Draven often fuses rock, orchestral and industrial elements into her musical style for motion pictures. She began her musical studies as a child growing up in East Java, where she learned how to play traditional Javanese instruments such as the gamelan and angklung. She received her classical piano training for several years before aspiring to become a rock guitarist after seeing a KISS video. Before her career as a film composer, Draven was the award-winning lead guitarist for Shrapnel Records' all-female metal band Phantom Blue, as well as the co-founder of the all-female tribute band The Iron Maidens and the founder of the industrial band Trecherie. She has been featured in Cosmopolitan magazine as a Fun Fearless Female, and has appeared in other publications such as Guitar World, Metal Edge, MTV Coffee Table Book and Music Connection.

After receiving her bachelor's degree in music, she got her start as a film composer while working as a post-production supervisor for a motion picture company in Hollywood, CA in 2001. Her film scores have been shown internationally and domestically on cable and network television channels such as Showtime, HBO, NBC/Universal Chiller TV, The Movie Channel, Here TV, DIRECTV, and streaming and VOD services such as VUDU, iTunes, Hulu Plus, Amazon on Demand, Amazon Prime, and Netflix. She is a member of the Society of Composers & Lyricists.

In addition to her busy schedule as a film, TV and new media composer in Hollywood, she plays guitar for the critically acclaimed show the Blue Man Group in Las Vegas.

As a composer, what is your creative approach when preparing to score a

horror film? Is your approach any different from other genres you work in?

After the director of the film communicates his/her musical ideas to me and after we have a spotting session, I usually will watch the movie several times on my own to get the feel of it, during which I will start to hear musical ideas in my head and I would write them down or record them on my portable recorder. Initially, some scenes would get my attention more and I would zero in on those scenes first just to get the flow going.

The overall approach is generally the same for me whether I work on a horror film, a drama, a comedy, or a commercial. Once in a while I will have the luxury of reading the script of a film before it was shot; that way I can get a head start in coming up with themes and musical ideas, and therefore I have a little bit of extra time.

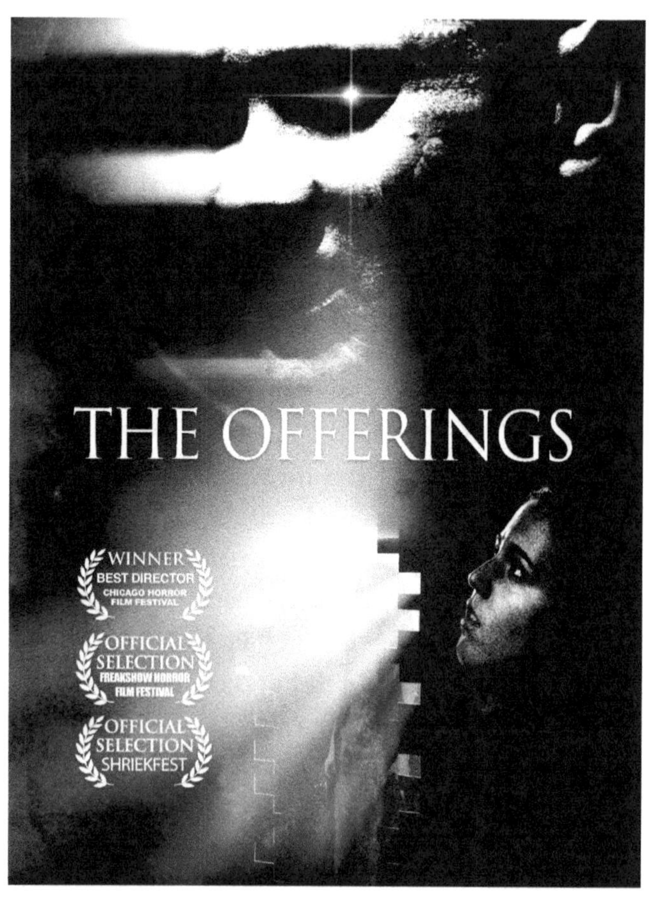

THE OFFERINGS (2009). Now on AMAZON Prime!

Your score for THE OFFERINGS (2009) took a traditional score and blended it with Asian instrumentation. What was that musical blending process like for you?

That was a fun yet challenging project because of the creative freedom I was allowed. I came from a background of growing up in Java where I was around a lot of ethnic music. Gamelan and Indian music were heard on a daily basis. I also grew up watching a lot of Kung Fu movies and TV series; the instrumentation they used in the soundtracks stuck with me. My early musical training was highly classical, and as a child I used to wonder of the possibility to merge classical and ethnic music. When I was presented with the opportunity to score The Offerings, I was really excited for the chance to make this blending as interesting and captivating as possible. I did a lot of scoring tests for some of the scenes to see if it would work. I tried the thematic approach where each of the characters had their own theme. There's a character of an ex-boyfriend that has this foreboding sense of presence, and a little sadness in the main protagonist, and the setting of this Asian woman's house has the feel of calm and peace, which later morphed into the feel of something sinister.

Because the setting was supposed to take place in the Southwestern U.S., I didn't want the score to be laced with all Asian instrumentation, so I started to experiment with piano and a little bit of drum sequencing. In the end for me it was about the race with time; I didn't have the luxury of having more than two weeks to score the entire film.

What do you think are the most important musical moments in a horror film?

Having a good understanding of what makes a scene scary is vital in scoring a horror film. A director sometimes relies on the music to emotionally enhance a scene, and it's my job to translate those emotions into music. I always remind myself that one thing to note about scoring a horror film is to also know when to leave out the music and to let a scene play without any music, as it sometimes can be twice as scary to have the silence than to have a lot of music.

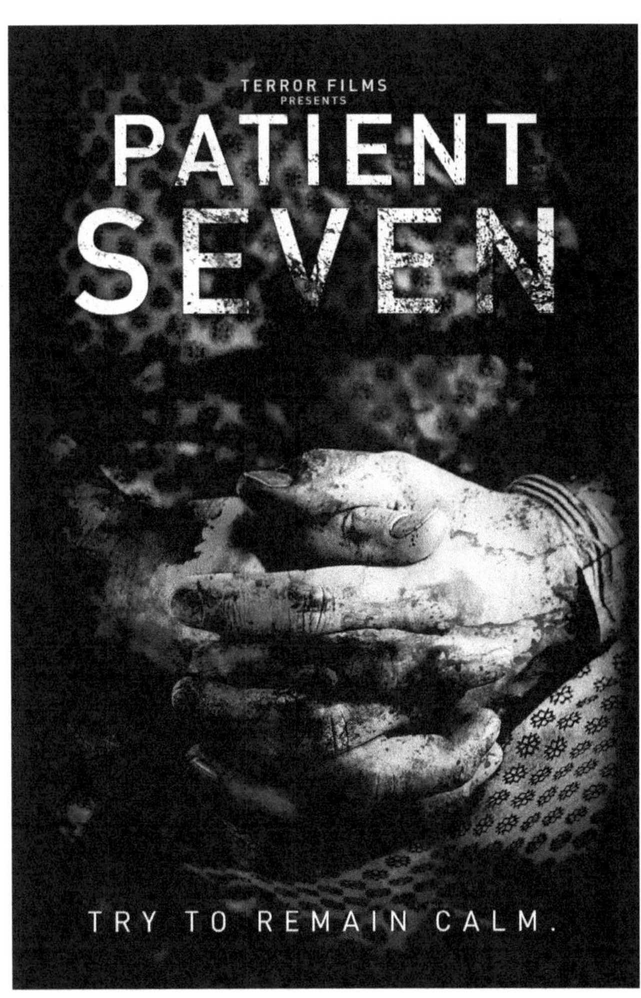

PATIENT SEVEN (2016) Starring Michael Ironside., Amy Smart, Alfie Allen Original Score by Jojo Draven. Now on Amazon & iTunes!

I see more and more indie filmmakers turning to library music to track their films, which I think is a shame. What would your advice be to a new filmmaker who may be considering bypassing an original score in place of stock music?

From my perspective, if I were to make a movie, for the best result I would want to use the best resources that I can find for the production. And then when it comes to post-production, I would want the best editor I can find to edit my film, the best sound designer to work on the sound, and undoubtedly a good composer to write the music. I see some filmmakers spend their budget on production but leave very little to nothing for the post-production. A filmmaker would be willing to pay a makeup artist their rate because they think it's important for the film, but expect the composer to donate their music for free, or end up using library music that doesn't quite fit the tone of their film. It's easy to overlook this need because a lot of people have the notion that what you see on the screen is more important than what you hear.

There's something magical about a piece of music that is created specifically for your film. It's a process of creativity, much like how a script is written and how a director brings what's on the screenplay to life. The composer brings a musical lifeforce to the film that can no doubt enhance the storytelling and audience reaction to the final product.

For a lot of new filmmakers, they might not have a lot of money to spend, but sometimes finding the right person for the job isn't determined by the size of your budget. There are a lot of composers just starting out that can do good work and would be willing to score your film. Sometimes you can even get an experienced composer to work on your movie if they like the subject matter and your movie is compelling and well crafted. If you look, you may find.

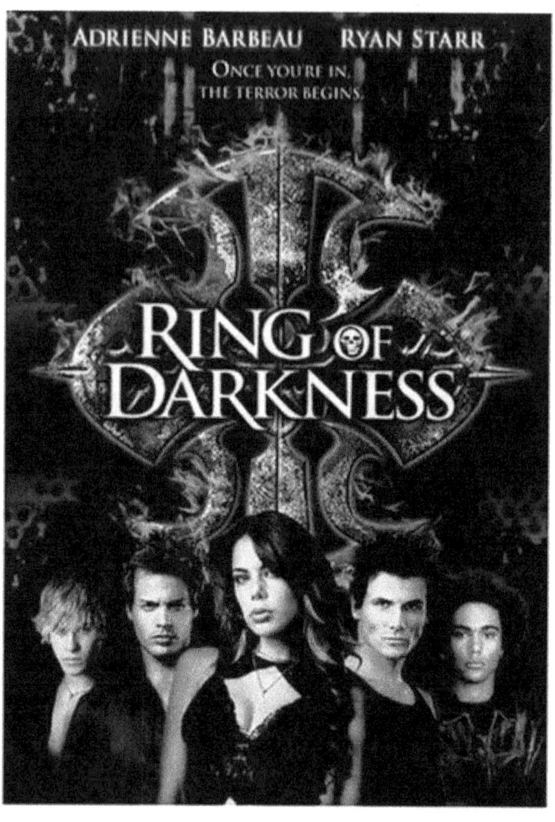

RING OF DARKNESS (2004)

What is the best way a beginning filmmaker can communicate their ideas to a composer musically?

I've found that establishing an overall musical tone first is key. Then during the spotting session it's helpful to be told what each scene is about and what emotions are present. Sometimes listening to cues from other films the director likes is helpful to guide the overall direction of the score.

In scores, what are some of the biggest mistakes you see musically speaking in low budget films?

Usually, to cover up bad production sound or a scene that doesn't work, filmmakers tend to look to the composer to fix this problem by adding a lot of music. As a result, the music can be overwhelming; there can be too much music (wall-to-wall) or instrumentation that doesn't quite work for the scene. Also, some scores might have too many themes, or too many different styles of music, which can invoke confusing feeling when watching the film. It's important to pick a musical direction and stick to your guns.

What are your personal favorite horror scores and why do you love them so much?

The music from Ridley Scott's ALIEN (1979) to me is this soundscape that is not only fitting perfectly to the film but is also chilling when heard on its own. It's very ominous and suspenseful. I also enjoy Alejandro Amenábar's score for THE OTHERS (2001); to me it captures the feel of movie so well.

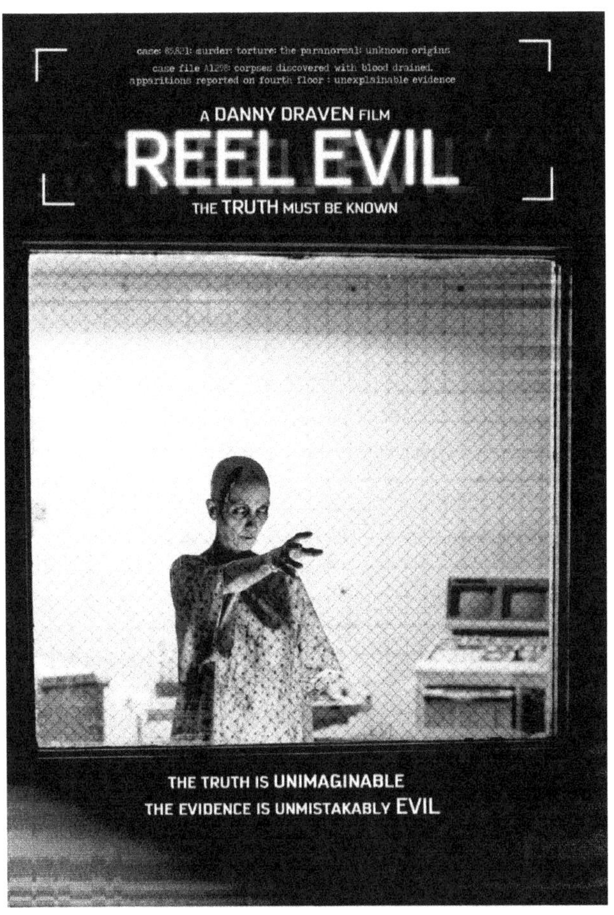

REEL EVIL a.k.a. SPECTERS (2013)
Photo Credit: Full Moon Features

Are there certain musical instruments that you would normally use for horror score instrumentation?

My favorites are the piano and the waterphone; they are my go-to instruments. I also use strings quite a bit, and I always find ways to implement some kind of percussion.

What was the best scoring advice you ever received and how has it helped your as a composer?

"Let the music support the emotions and visual cues of the scene" is probably the best advice I've ever received. A director said that to me one time. As a musician it's easy to get carried away and only think about how the music should go, but a scene can speak to you and give you a lot of ideas for music. A movie isn't about the music; it's about the story and the characters, and the music needs to support the director's vision and create an emotional effect in the audience.

ROBERT ENGLUND
ACTOR / DIRECTOR

www.RobertEnglund.com

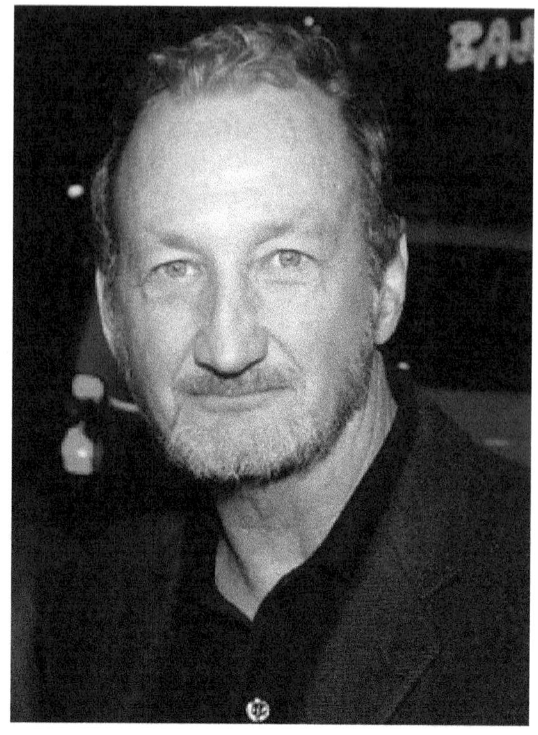

Robert Englund. Source: Wikipedia.

ROBERT ENGLUND returned to the West Coast where he had grown up after 5 years of success in regional theater. His very first audition landed him a starring role in the 1973 film BUSTER AND BILLIE directed by Daniel Petrie.

Far from living the classic hand-to-mouth existence of a struggling actor, Englund worked steadily through the 1970s playing best friends, bad guy #1, and southern rednecks and starring opposite Henry Fonda, Susan Sarandon, Jeff Bridges, Sally Field, and Arnold Schwarzenegger, among others.

In the 1970s, regarded as the second golden age of American movies, Englund was privileged to work for such classic film directors as Robert Aldrich, Robert Mulligan, J. Lee Thompson, Bob Rafelson, and John Milius.

During this time, Englund was living in Malibu, fishing off his porch at high tide, and surfing, when not slogging through traffic on the seemingly endless rounds of interviews and callbacks that fill the days of every working actor. He guest starred in scores of TV shows and worked alongside some of the biggest stars of that decade, including Barbra Streisand, Richard Gere, Burt Reynolds, and Charles Bronson.

Finally, audiences could put a name to his familiar face when Englund was cast as Willie the friendly alien in the hit miniseries and subsequent weekly TV show V . Within weeks, Englund went from questions like, “Didn’t I go to high school with you?” to “Aren’t you that lizard guy on TV?” Twenty-five years later Willie still generates fan mail from science fiction devotees both in the United States and around the world.

The series was a huge success. As a result Englund figured he would be eternally typecast as a sweet and lovable alien. To counterbalance this public image, he looked for a role that would allow him to demonstrate another side of his talents. During one hiatus from filming the series, he auditioned for a hot young director making an interesting low-budget horror movie for the independent studio New Line Cinema. Englund’s interview with Wes Craven landed him the role of the burn-scarred dream demon, Freddy Krueger, in A NIGHTMARE ON ELM STREET and launched him into horror history.

Englund's portrayal of Freddy Krueger blasted him into the pop culture vernacular as heir apparent to the horror icons of the past, destined to stand alongside Bela Lugosi's Dracula and Boris Karloff's monster in FRANKENSTEIN.

After more than 70 feature length films, four TV series, and countless episodic guest star roles, Englund is now directing as well as acting, and he is exploring the world of reality television and Internet programming.

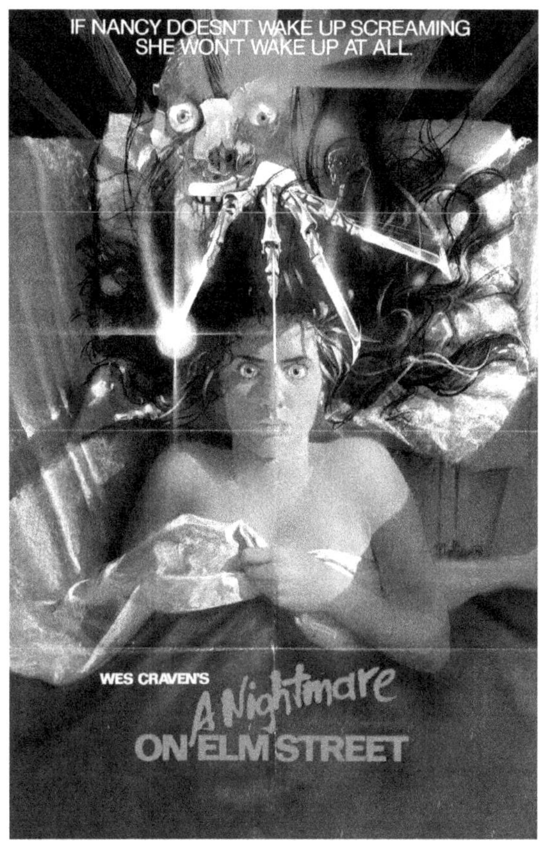

A NIGHTMARE ON ELM STREET (1984)

Your character Freddy Krueger from the NIGHTMARE ON ELM STREET films is one of the most influential screen monsters in the history of horror films. What are the mechanics underneath that made Freddy such an unforgettable screen monster, and why?

It is a combination of the character's sense of humor and Freddy's physicality in which I bring to the role as a trained actor. He's not only reminiscent of the familiar boogie man of myth and fairy tale but he also represents a very real sexual threat. These factors combined with the nightmare/bad dream trope make him a novel and contemporary villain.

In the horror genre, what are the biggest mistakes you see filmmakers make when creating a monster?

Instead of erring in the direction of originality, filmmakers tend to borrow from preexisting creations that everyone is familiar with. That could be monsters, creatures, or villains that they have already seen in other movies or read about in books or comics. Established monsters can be reinterpreted, freshened up, e.g. the vampires in 30 DAYS OF NIGHT (2007) and the damaged heroine/killer from MAY (2002).

What is the best way for a new director to communicate with an actor on set?

Directors need to respect the fact that all actors work differently. Directors should be able to adapt to each actor's needs. Some actors require discipline, some require pampering, and others should be left alone. All actors should be encouraged to bring their ideas to the project. It is also important that the director communicate so that all departments are on the same page.

What do actors really want from a director?

I don't know about others, but I want the director's vision communicated to me. I also want the director to be open to my ideas.

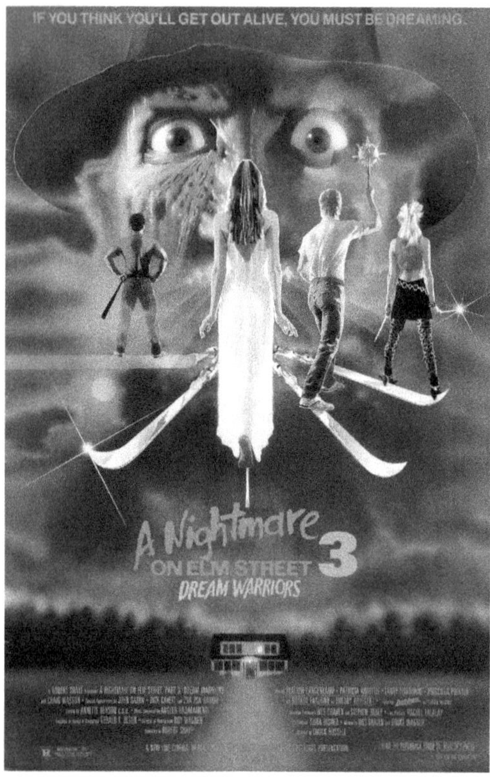

A NIGHTMARE ON ELM STREET 3: Dream Warriors (1987)

In your vast experience in the genre, what do you think are the key elements to a great cinematic death scene?

Surprise. I think my favorite death scene is Harry Dean Stanton's in THE MISSOURI BREAKS (1976) directed by Arthur Penn.

In the horror genre, what are your favorite screen monsters, and why?

The BRIDE OF FRANKENSTEIN (1935), the creature from the Id in FORBIDDEN PLANET (1956), the giant squid from 20,000 LEAGUES UNDER THE SEA (1954), the Cyclops from THE 7TH VOYAGE OF SINBAD (1958), Norman Bates from the original PSYCHO (1960), William Finley as Emil Breton in SISTERS (1973), John Cassavetes in ROSEMARY'S BABY (1968), the alien in ALIEN (1979) and its sequels, Klaus Kinski in NOSFERATU (1979), the stick man/insect in MIMIC (1997), and Angela Bettis in MAY (2002). They all surprised me with their original performances or designs, captured my imagination when I was young, or thrilled me as an adult.

What are some of the things that annoy you about low-budget films in today's digital revolution?

I am more annoyed by overproduced, money-wasting event films that rely on CGI and fail to deliver proper thrills.

In today's world of distribution, there is a glut in the marketplace with too many independent horror films being made. Some producers seem to recycle the same star actors, over and over again, ad nauseam. What are your thoughts on this?

There is too much product of all types these days. There are too many teen comedies, too many mediocre thrillers, too many chick movies, etc. When producers are fortunate enough to luck into a popular character, of course they are going to exploit it. Franchises are inevitable. The popularity of an actor dictates how many movies he will be in. The profits from a successful bad movie/franchise can fund several low-budget, independent movies. Movies beget movies.

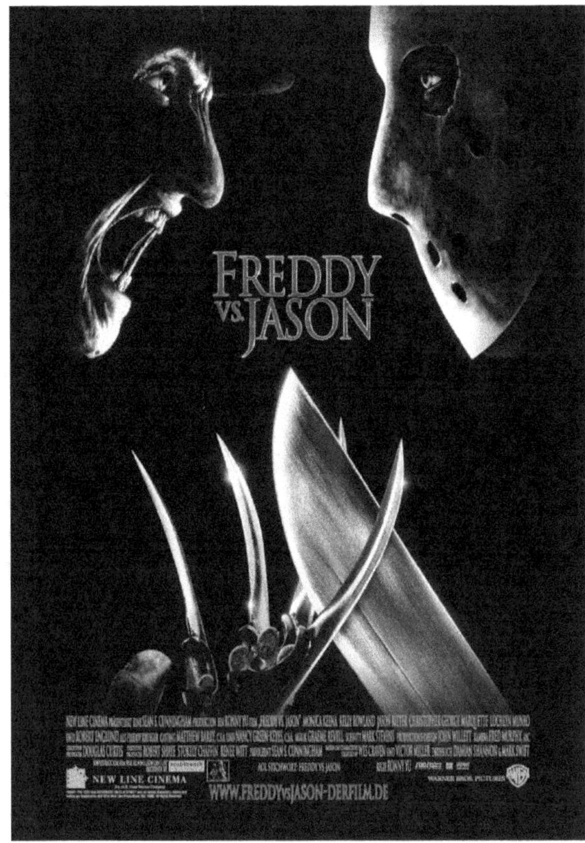

FREDDY VS. JASON (2003)

Where do you think the future of the horror film is headed?

I'd like to see some classic period horror revisited as a source, maybe some Edgar Allan Poe or Brothers Grimm.

What does Freddy Krueger think of my new book?

He couldn't put it down but ruined his copy turning pages with his glove on.

MICK GARRIS
DIRECTOR

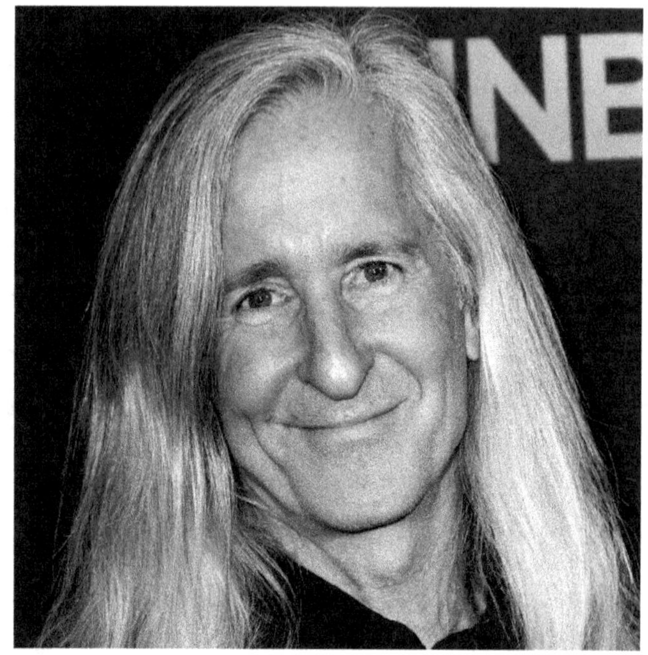

MICK GARRIS

www.mickgarrisinterviews.com

Mick Garris was born in Los Angeles, California, on December 4, 1951. At age 12, he was making his own 8mm home movies and when he got older be became a freelance critic for a number of film and music publications. He wrote about various bands and movies for newspapers and magazines like "The San Diego Door", "The Los Angeles Herald-Examiner", "Cinefantastique" and "Starlog" through the 1970s.

For eight years he was the lead singer in a band called The Horsefeathers, which disbanded in 1976. In 1977 Garris was hired as a receptionist in George Lucas' newly formed company Star Wars Corporation where, through industry contacts, he created and served as the on-screen host for a Los Angeles cable access interview program show called "Fastasy Film Festival," which aired on L.A.'s legendary Z-Channel. Guests included filmmakers like John Landis, Joe Dante, John Carpenter and Steven Spielberg and actors like William Shatner and Christopher Lee.

In 1980 Garris worked as a press agent for the newly merged Pickwick-Maslansky-Koeninsberg agency. He also began making a name for himself with photographing and directing "making-of..." features for such films as Scanners (1981), The Howling (1981), Halloween II (1981), The Thing (1982) and Videodrome (1983). In 1982 Garris was hired by MCA/Universal to write the script for Coming Soon (1982), which was a collection of horror movie trailers featuring Jamie Lee Curtis as the hostess and directed by John Landis. While struggling to find more work, Garris was hired by Steven Spielberg to be one of the writers and story editors for Spielberg's sci-fi anthology series Amazing Stories (1985). Garris worked as a writer again for Spielberg on the sci-fi fantasy *batteries not included (1987). He also directed for horror anthology TV shows, like Freddy's Nightmares (1988) and on the HBO cable series Tales from the Crypt (1989), as well as co-writer on the screenplay for The Fly II (1989). Garris directed Psycho IV: The Beginning (1990) as a prequel to the Anthony Perkins "Psycho" films, featuring Perkins in his fourth (and last) appearance as Norman Bates. Co-starring with Perkins was Henry Thomas (from E.T. the Extra-Terrestrial (1982) fame), whom Garris hired to play young Norman. That same year Garris was approached by MCA/Universal to create a syndicated TV series about werewolves which resulted in the series, She-

Wolf of London (1990) and ran for two seasons.

In 1992, Garris directed an original screenplay by Stephen King, Sleepwalkers (1992). The following year Garris received story and screenplay credit for the comic horror film Hocus Pocus (1993), and the year after that he took the reins at the request of Stephen King for the eight-hour mini-series The Stand (1994) based on King's best-selling horror novel. The mini-series, which had a grueling 20-week shooting schedule, was one of the most-watched shows of 1994. Garris and King again teamed up for a three-part made-for-TV rewriting of King's novel, The Shining (1997). Later that year Garris wrote and directed Quicksilver Highway (1997), based on a pair of horror stories by King and Clive Barker. Garris directed Höst (1998) (later changed to "Virtual Obsession"), based on a novel by Peter James, with a screenplay written by Preston Sturges Jr., about a computer genius stalked by a female colleague bent on digitizing her consciousness. Taking a break from horror films, Garris directed The Judge (2001), an adaption of the mystery novel by Steve Martini. Garris and Stephen King reunited for Riding the Bullet (2004), which he wrote and directed directed and was based on an internet short about a hitchhiker being picked up by a soul-searching angel of death driving a 1959 Plymouth. They also collaborated on Desperation (2006), based on King's 1997 horror novel.

In 2005 Garris was able to assemble a group of his fellow horror film directors in the anthology horror series Masters of Horror (2005), which he created and executive-produced. Garris' own contribution, "Chocolate", was based on his own short story, written 20 years earlier.

You're known for your adaptations of Stephen King stories such as SLEEPWALKERS (1992), THE STAND (1994), QUICKSILVER HIGHWAY (1997), THE SHINING (1997), RIDING THE BULLET (2004), DESPERATION (2006) and BAG OF BONES (2011). What is your collaboration process like with master storyteller Stephen King?

It started with him being on the other side of the country in Maine and me being in LA. We were doing a script he'd already written called SLEEPWALKERS which was the first script we had done together. The collaboration on that end was that they already hired a director who had re-written it into something nobody liked and then they brought me on board to bring it back to what Steve had done while incorporating what the studio was interested in making.

Stephen is a guy who once you have his trust, he doesn't interfere, but, when you have Stephen King, you're an idiot to not taking advantage of having access to him. So in the case of SLEEPWALKERS, it was the first time for me and it was a matter of developing that trust with him. He knew I was a writer as well, and there would be changes that the studio would want and I would offer to do them and always run it past him. I would tell him what I want to do, and then he would say let me have a crack at it, and the next day there would be pages in the fax machine, back

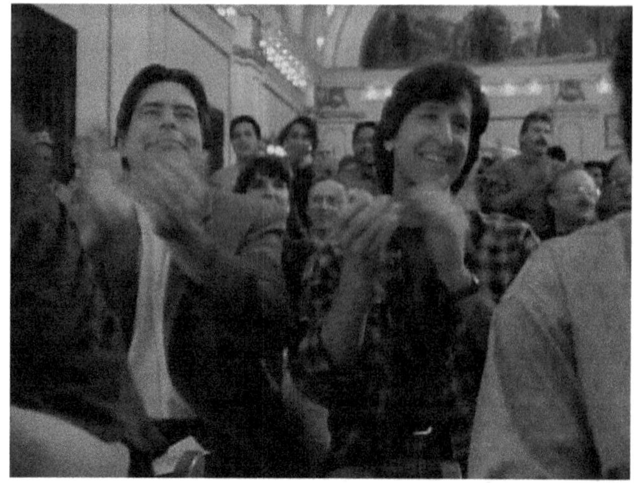
Mick Garris and Stephen King in a cameo.

in the day of fax machines, and they would be fantastic. It was a great collaboration from a distance. I never met him until he came out to do a cameo on set. It was lots of fun. Then we really got closer in the screening room in New York when my cut was done since he had approvals. He and Tabby (Tabitha King) were the only ones in the screening and he was hooting and hollering and laughing and jumping, every kind of great reaction that you'd want. So, it was a matter of developing a trust. We became friends after that when he said they're going to do a mini series of THE STAND and would you be interested in directing it? We became friends and it became easy to talk and communicate to each other and I really respect what he's done and he knows the difference between movies, TV and books. No matter what the movie is it won't fuck up the book, no matter what the movie is the book is still good. And we have developed a great trust between each other. I mean I trust him, explicitly! It's turned into as much of a friendship as a working collaboration. He is very playful when he is on a movie set. It's like a giant train set and he really has fun with it. That kind of collaboration is work and play at the same time. It's a very personal thing, it's not just about what we are making but an atmosphere on the set. My sets are usually very happy sets, everybody gets respect, we're all in it together and we all want to do the best work possible. King is very much on board and yet he really loves to have fun. It was really fun on THE STAND when Gary Sinise and I and one of the other actors, kind of play guitar, We are shooting the scene where Adam Storke is singing "Eve of Destruction" amongst all these dead cars and so in between takes we all have our guitars around our necks playing "Eve of Destruction"! It's really an atmosphere as much as it is an artistic endeavor.

I didn't know you play guitar. Me too. I went to Berklee College of Music before I went to film school. Rock on!!

Well, I don't play guitar well. I play guitar like I play piano, just chords, but I was in a band for 7 years when I was in my 20s. An all-original progressive rock band. We opened for the KINKS and some other bands and it was great fun.

What was the most influential element you learned about horror storytelling from Stephen King?

What I always felt intuitively and really learned was keeping it real. The characters in the world of our story are real. He writes his characters so believeably that we all identify with them. We are all his characters. We shop at the same stores, eat the same food, all the things that real human beings do. If you have a reality basis then you can take it somewhere else. Once you establish a real world then you can go to an unreal world and make it believable and the audience will buy into it.

My philosophy is: great horror is great drama plus. It's drama amplified. The stuff that I don't give a shit about are monsters that come from nowhere, slasher movies and things like that. They're just about the effect and not about the story of the characters. I started writing when I was 12 years old and story and character have always come first. As far as I'm concerned the most potent story is a reality-based story.

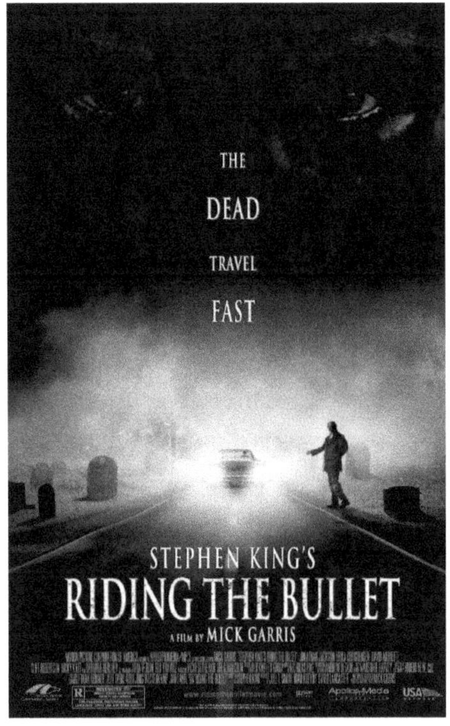

Stephen King's RIDING THE BULLET (2004)

It's an interesting fact that early in your career you shot behind the scenes footage for classic films such as THE HOWLING (1981), THE GOONIES (1985), THE FOG (1981), VIDEODROME (1983), GREMLINS (1984) and even INDIANA JONES AND THE TEMPLE OF DOOM (1984). What did the experience of being on set and watching these great filmmakers at work teach you about filmmaking?

Well it taught me a lot and didn't teach me a lot. One of the things I learned off the top was that most of the real work is not done on the set. All the discussions with the DP, the director, the actors, storyboards, production design, were all done before you get to the set. But, I learned protocol. There were echelons of priority.

You see different ways that different people work. Steven Spielberg works closely with the actors and the DP, where John Carpenter is more technically oriented, or another director may be more performance oriented or a blend of the two.

I bet you have a lot of rare behind the scenes footage that no one has even seen?

It was all shot on 16mm film. Universal may have all of the footage I shot, but probably don't. I have no idea where it is but most of the good stuff got in. I had hours of stuff, but it was mostly boring. I usually had 2 days to shoot. There is not a lot of buried stuff.

When working with actors, how do you determine what is a truthful performance and what isn't?

You feel honesty intuitively and you can tell if it put on. The main thing is how you work with actors since they all have different processes. When you see an actor that needs a bit of ramping up, you may opt do their coverage second. If this is an actor that does their best when they do the first or second take and then they loose steam, shoot them first. Then sometimes they'll have the same process or it won't matter. The honesty of it is the naturalness of it. I guess the best test is that if people who are observing can't tell the difference before you say action and after you say cut. A conversation may be going on and they're the same before action as they are after action. It needs to be honest and feel that they're not acting. The whole point is putting yourself in the circumstances. If it were you, Danny Draven, in this building that is collapsing because a mutant animal was burrowing down under and wants to drag you to the depths of hell . It's not you playing a guy who would be sucked down into hell, but it's your experience of it as if it were happening to you in reality. I think it's more intuitive that anything else!

Hitchcock says 75% of directing is casting. What are your thoughts?

Absolutely!

In a genre film especially, there is a lot of snobishness about it. So who you can get and who is willing to play an extreme film or role. Availability, pricing, enthusiasm… you don't want an actor who just wants to take a job, you want an actor who wants to be there. We got Pierce Brosnan to do BAG OF BONES, who hasn't done TV in 15 years, he's a guy who likes to try new things, and really went for it. It was a gamble. I did not know the guy, we met, had a great meeting. I didn't know if he was going to get into it, not doing this kind of genre before. But, he brought into it a great sense of reality, I know it had to be difficult for him because I know he lost his wife, and he plays a guy who looses his wife, and the reality of his reaction to his loss in the charter who was killed while he was in a book store and heard the bus crash outside. It went so far and so emotional that I was tempted to pull it back, but I dare not, because the reality that he brought to it came from a much deeper place.

I'm way too embarasable to be an actor, you have to be beyond embarrassment. To be a great actor you have to be willing to be naked for your psyche to be exposed . That's where the honesty comes from, it comes from experience. A 20yr old who's had everything will not have the depth of someone who's lived a longer life and obstacles to overcome. As a writer, actor, director, musician, or a painter, the deeper you experience life the deeper your heart becomes. In Pierce's case, it was a sense of loss that brought honesty to the role and the ability to confront that loss he experienced in real life and bring it to the screen.

Did you ever take acting classes?

No, I've sat in on a few acting classes. A great actor is beyond ego, someone who is willing to be small or large, willing to expose the psychological issues that they have dealt with or would have if they had been in that situation. A lot of people become actors or join bands for the same reason: to get laid or to be famous. Those are the one who don't have success. Fame and fortune also can make an artist reach less and be less adventurous. It can either liberate you or limit you.

The great acting teacher Stanislavsky once said to his students "do you love the art in yourself, or yourself in the art." Wise words indeed.

I haven't actually heard that. That's very profound. Humility goes a long way.

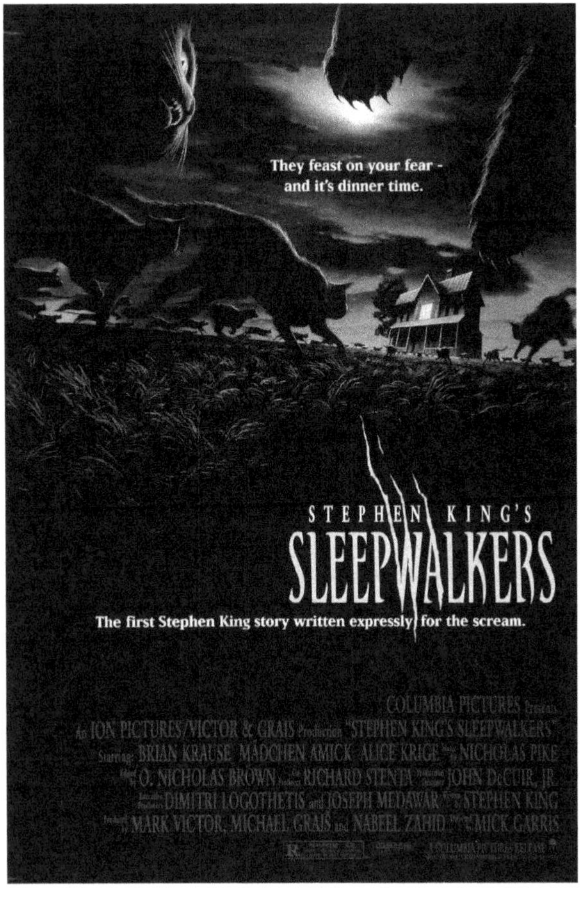

Stephen King's SLEEPWALKERS (1992)

In a horror film, what would you say are the key elements to truly scaring an audience?

There's the technical aspect brought up with unnerving sound design, dread and making you go "BOO"!. But making you jump and go boo is the easiest part. Again, I'm going to go back to reality, The more real it is the more sense of fear that you can identify with the actors and the actors expressing that fear is key. Like misdirection in comedy, you lead someone down one path and take them to an unexpected place. That is building a sense of identity on the audience part. If you can identify what the charter is going through and scare the character, you can take the audience with you. The sense of reality and surprise, you can be surreal as opposed to just real , that's why the Horror genre is my favorite genre, because you can be expressionistic as well as real. You can enter into the realms of the psyche inner life as well as outer life and blend those two together. So many fears are universal and a commonality of fear among all cultures. In traveling to different countries and festivals around the world I have seen that, but sometimes they are expressed in different ways.

I love when you take an Asian concept of fear and their approach to ghosts and how they feel about them and bring it to a Western consciousness. The fear itself is communal, but the taste may be different. You can bring something new to something that is already founded within you. That is when you can take someone by surprise and surprise is a big part of fear, the unexpected. Comedy and Horror are similar because they are best shared with an audience that go for a laugh or a scream and are all intertwined with one another.

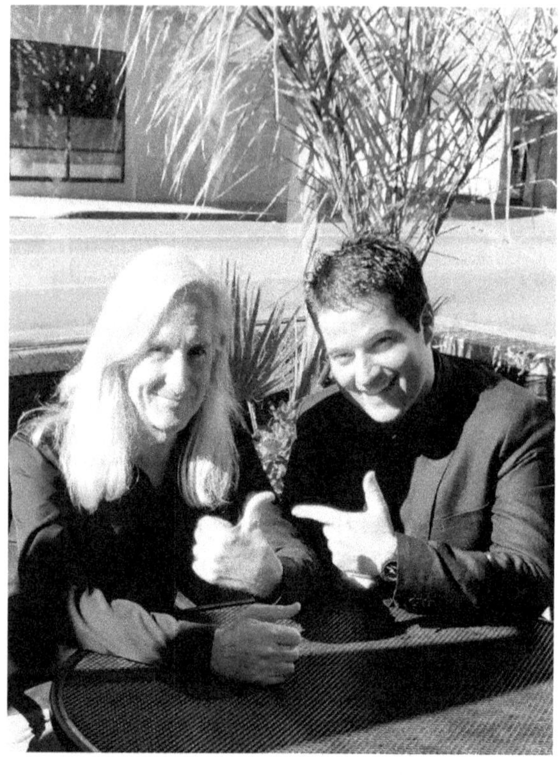

Mick Garris and Danny Draven in Los Angeles 2015.

My mentor Stuart Gordon used to tell me that comedy is the antidote to fear. And one of the best ways to relieve that tension in a movie is with a laugh.

It's the Hitchcock thing: disarm! There is also a defensiveness that comes with making a horror film, that if you just tell someone the ridiculous things that happen that could not happen in real life, it's hard to take them seriously, so if you disarm with a joke, there is a relief to make them laugh after a shock. The more organic the fear is, the more deeply rooted it is. I remember John Carpenter saying this when I interviewed him. He said that he could run black leader through a projector and have a white cell and a really loud noise and it will make you jump. It works for a few seconds and then you forget about it.

Horror is to film what heavy metal is to music. You want to embrace something you know your parents won't. It's a great breaking away thing and a spit in the eye of mortality, because you have never experienced mortality. I think it's good for you, but I'm not a fan of extreme horror, but extremism in the hands of an artist can be fantastic. When in the hands of hacks, it's all about splatter.

Can a great horror film be done on a low budget?

Horror does not have to cost money, it doesn't require movie stars and you can easily sell the concept. It doesn't cost anything to do something well. It's the ideas that are rich and ideas are cheap. You don't need a $50 million dollar budget to make a great horror film. Yes, if you hire name actors, they're special and they're worth what they get paid. They bring an entire history of who they are to the screen, and you have some expectations there. They are incredibly valuable when they play against those expectations in a different role.

A good idea costs nothing! Sometimes it takes money to tell the story but ideas are cheap. Talent is more rare than we'd like it to be but talent costs nothing, until it's had a value placed on it by an employer or a studio or network. It's really hard to get ideas made, especially original ones. It seems to be a bit more open in the independent world, but that leads to the democratization of film making by the resources everybody has at their fingertips. You can make a movie on your iPhone or edit easily on your desktop. Democracy in all things is great, but not so much in art. The good news is "anybody can make a movie" the bad new is " Anybody can make a movie." How do you find the jewels amidst the dross?

What is the biggest mistake you see young directors make on their first films?

The main one is hiring your best friend as your lead. Go to a University or a film class, an acting class or a local theater and find the best people you can. The first mark of amateurism apart from production value is BAD acting. Know the difference between good and bad acting. Since the 70's we have been in a long era of movie "brats" where people make movies based on movies, rather than movies based on life. They are imitating things that have come before. Your shots need to be eloquent not cool or impressive. A shot that best expresses the emotional tone the scene is trying to set to amplify the drama. If your best friend is a really funny guy at your parties, it doesn't mean he will carry your movie. The performances in a film are what carry it more than anything else. More than the script or the effects. Your willingness to spend time with these people is the first sign of amateurism.

For you, what makes a great movie monster or villain and why?

Something new! No evil person thinks they are evil. It works great when you can take a character with evil intent and present it in a way that I haven't seen it before. For instance, Ron Pearlman in DESPERATION, he was so great and so delicious and then the movie takes a nosedive after he's gone. Its being captivated by the character since everyone knows that the most interesting & memorable charters are the villains.

What is your favorite horror film of all time?

I don't have one favorite film of all time since it's kind of a shifting thing. I will tell you that David Cronenberg's DEAD RINGERS is one of them. It took me somewhere I've never been or knew I wanted to go. Genius! Jeremy Irons performance in that movie was so good, and the surgical instruments he used to mutilate women, what a great concept.

Tell us about mickgarrisinterviews.com and what students may be able to

learn from your site?

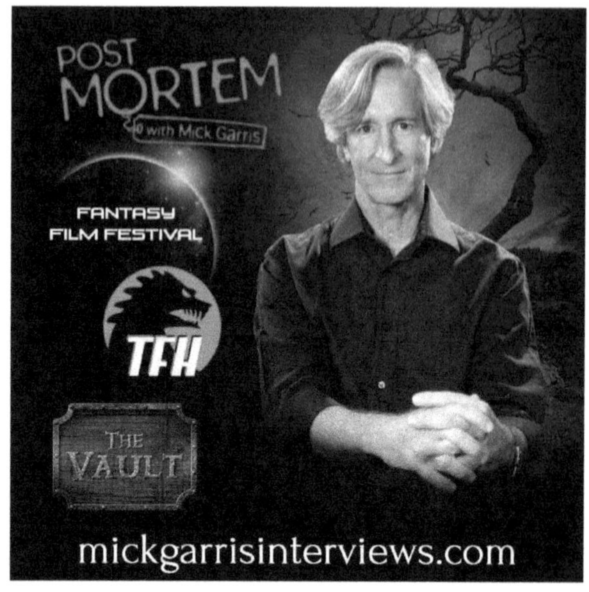

The whole point of putting these interviews online was to just give it to everyone. Every interview I heard something I'd never heard before. Most were my friends so they were comfortable being interviewed and it was not about anything specific or general about their careers. It was great because they were comfortable and unguarded. It was uncensored with no commercials and we didn't need to worry about offending anyone. They became very open. Carpenter is very open guy, very cynical and funny in a good way. The website is completely free.

It's a resource that I wish I had when I was starting out. I read, Famous Monsters. But there wasn't websites and video blogs and podcasts like today. I'm not looking to get money off this stuff, I just want to share it. These people are all so good and these hour long interviews are worth sharing.

What's the best advice you ever received in the movie business?

One thing I will always remember was when I was working on AMAZING STORIES. I had written several of them and worked as story editor on the first season. The second season, Steven Spielberg gave me the opportunity to direct an episode. One of the best things he said to me was: "Don't worry about getting fired, take chances, do something that you'd be afraid of being fired to do, because I'm not going to fire you. Be adventures, take chances, break the rules…" It gave me so much freedom. That was the first time I felt like a director. It has a visual style that is very distinct. I took what he said to heart. I never want to be timid or sedate about anything. It's easy to be if you make a comfortable living as an artist and you stop reaching. Thank you Steven for that!

If the Critters would face off against the Gremlins, who would win?

Money always wins. Gremlins would beat the shit out of them!

LISTEN TO THIS FULL UN-EDITED AUDIO INTERVIEW ON MY YOUTUBE CHANNEL FREE AT:

https://www.youtube.com/c/DannyDraven

STUART GORDON

DIRECTOR / WRITER / PRODUCER

Stuart Gordon is a legendary film director in the horror genre who started his film career in 1985 with the hit RE-ANIMATOR (1985) for Empire Pictures. He has since become a household name in the horror genre for his unique style and vision as a filmmaker.

Some of his credits include RE-ANIMATOR (1985), FROM BEYOND (1986), DOLLS (1987), ROBOT JOX (1990), THE PIT AND THE PENDULUM (1991), FORTRESS (1993), CASTLE FREAK (1995), SPACE TRUCKERS (1996), DAGON (2001), Stuart Gordon Presents DEATHBED (2002), KING OF THE ANTS (2003), EDMOND (2005), and STUCK (2007). Gordon has also directed for Showtime's Masters of Horror series, including the episodes "H. P. Lovecraft's Dreams in the Witch-House" (2005) and "The Black Cat" (2007), and the episode "Eater" (2008) for the horror TV series Fear Itself .

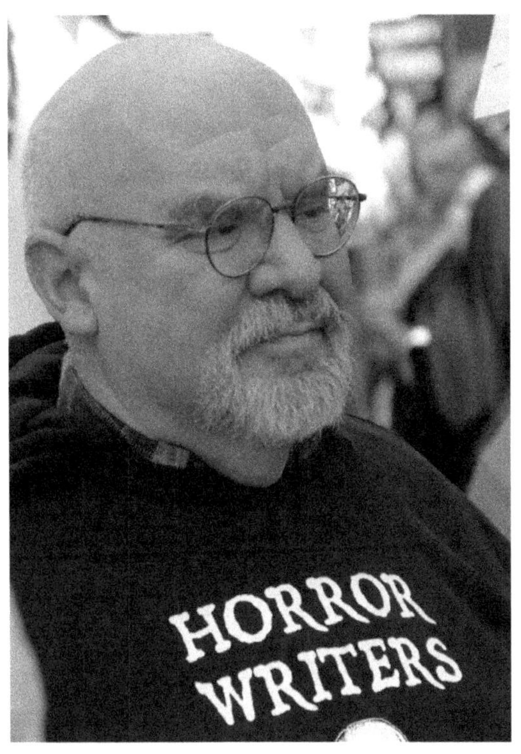

STUART GORDON
Source: Wikipedia

How did your background in the theater help you as a director?

I had a lot of experience in theater working with actors, writers, and playwrights. All of that was very useful to me. We did a lot of plays that were fantasy or horror based, and we did all of the effects live on stage. A lot of those effects were used in RE-ANIMATOR (1985), which was my first film. I didn't know anything about filmmaking; not even the basic things like screen direction (or crossing the line). On the set of RE-ANIMATOR (1985), I was run over several times by the dolly because I didn't know where to stand. Luckily, I had a great director of photography, Mac Ahlberg, who I still call "The Professor," because he gave me a crash course in filmmaking.

Your film RE-ANIMATOR (1985) is a classic because of its combination of extreme gore, sexuality, and macabre humor. The film masterfully balances gross-out horror and macabre humor. Why is laughter an important element in horror films?

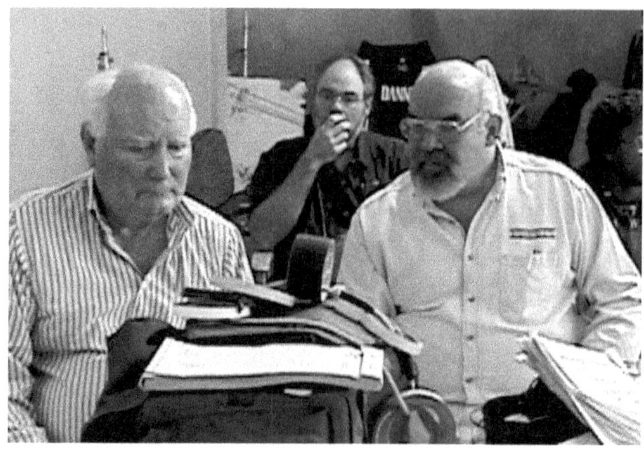

Director of Photography Mac Ahlberg and Stuart Gordon on the set of Danny Draven's DEATHBED (2002).

You will never find an audience that likes to laugh more than a horror movie audience. Laughter is the antidote to fear and helps them relieve the tension. People are always trying to find something to laugh at. I always thought it was a good idea to give them something that is not going to be at the expense of my movie. You don't want them to laugh at your monster thinking that the whole movie is ridiculous. It's great to have those moments when you can break the tension with a laugh and then crank up the suspense again. A good example is in the movie JAWS, when they are out on the water and they say, "we should have brought a bigger boat" after seeing a big shark's head coming out of the water. It gets a huge laugh and then you're right back into the danger.

The humor comes out of the characters; it's not winking at the audience. You have to be careful not to mix comedy with horror or they will cancel each other out. I think you have to take the movie seriously. Your audience wants you to do that. If they sense that the director thinks the whole movie is silly, or that he thinks he is slumming by doing a horror movie, they will have nothing to do with it. They want to know the people who made the movie are fans of the genre and take it seriously.

How important is sexuality in horror films?

I always felt that sex and horror go hand in hand. They are basically two sides of the same coin. You can go back to some of the old drawings in the middle ages and they have something called "Death and the Maiden." They would use the characters, "Death," as a picture of a skeleton caressing a beautiful naked woman. I think what it is, is life and death. Sex symbolizes life and procreating. Horror movies are really about death, and it's the conflict between the two. Even in the older horror movies there are scenes of the monster picking up the woman and carrying her off. They never used to show you what happened when they carried her off, but now we do.

I am sensing a backlash recently. Kids are getting more puritanical. In one of my movies I was looking at some of the comments about it on IMBD, and one of them wrote, "How bad is the nudity?" It was somebody who wanted to watch it with his girlfriend but was afraid if it was too sexually explicit she might think he was a pervert or something. It was just really weird. I think now, there is sort of an anti-sex feeling in horror movies as well.

I think things are changing. I feel if there is a reason for the nudity, in terms of the story, fine, then do it. If the audience feels that you are doing it just to add T&A to your movie, they tend to turn off to that.

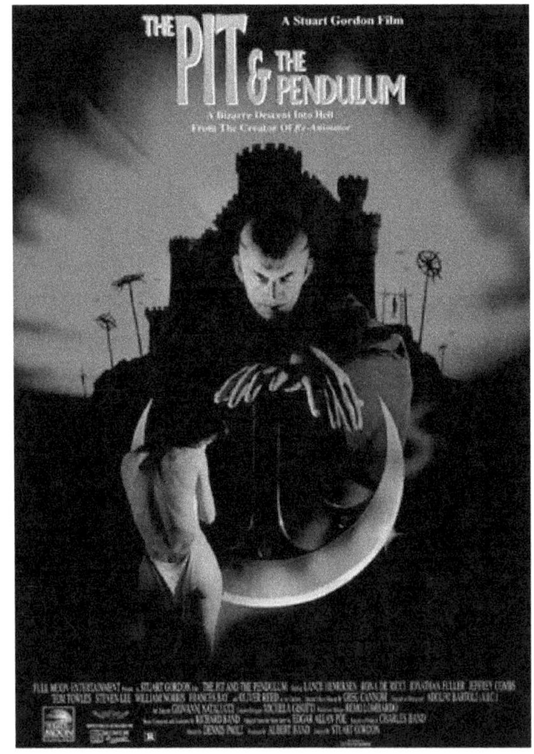

THE PIT AND THE PENDULUM (1991)

What are the mechanics of a successful scare?

It depends on what you are calling a scare. Stephen King once said, "The strongest emotion one can create is horror, a sense of dread." The sense that something awful is going to happen is true horror . The next level he said was "shock," when something jumps out at you and goes "BOO!" The lowest level is "gross out," something that is just plain disgusting. Those are the ways he broke it down. I think for me, in regards to scaring the audience, is creating characters and a story you care about. Once your audience is involved, you can put your characters in dangerous situations and they will get scared for them.

What is the best way for a new director to communicate with an actor on set?

I think it's helpful if the director knows what goes into acting. I always advise new directors to do some acting or theater classes. If you take an acting class, you will know how to speak the language of the actor. It's important for the actor to know that the director understands what they are going through.

The thing I have learned over the years is ask questions of the actors and let them solve the problems, so it's coming from them. You ask questions like, what would you do if this were to happen? The actor has to believe that this is all really happening to him and put himself in that situation. Giving an actor a direction by saying "be more scared" isn't helpful because you are just asking him for results of what you are looking for, as opposed to asking, "what is it about the situation that would scare you?" Something you can also do is the what if situation. "What if you are being followed by somebody? Suppose you heard the person breathing, not knowing if it was human or animal." By this, you're putting their imaginations to work, putting them in that situation.

Good directors don't say a lot to the actors, but they say just enough and encourage them. The director is kind of a surrogate audience for the actor. So it's encouraging to say "wow, you did great!" to the actor to put them at ease. It's important for them to be relaxed, to create a comfortable environment on the set, even though you are under a lot of pressure to work quickly. You should never rush the actor. You try to make them feel they have all the time in the world to do what they have to do.

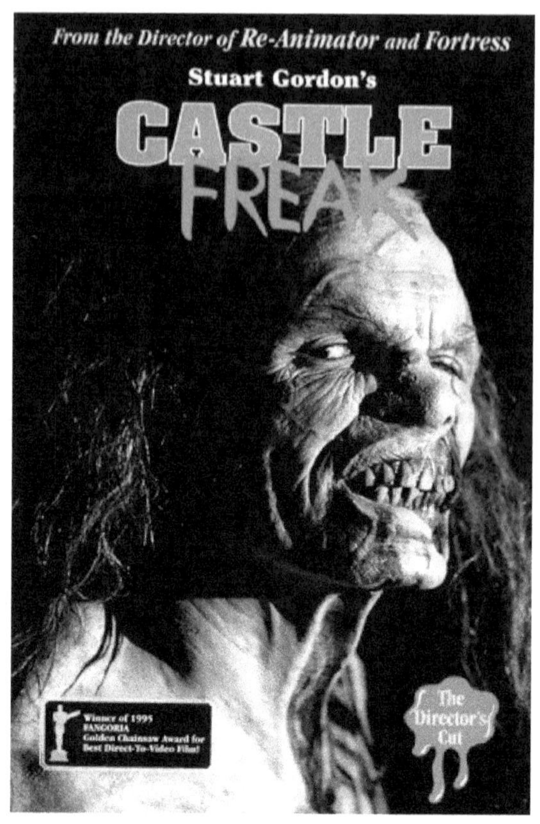

CASTLE FREAK (1995)

I think in movie making the actors are the most important part of the process. It's all about the acting for me. The technical part is important, but movies are all about the actors, that's what makes them so powerful. Actors become like family to the audiences, and we care about them.

When directing horror films, what criteria do you use when determining where to put the camera?

The best answer I've heard came from Steven Spielberg, who said that he likes to put the camera where he sits to watch the rehearsals. I think that's a very practical way to look at it. I also recommend rehearsing with your actors before production to work out all the character motivation and other details.

For RE-ANIMATOR (1985), I was influenced by Roman Polanski's work. He shoots his movies by making his audiences feel they are a character in the film. One of my favorite shots is the overthe-shoulder shot. It gives the audience a real sense of being in the movie instead of watching it from a distance. Alfred Hitchcock had a great line, too. He said, "I want to be on the train, I don't want to be a cow in the pasture watching the train go by." What I like in movies is when you forget you are watching a movie. You're engaged and you're in it. As an audience you want to forget that these are actors and there is a script. When you start to say to yourself, "WOW, what a great shot!" you're out of the movie. The positioning of the camera can really have an affect on how the audience takes in the scene.

One of the other things I've learned is that horror is slow. Horror is about anticipation. The longer it takes someone to walk up the stairs the better, because you know something is at the top waiting for them. You need to slow it down. I read somewhere that when David Cronenberg makes movies, his scripts are very short because he knows he will play things as slowly as he possibly can.

Do you storyboard?

Yes, I do storyboard, but not everything. I storyboard effect sequences and stunt scenes. I think it's important to show departments what you have in mind and how you are planning on shooting it. When dealing with special effects or mechanical prosthetics, they will know where the camera is going to be. This way they can hide the machinery or see how they can accomplish the shot.

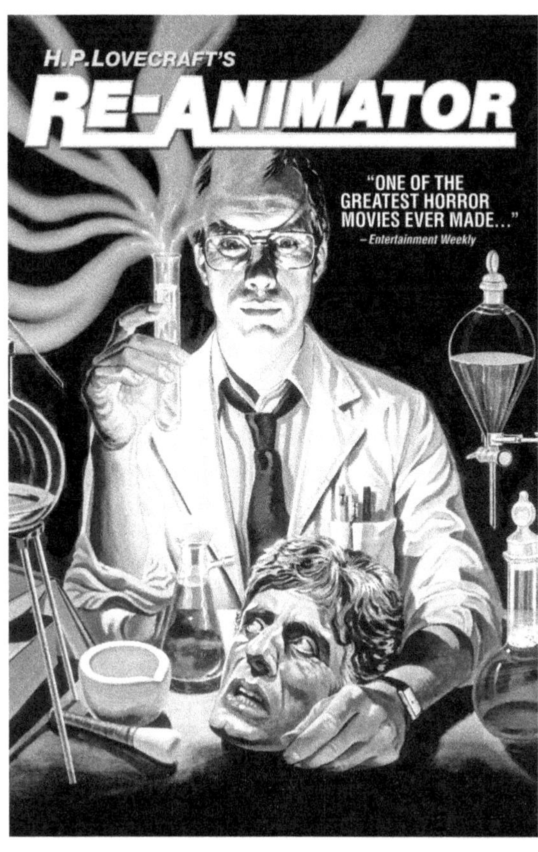

H.P. Lovecraft's RE-ANIMATOR (1985)

In one of my earlier movies, we had an effect where we had a thing coming out of this guy's forehead [FROM BEYOND, 1986]. Sometimes we used a dummy and sometimes we used the actor, puppeting from the side of his face the camera couldn't see. So we had to have a drawing on how we planned on shooting it.

It's a good idea to sit down with the effects guy before you storyboard so you know what the effects are and how they are planning to accomplish them. I usually don't storyboard everything because I like to see what the actors are going to be doing. They may not want to come through the window and would prefer a door. Well, then your storyboard ends up in the trash can. That's why I think rehearsals are important. I don't even do my shot list until after I rehearse with the actors.

In today's digital revolution, there are more horror films than ever being made. What do you think are the biggest mistakes of new filmmakers when making their first horror film?

I see more movies concerned with the gore effects than the actors or the story. The most important thing—and this is true about all movies, not just horror movies—is the script. You really have to get your script right and create a story that is really captivating and that every scene flows into the next one. I've seen a lot of movies where the script is just nonexistent, but you can tell they spent a lot of time focusing on the makeup FX. This is not only true with little films, but big Hollywood blockbusters. No matter how wonderful your actors and effects are, if the script is bad, you're doomed.

In your experience, what do you think are the most vital elements a horror film must have to be successful with an audience?

A story with characters that you care about, I think, is one of the most important. One of the things I see a lot are people that make movies about other movies. They borrow scenes from other films. You think you are seeing retreads from other movies and scenes you've seen a million times. What's important is to come up with something fresh and new. I also think you need to go beyond what has been done before in the past. I think good horror movies are transgressive and do things that are taboo. There are so many horror movies out there. You have to do something that separates your film from the rest of the pack, something that has people talking about how they can't believe what they just saw.

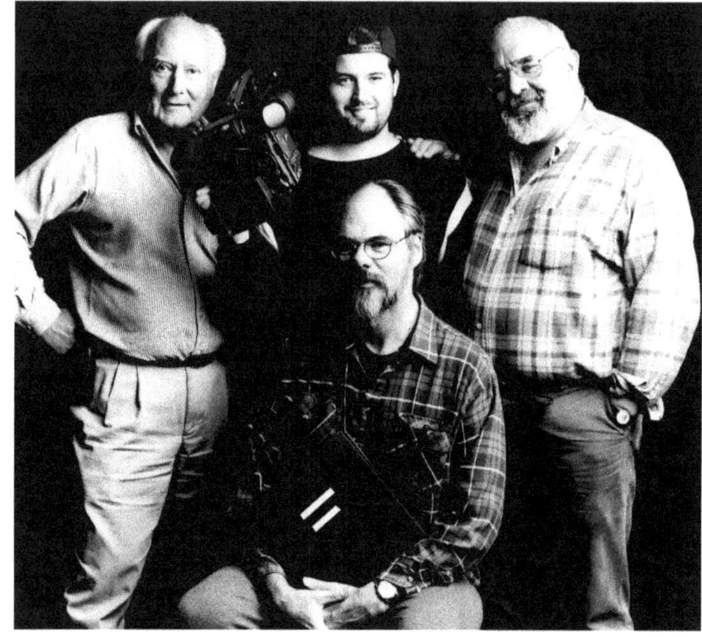

On the set of Stuart Gordon Presents DEATHBED (2002) Cinematographer Mac Ahlberg (far left standing), Producer/Director Danny Draven (center with camera), Stuart Gordon (far right standing), and screenwriter John Stysik (middle sitting down).

Photo Credit: Ward Boult (2002)

It's interesting how time has a way of dulling everything down. Amazingly, about 30 or 40 years ago, NIGHT OF THE LIVING DEAD (1968) was being shown at midnight screenings, with scenes of zombies eating flesh and intestines. No one had ever seen this before, and it was very disturbing. Audience members vomited and fainted. Now that movie is shown uncut, on television, at 3 p.m. in the afternoon.

In PSYCHO (1960) Hitchcock sets up the whole story with Janet Leigh stealing money from her company and being on the run. This whole story line builds up to her getting stabbed to death in the shower. The stabbing in the shower was a famous scene, but the scene would not be as powerful as it was had he not done all the setup for it, getting us involved with the character's predicament. This makes the audience feel as if they are getting stabbed in the shower. That's why it's so shocking.

The greatest tool that a filmmaker has is the audience's imagination. If he can manipulate, tease, and engage them, he will get their imagination spinning. With a great filmmaker, you feel you are in the hands of a guy who is not going to stop. He is going to go way beyond anything you have ever seen before. You get this weird feeling where you are excited and also terrified, wondering if you can

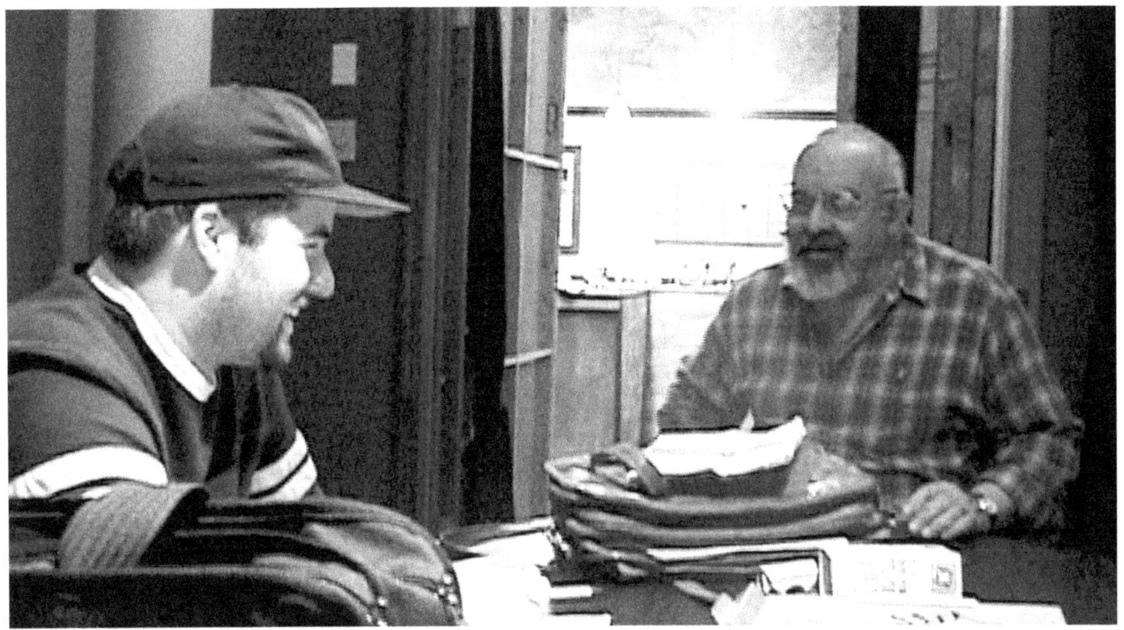

Danny Draven (left) and Stuart Gordon (right) going over the day's shooting schedule on the set of Stuart Gordon Presents DEATHBED

handle this. I think that is the goal of the filmmaker. When you realize that the filmmaker is smart and talented and that you are under his spell, it's a great feeling.

In ALIEN (1979) you don't see the whole monster until one of the last shots in the movie. You see little pieces of it, a little mouth or pieces of a hand. You're not even sure what you are looking at half the time. It makes it mysterious. The idea is that once you show the monster, the movie is over. It's the fear of the unknown that is the strongest fear. Once the unknown becomes known, then you can handle it.

In 2002, I produced and directed a film with you for Full Moon Pictures called Stuart Gordon Presents DEATHBED for a budget of only 35 thousand and shot in 8 days in Los Angeles. As someone who regularly works on larger projects, this was somewhat of a different world you entered into working under these constraints. What kinds of things did you learn from working on this ultralow budget level and fast-paced schedules?

I learned a tremendous amount! That was a really good experience for me. I felt like I was seeing the future of film making. Seeing how you produced and directed DEATHBED was a revelation to me. It made me realize that the whole world that I had known was about to change in a big way. I remember you guys were making movies out of an apartment complex, which seemed to be a mini-production studio. We did Foley and ADR in the bathroom, sound design in another apartment, and our commentary in your living room.

What I feel that will never change is the importance of story, strong performances, and imagination. That is what you need no matter what the format is. It all comes down to the script, actors, and the director being able to tell that story.

I always tell my students that the problems are always the same no matter what the size of your budget. You never have enough time or enough movie. When James Cameron did TITANIC, he wanted to build the whole Titanic full size and couldn't do it. He had to build half of it. There was a scene where he had to show the other side, and he ended up just flipping the negative. He had all the signage written in mirror image because he knew he was going to flip it. The whole scene where the passengers were boarding the ship was all shot with a negative flipped because the ship was facing the wrong way. Amazing!

My mother used to always say, "There are two ways to solve a problem: one is to throw money at it; the other way is to be clever."

LISTEN TO THIS FULL UN-EDITED AUDIO INTERVIEW ON MY YOUTUBE CHANNEL FREE AT:

https://www.youtube.com/c/DannyDraven

DENISE GOSSETT

FESTIVAL DIRECTOR
SHRIEKFEST

www.shriekfest.com
www.denisegossett.com

Shriekfest is an international horror/sci-fi film festival and screenplay competition -- and the longest running horror festival in Los Angeles!

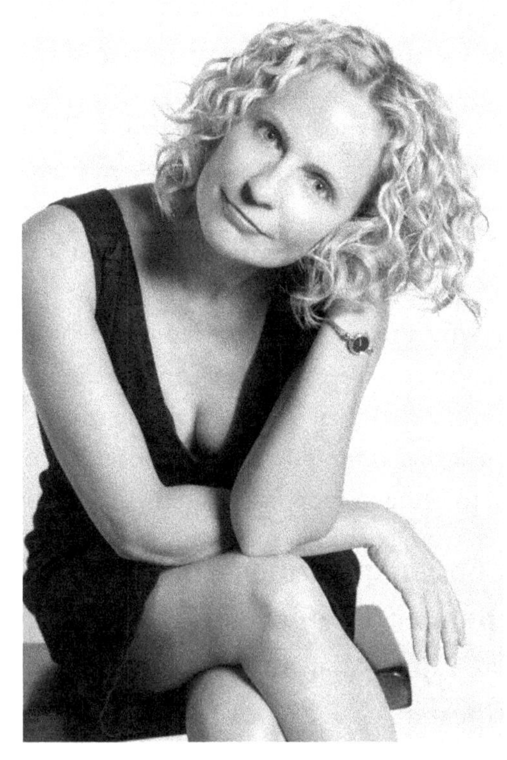

DENISE GOSSETT

What are the common mistakes you see filmmakers make when submitting to a film festival?

Not having a complete package...and that means a good story, good production value, good acting, good FX, good sound, good cinematography...the whole thing. So many are just too long. I know it's hard to edit down your baby, but, quite honestly, if it doesn't move the story along, it doesn't belong in your film.

Once accepted to the festival, what should all filmmakers have ready and why?

They need to have their screeners ready with a back up copy. We like to put posters up at the festival, flyers can go out, business cards, some filmmakers like to do trinkets to publicize their films, have a Twitter page and a Facebook page. All of this is important, grab your fans now and when it's time to sell your film, you'll already have a huge fan base. When you are in a festival, make sure you use that time and that audience wisely. And this shouldn't end when the fest ends either...keep that marketing going.

What does the festival look for in a horror or sci-fi film in order to be accepted to the festival?

Complete package. I can't tell you how many times a film has a good story and then bad acting or great acting and bad filming or story. We like unique ideas as well. It doesn't have to be a high budget film to be good or to be accepted, but it does have to be good.

Can you give us a glimpse of how the judging process works, and what criteria may be used to determine the winners?

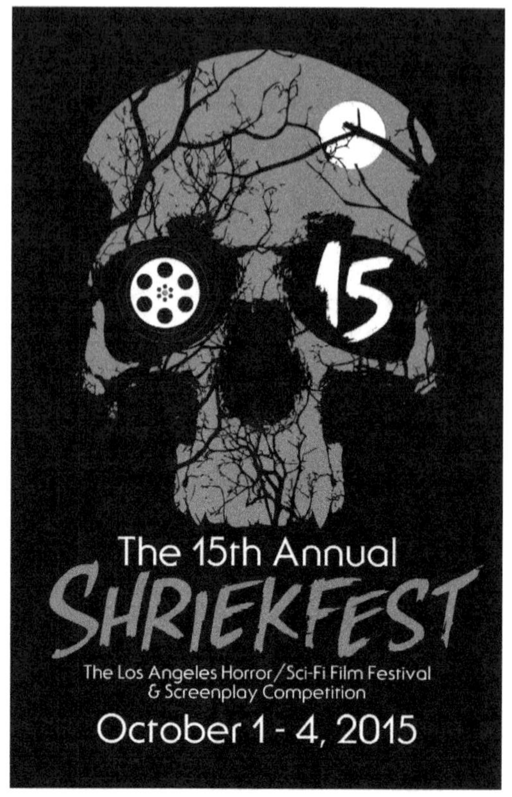

SHRIEKFEST Poster!

I have over 40 judges and they each help narrow down the choices. It's a lengthy process. We have voter sheets to help narrow the films down. Once we get votes back, entries now go in yes, maybe, and no piles. From the yes piles we choose the official selections! Now, every year there are great yes's and maybes that don't make the cut due to time constraints...the festival itself can only be so many days. From the official selections, we pick the winners and sometimes if there are ties, I have to bring in more judges to help with those ties.

Do film acquisitions executives lurk in the audiences at your festival, or is it mainly horror and sci-fi fans? Any distribution deals happen after a Shriekfest screening?

Oh yes! All the time. All the big companies send some sort of rep. As a matter of fact, they trust Shriekfest now and often filmmakers will get deals before they even screen at our festival! Once we've announced our selections they often get contacted right away! So, now, when their film screens any distributors who weren't quick on the draw lose out.

Do the winners of awards from festivals like yours, who then display "Best Picture" or "Best Actor" on the box art usually help the film in terms of sales or finding distribution?

Yes, it helps in many ways. A win at a festival opens up doors to agents, distributors, publicity, and fans. All the things a filmmaker wants. Just be careful which festivals you screen at, if they don't have a good reputation that win may not mean as much. Distributors want to make money, so, if your film has wins and has a fan base they can use all of that in their marketing of it.

There seems to be a never-ending list of genre film festivals emerging every year. A low-budget filmmaker can spend thousands in expensive submission fess and press kits just trying to get accepted. What criteria can filmmakers use to judge the quality of a film festival and make sure it's not a backyard operation?

Great question! Draven, they are popping up everywhere. It's actually frustrating to me because I hear horror stories from filmmakers about them. If your film is just ok, try a first year or second year fest and maybe you can get in or grab a win. If your film is good, try the festivals that have been around longer so you get the bang for your buck. Research festivals too, attend them, see what is par for each one.

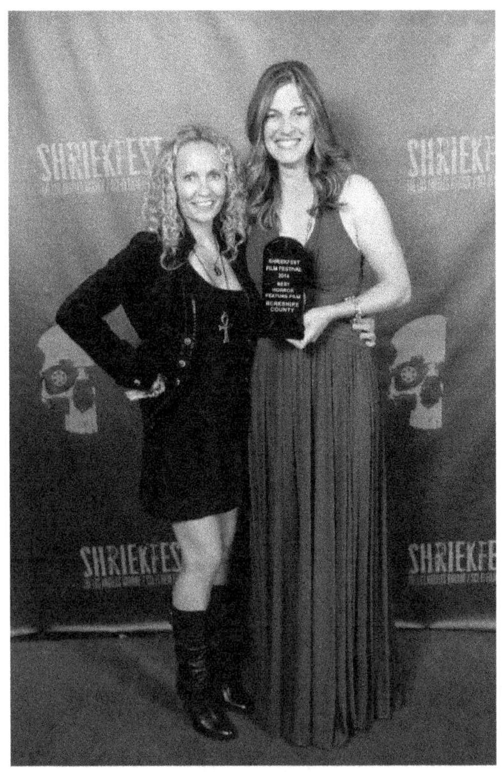

Denise Gossett and Audrey Cummings, 2014 winner for Best Horror Feature Film for BERKSHIRE COUNTY (2014). She was the first female ever to win this award.

What is a press kit, and why is it important for a film festival?

A press kit is a packet or a digital file (EPK or Electronic Press Kit) filled with cast pics and bios, crew list, on set pics, synopsis, a listing of festivals it has screened at and any awards, websites, social media, etc. For our festival these are NOT needed...do NOT submit these with your entry, it's just a waste of time and money. Once you are accepted you may send them to us. These can be given to distributors, agents, etc. I think they are very important, but they are most important when you have already made some sort of contact with the person. You don't want to waste these by passing them out to everyone that attends. If you want something to pass out, make postcards with your film poster on them and your contact info.

What is your advice for a filmmaker who wants to network at the festival?

Look for name badges and just start talking to people. If you saw someone's film, talk about that or if you have a film screening talk about that. We have an opening night party that is full of industry people 400-500 people attend it and that is the start of the fest, so, it kinda breaks the ice and gives everyone a chance to mingle and pass out their postcards or flyers. I do my best to make Shriekfest like a family, so, if we see someone just standing around, we will introduce them to others or bring them in the conversations. Shriekfest is a great place to network and people team up every year from it. I love that the most!

What is the most common submission format for filmmakers? And what is the ideal format for presentation at the fest?

Online submissions are the most common, which is great, so easy to get them to the judges, but, some people still submit on dvd. For the screenings the most common is Blu Ray, but we also do DVD or a digital file.

Does a film with a star or a higher production budget get priority over micro-budget productions?

NO, a huge NO. Every year we have submissions come in with stars and if the movie is not good, it doesn't get in. It's amazing how many pretty movies are out there with stars in them that have horrible stories. We are not going to show horrible stories just because there is a star in them. You would be shocked at the "stars" we have rejected.

In all your years as a festival director, what is the best advice you can give a new filmmaker with a completed movie ready to show?

Research the festival route you want to take. Ask other filmmakers which festivals to stay away from. Start that marketing campaign, get that twitter and facebook account going...rack up your fans. Do NOT post your film online yet...you can post trailers, but, not the actual film. Create a buzz, but don't give it all away, even if it's a short film. Be professional. Keep track of where you submitted and when the festivals are...I can't tell you how many filmmakers/screenwriters have emailed me and said Denise, did I submit this year yet? Don't expect a festival to keep track of that for you. That is the business side of your job as a filmmaker. Log everything, keep a database. But, most of all, believe in your project, have passion, be kind, generous, and help others spread the word on their projects too. It is a wonderful community if you treat it right.

KANE HODDER

ACTOR / STUNTMAN

www.kanehodderkills.com

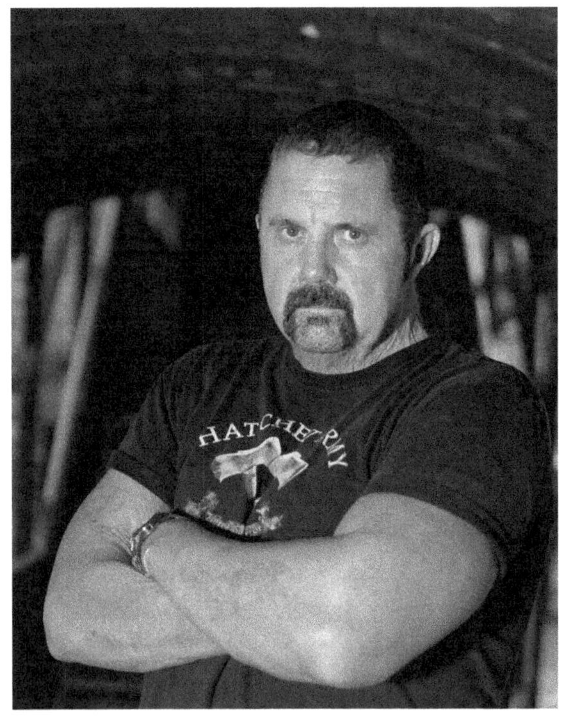

Kane Hodder unmasked.
a.k.a. Jason from the Friday the 13th Films (7,8,9,10)

Kane Warren Hodder was born in Auburn, California. As a child, he was relentlessly bullied and suffered terribly, until he and his family moved to the tiny South Pacific Island Kwajalein, one of the Marshall Islands. Here Kane attended junior and senior high school and loved life on this small jungle island.

When Kane eventually returned to California, he started getting stunt jobs on feature films and then made his way into the acting world, eventually to portray the best known, most memorable and terrifying JASON VOORHEES, four consecutive times in the Friday the 13th film franchise.

To date, Kane Hodder has starred in FRIDAY THE 13th Part VII: The New Blood, FRIDAY THE 13th Part VIII: Jason Takes Manhattan, JASON GOES TO HELL: The Final Friday and JASON X.

Kane is also well known for his role as Victor Crowley in HATCHET, which rolled into the film franchise HATCHET 2 and HATCHET 3.

Kane Hodder is the true definition of dichotomy: he is possibly the most beloved horror icon in the film industry, as well as with his millions of fans. Kane towers at 6'3" and has an intimidating and unforgettable, powerful presence. And a heart of gold.

Kane Hodder has starred in more than 200 films and television shows, as well as being stunt coordinator on hundreds of films. Kane is also a published author.

In the mid 1980's, Kane was performing a stunt that went horribly wrong, leaving him with first and second degree burns over 75% of his body. It was a long and painful road to recovery. He has the word "Kill!" tattooed on the back of his bottom lip. He is an avid poker player and often plays celebrity tournaments.

Kane spends much of his time, when he is not filming, working with children in burn centers, as well as with numerous charities. Despite the roles he portrays, Hodder is often described as a very kind, compassionate and generous soul, who truly cares for those who suffer life's cruel blows. He loves and appreciates his fans. Kane also has the most wicked and wonderful comedic timing...a real cut up (pardon the pun!)

Kane Hodder is often compared to legendary film stars such as Vincent Price, Bela Lugosi and Boris Karloff.

"*Attitude is everything when it comes to the character. I'm a real natural when it comes to looking scary. If you're not seriously trying to frighten people, then the fear these movies are intended to generate doesn't come across. I truly try to scare the shit out of people all the time. Between takes, in the make-up trailer, you never know when I'm going to go "Boo!" That's the main reason I keep getting asked to play Jason" – KANE HODDER*

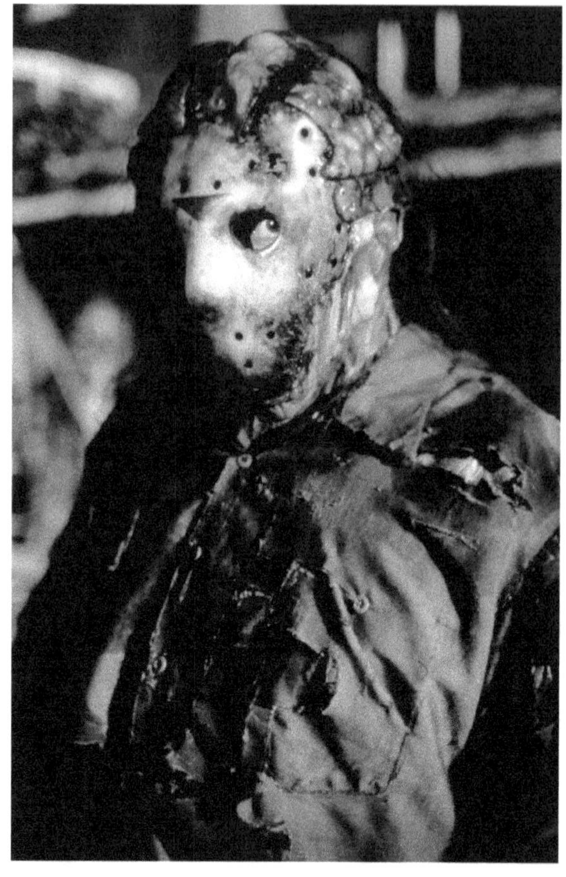

Kane Hodder as Jason Voorhees

Your character Jason Voorhees from the Friday the 13th films (7,8,9,10) is one of the most influential screen monsters in the history of horror films. What are the mechanics underneath that made Jason such an unforgettable screen monster, and why?

I think that the biggest reason that Jason has become such an unforgettable horror icon is the hockey mask. It's a terrifying, expressionless image, that never changes, regardless of what the character is doing. Combine that with the fact that he has existed for 12 different movies, and you have a lengthy history and story that different generations have experienced. Jason was already well known around the world, before I ever wore the mask, and that is why I will always feel that it was an honor to play the character, and I always felt that I had an obligation to give the very best performance that I possibly could.

In your vast experience in the horror genre, what do you think are the key elements to a great cinematic death scene?

I think that the absolute key ingredient in making a memorable death scene is creativity. My favorite kills are the ones that you had never seen anything like it before. It's pretty hard nowadays to come up with something new in regards to cinematic death, but fortunately we have writers like Adam Green who can still do it. I also try to add my own "flavor" to a kill, as well.

In the horror genre, what are your favorite screen monsters, and why? Were any of films or characters influential for you when playing Jason Voorhees or Victor Crowley?

As a kid, I enjoyed the classic monsters like the Wolfman, Mummy, Dracula and The Phantom of the Opera. But my favorite was always Frankenstein. I'm sure it won't surprise people that those memories had something to do with the way I played Jason. I always loved the unstoppable, slow moving machine. I always found that to be more frightening.

How important is movement and onscreen presence for some of the madmen you have played onscreen?

With a non-speaking, non-facial expression character, the importance of body movement is of ultimate importance. Virtually 100% of the performance relies on movement and not just movement, but NATURAL movement. It has to not look like you are acting, or it just won't work. A lot of actors in this type of role will try too hard, and then the character loses all its power.

In the horror genre, what are the biggest mistakes you see filmmakers make when creating a monster on a low budget?

I think the only mistake you can make while developing a horror character is too make it too similar to something that already exists. When someone comes up with a new idea regarding its killer, or overall premise, the chances of success are much higher, regardless of the budget.

What is the best way for a new director to communicate with an actor or stuntman on set? How do you like to be directed when you are in full makeup and costume as Jason or Victor?

New directors have to know the material they're shooting, inside and out. I always enjoy when a new director has also written the story as well. Nobody knows the material better than the writer. New writer/directors usually have more self confidence and that works well. When I'm in character, I prefer a director to talk to me off to the side, away from the other actors, so that they can't hear what the director is saying, or what my response might be. It keeps them a little off balance. It seems a little "method", but I think it has worked fairly well for me over the years.

LLOYD KAUFMAN

DIRECTOR / PRODUCER
TROMA ENTERTAINMENT

www.troma.com

www.lloydkaufman.com

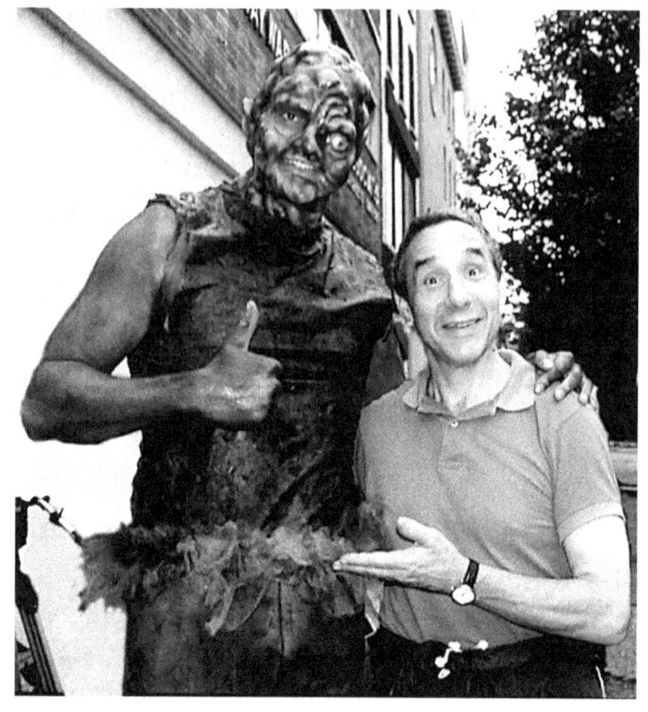

TOXIE & LLOYD KAUFMAN

LLOYD KAUFMAN, entertainment industry veteran, is president of the New York-based production and distribution company Troma Entertainment, the longest-running indie film studio in history, which he and partner Michael Herz founded in 1974 shortly after they graduated from Yale University. In 35 years, Kaufman and Herz have built Troma up to legendary status as a bastion of true independence and a strong consumer brand through a visionary body of work that has had a huge impact on pop culture and today's mainstream filmmaking. New York Post film critic Lou Lumenick recently wrote that Kaufman "has been cited as a major influence by Peter Jackson, Quentin Tarantino and Takashi Miike, among others." Other writers and directors who have cited Kaufman as a major influence include Sam Raimi, James Gunn, Kevin Smith, and Eli Roth, to name a few. In addition, Kaufman has mentored many young independent filmmakers, and Troma movies or releases have given numerous now-famous talent their first start in the film industry, including Trey Parker and Matt Stone, Samuel L. Jackson, Kevin Costner, Oliver Stone, Marisa Tomei, Vincent D'Onofrio, and Jenna Fischer. Other major figures whose first work appears in a Troma film include Robert De Niro, Dustin Hoffman, and Carmen Electra.

Kaufman and Herz created Troma Entertainment with a series of highly original comedies, such as SQUEEZE PLAY!, WAITRESS!, and other titles that served as independent precursors to such later smash hits as NATIONAL LAMPOON'S ANIMAL HOUSE and PORKY'S. In 1984, Kaufman achieved new levels of success with his breakthrough movie THE TOXIC AVENGER, which led to the animated spin-off television series Toxic Crusaders, several different comic book titles published by Marvel and Troma's own independent comic book imprint, and three sequels. Its multiplatform success was followed by a string of commercial and artistic triumphs that blended fantasy, heavy action, and comedy in a style that the Cinémathèque Française described as "Tromatic," including the CLASS OF NUKE 'EM HIGH trilogy, SGT. KABUKIMAN N.Y.P.D., and TROMA'S WAR. Kaufman most recently wrote and directed POULTRYGEIST: NIGHT OF THE CHICKEN DEAD. Kaufman's TROMEO AND JULIET, written with James Gunn, became a theatrical and critical hit, earning the grand prize at the Fanta Festival in Rome and the audience award at Raindance in London, among others.

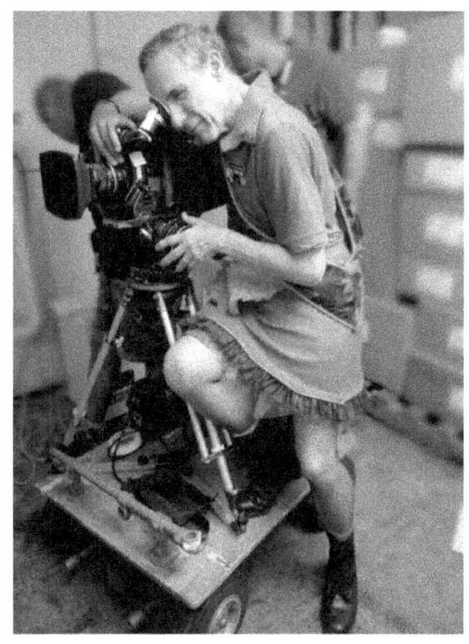

Kaufman on set.

In 1999, Kaufman founded TromaDance Film Festival in Park City, Utah, now in its 10th year (www.tromadance.com). His popular Make Your Own Damn Movie master classes have been given at universities and venues throughout the world.

In addition, Kaufman has been honored by various international film festivals and Troma retrospectives across the globe, including the San Sebastian Film Festival, the British Film Institute, the Cinémathèque Française, the American Cinematheque, the Chicago International Film Festival, and the UCLA Film Archives. Fluent in French and able to "get around" in Mandarin, he has also served on the boards of Trinity School and ECO, the environmental foundation. Kaufman has also made films pro bono for his Yale University class and for Jacques d'Amboise's National Dance Institute. The author of three books, with two additional books in the making, Kaufman is married to Patricia Swinney Kaufman, the New York State Film Commissioner. He is also the elected chairman of the Independent Film & Television Alliance (IFTA), the global trade association of independent distributors and producers of motion picture and television programming.

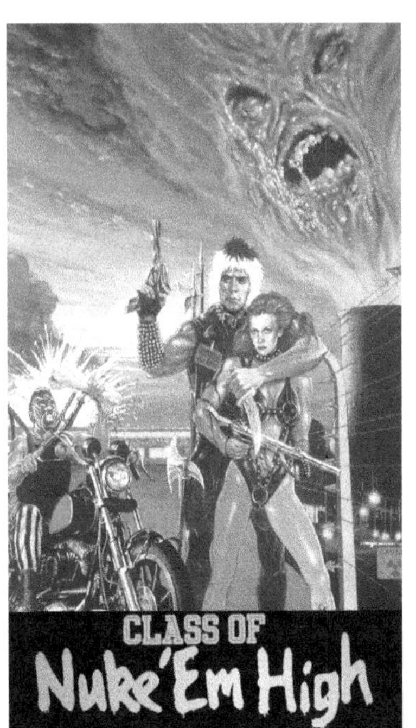

CLASS OF NUKE'EM HIGH (1986)

Troma Entertainment is one of the longest-running independent film companies in the world and has distributed hundreds of films. As a distributor, what do you look for in a film you are considering for distribution?

It has to be something that when people go to the movie theater and they know in advance that they may love THE TOXIC AVENGER (1984), or they may hate POULTRYGEIST:

NIGHT OF THE CHICKEN DEAD (2006), or they may never forget TROMEO & JULIET (1996), that they will have been on an adventure in the cinema. They feel challenged that they've seen something they've never seen before. They won't be getting baby food or fast food movies. Ninety-nine percent of the films made are formulated baby food, and it's very boring. If it's not baby food, then you have fast food films like SPEED RACER (2008), which like fast food that tastes good going down, but then you immediately get diarrhea. So, we are making movies that people can chew on and have flavor. Our movies are like the jalapeño peppers of the cultural pizza.

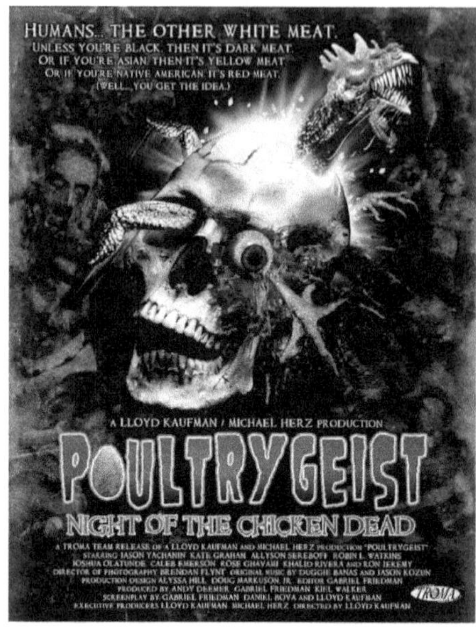

POULTRYGEIST (2006).

You have been making films for over 35 years and are among the most influential independent filmmakers of our time. In retrospect, what are the biggest pitfalls you see new filmmakers make when trying to sell their finished movie?

You should do what you believe in and what is in your heart, "To thine own self be true." The mistake most filmmakers encounter is not abiding by the "To thine own self be true" maxim, which as you know was coined by the great William Shakespeare who wrote the best selling book, 101 Money-Making Screenplay Ideas, otherwise known as Hamlet .

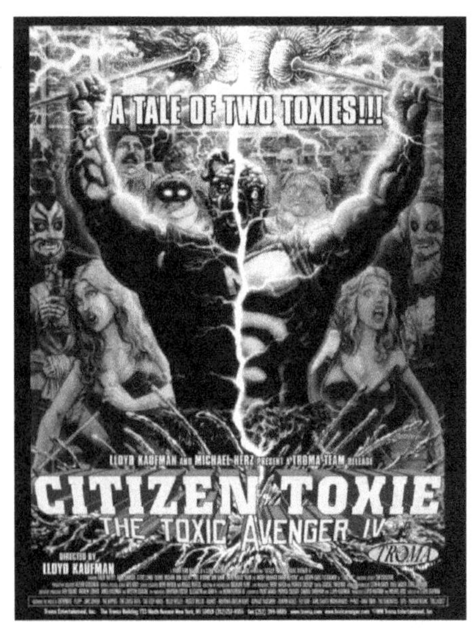

CITIZEN TOXIE (2000)

Another mistake is that when the movie is finished, some filmmakers feel it's beneath their dignity to go out and whore for their art. They're willing to compromise, and they are willing to copy other filmmakers, or try to make the next TOXIC AVENGER (1984) or the next Quentin Tarantino movie, but then they feel selling is dirty. They don't want to get their hands dirty by getting out there and selling the film.

Picasso was a genius, but he was also a great salesman, promoter, and merchandiser, whereas van Gogh, who was equally brilliant, didn't get involved in promotion. Charlie Chaplin sure as hell promoted and he died a rich man.

Buster Keaton didn't get involved in that stuff and he went bankrupt. They both were equally brilliant.

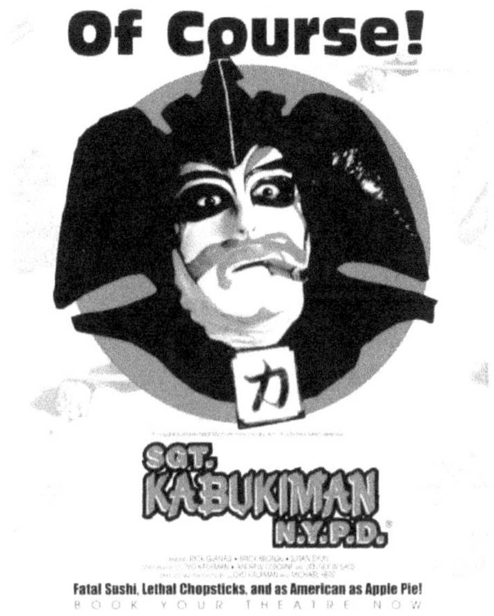

SGT. KABUKIMAN N.Y.P.D. (1991)

What is the best way for a low-budget filmmaker to finance a film?

The best way to get the money to make your own damn movie is to get your own damn script, and one that is really good. I never had the money to hire top-quality writers, so I write my own scripts. A good script equals power and is probably the best way to get mainstream financing.

You must speak to everybody. Tell everybody you know about your movie, even your bus driver. A perfect example is when I was making my first feature called BATTLE OF LOVES RETURN (1971). I was coming out of a movie theater—I think I was seeing STRAP-ON SALLY: PART 6—and I ran into one of my Yale classmates. Instead of exchanging just platitudes, he asked me how I was doing and what I was doing. I told him I was making a movie and I need someone to finance it, and bingo, he became my executive producer. If I would have been embarrassed to ask, BATTLE OF LOVES RETURN (1971) would not have happened, which was Oliver Stone's first film as an actor.

My wife and I put up 80 percent of the money for POULTRYGEIST: NIGHT OF THE CHICKEN DEAD (2006). Her retirement money is in that film, but I told her she was investing in TRANSFORMERS: PART 6. Don't tell her.

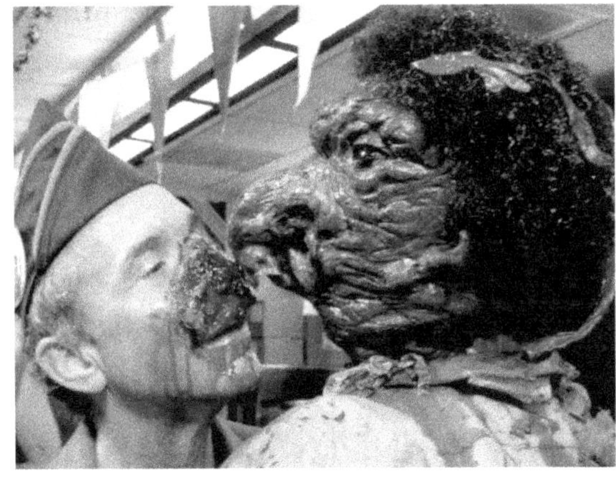

Kaufman and pal on set.

It's tough for independent filmmakers. I have always been upfront with investors. I have never tried to hoodwink anyone, and I've always told investors that they must be prepared to lose every dime. If you don't say that, then you may get your movie made, but may not get another one made after. So right now a $500,000 movie that is totally independent and distributed independent is very, very questionable whether it will turn a profit. This is because the industry is so consolidated.

In our modern times, the tools for making a film—such as affordable digital cameras and post-production on your desktop—has given just about anyone the ability to shoot their own movie. It has also caused a glut in the marketplace. What are some of the things a filmmaker should do before shooting to ensure their film will stand out above the rest?

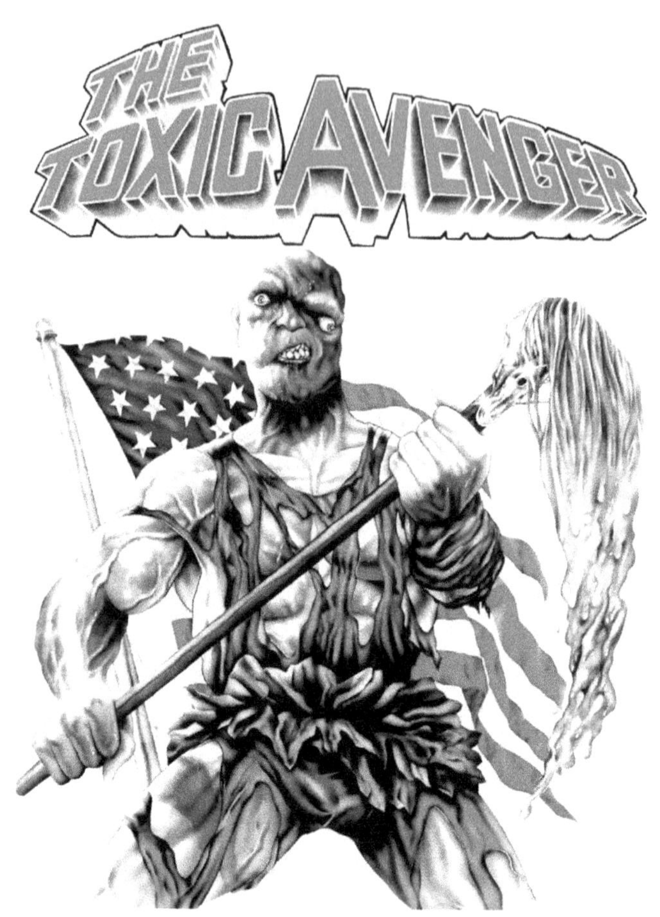

THE TOXIC AVENGER (1984)

There is economic blacklisting in the mainstream industry because the media is consolidated and controlled by five or six devil worshiping, international media conglomerates. As a result, the independents are economically blacklisted. We cannot get our films on television in America, unless we come in through one of the vessels of the majors.

There is a trade association—which I was elected chairman of—for independent movie companies called THE INDEPENDENT FILM & TELEVISION MOVIE ALLIANCE. We are the equivalent of MPAA for independents. I ran for chairmanship because the consolidation of the industry has gone too far.

It is very important to maintain neutrality on the Internet. The Internet has to be kept open and free democratically because it's the last democratic medium. The phone companies and major studios are against Net neutrality because they want to get rid of it and want to control the pipes that go into your home. We have to preserve Net neutrality. If that goes, then we have a problem.

After reading an article that claimed horror films were dead, you had the idea to combine horror and comedy and THE TOXIC AVENGER (1984) was born. This genre combination has become a popular one. In your experience, what

are the key components to have in a horror–comedy?

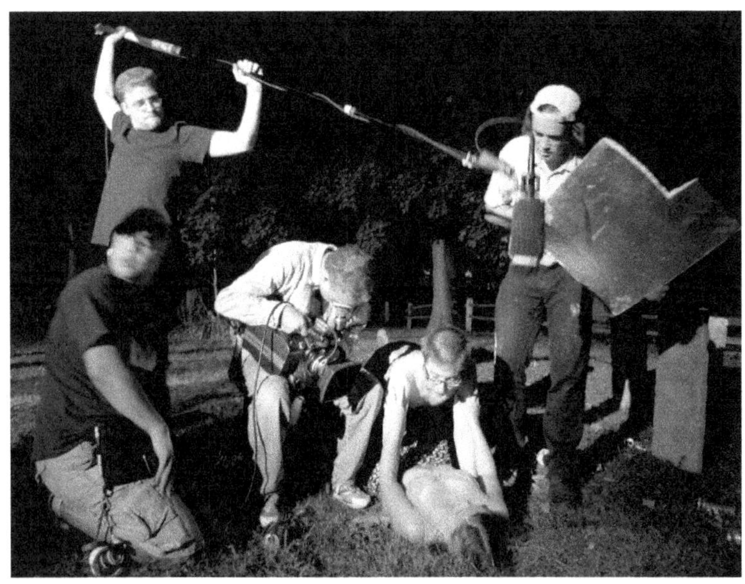
Kaufman on set as his own cameraman.

Peter Jackson and James Gunn and a few others suggested we invent the slapstick–gore movie. This is not a very smart way to go because both horror and comedy ride the back of the bus, and certainly comedy is very subjective. What is funny in New York may not be funny in Hungary, or even Arkansas. You'll reach a much wider audience by not combining slapstick satire with horror and gore.

In the case of TROMEO AND JULIET (1996), we mixed eroticism and Shakespeare, horror and slapstick satire. In POULTRYGEIST: NIGHT OF THE CHICKEN DEAD (2006), we took it a bit further. We had singing and dancing along with horror, slapstick, and erotic scenes. What we do is comedy, and comedy is probably the most difficult economically from a distributor's point of view. I don't think there are rules to this game. What you do is what you believe in and what interests you!

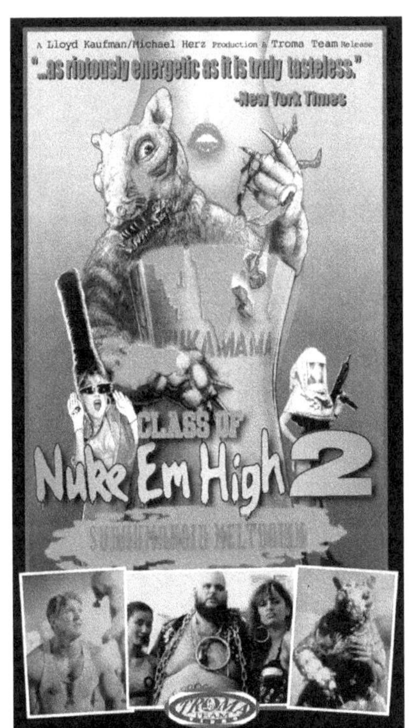

CLASS OF NUKE'EM HIGH 2 (1991)

Is it necessary to have a star in the film for it to be sellable, or are there certain nonactor related elements that can be just as valuable to a distributor?

Personally, I don't care for stars unless you have three or four who can actually produce ticket sales, and there are very few of them. Stars are useless. In fact, they are a determent. With THE TOXIC AVENGER (1984), we created our own star. Today, without any advertising, he is more famous than probably 99 percent of the young actors who were heavily promoted or started in 1984.

The smart way to make a low-budget independent movie is to aim at some kind of audience. If you put a gun in the movie then people will look at the screen. If it is a monster, then someone will buy a ticket. If you have a vampire, there is an audience for every vampire movie, and they will go to see, buy, or rent it no matter what. So that might be a better backstop than having Stanley Tucci in your film.

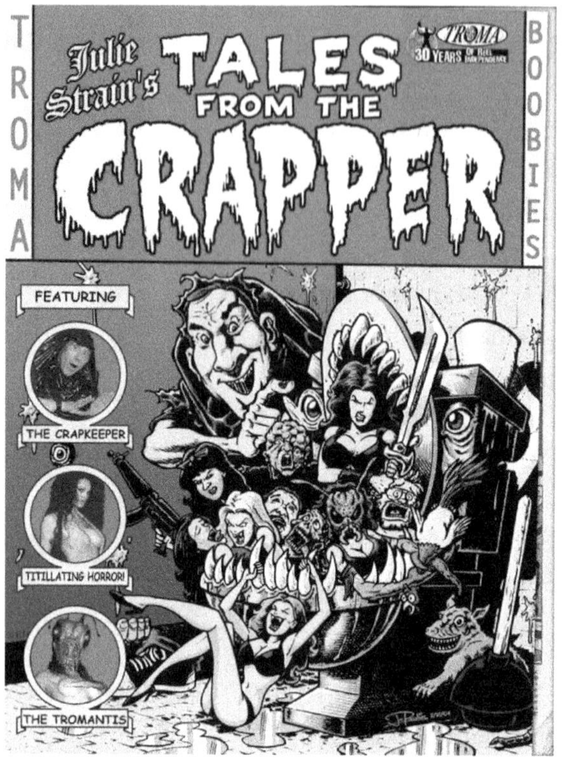

TALES FROM THE CRAPPER (2004)

The only kind of formulaic advice I would give is to try to have something in your movie that ensures someone will buy tickets.

Are film festivals a scam or a necessity?

We setup Tromadance (www.tromadance.com) in 1999 as a reaction against Sundance. We felt that Sundance was exploiting independent filmmakers into sending in their money. A lot have paid entry fees and never even got a "F&%$ You" letter. That is what inspired us for Tromadance. Everything is free. You can submit your movie for free and watch them for free, and there is no VIP policy. It is also during Sundance, so you may see some celebrities and studio executives walking the streets of Park City, Utah. The big film festivals like Sun-dance, in my opinion, are fixed.

When POLTERGEIST played, the theater was packed. We had one screen in a theater in Manhattan. The week we opened we had the second highest gross in the country on that screen, and the third week, we were replaced by a studio blockbuster that took all the screens in the country. Luckily we found another movie screen, but all your momentum is destroyed if you have to change screens.

LISTEN TO THIS FULL UN-EDITED AUDIO INTERVIEW ON MY YOUTUBE CHANNEL FREE AT:

https://www.youtube.com/c/DannyDraven

ROBERT KURTZMAN

PRODUCER / DIRECTOR / SCREENWRITER / CREATURE AND VISUAL FX CREATOR

www.creaturecorps.net

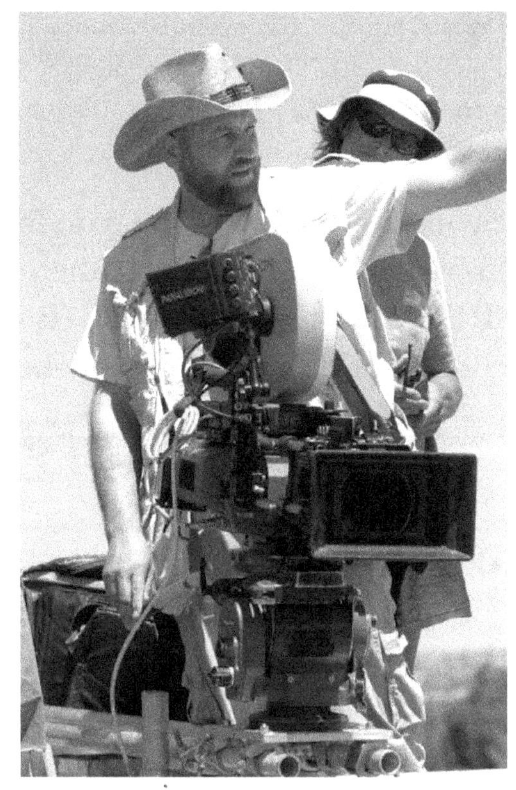

ROBERT KURTZMAN

ROBERT KURTZMAN, Hollywood special effects legend and filmmaker, began his career in 1984 when he moved from Ohio to Hollywood and started working as a freelance artist for many of the industry's top special effects creators. His early credits include PREDATOR, EVIL DEAD II, FROM BEYOND, THE HIDDEN, PHANTASM II, INVADERS FROM MARS, NIGHT OF THE CREEPS, and RE- ANIMATOR. In 1988, Robert formed the award-winning KNB EFX Group, Inc. with partners Greg Nicotero and Howard Berger. Over the next 15 years, KNB became one of the most prolific effects studios in Hollywood with hundreds of feature film and television credits, including the SPY KIDS movies, THE CELL, UNBREAKABLE, HOUSE ON HAUNTED HILL, SPAWN, THE FACULTY, Sam Raimi's ARMY OF DARKNESS, DANCES WITH WOLVES, JINGLE ALL THE WAY, THE GREEN MILE, GHOSTS OF MARS, RAT RACE, 13 GHOSTS, VANILLA SKY, THE TIME MACHINE, AUSTIN POWERS: GOLDMEMBER, THE HULK, GHOST SHIP, EVOLUTION, BUBBA HO-TEP, WYATT EARP, John Carpenter's VAMPIRES and IN THE MOUTH OF MADNESS, MISERY, Steven Spielberg's MINORITY REPORT and AMISTAD, Quentin Tarantino's RESERVOIR DOGS, PULP FICTION, KILL BILL Volumes 1 and 2, as well as the television series Hercules, Xena, Picket Fences, Outer Limits, ER, Chicago Hope, and many more.

In 2003, Kurtzman founded Precinct 13 Entertainment/Creature Corps, which is a full-service production facility that handles film, commercials, and music videos as well as special makeup, creature construction, visual effects, editorial and post. P13 and Creature Corps have worked on a wide array of projects with credits that include the effects supervision on HOSTEL, THE DEVIL's REJECTS, 2001 MANIACS, Mad TV, and CHILDREN OF THE CORN.

Robert's foray into production began with FROM DUSK TILL DAWN (1996). He wrote the original story, which was adapted by Quentin Tarantino, coproduced the film, and created the eye-popping special effects. His directorial debut was THE DEMOLITIONIST, which was quickly followed by WISHMASTER, a film he directed for Artisan Entertainment and executive producer Wes Craven. WISHMASTER opened as the number one horror film and went on to become the year's most successful independent release.

After leaving KNB EFX Group, you formed Precinct 13 Entertainment, a makeup/visual FX studio. Since then you have independently made films such as BURIED ALIVE (2007) and THE RAGE (2007). How is working on huge Hollywood films different from low-budget ones in terms of makeup FX?

On big films you have more time and money and a much bigger crew. You're used to having more research and development (R&D) time to create innovative effects. These days, even on the big films, there really isn't any R&D. You're usually up against an almost impossible deadline when you start the show, but the bigger the show and the more time you have, the more polished the work will look.

On small films you have to really think on your feet and come up with easy, innovative ways to shoot the effects because the schedule and money are so tight. You have to use techniques that are tried and true. Getting your feet wet doing low budget films ultimately prepares you for working on bigger films as the techniques you learn on small pictures always come in handy, even on blockbusters. Sometimes it's the simple things that work best.

What are two of the biggest pitfalls you have encountered in making independent films, and what is your advice to help others avoid the pitfalls from happening to them?

Jumping into a film without being prepared and organized.

Never start a film without having secured all the monies and having it in the bank. I've been involved with productions on an FX level that start the film and then halfway through prep or production they have an issue with an investor and someone pulls out on financing. When this happens production usually continues as though nothing is going wrong, and they scramble to fill the financing gap. The work continues, but soon they start not making their payments to the crew on time. They'll have 8 million excuses and will promise you they will make good. However, it doesn't always go down that way, and a lot of times the production folds with crew and talent hung out to dry being owed a lot of money. So as a filmmaker, always have the money in the bank before starting. Putting funding together in pieces is not a good idea.

On your independent films, do you shoot on digital or film?

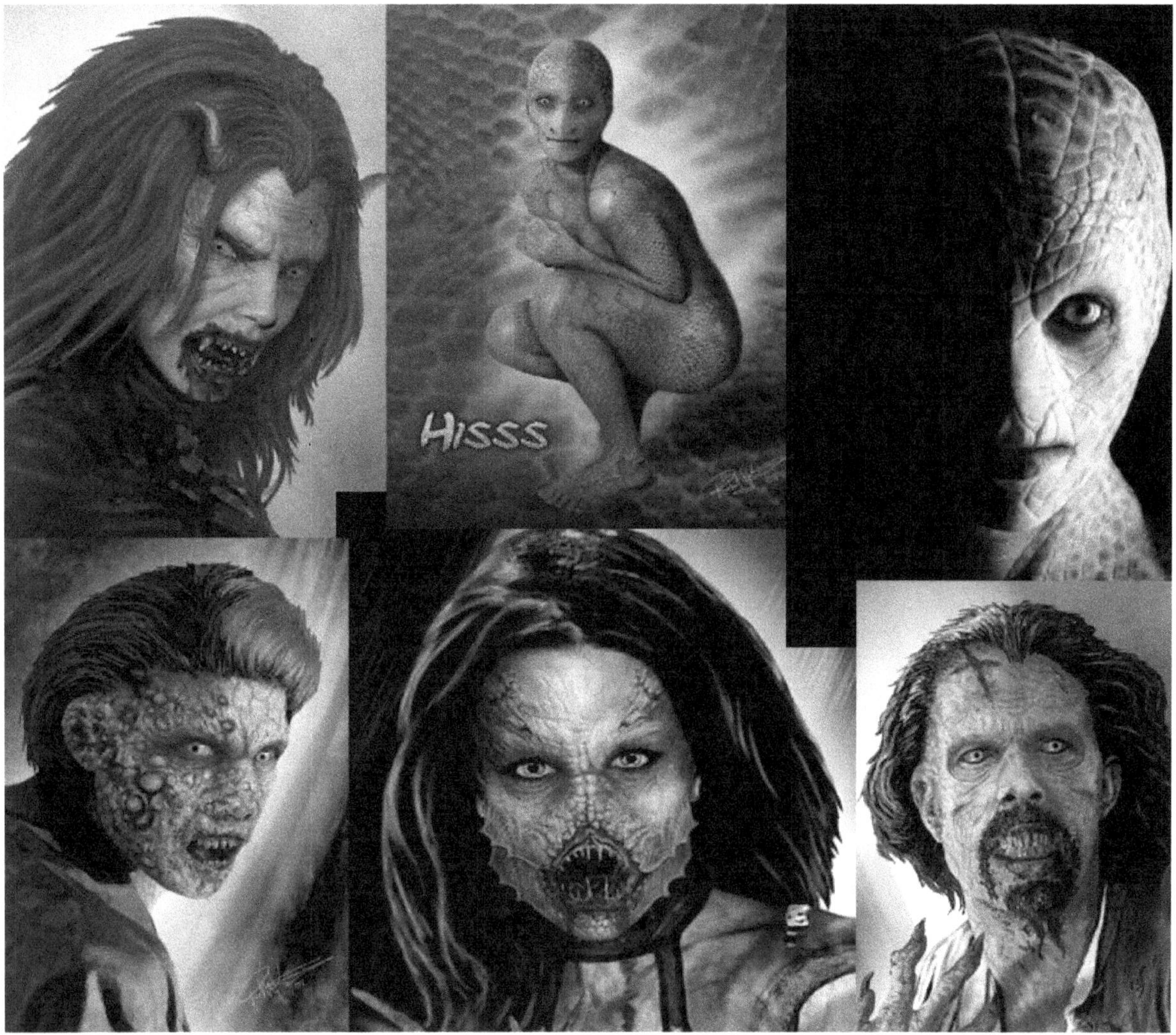

Robert Kurtzman's Monster Creations

Both. It depends on the film and the financiers. I personally like to shoot digital for various reasons. It streamlines the post process when dealing with digital FX work, and I'm able to move much quicker shooting. I don't have to worry about the cost of shooting too much coverage and burning film. Also, I can let the camera roll and keep the actors in the moment without having to cut. I shot my last film for MGM using the Viper (the same camera David Fincher uses on films like ZODIAC), and we were able to get double the amount of coverage, which is a real asset when you get into the edit room.

In your experience, what makes a great movie monster and why?

It's all about the story. You can have a great monster, but if it's shot like crap and the story sucks then so does the monster. So it's a combination of things that have to come together to make a great monster movie. Design and execution are key. Also, the less you see the better.

A monster isn't scary unless you can build the suspense around it. It's just a piece of rubber without lighting, music, sound effects, and actors who can convey fear, so all this has to come together to make a great movie monster work.

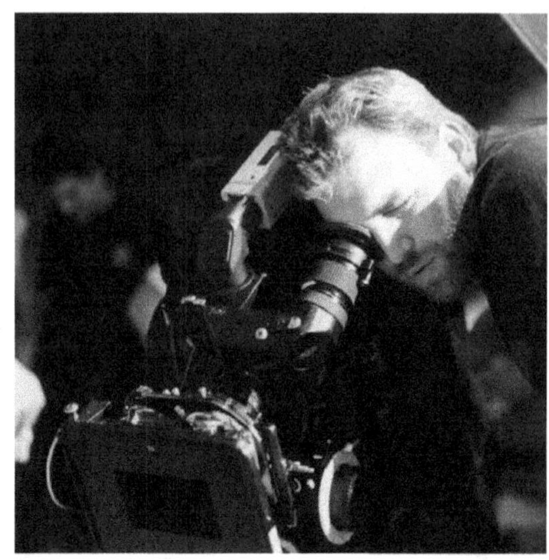

Robert Kurtzman on set.

In a new age of digital gore, what are your thoughts for using computers in place of on-set FX? Is one better than the other, or do they compliment each other?

It's a tool and an asset if used properly. One isn't better than the other. There are things that each is great for, and limitations to both. A mix of the two, whenever possible, makes for the best results.

For low-budget horror films, what do you think makes the most effective types of monsters? What should filmmakers with big ideas but microbudgets stay away from?

It's best on low-budget films to use more practical effects. Sometimes you have to use digital because you can't afford a crane to fly a puppet around on and you'll never get the puppet to do what you need and your day goes down the tubes while you try to get impossible shots. So shooting plates and adding animated creatures in postproduction is the only way to go. But CGI isn't cheap, as everyone thinks, and if you don't have a post schedule long enough to achieve the effects, then you should rethink your approach to accommodate your budget and schedule.

If you could choose three horror films that best demonstrate the use of simple, effective, low-budget FX, what would they be and why?

KURTZMAN: NIGHT OF THE LIVING DEAD (1968): Very minimal effects but very effective.

THE HOWLING (1981): A low-budget film with a very small FX budget that was able to break new ground in FX techniques. The lighting and staging of the FX were key in creating a successful creature transformation.

FRIDAY THE 13TH (1980): Great gore gags on a shoestring budget. Tom Savini used staging and misdirection to set up great scares and kills using very simple but effective techniques.

What do you think are the three most important elements for a low-budget horror film to have?

Good story. Great suspense. Great cast!

There are different kinds of horror films, so you have to consider what the filmmakers are going for. Some are meant to be fun rides and others more cerebral. The most important thing is for the filmmakers to have passion for the material, which ultimately shows in the filmmaking.

What is the Robert Kurtzman secret to homemade fake blood?

Karo Syrup, food coloring (red, green, blue) and a dash of clear dish soap to get it to not bead up and flow properly. You just have to eye the coloring to get the right look so it's not too pink or bright red. Every filmmaker likes a different look depending on how they are lighting the film. It's very easy to make the blood too dark and it shows up black on film, so its good to test out the blood on film to make sure it looks good.

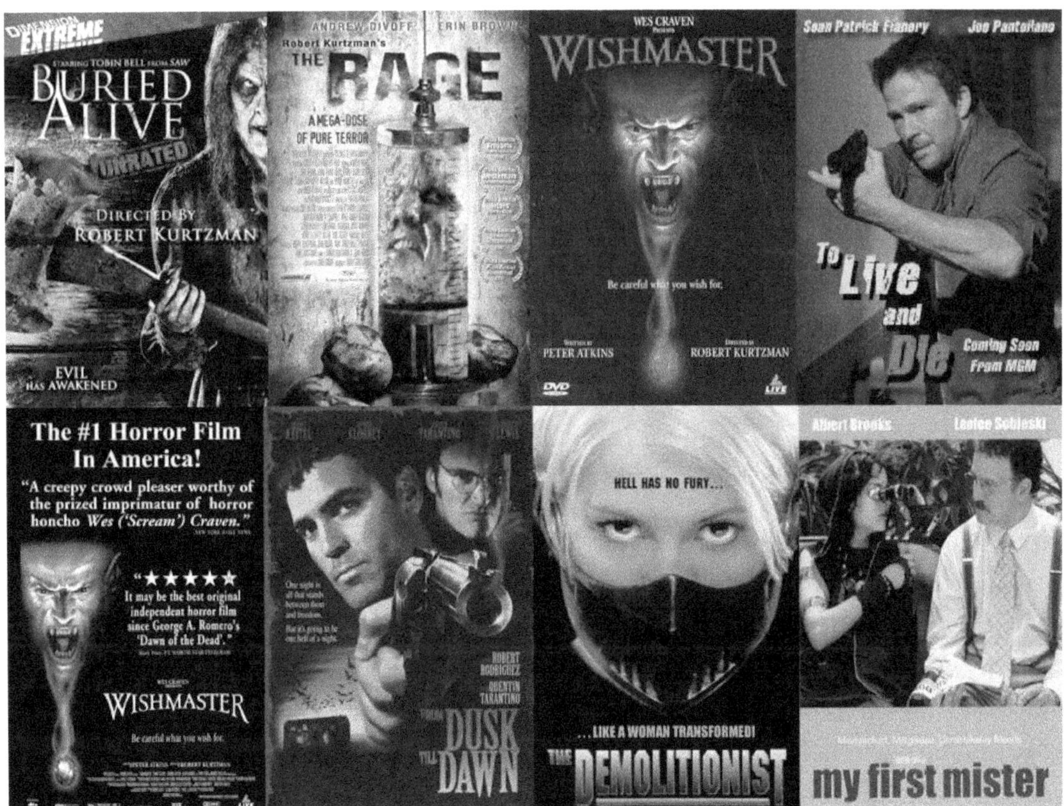

Robert Kurtzman's movies.

JOHN D. LEMAY

ACTOR

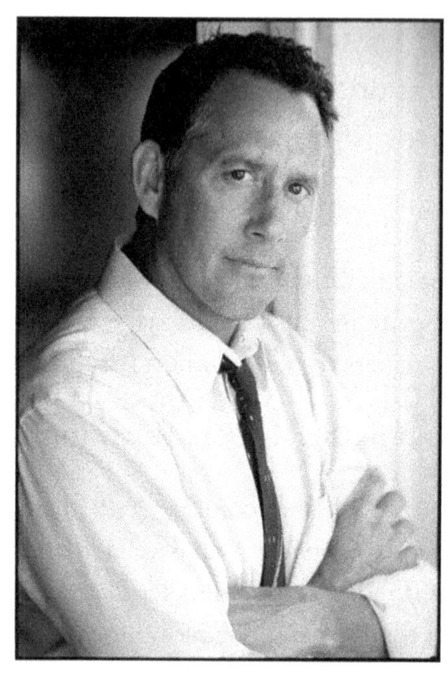

JOHN D. LEMAY

John D. LeMay is a California-based actor whose career in theater began in Normal, Illinois, where he participated in singing and acting in school plays as a young student. After completing a bachelor of science degree at Illinois State University, where he completed a double major in music and musical theater, John moved to Los Angeles in 1985 and made various guest appearances in popular TV series, which included Remington Steele, The Facts of Life, and Rod Serling's The Twilight Zone . In 1987, he landed the leading role in Paramount television's horror syndicated series Friday the 13th: The Series as Ryan Dallion, a young antique sleuth who worked with his distant cousin and their retired magician friend to hunt down cursed objects. Friday the 13th: The Series was filmed in Toronto, Ontario, Canada. Although John left to pursue other career goals at the end of the second season, he is best known for his work in the series as Ryan Dallion and is the all-time fan favorite. His web site generates a great deal of interest for both his work from the series (also known under the title Friday's Curse in the United Kingdom) and his 1993 starring role in New Line Cinema's FRIDAY THE 13TH film series, part 9, JASON GOES TO HELL: THE FINAL FRIDAY. John has also returned to the stage as a member of the Acting Company at the Alliance Repertory Theatre of Burbank, California and received outstanding critics' reviews for his starring role as a lawyer turned filmmaker in the Alliance production of Spec . Recently John has returned to his musical theater roots, appearing in the Ovation Award winning production of Jekyll and Hyde .

In Friday the 13th: The Series (1987– 1989), you played cursed antique sleuth Ryan Dallion. When creating a character like Ryan Dallion, how much of yourself goes into the role, how much is the writers', directors', and producers' input, and how much just happens organically on the set when interacting with the other actors?

For the role of Ryan Dallion in Friday the 13th: The Series, the character cues were initially from the casting director and the information relayed to me from the character breakdowns describing him like the character David Addison, Jr., that Bruce Willis played in the TV series Moonlighting (1985–1989). The writing for the character, and the scenes I auditioned with reinforced that idea so, I channeled my best Bruce Willis imitation with his devilish, cocky and flirtatious demeanor. That landed me the role.

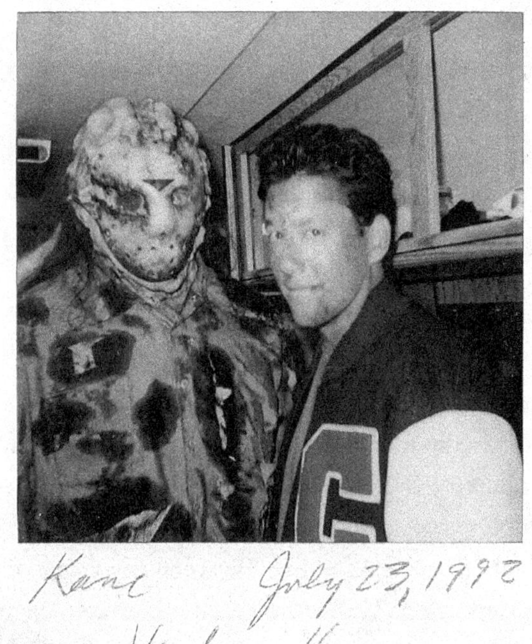

Kane Hodder as Jason Voorhees and John D. LeMay as Steven Freeman on set of JASON GOES TO HELL: THE FINAL FRIDAY (1993) inside the Voorhees house on July 23, 1992.

After I got the series I spent some time with an early director, Timothy Bond, who cautioned me by saying, "Hey, you don't have to do this Bruce Willis thing because you will just be a second-rate Bruce Willis, so just be the best John D. LeMay you can be instead." It was great advice and I have been forever thankful for it. The best actors are the ones who can bring as much of themselves to the part as possible. In an audition it's who can walk into a room and be the most authentic, present, and real. Those actors will own the room. I think the shift was noticeable, and the character emerged after about the fourth episode in the series.

Also, early in production of the series, the producer, Ian Patterson, came up to me and requested I show more fear in response to the scary bits: "John, you are not being scared enough; there are scary things happening here, you can't be stoic watching a monk get smashed in a bed, or getting beheaded by a flying guillotine." I was again very thankful for the advice. Reacting to special effects that were to be layered in later was new to me, and the series helped me climb a tremendous learning curve.

When you are a regular on a series, the stories keep evolving in ways that always surprise you. As an actor you try to create as much backstory as possible for yourself, but a lot of that is secondary to the writers' impact every week when you get a new script. For storytelling purposes, a lot of backstory information comes to you in bits and pieces. You have to be flexible and willing to go with it. Consequently, I found the key to grounding myself was the interaction with other actors on the set. Those relationships really helped define who I was week in and week out.

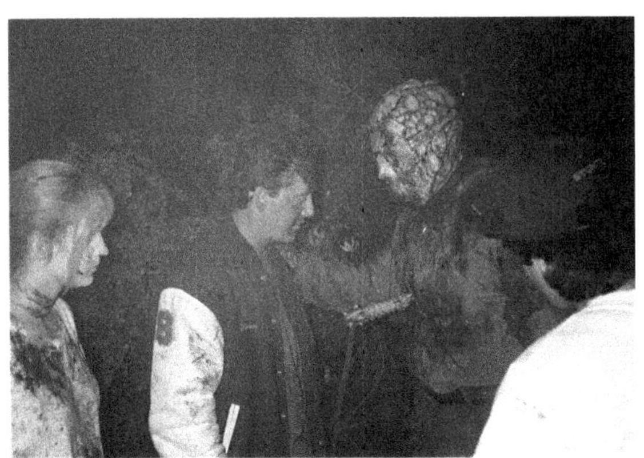

John D. LeMay and Kane Hodder on set during a fight scene.

The series also stars Louise Robey as the beautiful redhead Micki Foster and Chris Wiggins as the wise Jack Marshak. When all three of you would

have scenes together, what is the process you went through among yourselves to make a scene playable?

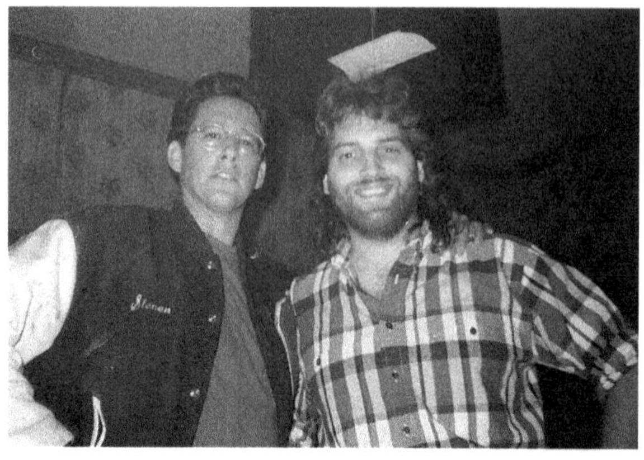

John D. Lemay and Robert Kurtzman on set.

Early on we discovered what our job was and how we plugged into the story line. It didn't take too long before we all got into a comfortable rhythm with each other. I remember how important it was for me personally to stay loose. The schedule was an assault on our bodies and minds. It was an exhausting shoot and similar to Guerilla filmmaking. We had to make sure we all stayed healthy week after week. Scenes between the three of us became an exercise in economy. It's all about self-preservation. We learned to work effectively as a unit. I was a bit disappointed to find out that all of our lines were basically interchangeable—it wasn't about character. Our job was to relay exposition and move the story along . . . quickly. Back to more gore.

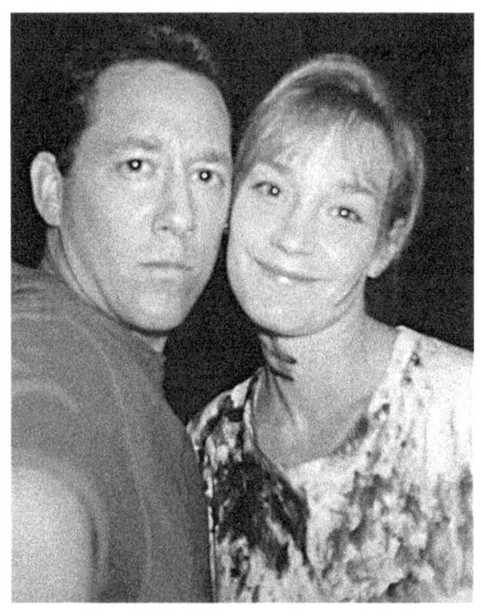

John D. LeMay and co-star Keri Keegan—who played Jessica Kimble—on the set of JASON GOES TO HELL: THE FINAL FRIDAY (1993).

What is it that actors really want from their director?

Respect! [Laughs] No really . . . we want the director to have good communication skills and make us feel like a collaborator in the process. It's the actor's job to get from point A to point B and have it make sense, and if the actor is having a problem doing that, they may turn to their trusted director to help solve the problem. Specifically with respect to genre films with special effects, the actor needs a director who can relay what the effect is supposed to look like and where it is supposed to be happening. It is then up to the actor to use his or her imagination and hope the effect is a reasonable facsimile of what the director describes and you the actor imagined. Budgets play a role here. I have had my share of disappointments where the effect has been underwhelming and my performance overwhelming. I may not trust that director next time, and they certainly would forever lose my respect. [Laughing]

For the aspiring directors out there who may be technical geniuses but lack the

ability to direct actors, what would be your advice to them?

Cast the right actors and be prepared. The actor gets cast because they bring certain qualities to the process. Hopefully the director has the performer who best suits the role. I imagine that is half the work for the director. A director can't and shouldn't be spending their time on set coaching his actor on how to be the character. They need to be prepared to answer technical questions and assist the actor if they have trouble making sense of a direction, or character motivation.

To understand the process better, an acting class would be a great place to start. There are often acting instructors who will allow you sit in and observe a class. Second, being a technical wizard is a plus and very important for a director, but human beings make films and human beings watch them. Get away from the playback and talk to your performers. Try to avoid yelling directions and never berate your actors in front of the cast and crew.

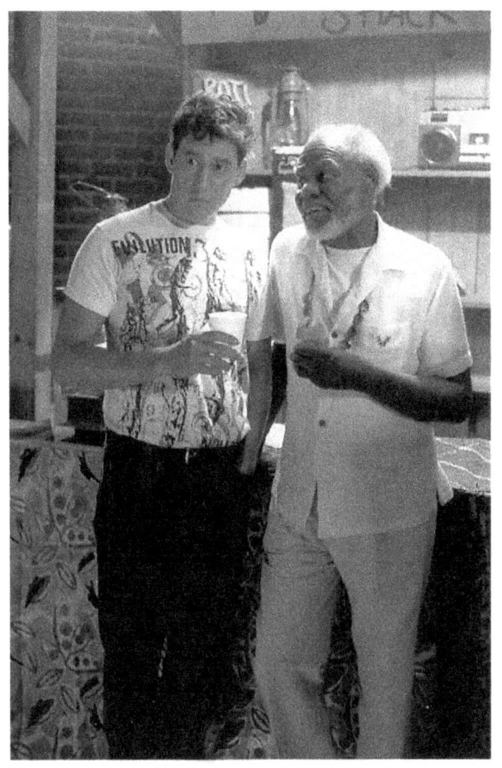

John D. LeMay and Joe Seneca on set of Friday the 13 th: The Series, the "Voodoo Mambo" episode (1988).

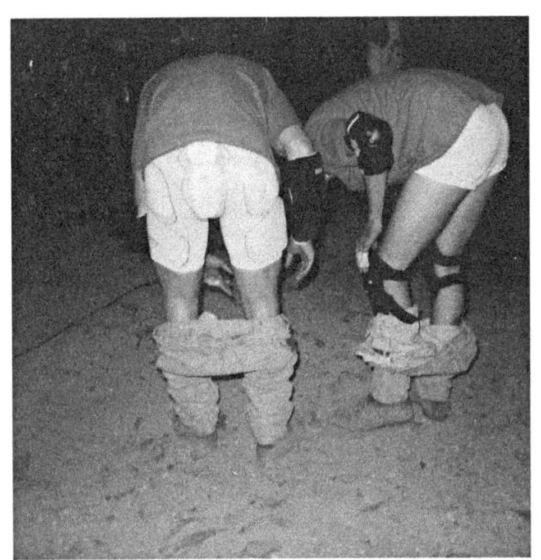

John D. LeMay and his stunt double preparing before a scene.

You did a lot of hand-to-hand combat scenes with Jason Voorhees (played by Kane Hodder), one of horror cinema's toughest screen villains. Can you describe the creative and technical process behind your favorite fight scene in the film?

I was pretty confident in my stage combat skills. For two seasons of Friday the 13th: The Series I did a lot of stunts, working with stunt coordinator T. J. Scott in Canada. In the series, I fought many emissaries of the devil, and these were not your ordinary fights. You had to have a lot of luck going for you. Once the technical aspects of the fight are set, it is up to the actor to create

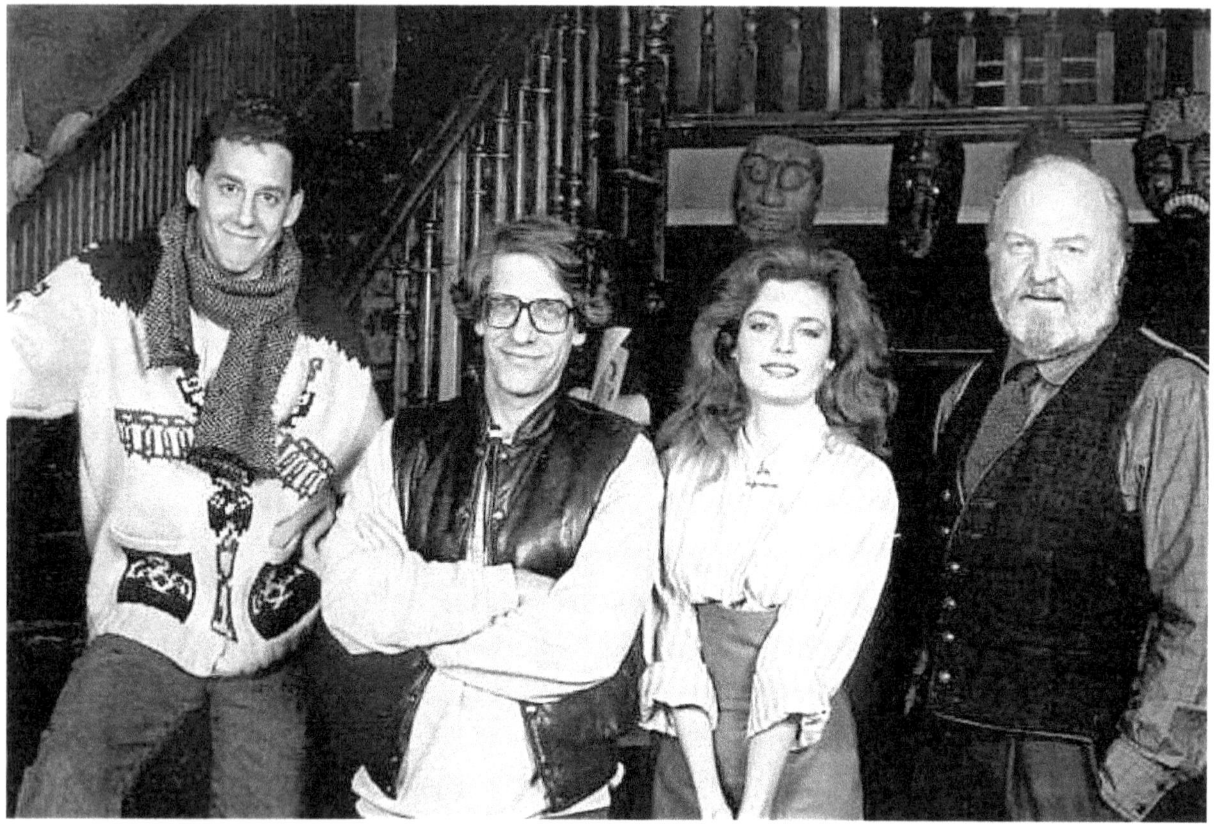

(L–R) John D. LeMay as Ryan Dallion, director David Cronenberg, Louise Robey as Micki Foster, and Chris Wiggins as Jack Marshak.

an environment in which the impossible seems possible.

Kane Hodder was the stunt coordinator on JASON GOES TO HELL, so he choreographed the fight at the Voorhees' house. You have to be on your game with Kane. He is a big guy and you can't read his face under the hockey mask. He has big arms so you don't want to miss one of his arm cues. Oftentimes you get your cues from someone's face; his was all physical cues. A major disadvantage and a bit scary to boot. The adrenaline is always pumping when they yell "Action." Having Kane there (with his black Jason eyes) certainly raised the adrenaline bar. My stunt double got thrown into the jungle gym in the film, so I can't take credit for that. As luck would have it, I was assisted by a conveniently-placed shovel. Not that it helped much. Actually nothing really worked with Jason. The guy just keeps coming. It really was an exhausting fight. I was glad to make it out alive.

In terms of acting, how is working in film different from television?

I really don't see any difference, at least in the projects that I've done in the horror genre. The speed was a bit more hyperactive on the TV series. It always seemed like we were racing to get a shot done. Sometimes you are shooting two different episodes at once, doing pickups from an episode that wrapped last week.

If you could chose one horror film or performance in the history of horror cinema that influenced you as an actor, what would it be and why?

As a kid, I watched the old black and white Universal Studios horror classics like WOLFMAN, DRACULA, and FRANKENSTEIN. Currently, I love watching ABBOTT AND COSTELLO MEET FRANKENSTEIN with my daughter. Classic.

Would have to say I am more a fan of psychological thrillers. One of my favorites is Anthony Hopkins' performance in THE SILENCE OF THE LAMBS (1991). That film had magic; he is a great actor.

Last year I enjoyed watching some old Halloween chestnuts on Turner Classic Movies. There are tons of great films in the genre I have yet to discover. Look . . . when you lived through a horror film, it takes a while before you want to risk triggering the nightmares all over again.

On the film set, what is the worst direction you have ever received from a director?

"Move here and say the line like this."

LISTEN TO THIS FULL UN-EDITED AUDIO INTERVIEW ON MY YOUTUBE CHANNEL FREE AT:

https://www.youtube.com/c/DannyDraven

HERSCHELL GORDON LEWIS
DIRECTOR

"The Godfather of Gore"

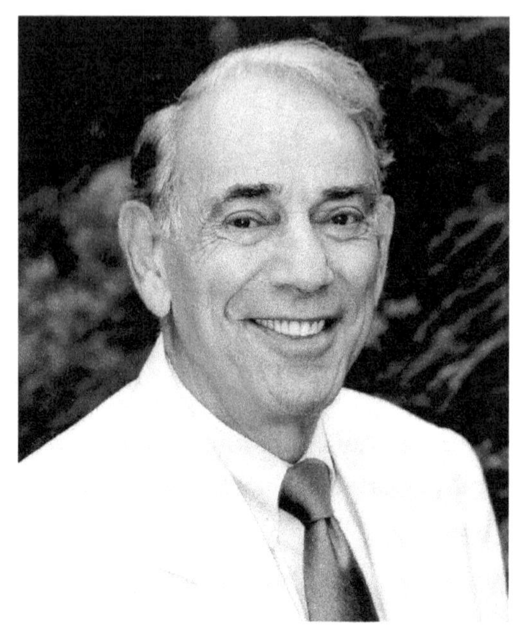

HERSCHELL GORDON LEWIS

HERSCHELL GORDON LEWIS — The incredibly popular, violent horror films of recent decades, such as TEXAS CHAINSAW MASSACRE, FRIDAY THE 13TH, and A NIGHTMARE ON ELM STREET, owe much of their existence to the undisputed Godfather of Gore, Herschell Gordon Lewis. In 1963, Lewis, with his monumental splatter movie BLOOD FEAST, single-handedly changed the face of horror cinema forever. As well as virtually inventing the gore generation, Lewis also produced a number of exploitation movies, as well as sampling the full gamut of exploitation subjects ranging from wife swapping and ESP to rock 'n' roll and LSD. A TASTE OF BLOOD (1967) details all these, plus gore classics such as TWO THOUSAND MANIACS (1964), THE GORE GORE GIRLS (1972), COLOR ME BLOOD RED (1965), and THE WIZARD OF GORE (1970), placing them in context amid the roots and development of the exploitation film. Lewis sadly passed away in 2016.

Your film BLOOD FEAST (1963) is generally recognized as the first splatter film. In modern times, we have computers to help us do digital gore FX and make deaths even more realistic to the eye. In the gross-out wars of Hollywood, have you ever felt that filmmakers go too far?

On the contrary, I feel they don't go far enough. Too many splatter films are derivative. We get the feeling we're watching the same tired effects over and over again. More to a negative point, these offerings are humorless. Ugh.

There are a lot of movies being made for little money but generating high returns because of great titles, trailers, art campaigns, and concepts. What are the three most important elements in a horror movie marketing campaign, and why?

The three most important elements: (1) showmanship on the level of P. T. Barnum, (2) promise of an experience the moviegoer hasn't ever enjoyed before, (3) wording that maximizes the relationship between producer and viewer.

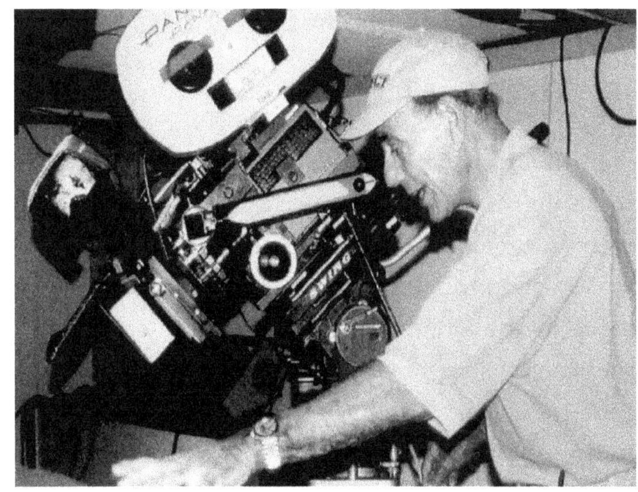

Lewis on set.

What is it in the human psyche that attracts people to violent films, and is this a good or a bad thing?

Bloodlust is implicit in the human psyche. Psychologists have proved over and over again that being able to satisfy that bloodlust as a spectator is a powerful preventive against the need to satisfy bloodlust by aggressive action.

What are your thoughts on the state of the horror genre today? Is it better or worse than when you were making films?

Since I intend to make another movie, I'd say, competitively, it's worse. Imagination seems to have gone the way of all flesh.

What is your advice for independent filmmakers trying to self-distribute and market their movies online?

Before you make that first phone call or send that first email, be positive you have an adequate answer to the self-question: Do I have a salable product, and if not, what can I do to make it salable?

What advice can you give new filmmakers who want to start their career in low-budget horror films?

Don't let your ego drive the product. What you think is entertaining may be light-years removed from what an outsider regards as entertaining.

NOTES ON WRITING WEIRD FICTION

BY H. P. LOVECRAFT

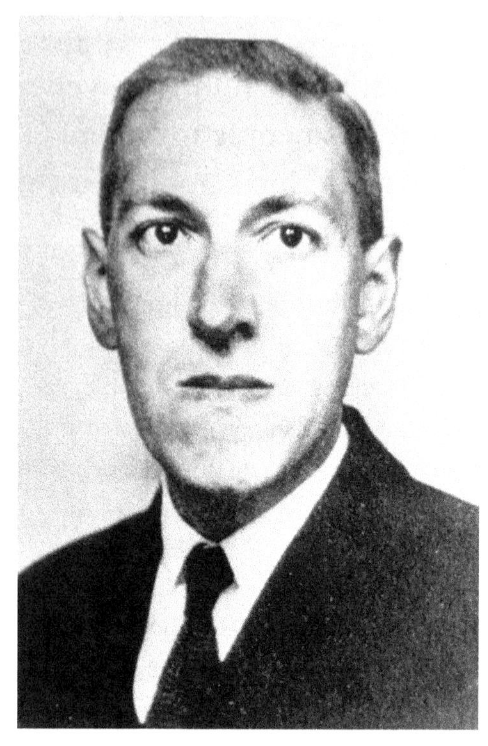

H.P. Lovecraft (1890-1937)

My reason for writing stories is to give myself the satisfaction of visualising more clearly and detailedly and stably the vague, elusive, fragmentary impressions of wonder, beauty, and adventurous expectancy which are conveyed to me by certain sights (scenic, architectural, atmospheric, etc.), ideas, occurrences, and images encountered in art and literature. I choose weird stories because they suit my inclination best—one of my strongest and most persistent wishes being to achieve, momentarily, the illusion of some strange suspension or violation of the galling limitations of time, space, and natural law which forever imprison us and frustrate our curiosity about the infinite cosmic spaces beyond the radius of our sight and analysis. These stories frequently emphasise the element of horror because fear is our deepest and strongest emotion, and the one which best lends itself to the creation of Nature-defying illusions. Horror and the unknown or the strange are always closely connected, so that it is hard to create a convincing picture of shattered natural law or cosmic alienage or "outsideness" without laying stress on the emotion of fear. The reason why time plays a great part in so many of my tales is that this element looms up in my mind as the most profoundly dramatic and grimly terrible thing in the universe. Conflict with time seems to me the most potent and fruitful theme in all human expression.

While my chosen form of story-writing is obviously a special and perhaps a narrow one, it is none the less a persistent and permanent type of expression, as old as literature itself. There will always be a certain small percentage of persons who feel a burning curiosity about unknown outer space, and a burning desire to escape from the prison-house of the known and the real into those enchanted lands of incredible adventure and infinite possibilities which dreams open up to us, and which things like deep woods, fantastic urban towers, and flaming sunsets momentarily suggest. These persons include great authors as well as insignificant amateurs like myself—Dunsany, Poe, Arthur Machen, M. R. James, Algernon Blackwood, and Walter de la Mare being typical masters in this field.

As to how I write a story—there is no one way. Each one of my tales has a different history. Once or twice I have literally written out a dream; but usually I start with a mood or idea or image which I wish to express, and revolve it in my mind until I can think of a good way of embodying it in some chain of dramatic occurrences capable of being recorded in concrete terms. I tend to run through a mental list of the basic conditions or situations best adapted to such a mood or idea or image, and then begin to speculate on logical and naturally motivated explanations of the given mood or idea or image in terms of the basic condition or situation chosen.

The actual process of writing is of course as varied as the choice of theme and initial conception; but if the history of all my tales were analysed, it is just possible that the following set of rules might be deduced from the average procedure:

1. Prepare a synopsis or scenario of events in the order of their absolute occurrence — not the order of their narration. Describe with enough fulness to cover all vital points and motivate all incidents planned. Details, comments, and estimates of consequences are sometimes desirable in this temporary framework.

2. Prepare a second synopsis or scenario of events—this one in order of narration (not actual occurrence), with ample fulness and detail, and with notes as to changing perspective, stresses, and climax. Change the original synopsis to fit if such a change will increase the dramatic force or general effectiveness of the story. Interpolate or delete incidents at will—never being bound by the original conception even if the ultimate result be a tale wholly different from that first planned. Let additions and alterations be made whenever suggested by anything in the formulating process.

3. Write out the story— rapidly, fluently, and not too critically— following the second or narrative-order synopsis. Change incidents and plot whenever the developing process seems to suggest such change, never being bound by any previous design. If the development suddenly reveals new opportunities for dramatic effect or vivid story telling, add whatever is thought advantageous—going back and reconciling the early parts to the new plan. Insert and delete whole sections if necessary or desirable, trying different beginnings and endings until the best arrangement is found. But be sure that all references throughout the story are thoroughly reconciled with the final design. Remove all possible superfluities—words, sentences, paragraphs, or whole episodes or elements—observing the usual precautions about the reconciling of all references.

4. Revise the entire text, paying attention to vocabulary, syntax, rhythm of prose, proportioning of parts, niceties of tone, grace and convincingness of transitions (scene to scene, slow and detailed action to rapid and sketchy time-covering action and vice versa...etc., etc., etc.), effectiveness of beginning, ending, climaxes, etc., dramatic suspense and interest, plausibility and atmosphere, and various other elements.

5. Prepare a neatly typed copy—not hesitating to add final revisory touches where they seem in order.

The first of these stages is often purely a mental one—a set of conditions and happenings being worked out in my head, and never set down until I am ready to prepare a detailed synopsis of events in order of narration. Then, too, I sometimes begin even the actual writing before I know how I shall develop the idea—this beginning forming a problem to be motivated and exploited.

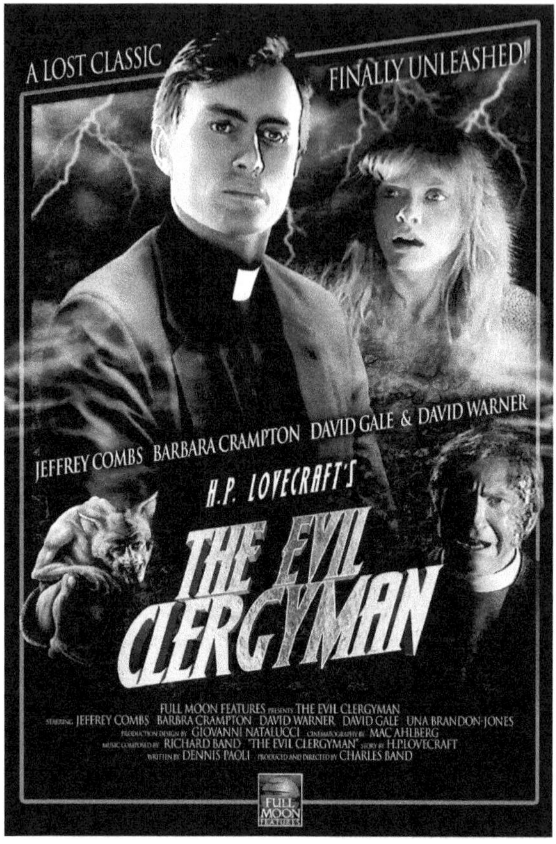

H.P. Lovecraft THE EVIL CLERGYMAN
From Full Moon Features

There are, I think, four distinct types of weird story; one expressing a mood or feeling, another expressing a pictorial conception, a third expressing a general situation, condition, legend or intellectual conception, and a fourth explaining a definite tableau or specific dramatic situation or climax . In another way, weird tales may be grouped into two rough categories—those in which the marvel or horror concerns some condition or phenomenon, and those in which it concerns some action of persons in connexion with a bizarre condition or phenomenon.

Each weird story—to speak more particularly of the horror type—seems to involve five definite elements: (a) some basic, underlying horror or abnormality—condition, entity, etc.—, (b) the general effects or bearings of the horror, (c) the mode of manifestation—object embodying the horror and phenomena observed—, (d) the types of fear-reaction pertaining to the horror, and (e) the specific effects of the horror in relation to the given set of conditions.

In writing a weird story I always try very carefully to achieve the right mood and atmosphere, and place the emphasis where it belongs. One cannot, except in immature pulp charlatan-fiction, present an account of impossible, improbable, or inconceivable phenomena as a commonplace narrative of objective acts and conventional emotions. Inconceivable events and conditions have a special handicap to over come, and this can be accomplished only through the maintenance of a careful realism in every phase of the story except that touching on the one given marvel. This marvel must be treated very impressively and deliberately—with a careful emotional "build-up"—else it will seem flat and unconvincing. Being the principal thing in the story, its mere existence should overshadow the characters and events. But the characters and events must be consistent and natural except where they touch the single marvel. In relation to the central wonder, the characters should shew the same overwhelming emotion which similar characters would shew toward such a wonder in real life. Never have a wonder taken for granted. Even when the characters are supposed to be accustomed to the wonder I try to weave an air of awe and impressiveness corresponding to what the reader should feel. A casual style ruins any serious fantasy.

Atmosphere, not action, is the great desideratum of weird fiction. Indeed, all that a wonder story can ever be is a vivid picture of a certain type of human mood . The moment it tries to be anything else it becomes cheap, puerile, and unconvincing. Prime emphasis should be given to subtle suggestion—imperceptible hints and touches of selective associative detail which express shadings of moods and build up a vague illusion of the strange reality of the unreal. Avoid bald catalogues of incredible happenings which can have no substance or meaning apart from a sustaining cloud of colour and symbolism. These are the rules or standards which I have followed—consciously or unconsciously—ever since I first attempted the serious writing of fantasy. That my results are successful may well be disputed—but I feel at least sure that, had I ignored the considerations mentioned in the last few paragraphs, they would have been much worse than they are.

SAM McCURDY, BSC

DIRECTOR OF PHOTOGRAPHY

www.sammccurdy.com

SAM McCURDY is a London-based cinematographer. He often shoots films in the horror genre and regularly works with director Neil Marshall. McCurdy's credits include shooting the British werewolf film DOG SOLDIERS (2002), THE DESCENT (2005), COLD AND DARK (2005), THE SICK HOUSE (2007), THE HILLS HAVE EYES II (2007), DOOMSDAY (2008), DREAD (2009), THE DESCENT: PART 2 (2009), CENTURION (2009), GAME OF THRONES (2012), MERLIN (2012) and A UNITED KINGDOM (2016).

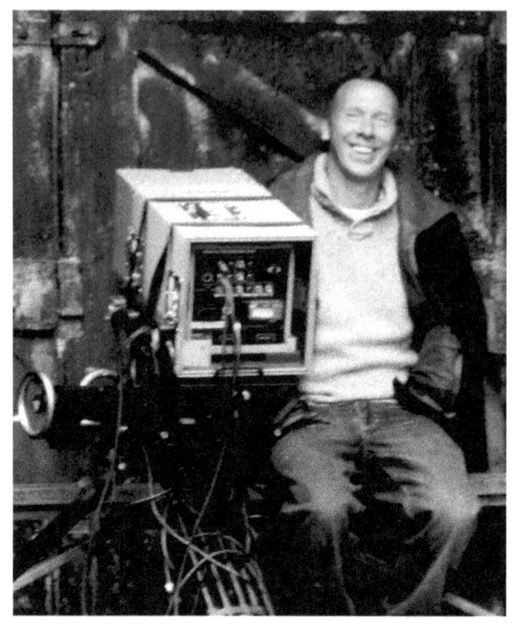

Sam McCurdy on set.

From the time you are hired to shoot a film, what is the director of photography's work flow on a film?

For me personally, I always start with the script. I break it down into two parts: how the story is going to work visually and how best to achieve the results. The next step is we scout possible locations, sets, and studios. Based on what we find, I then begin designing the lighting plans. Because there is a lot of preplanning, shooting the movie always seems the easiest part!

As a director of photography, what are your responsibilities on set?

On set, my main responsibilities are dealing with camera, lighting, and grips. How the film looks and feels is the responsibility of the director of photography.

Is lighting and photographing a horror film different from other genres?

I was always told that the two hardest genres to get right were horror and comedy. Horror is very different from any other genre. I guess because if you make any mistakes, it just won't work. I love shooting horror films. It allows you to try things you would never have the opportunity to do in any other genre. And I love the dark! Shooting the darkness is a difficult task, I think. When you get it right and you only allow the audience to see what you want them to see then it feels great.

What are your thoughts on shooting digital versus film?

Both formats have their place in filmmaking. The difference is in other people's attitudes towards them. As long as people put in the same amount of effort on a digital format as they would a film format they can both work. I recently shot a digital movie and found it very forgiving as a format, and I feel the look suits the movie, so the right format was chosen.

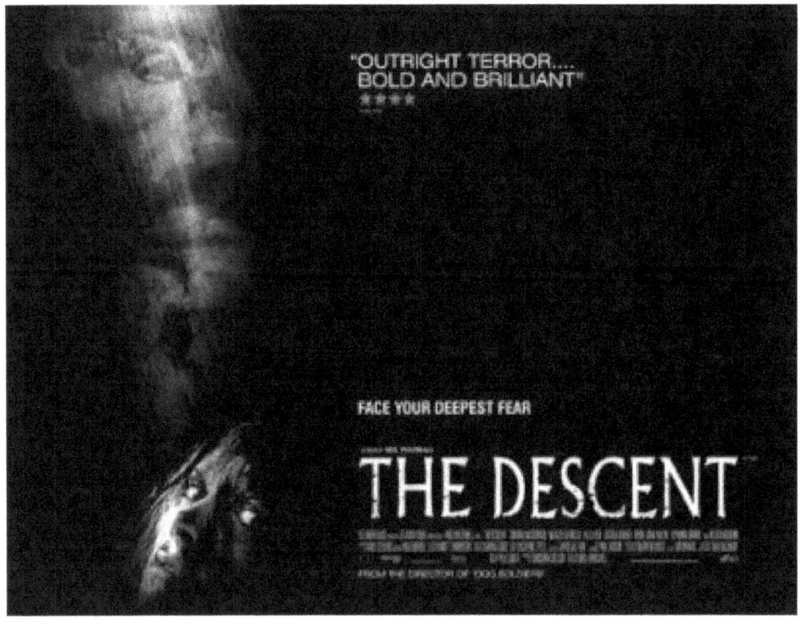

THE DECENT (2005)

After you shoot a film, how much of its final look is done in post? Can you describe what the post process is for films like THE DESCENT (2005) and THE HILLS HAVE EYES II (2007)?

A lot of movies spend a lot of time in postproduction these days, and this can be a good and a bad thing. The digital intermediate stage is now a director of photography's new tool and long may it continue. However, with the films THE DESCENT (2005) and THE HILLS HAVE EYES II (2007), a lot of the work is done in camera. The lighting, the coloring, all of these are talked about in the beginning, and hopefully this means you spend less time in postproduction.

In terms of cinematography, what are the biggest things that annoy you when you see a low-budget horror film?

I guess the things that annoy me the most are the lack of respect to a script. Sometimes you can see that someone is just painting by numbers, so to speak.

What are a few of the biggest pitfalls you have encountered in shooting independent films, and what is your advice to help others avoid it happening to them?

I guess the pitfalls are financial mainly. Independent cinema by its nature means you have to make do with what you have. My advice is to always prepare as much as you can beforehand. Even if you have no money, there is no excuse for not doing as good a job as possible. Always prepare before you shoot, think of all the things you want to do and work out how to do them before you're on set.

If you could pick one horror film that was influential to you in terms of having exceptional cinematography, what would it be and why?

HALLOWEEN (1978) has always been, and will always be, my favorite movie. It is one of the reasons I'm a cinematographer today. For a low budget movie, it has everything such as great ideas beautifully executed (excuse the pun), exceptional photography, simple and thought-out camera moves, simple frames that allow a viewer to watch the screen, and an exquisite composition that makes you want to watch. I love this movie. HALLOWEEN isn't just a great horror movie—it's a great movie!

MIKE MENDEZ
DIRECTOR

A native to Los Angeles, Mike Mendez was in the backyard making movies since the age of 10. At the age of 23, Mike made his first feature film "Killers," which was accepted into the Sundance Film Festival in 1997. The film was picked up by Alpine Pictures, who distributed the feature in the U.S. The film also received a worldwide theatrical release.

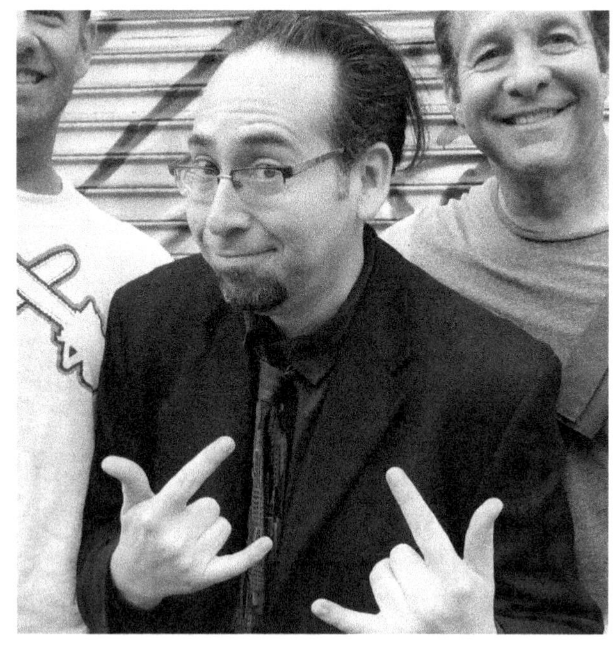

MIKE MENDEZ

He followed that up with the horror comedy "The Convent," which was also accepted into the Sundance Film Festival in 2000, as well as over 30 other film festivals worldwide. The film was released by Lionsgate in the U.S.

In 2002, he produced a documentary for Universal Television and Showtime entitled "Masters of Horror," featuring interviews with some of the genre's most legendary filmmakers. In 2006, Mike's film "The Gravedancers" premiered at the Tribeca Film Festival and was released in theaters nationally by Lionsgate & After Dark Films as part of "8 Films To Die For".

Along with producing short films for X-box and working on the television series "Beavis & Butthead", Mike's newest films are "Big Ass Spider!" for Epic Pictures, which premiered at the 2013 SXSW Film Festival. Starring "Heroes" alumni Greg Grunberg, it had a limited theatrical worldwide,. His latest films are TALES OF HALLOWEEN (2015), LAVALANTULA (2015), THE LAST HEIST (2016) and DON'T KILL IT (2016) starring Dolph Lundgren.

Your first film KILLERS was accepted to Sundance in 1997 which is a wonderful accomplishment for a young emerging talent. Did getting your film accepted to a top-tier festival help your career move forward? Would you suggest the same for new talent?

My goodness you did your homework. Yes, getting into Sundance changed my life. I felt I had crossed over from struggling, broke student filmmaker to struggling, broke indie filmmaker. There was a huge difference though, people took me at least semi-seriously for the first time. It got me my agent, got me into meetings even led me to my first paying writing and directing job. The heat you get from those festivals is crazy, for at least a second all eyes will be on you as new emerging talent.

The heat tends to cool off very quickly, but it was great to have that experience. Yes, I would highly recommend it to new filmmakers. The tricky thing is I think it's much harder to get into than when I was starting out. There's so many politics when it comes festivals, who's in it? Who's the director? Who's distributing? It's tough out there, but in the 90's you could submit and have a shot at getting in, at least that's what happened in our case.

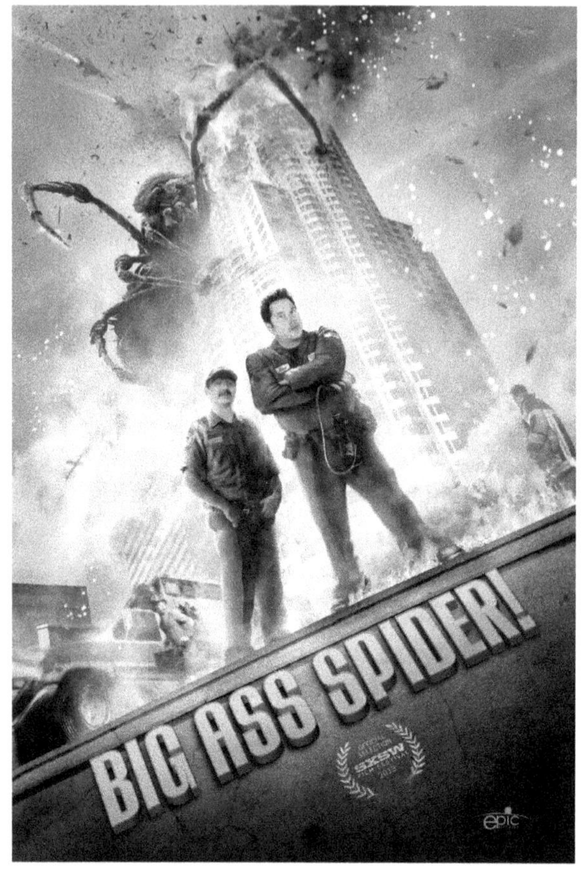

BIG ASS SPIDER (2013) from Epic Pictures.

When directing talent everyone has a different approach. Could you share a few tips from your own experiences that may help a new director who may be directing actors for the first time?

Well, get the best actors you can. They'll make you look good. In all seriousness though, it makes such a difference, capturing real chemistry or a great performance is like finding gold. For me, I always looking for finding magic. When a scene is working and the actor's are bringing more to it than you envisioned, it's magic, plain and simple. Your job is to capture that, it's not something that can truly be found in the editing room. It's right there, in the room, that's where the magic is happening, so you better have your cameras rolling to capture it.

From a directing perspective, what criteria do you use to judge how to make a scene scary?

Tough question cause it's so hard to make things scary. I'm always trying. I'd say it's atmosphere and a connection to your character. To be scared for a character, I think you have to like an empathize with them, they're your way in. Then I think it's creating atmosphere, with sound and lighting. Then it's a loud bang and a quick motion to relieve the fear.

Of all your films, which scene in which movie is your favorite and why?

I think that constantly changes. Someone told me your favorite film should be your latest one. Your least favorite the one you did right before, because now you can really see the flaws. So I don't know. Movies are like your kids, you love them equally.

How important is the director and cinematographer relationship on set and what is this collaboration like for your films?

The D.P is extremely important. Between him and the production designer, that's the look of your movie. So as a rule of thumb, in every department really. I just try to hire people that are far more talented then me. Hiring good people and surrounding yourself with them is a great start in delivering a good final product. I do like to start them off on a pretty detailed direction, but from then on I welcome a collaboration all the way through.

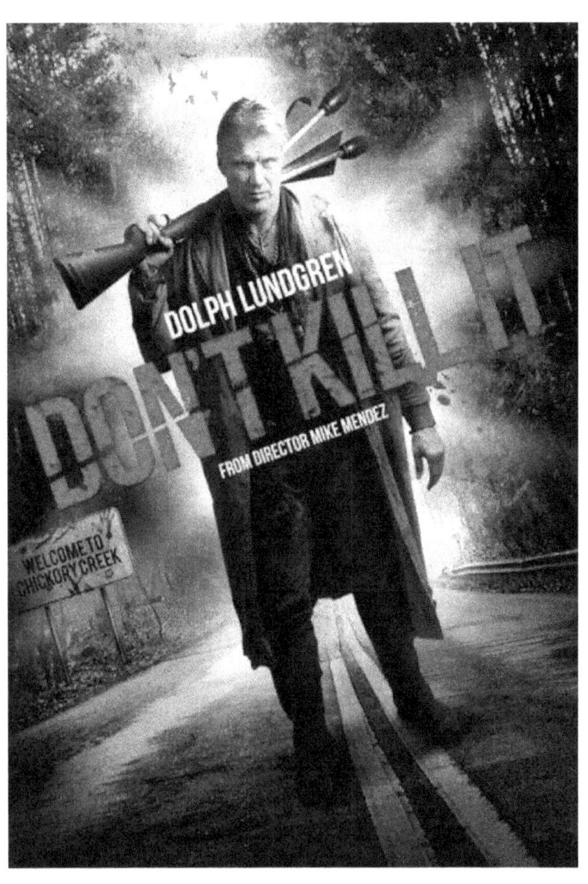

DON'T KILL IT (2016)

Do you storyboard your films and do you feel it's helpful?

I storyboard my movies myself. It'd be great to have someone to work with and get down the ideas faster, but sadly on the budgets I've been working on, you have to do most things yourself. Storyboarding is actually my favorite part of the movie making process. It's the only time that it's just you and the movie to be. There's a blank slate in front of you. The possibilities are endless. From a more practical level, it helps me schedule and plan the entire shoot. I know that I need to get these shots to tell the story the way I want to tell it. So, it ends up becoming more of a to do list, that I check off as I go through the day.

Some directors do shot lists while others may "wing it." Could you share with us your preparation approach and why it works for you?

Shot listing and scheduling is all related. It starts off as a picture in my head, then I crudely draw it on paper, then that tells me what I need and what kind of location is needed. From there I break it down further into shot lists which for are basically an ordered list. If I know the day is going to be a real crunch, which they are 95% of the time, I try to break it down even further by trying to break down which way the camera is pointing and what needs to be relit. That helps me plan it out so I can hopefully make my day.

What were your biggest challenges working with a lot of visual FX on BIG ASS SPIDER! (2013) and LAVALANTUALA (2015)?

I learned a lot about VFX on "Big Ass Spider". You take things for granted, and just sort of think, oh leave some empty space and we'll fill it in. Which is basically kind of true, but you learn about tracking and roto-scoping and all the time consuming techniques used within each individual fx shot. So if anything on "Lavalantuala" I was better prepared to know how to minimize work in each effects shot.

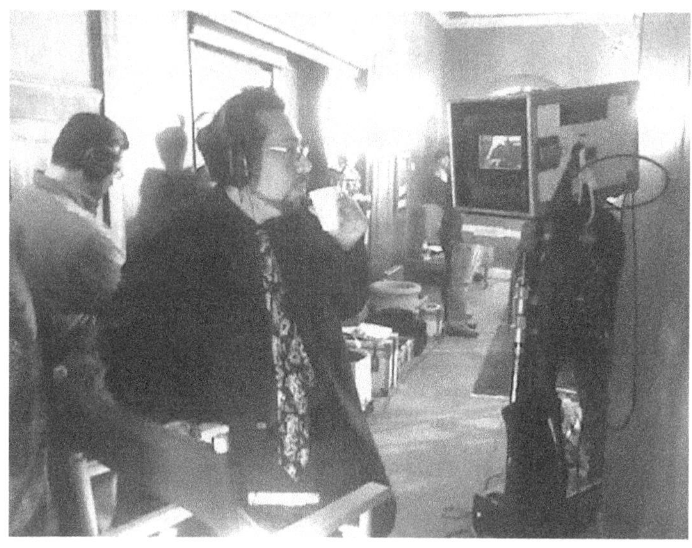

Mike Mendez on the set of GRAVEDANCERS (2006).

Who is your favorite horror movie monster and why does this monster work for you as a fan and as a professional director?

My favorite movie monster is the Alien Queen. Still an incredible achievement in sculpture and rod puppetry. You really don't see creations like that on the big screen. I'd love to capture that on the types of movies I do, but you need A-list dollars to pull that level of stuff off. Sadly most A-list movies spend it on CG. So the Alien Queen feels like an artifact from a time gone by. Amazing work.

A lot of emerging filmmakers debate if they should go to film school or not. What do you think of the value or lack of value of film programs being offered?

Film School is great for the connections, for the contacts, but ultimately as the great Lloyd Kauffman said, "Make your own damn movie!" It's the best film school of all

MARK ORDESKY
JANE FLEMING
PRODUCERS

COURT FIVE
www.courtfive.com

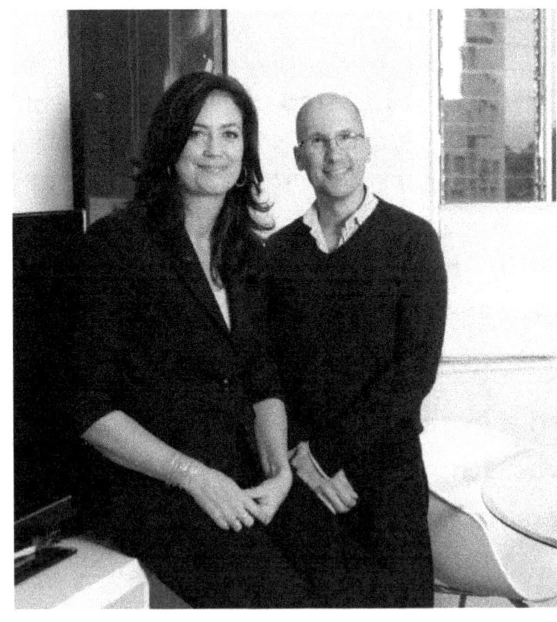
Jane Fleming & Mark Ordesky

New Line Cinema veterans Jane Fleming and Mark Ordesky are founding partners in Court Five, a multi-platform media company that develops and converts diverse intellectual properties and brands into bold filmed entertainment. The studio output of the Court Five partners exceeds $4 billion in global box office, ranging from The Lord Of The Rings trilogy (which Ordesky executive produced), The Golden Compass and The Frozen Ground; Oscar, Golden Globe and Palme D'Or winners like Shine and Dancer In The Dark; and multiple films from beloved action superstar Jackie Chan. Most recently, Court Five had its ground-breaking television series The Quest on ABC. Fleming and Ordesky are members of the Producers Guild of America. Ordesky is also a member of the Academy of Motion Picture Arts and Sciences and a board member of the American Cinemateque. Fleming is a two-term president of Women In Film, whose purpose is to empower, promote and mentor women in the entertainment and media industries. She continues to serve the organization as its President Emeritus.

In the 1890s, film and special FX pioneer Georges Méliès made the film LE MANOIR DU DIABLE, released in the United States as THE HAUNTED CASTLE (1896). which is often credited as the first horror film. Ever since then studios have been making horror to shock, thrill and sell tickets to voracious consumers of horror-themed content. In fact, gothic horror in the mid-thirties kept Universal Studios from financial ruin when films like DRACULA, FRANKENSTEIN and SON OF KONG were a major success, then they started pumping out horror films to turn a hefty profit. In our business Horror no doubt has influenced our art form and our psyche. When you were executives at New Line how important was the horror genre and franchises like NIGHTMARE ON ELM STREET to the company's success?

ORDESKY/FLEMING: The importance of A NIGHTMARE ON ELM STREET cannot be overstated. New Line was The House That Freddy Built, particularly in the early 90s prior to the HOUSE PARTY and TEENAGE MUTANT NINJA TURTLE franchises. One was conscious every year at New Line of the need to make and market a successful NIGHTMARE ON ELM STREET movie, not just for the film's sake but for the robust merchandising and home entertainment values each film supported. That revenue kept New Line growing heading into the 90s before the Jim Carrey movies and other New Line hits.

I'm a geek and I love LORD OF THE RINGS trilogy, so I can't interview you two without asking a least one question about your time in Middle Earth. Personally and/or professionally what was the most important life lesson you leaned during the making of such an influential trilogy in American cinema?

ORDESKY/FLEMING: The biggest lesson, which remains top of mind to this day, is never deny a conviction when you're fortunate enough to have one. THE LORD OF THE RINGS sprang from profound passion and belief in the power of Tolkien's books and fans, and in Peter Jackson as the perfect filmmaker even though he'd never made films of such scale before.

You two were the active producers on the Bigfoot film EXISTS (2014), which was directed by Eduardo Sanchez, who most consider the father of the "found footage" sub-genre of horror. How did this film come about and why Bigfoot? Also, why chose a "found footage" shooting style as opposed to a traditional shooting style?

ORDESKY/FLEMING: EXISTS sprang from a passion for Bigfoot which we shared with Eduardo and his Haxan Films team. Bigfoot and Eduardo were a natural fit, as THE BLAIR WITCH PROJECT was inspired by the 1972 Bigfoot classic THE LEGEND OF BOGGY CREEK which we all loved. What we set out to do with EXISTS was to reinvent Bigfoot for a new generation. As far as why found footage, Ed and we don't consider EXISTS "found footage" per se. It is first-person which is something all found footage films share. We felt it made sense that since every Bigfoot sighting video is essentially first-person, we should shoot the film first-person. We also wanted to subvert the expectation of found footage horror sub-genre, which often focuses on fear of what you don't see. With EXISTS we wanted to bring a big-budget Bigfoot to found footage so you could be scared of what you do see.

Mark, in your early beginnings, you worked for the indie film company Republic Pictures doing video acquisitions. A job that allowed you to see Peter Jackson's film BAD TASTE, which was your first introduction to the filmmaker. As an acquisitions exec what were the key elements you were looking for in the b-movies that were being sent to you?

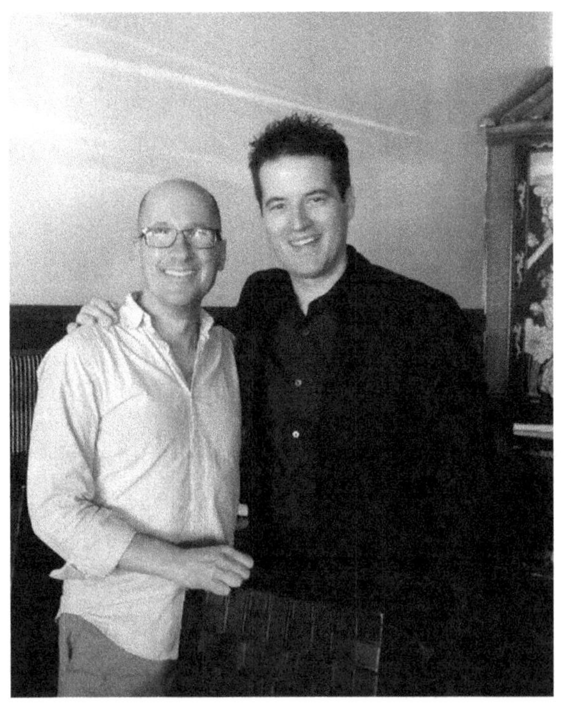

Danny Draven & his producing mentor Mark Ordesky in Beverly Hills, California in 2015.

ORDESKY: Doing B-movie acquisitions at Republic remains such a happy memory. There was a wonderful purity in chasing distribution rights to films for which I was a natural audience. My primary criteria then remains a sound criteria for contemplating films now: a compelling central idea, execution that exceeds or subverts audience expectation, and stars people want to see or new faces they'll always remember discovering.

You were both part of the team of executive producers on THE QUEST, a hybrid fantasy reality TV series which aired on ABC in Summer 2014. What was your biggest challenge working in television as opposed to feature film production?

ORDESKY/FLEMING: The biggest challenge of THE QUEST was also its greatest thrill: Creating and maintaining the "live" component of the production so that contestants had as immersive and natural an experience as possible—with little sense of the complicated behind-the-scenes machinery. Every day was an exciting high-wire act, a mammoth endeavor in timing and coordinating cameras, actors, extras, animals, stunts, prosthetics, and all manner of practical, lighting and sound effects. Our sole purpose was to surprise and challenge 12 real people, and capture their transformation. All without second takes!

What is your favorite horror film of all time and why does the film work for you?

ORDESKY/FLEMING: Just one? Difficult! If just one then THE EXORCIST for us both. It was so shocking and disturbing. You'd never seen anything like it in its time. And the horror was deepened by the nuanced explorations of its characters and themes. Unforgettable. That said, ROSEMARY'S BABY is also so incredibly terrifying because it revealed to us how hideous human beings can be.

If you had to pick one factor when green lighting a feature film project, what would that element be and why?

FLEMING: Actually a proper greenlight decision must consider a balance of multiple elements or else it has failed the test. At New Line, where Mark and I shaped the greenlight process, no decision was made without considering both the financial implications and the creative imperative. If one runs a business by creative instincts alone, it will most likely fail and if one runs a business by bottom-line analysis alone it will most likely fail. The perfect greenlight is one in which the creative imperative is clear, a market for the project is identified, and a budget is scaled to meet that identified market demand.

What are some of the mistakes you see younger filmmakers make when directing for the first time?

FLEMING: I think anyone that is brave enough to step up to the plate and be convincing enough to have people part with money to make the film deserve a medal. That said, if I had to pick one mistake first-time filmmakers can make is that they fall in love with every scene and therefore, put equal emphasis on every shot. This ends up eating up their shooting days and they are forced to rush important emotional scenes. More experienced filmmakers know how much gets left on the editing room floor and understand how to emphasize their attention on set.

How important is networking in the film business?

FLEMING: Our business is a relationship business. People want to work with people they like and trust. Networking is a critical part of that. Where people get networking wrong is that they are always networking "up" when it is more important to network peer to peer. Find your like-minded creative partners. It is in the team that you will create great things. Once you create great things, agents and studio execs will find you. Proof is in the pudding and no matter how many great friends you have at the top, if you don't have the goods there is very little they can do for you.

Jane, you have been the president of Women In Film (www.wif.org) and very dedicated to advancing the professional lives of women working in film. It's no secret that the horror genre has been male dominated since the beginning, but women are such a big part of the fan base.   I'm excited to see new female

artists emerge creating films like JENNIFER'S BODY (2009), written by Diablo Cody and directed by Karyn Kusama and more recently Jennifer Kent's scary-as-hell film THE BABADOOK (2014). What would your advice be for a young woman who is about to embark on a filmmaking career in Hollywood?

FLEMING: It would be the same advice I would give to anyone. Be prepared. Be distinct. Be determined. For women, I might specifically add to be fearless when asking for money. Women In Film and the Sundance Institute have been doing groundbreaking research on why women face bigger challenges getting their films made and the primary block is access to capital. We need to break down those barriers.

Mark, I know you're still a fan and player of Dungeons & Dragons. If you could look at a new filmmaker through the eyes of a Dungeon Master, what qualities would you give him to aid him on his journey to success?

ORDESKY: You mean other than perfect 18s in all character stats? All kidding aside, I think the best quality would be fearlessness. In film-making as in D&D, fortune favors the bold. And If you perish pursuing a grand film-making quest, as in D&D, resurrection is not only possible, it's a way of life.

JOHN OTTMAN
COMPOSER / EDITOR

www.JohnOttman.com

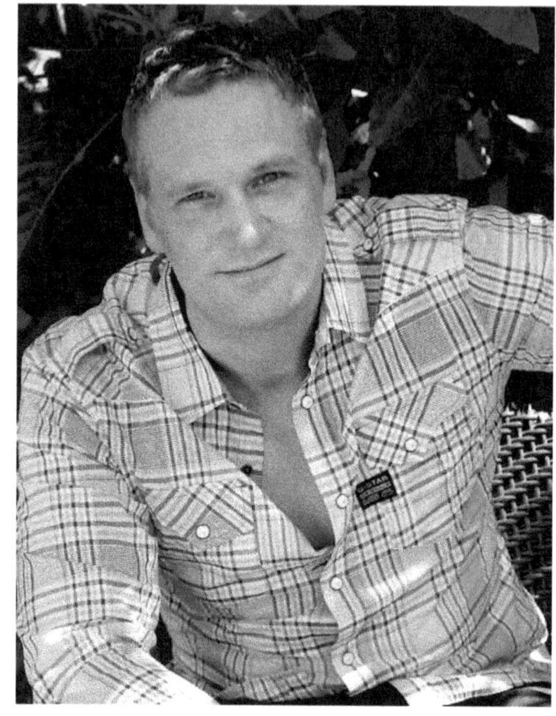

JOHN OTTMAN

John Ottman holds dual distinctions as a leading film composer and an award winning film editor. Ottman has often completed both monumental tasks on the same films. Such remarkable double duties have included The Usual Suspects, X-Men 2, Superman Returns, Valkyrie, and Jack the Giant Killer. He has also held producer roles on several of these films, as well as directing, editing and scoring Urban Legends 2.

From an early age in San Jose, California, Ottman began writing and recording radio plays on cassette tapes. He'd perform many characters with his voice (and some sound effects), and called upon his neighborhood friends as extra cast members.

By the fourth grade, Ottman was playing the clarinet and continued doing so throughout high school. But his real concentration turned from audio productions to making films. He turned his parents' garage into a movie studio, where multiple sets were interchangeable to accommodate productions - invariably some sort of science fiction film. By high school, his films evolved to hour-long productions complete with large sets and lavish scores edited together from his favorite soundtracks.

Having been a veteran of numerous short films, Ottman excelled at USC film school, receiving accolades for his direction of actors and for how masterfully he edited their performances. It was in this directing course that a graduate filmmaker asked Ottman to re-edit his thesis film. John modified the story from raw footage and also designed the film's extensive sound. The film ended up winning the student Academy Award. On that film, Ottman met a production assistant named Bryan Singer.

Singer, only aware of Ottman's editing (Ottman stayed awake into the wee hours learning midi gear and composing music), asked him to edit a short film starring Ethan Hawke - a childhood friend of Singer's. Ottman ended up co-directing the film (Lion's Den) as well as editing and doing the sound design.

Ottman edited Singer's first feature, Public Access. His effective sequences and editorial montages became the highlight of the picture. In the eleventh hour, the film lost its composer. Singer asked Ottman to write the score, after much prodding from the editor. Public Access received the Grand Jury Prize at the 1993 Sundance Film Festival, with the score and editing being lauded in reviews.

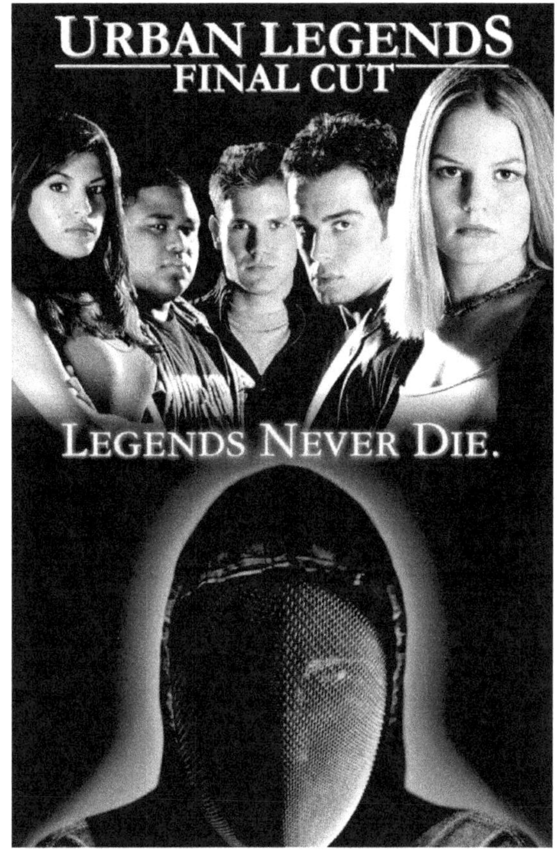

URBAN LEGENDS: Final Cut (2000)
Photo Credit: Columbia Pictures

With The Usual Suspects and future Singer films, Ottman held to a promise that, despite his scoring dreams, he would commit to the months required to also serve as editor on Singer's films. The wary producers of The Usual Suspects gave the go-ahead for him to both edit the complicated picture and write the score, the demands of which no one had undergone. The film was edited in Ottman's living room on a Steinbeck flatbed and a splicer. The Usual Suspects and Ottman's work received widespread acclaim, earning Ottman the British Academy Awards for his editing, a Saturn Award for his score, and a nomination by the American Cinema Editors.

Since then, Ottman has scored numerous films with the intent of keeping thematic film scoring alive. Ottman also made a brief foray into television for which he received an Emmy nomination ("Fantasy Island.")

You've edited, scored and directed the horror film URBAN LEGENDS: FINAL CUT in 2000. As your first horror film as a director, what did you learn from the experience? Any advice for someone who is about to direct for the first time?

I'd been making small films for so many years, plus the years I spent as a filmmaking partner with Bryan Singer, that there was fortunately never a deer-in-headlights moment for me. I was pretty attuned to the political and creative challenges ahead of me. As an editor, I'm big on shot lists, storyboards and being ridiculously prepared, designing scenes ahead of time and so forth. What I did discover is my love for working with the actors. Obviously, I was dealt a teen horror film at a time when they were being made fun of, ala Scream. Working on the script and changing the story line in pre-production was as important as anything I did in production, or post. The main challenge was to try and make what is basically a ludicrous story, plausible. This extended to production design, location scouting, casting and working with the actors. I enjoyed huddling with them trying to figure out ways to best relay some silly dialog and make it as buyable as possible. Because I do so many different roles on a film, I've sort of trained myself to compartmentalize all of those tasks and not let one influence the other too much. That's probably the advice I would give a new director. Once you've shot the film, you need to forget the fact that there was, for instance, a big day where you rented an enormous crane for this incredible establishing shot etc. You need to divorce yourself from all of the experiences you had on set and other preconceived notions so that you can maintain objectivity in post-production. The other advice is to learn the craft of picking your battles. You know you're going to lose some and you're going to win some. So you have to figure out what babies you can stand killing in order to get something you really want. It's all a fine line of maintaining your passion and vision, while simultaneously being an effective diplomat.

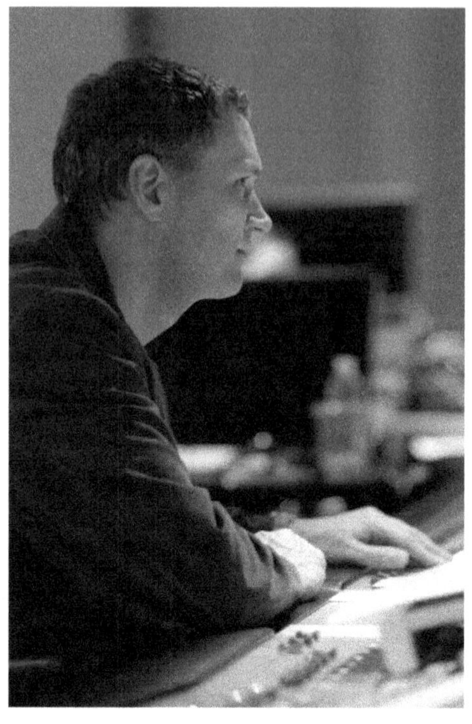

Ottman in the studio composing for SUPERMAN RETURNS (2006).

As a composer, what is your creative approach when preparing to score a horror film? Is your approach any different from other genres you work in?

My philosophy is that the more you believe the world of the movie and identify with the characters, the more scared out of your pants you're going to be when they're in jeopardy. Horror scores that simply go for the surface clunks, bangs and creeps with no subtext often reduce the film to the ordinary. Those that strive to tell an actual story tend to endure. Naturally, horror scores must create unease, but there's a tasteful way and a lazy way. I remember being brought in to watch the film, Orphan. The temporary music was simply service-level stings, drones and such. But when I watched it, I saw a story of a mother, Kate, who has a painful past, having lost her daughter, Jessica, to an accident years before. Her current daughter, Max, is deaf, but is clearly one of the joys of Kate's life. This was, of course, an invitation for me to create a theme that bonded Kate, Jessica and Max. Even better, there was an early scene where Kate is composing a piece of music on the piano. I felt that the music she's writing should be the theme of the film as well as her music for Jessica and Max. So we stripped out the sound of whatever she was playing on set, and replaced it with a rudimentary version of the theme I wrote. Because it was a piece of music she was writing, I decided to give it a classical feel in three basic "movements." Part A, a simple classical piano and cello movement. Part B is Jessica's mournful theme, and then Part C is Max's innocent theme, characterized by added electric piano, harp harmonics and muted synthesized textures reflecting her deafness – literally a "ringing in the ears" at times.

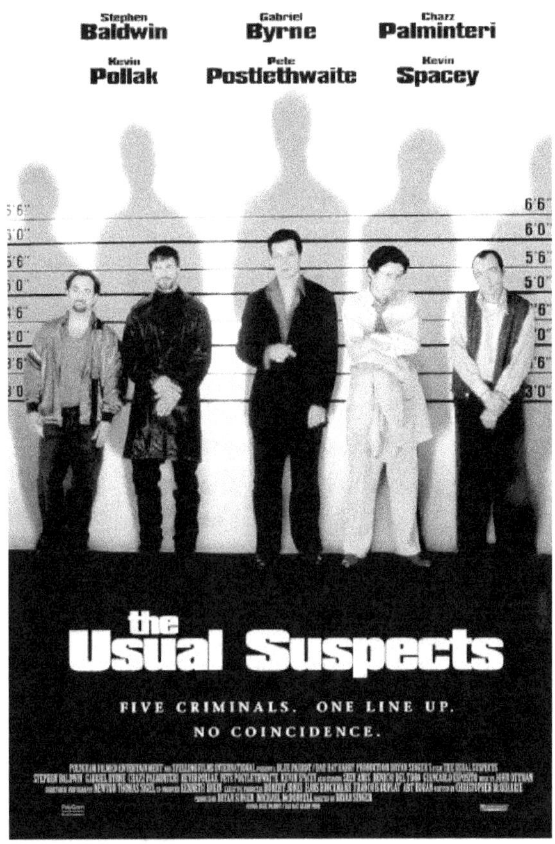

THE USUAL SUSPECTS (1995)
Photo Credit: MGM

Writing Kate's piece not only gave me the opportunity to write music that could stand on its own, but it also served as a way to relate to her character, thereby making her and Max's endangerment more scary later. So by searching for the subtext of the story, the music elevated the film beyond mere horror schlock. Even with silly fare like House of Wax, I tried to create a history behind the evil character, harkening the music of his childhood wherever I could. Besides, child-like tunes in horror films is always scary! Evil characters are bad for a reason; they were children one time and something made them go awry. Even Keyser Soze has melancholy woven into his dark theme. It just makes the film and characters, no matter how evil, richer and a little more "legit."

The bottom line, for any genre, is that if there is a subliminal sense that the music is actually telling a story and bringing believability, the film will benefit greatly. Thus, the power of thought-out motifs and themes.

You have a long working history with director Bryan Singer which started with your score for PUBLIC ACCESS (1993) and the more widely known film THE USUAL SUSPECTS (1995) and continues to this day with X-MEN: Days of Future Past (2014). What is the collaboration process like between you and Bryan? What about with other directors?

I guess I've been lucky in a sense that Bryan, and even other directors, have been more reactors than planners when it comes to the film's score. I spend time alone analyzing the film until I feel that I've "cracked" it. I then present a concept, or an overture of sorts, highlighting the themes, … and they react. Also, no matter how experienced a director is, they are plenty insecure and often have at least a degree of self-doubt. This is why they seek out the expertise and opinion of others. The composer, especially, is a newcomer to the film late in the game. The composer has an objective eye and is often looked at as a sort of a one-man test audience. As long as a composer can communicate story, character or pragmatic reasons why he wants to go a certain direction, he will have the ear of the filmmakers.

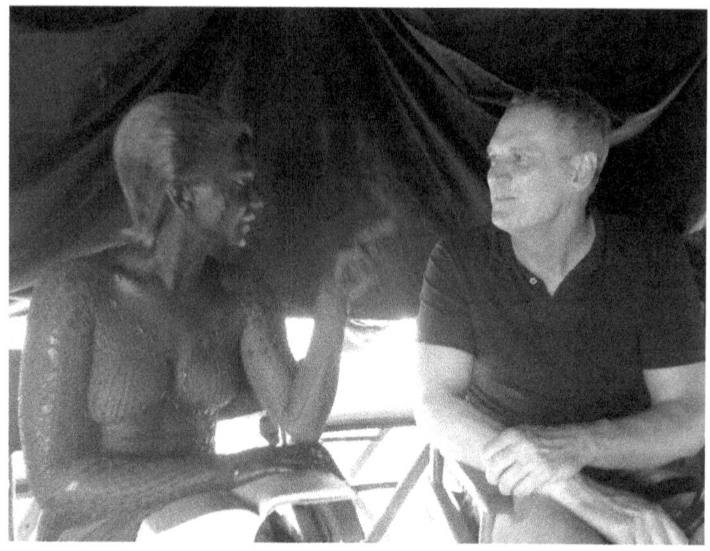

Ottman on set during the making of X-MEN: Dayos of Future Past (2014) with actress Jennifer Lawrence as Mystique.

Regarding directors as responders to score, the same can be said for the film's editing; at least in my relationship with Bryan. Bryan likes to walk in the editing room and be surprised, moved or excited by a scene with no prior prodding me in any direction. He doesn't want to disrupt some sort of vision or solutions I might have for a sequence. Throughout the years we sort of created each other's sensibility and taste, so I know that when I create something that gives me chills, he will most likely react the same way. And if he doesn't, I'm pissed! He has referred to me as an architect, and in essence, reacts to my "designs." Sometimes, probably like many editors, I resent directors who are able to actually have a life, go on vacations and dinners and so forth. But I guess the alternative would be them breathing down my neck while I'm trying to work, which would destroy any of my mojo or inspirations. So Bryan knows to stay away. This also goes back to a director maintaining objectivity by keeping an odd distance and forgetting on-set dramas and preconceived notions of what scenes were supposed to be. I can't say this is a normal editor-director relationship. They all vary depending on personalities, style and years together. Ours is collaborative, and he trusts me to hold down the fort, as it were.

Do you record live orchestra or do you use software packages for your scores (e.g. Logic Pro X, Digital Performer)?

I write on Digital Performer, but whether the music will be reproduced with an actual orchestra depends on the type of score and budget. Even on a large budget film such as on Days of Future Past, I felt it was better to blend the orchestra with synthesized elements. So it was really a fusion between the two because this particular film needed a more modern and dark feel. Ironically, its actually much more labor-intensive to write a score incorporating lots of electronics, because those electronics have to be searched out, massaged, manipulated and mixed as the final product. Whereas a complete orchestral score can be written much more rapidly, perhaps even a tad sloppily, because it's all going to re-performed by musicians.

What do you think are the most important musical elements for a theatrical score to have present?

There's really no golden element for any film score except that in most cases, the best scores are those that have had a lot of intensive soul-searching in terms of the story the score is trying to tell and the "sound" the film should have. Just walking into a picture and writing music is like walking down a foggy back alley. How can you possibly know where you're going? Yet too many scores are written in haste this way today. The best scores are where an intensive and disciplined amount of time is spent deciding upon themes and motifs ahead of time and analying where they are going to go as the story develops… kind of like writing a good symphony.

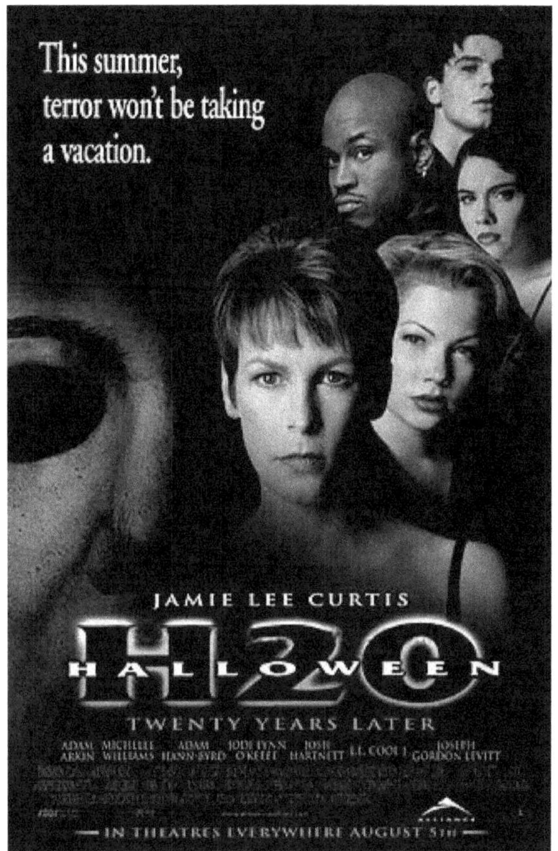

HALLOWEEN H20 (1998)

The agony a composer goes through up front to think all this through pays off big time in the end, because it also makes the score much easier to write once these themes have been layed out. And the film is the benefactor in terms of symmetry, cohesion, clarity and refinement.

I see more and more indie filmmakers turning to library music to track their films, which I think is a shame. What would your advice be to a new filmmaker who may be considering bypassing an original score in place of stock music?

First of all, I always say that if there's a way to accomplish things without score, that this should be the goal. Imagine the White House sequence in X-Men 2 or the Quicksilver kitchen sequence in Days of Future Past being scored with film music. They would just be reduced to typical sequences, and not the classic scenes they became. So if, in an independent movie, classical or some interesting use of source music is being used in lieu of typical score, it actually may elevate the film. I wasn't aware so many independent movies were having to use library music four score. If in fact, an independent filmmaker requires an original score, my only advice would be to try their best to help the composer have what he needs to produce something of quality sonically. The technology has advanced to such a degree, that even up-and-coming composers have pretty good tools and samples at their disposal to create a quality sound. But these tools don't do this by themselves. It still comes down to an artist weaving things artistically and carefully to create a convincing sound. These are the kinds of people directors need to seek out. But if the director is truly looking for something "orchestral" the composer is going to need to sweeten with some real instruments to make it convincing. That is where they need the support of the director/producers.

When you collaborate with a director what is the ideal way in which he or she can communicate his ideas to you musically?

The best way for a director to communicate ideas or reactions is to speak in non-musical terms. It's most valuable to a composer if a director relays what he/she feels and re-states what goal is for a scene. For example, "Sally needs to seem more ambivalent here", or "I'm not feeling the graveness of the situation there."

What skill do you wish all directors had more of in the edit room?

Well, filmmaking is about communicating ideas and feelings, whether it be to an actor, composer, editor, visual fx supervisor, costume designer and on and on. I guess what anyone wishes from a director is for them to be able to describe their reactions or what they want succinctly.

How long do you normally get to complete an original score? What about an edit for a Hollywood film?

Normally a composer has at least a few weeks to write a score; and for large films, three or four months. There are also emergency situations where a composer is called in at the last minute to rescore a movie, or is just hired too late in the game. I have had as little as two weeks to write a score. On a large-scale film with a hundred or more minutes of music, this, of course is nearly impossible without more time or a team of writers. The latter "factory" situation will produce a score of much lower artistic merit or integrity. Rarely these days are composers ever writing to finished picture. Writing a score involves many revisions to new picture or changing ideas. Or, in today's digital editing world, a composer decides whether the music can be edited to a new scene edit.

The editing of a movie is a saga. From beginning to end, an editor is normally on a film anywhere between one and two years. The editing begins as soon as shooting commences, or even beforehand if the editor is involved in designing the scenes with storyboards, the visual fx team, etc. During production the editor is still designing future scenes with the storyboard artists or previs team while simultaneously trying to keep up during the shoot, editing scenes as they're being shot. The editor must declare whether a set can be torn down, what pick-up shots are required, many times coordinating shots with the second unit director or going off with a splinter team. The more the editor can anticipate what may explode in his face later, the fewer re-shoots may be required down the road. The authority of editor varies upon the relationship with the director and is involved in every one of thousands of facets all the way through to the last day of the final dub.

When you score, how do you determine when you may have too much music and to just have silence?

The score is basically plotted out when the film is tracked with temporary music. Further decisions where music begins and ends is determined in what is called a "spotting session." This is where the director, and/or producers, sit with the composer through the movie and decide where music cues begin and end, as well as where they may have specific problems they want to address, or even specific musical approaches they would like to request in areas. For me, as I stated before, the goal is to not over-score. Music is too often seen as a security blanket, when it's not even required; especially if the scenes are strong and provocative on their own.

Many may find it surprising that, as an editor, I do not track with any music until my entire cut is together. I love to watch the whole film dry. Besides, I'm also involved in the sound design of the picture, so I like to hear everything except music. Often when music is added early to sell a scene, it can mask and delay the discovery of a problem till months later. I would rather confront the issues head-on, mainly because I don't have the time to have a problem-plaqued film on my hands later – I need the time to score the film while I'm trying to manage it at the same time. So, after I have my assembly together, I spend a couple of weeks tracking it with temporary music. This way the temporary score has not been hacked up over the course of months, allowing it to maintain some sense of continuity. That makes for much better viewing experience when we present to the studio or test it for an audience.

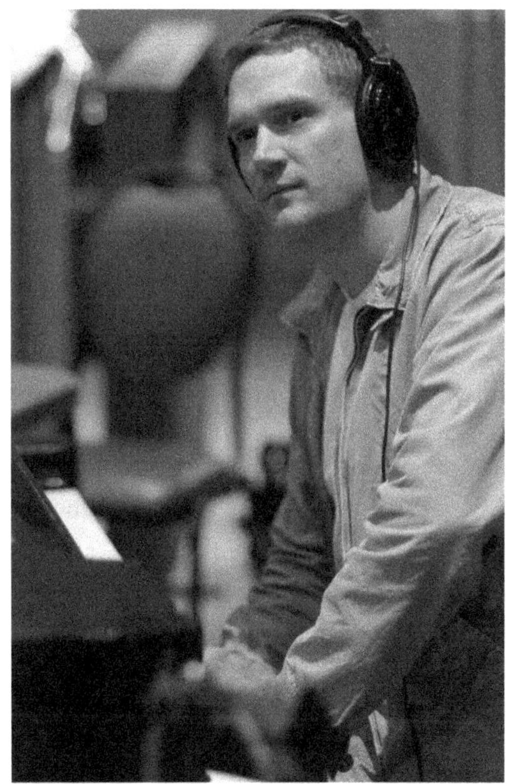

Ottman in the studio composing for SUPERMAN RETURNS (2006).

In scores, what are some of the mistakes you see musically speaking in low budget, indie or even Hollywood films? Any pet peeves you can share with us?

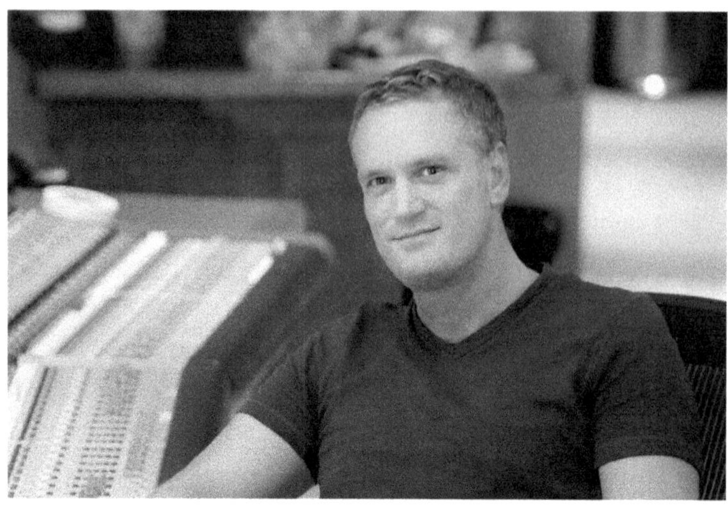

Ottman in the studio composing for JACK THE GIANT SLAYER (2013)

My main pet peeve is that in many of today's films, everything is climax and no foreplay. Truly captivating stories require peaks and valleys. This requires harder work and more foresight into plotting out how that score is going to evolve. If a composer is just cranking out film after film and walking into scoring a film flying blind, or walking down that foggy alley, the mistake is often made that every moment is scored as a supreme one. This also happens when teams of composers are hired on a project. A point of view often gets muddled. The hope is that when it's played back at the final dub of the film, the director can eliminate some music, try to assess that the score is not evolving intelligently and make music-editorial changes. Sadly, the everything–played–at–the–extreme–moment syndrome (and that includes sound effects), pervades modern films. It boils down to them having a lack of a point of view, paranoia … and lack of confidence in the film itself.

When you edit a film, what is the creative process like from the time all the footage is in the can to the time you lock picture?

I always make the analogy that the editor of a film is much like the editor of a magazine or newspaper. From the time the film is shot to the end, the editor is faced with an unending barrage of issues, whether it be political ones, studio notes, test screenings, looping the actors, sound effects reviews, planning a re-shoots, on and on. The film is constantly in flux, and because of our digital world, it's often in flux all the way into the dub stage. Changes are so easily made these days, that films require the till of a steady hand and a conviction of direction. In other words, today, a film can easily lose its way.

What programs to you use for editing?

I use an Avid, because that's all I know.

What are your personal favorite horror scores and why do you love them so

much?

Well, I would say Alien, however I'm not sure you would classify that as a strict horror movie. The theme for that film is a masterpiece, blending elegance and darkness. In terms of straightforward horror, Halloween and Silence of the Lambs come to mind. Halloween may be unabashed horror, but strong thematically, even complete with motifs that converge and often carry the evil felt in the film. Silence is an example of one central theme having great malevolent gravitas or "importance" recurring throughout the film, filling us with dread. No where are there bangs and booms; but instead, unrelenting deep dark emotion throughout engrossing the audience.

If you had to pick two all-time favorite horror films, one old and one new, what would they be and why?

The funny thing is I don't really see many horror films. Again, I go back to not only one of my favorite "horror" films but also one of my all-time favorite films ever; and that is the original Alien. I could write a dissertation on why this film is a masterpiece. Because it was so realistic, much like a sort of 2001: A Space Odyssey in one sense, it was even more terrifying and probably the last film I ever saw in a theater where I was completely breathless. I believed it. The environment was perfectly designed for paranoia, and it was one invincible scary-ass creature lurking about. Bravura filmmaking and performances made a basically a big-budget horror masterpiece.

The Dead Zone is another film that may not be strict "horror", but one of my favorites. This should have easily been an Oscar for Christopher Walken, but unfortunately the genre wasn't taken seriously at that time. Martin Sheen is also fantastic as a bad guy. Like Alien, it was such terrific filmmaking across the board, plus a unique screenplay that violated many tenants of story structure. The story was as emotional as it was riveting.

If you could be one character in the X-MEN when you compose, who would it be and why?

I'd probably be Magneto so I could lock the doors and not let anybody in.

DEBBIE ROCHON

ACTRESS / DIRECTOR

DebbieRochon.com
ModelHunger.com

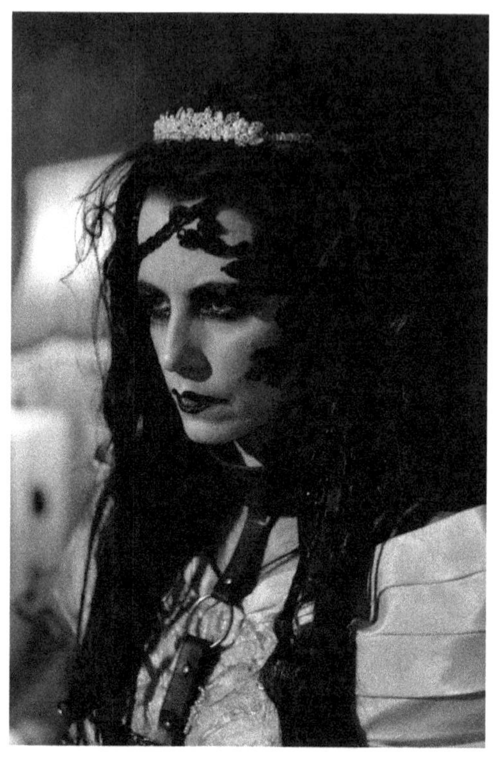

DEBBIE ROCHON in NIGHTMARE BOX.

Since 1988 she has worked in over 200 independent straight-to-DVD horror flicks in lead, supporting and minor parts. Although she is mostly associated with creepy features and thrillers, she has garnered acclaim for her turns in comedy and drama. She has also co-hosted a number of radio shows in New York City that focused on film and pop culture including Oblique Strategies with Peter Schmedig on WBAI a terrestrial radio station which aired from 1994-1996, she has co-hosted and co-produced the Internet radio show Illumination Gallery for Pseudo Radio from 1996-1998, she has worked for the Internet radio station Eyada.com from 1999-2001 producing many film and media related radio programs, Debbie then co-hosted and co-produced the Fangoria Radio show with Dee Snider, frontman for Twisted Sister, on Sirius satellite radio from 2006-2010. Debbie currently acts in film and writes for Fangoria magazine which features her Rondo Award nominated column Diary of the Deb, she also pens for The Phantom of the Movies' Videoscope magazine. Her directorial debut MODEL HUNGER is now available.

What do you think makes a great female protagonist in a horror film?

One of my favorites to this day has to be the role of Sally as played by Marilyn Burns in the original horror classic THE TEXAS CHAINSAW MASSACRE (1974). She portrayed all of the qualities that are essential for a strong but realistic female in a horror movie. She was not invincible; she was given obstacles that were physical, mental, and emotional. She was tested and rose to the occasion. I cite her even above the stunning performance Sigourney Weaver gave in the ALIEN film series because what Sally endured was realistic. It could really happen. She wasn't ubertough, but she had a will to survive that superseded all else. She was scared and abused, but she never gave up. She always continued to have the hope and kept an eye open for the first possible means of escape. The role and performance in this case were extremely believable therefore win my highest accolades. She didn't just scream, she didn't just get up and kick ass; she suffered greatly and found strength within herself to endure until hope turned into reality for her. Even at the end of the film she isn't OK and just happy to be getting away. She is traumatized and shaken and you could well imagine her spending the next couple of years on some serious mind-numbing drugs. For me, that was one of the performances that made the entire film work. All the qualities were born out of real human, female behavior.

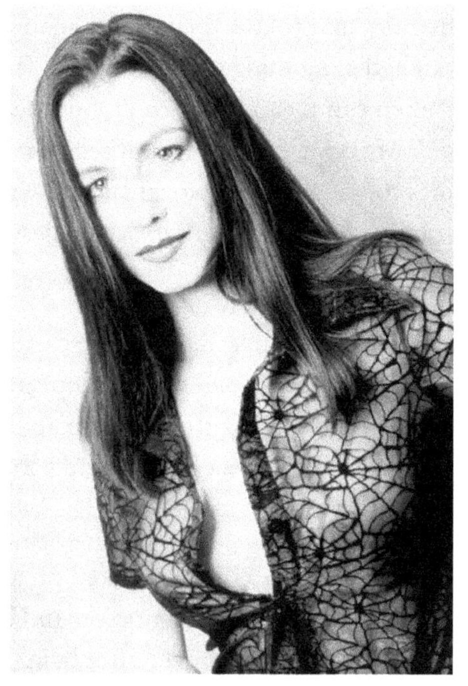

DEBBIE ROCHON
Photo By Gary Cook

What do you think makes a great female antagonist in a horror film?

I think I have to mention one of my favorites, which isn't considered a horror movie. I think the film PLAY MISTY FOR ME (1971) featured one of the scariest antagonists ever because it was very realistic. The more believable the character and story is, the more deeply disturbing a film can be. Jessica Walter knocked the ball out of the park in this film as the obsessed fan of a talk show radio host. The host, played by Clint Eastwood, makes the mistake of having a one-night stand with her, and all bets are off. She becomes impossible to get rid of as she destroys his life one bit at a time. In the horror world I think you have to acknowledge the great Betsy Palmer for her convincing portrayal as the overprotective murderous mommy in the horror classic FRIDAY THE 13th (1980). There is a fine line between playing crazy and just acting plain campy, and these actresses, both with extensive stage and film credits prior to the aforementioned titles, brought a three-dimensional character to the screen. That is what we all find most disturbing. It's not the unbelievable, but the believable, horrors that could happen next door.

In my opinion, there are a lot of horror movies that integrate both protagonist and antagonist. For example, actress Ellen Page in the film HARD CANDY (2005) is both the hero and the torturer in the film. Ms. Page's character took it upon herself to teach a pedophile a lesson even though she was never actually assaulted by him personally. This probably falls into the antihero category.

In your experience, what are the biggest mistakes you see directors—veterans or beginners—make when working with actors on the set?

There are many, but I think the biggest mistake is shooting from a script that isn't ready. Viewers can forgive a lot of things, but a poorly crafted story is the biggest cinematic sin. People will hang in there through less than perfect camera work, sound design, and even a wooden performance here or there, but if the story is boring or isn't believable, the movie is dead meat. This doesn't mean you can't have outrageous circumstances with bizarre worlds in your movie, but you have to lay down the rules and follow them. How many times have you watched something and wondered, "I thought the women can fly and men can't, but that guy just flew . . . ?" My point being you can set down the craziest rules to your filmatic world and we will follow you. You just have to adhere to your rules and everything will be fine.

I think the next mistake is in the casting department. Once the story is solid you really need to believe the people on your TV otherwise the audience's suspension of disbelief is shattered and you've lost them.

In my experience, I once worked on a film where the filmmaker didn't have insurance, and because of this, my life was altered forever after being injured on a set. I wouldn't want to be a director whose cast was hurt on my set. Besides the legal ramifications, I would find it hard to live with disabling someone permanently. You need insurance on your set or you have no business making a movie. Horror movies are action movies in a lot of ways (e.g., running, jumping, physical stunts) and it's insane to think you don't need it.

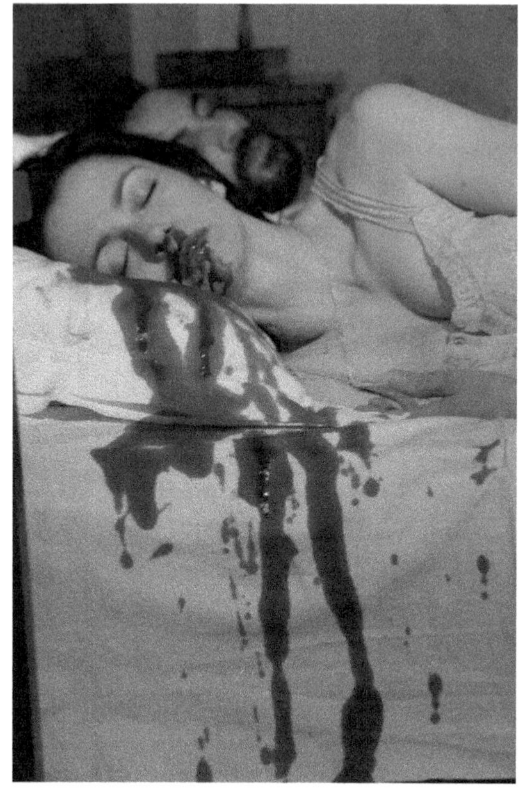

From COLOUR FROM THE DARK. Rochon loses her mind in this bloody good adaptation of an H.P. Lovecraft story.

Have you ever worked with a female horror film director, and if so, how do they differ from their male colleagues?

There are very few, I have to say, and there have been long stretches between working with them. The first female director I worked with was Roberta Findlay when I made two films in the late 80s . . . LURKERS (1988) and BANNED (1989) . She was a screamer, but her style was very frank and New York-esque. Her brashness was mostly just accepted, and we all didn't know any better anyway being novices! It ended up being rather funny to watch her direct the cast and crew. She had to be tough because I don't think anyone would listen to her otherwise. I like the energy of working with most women, so I think the comfort level is higher for me. But some actresses get a lot of their self-esteem from male-specific encouragement. I think both sexes have a lot to offer the role of director. I have just never had the patience for actresses who need to have the full attention of a male director for ego reasons just to be "The Belle of the Ball." I like anyone who works hard, has a vision (even if they're good at making "product" versus "art"), and concerns themselves with the making of the movie, not the movement in their pants.

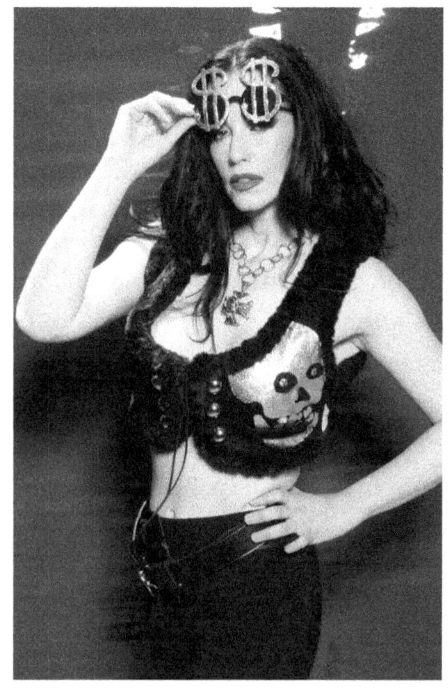

The money glasses are a little rose-colored as there is little money involved in making cult movies.
Photo by Gary Cook

The horror genre has a reputation for exploiting and objectifying women, usually to cater to the predominately young male audience. What are your thoughts on this issue, and do you feel you have been exploited?

No, I don't feel exploited whatsoever. I think both sexes have equally participated in the exploitation of women. I think there's a place for sexy movies, but as you get older your taste matures. I have no problem watching nudity in film, but what I enjoy now is different than when I was a teenager. I love a good scary horror movie with a solid story, or a well-executed horror–comedy, or even just well done, straight up camp. Exploitation doesn't do anything for me. I have done a lot of exploitation over the years and it didn't corrode my brain, so I think I came out alright. It does ruffle a lot of feathers. You will find people who use it as some sort of proof that you are inferior to them because you've been naked on screen. You can become an easy target to mean-spirited people. I feel like, God willing, if I make it to 90, I will show all the people in the horror-movie old age home how good I used to look.

If nudity is required in the script, how does an actress deal with this sensitive issue? What is your experience and how do you deal with this subject?

I think what saves the most time is to just tell the casting people or director immediately that you don't want to do it if nudity is involved. Never take the part thinking you will deal with it later. Maybe the director won't care and will hire you anyway. Maybe he won't hire you because he's required to deliver X amount of nude scenes per 30 minutes. Never piss everybody off by accepting the role then dropping the bomb that you're not going to strip down the day of the nude scene because you aren't comfortable with it.

I have taken roles that have required nudity, and when it was time for the nude scene, I would either just do it without obsessing over it beforehand, which really just gets you all worried and worked up anyway, or the opposite happens—I am dreading it. However, I never say a word and just do the scene as well as I can in hopes I will then only have to do minimal takes. I have told directors I wasn't interested in doing a role because of the nudity involved, I have no problem with turning work down. If I like the script, I have usually said yes to nudity because the rest of the movie made it worth it. At the end of the day, I have always looked at the overall picture but also took my bills into consideration as well. I always wanted to be a working actor. Nudity comes with the territory in film.

Is the independent horror genre dead?

The independent horror genre is both dead and undead! I think we need a new, cutting-edge revolution in how we get movies out to viewers. Times have completely changed. No more drive-ins, no more VHS, very little DVD distribution, no TV sales, and very little action on the video on demand download front. I don't know what the next thing will be, but whatever it is, it will save independent horror (and non) movies. This is the frontier that we need to be focused on; what's the new venue? I understand when people say that the indie scene is dead. Most sales have come to a complete standstill, and the self-distribution model hasn't completely taken hold yet. I think something will happen, it always does. If indie film does end up being viewed on iPods or BlackBerries then the filmmakers will adjust to it and shoot more close-ups! We are survivors and will mutate with the times.

What are some of the most annoying, penny-pinching things low-budget film producers do when making a film?

I really don't require much, but if a set doesn't have coffee, water, and a little craft service area, then they really shouldn't be making a movie. These are the basics for your cast and crew to keep them going! I know when Lloyd Kaufman is making a Troma movie he insists on using small cups instead of large ones, but I think that's very smart! How many times do you see half consumed beverages being thrown out? That's why he does it. There's a difference between being a miser and being smart.

I even had one incident where we wrapped the film at about 7 am after shooting all night long—keep in mind this was the last day of the film shoot—and the director said everyone should see the producer after they change to get paid. I changed as fast as a lightening bolt and ran downstairs and poof! The producer was gone. He was never to be seen or heard from again! That was a long time ago but you would be surprised how low some can go. If ever in that situation get the money before you get changed!

TOM SAVINI

SPECIAL MAKEUP FX ARTIST / ACTOR / DIRECTOR

www.savini.com

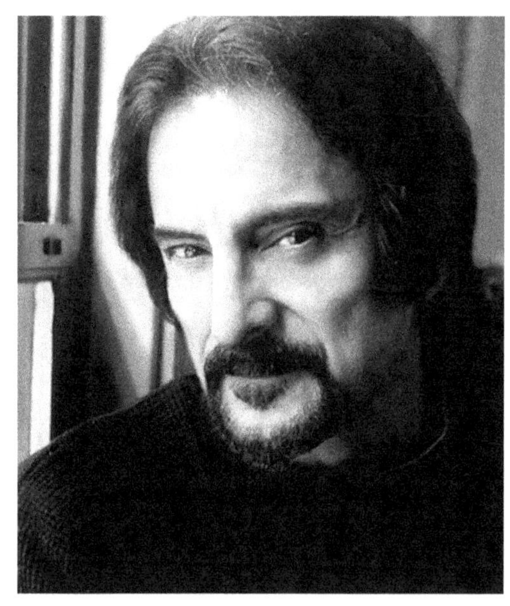

TOM SAVINI

TOM SAVINI is an actor, director, and makeup effects artist responsible for the creation of Jason in the FRIDAY THE 13TH movies, Leatherface in THE TEXAS CHAINSAW MASSACRE, and special effects and monsters in more than 37 horror movies. As an actor he played Sex Machine in the film FROM DUSK TIL' DAWN, the fingerless Tolo in GRINDHOUSE, has appeared on The Simpsons as himself, and was a villain in the TV series Sheena: Queen of the Jungle . He also directed the 1990 remake of NIGHT OF THE LIVING DEAD, THE CHILL FACTOR, and TALES FROM THE DARKSIDE. He currently owns the Tom Savini Special Make-Up Effects Program at the Douglas Education Center in Pittsburgh, Pennsylvania.

When directing horror films, what is it that actors really want from a director?

That depends on the actor. Some actors want you to leave them alone, and if you've hired good actors, you should leave them alone and sit back and enjoy their performance and make sure the camera gets the emotion they are trying so hard to feel. Other actors need guidance and someone to help them sculpt a performance, and know a little better what you want from them...what you want to see as the director. I think they all want to know if they're doing a good job or not, and as a director you may have to manipulate and be a bit of a psychologist to make them feel comfortable and that they are doing just fine.

What are two of the biggest pitfalls you have encountered in making independent films, and what is your advice to help others avoid the pitfalls from happening to them?

When I first started directing I read every book I could get my hands on. I felt like I knew what I was doing, but I wanted to see what other successful directors had to say about the process. I yellow highlighted the stuff in the books I thought was important, and when I was finished I copied all the highlighted stuff onto a legal pad. The very first thing was "producers and technicians will ruin your film... IF YOU LET THEM." The important part being "if you let them." Be always aware that a good director listens to everyone. I've seen it. They might not do everything suggested, but if you're smart you realize that one person can't think of everything and there is a lot of value in brainstorming ideas. But it's your vision and some things are just instinct and from the heart and don't let anyone interfere with that. Film is forever.

In your experience, what makes a great movie monster and why?

To me, the great movie monsters were Frankenstein, the Wolfman, The Creature from the Black Lagoon, Regan from THE EXORCIST (1973), The Alien, Hannibal Lecter, Jason, Leatherface, and many more. They were great because they did what they were supposed to do...scare the living hell out of you.

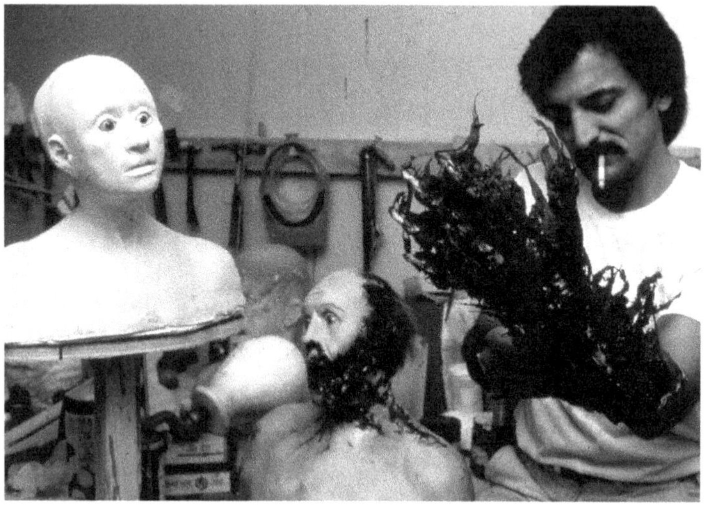

Savini in the makeup shop.

When you are doing special makeup FX on a horror film, what is your interaction like with the director? Can give us some insight on how this process works in the professional world?

The good directors let you do what you do and just put the camera in the right place for people to see it and give you the freedom to do your magic. Sometimes you have to educate a director that these are magic tricks and require maybe a setup shot to establish the weapon as lethal before you use the rubber one, or that moving the camera as the effect is happening might be detrimental to the effect of the illusion. Eventually my contracts included the clause that I direct the effect in the scene, and that helped so much in creating the magic. You don't just walk on the set and say here's what I'm going to do. There is a lot of conversation between the time you get the script and break it down into a list of effects that need to be done. I always have a lengthy conversation with the director to see exactly what he wants to see and that is my goal, and by the time you get to the set there are no surprises and in my experience that's what makes things go smoothly and a lot of fun for me and the director.

For low-budget horror films, what do you think makes the most effective types of monsters? What should filmmakers with big ideas but micro-budgets stay away from?

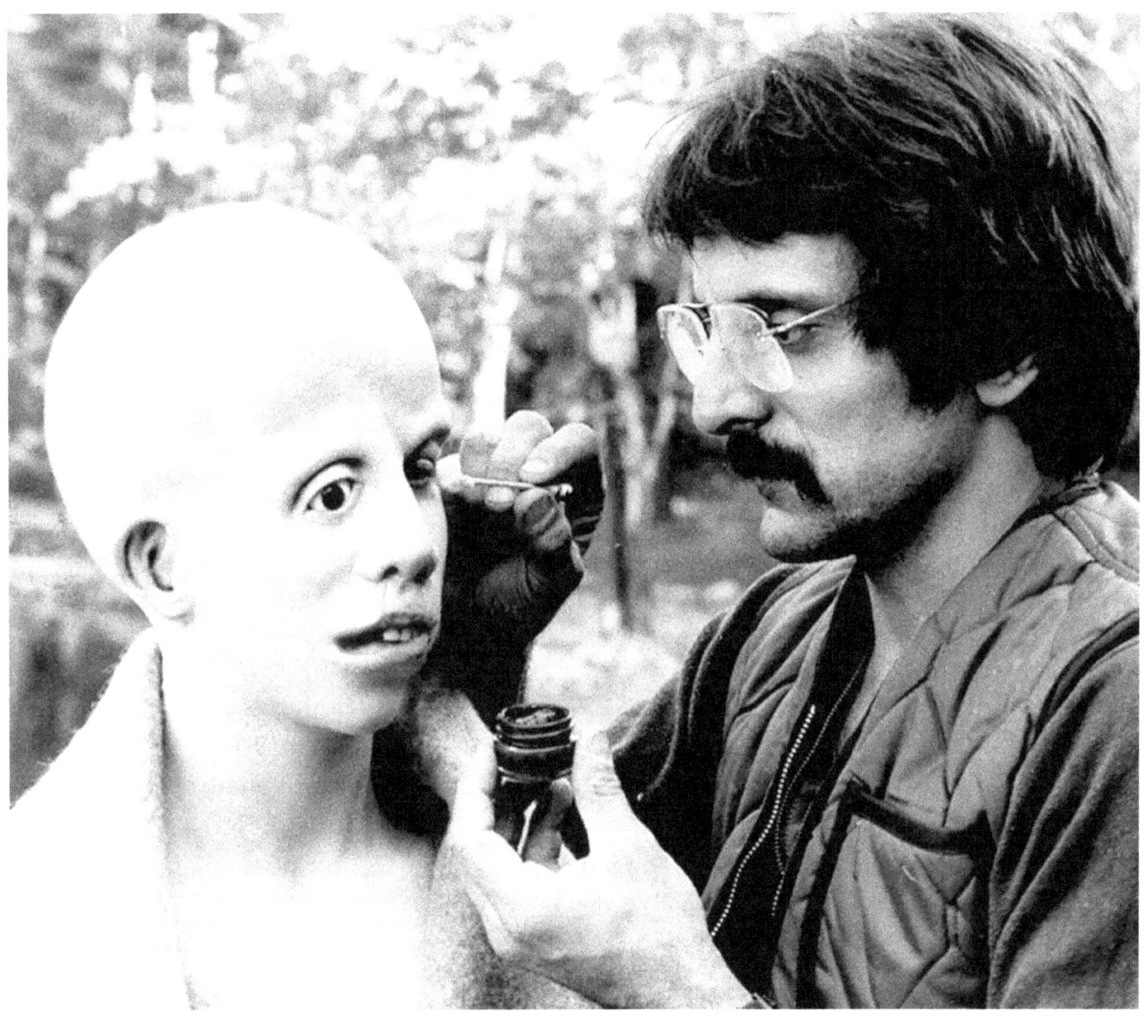

Savini on the set of FRIDAY THE 13TH. (1980)

I don't care what the budget is. Limitations always— always —make you more creative. It's your job to create what is required, and your mindset should be what do I need to see to make an audience believe what they are seeing is really happening. Then you create the pieces. Zombies are easy to do but hard to make scary; big hairy creatures might not be a good idea unless, like the shark in JAWS or the alien in ALIEN, you never see the whole thing until it matters. Once you see the monster your feeling is "oh is that it... well I can deal with that." So you postpone seeing it and build suspense, but of course the answer depends on the budget.

If you could choose three horror films that best demonstrate the use of simple, effective, low-budget FX, what would they be and why?

THE HAUNTING (1963), there was not one makeup effect or monster and it scares the hell out of you. It was psychological and went deep into your insecurities.

THE TEXAS CHAINSAW MASSACRE (1974), there probably was not a budget for makeup effects and lots of blood, but you never saw anything and the effect was truly horrific as you had to imagine the effect of what you were hearing off camera.

THE LEOPARD MAN (1943), again what you didn't see stuck with you and haunted your mind in the way the horrible stuff was presented.

What do you think are the three most important elements for a low-budget horror film to have?

A threat of some kind. A threat that makes you afraid of it and then the threat is placed in your vicinity. Suspense, anyone can jump up and say "boo" and you can just about scare anyone with that, but the really true and deep jolting scares come from suspense. A buildup of an outcome, a plunge into the unknown and then an unexpected turn of events that is shocking.

What are your thoughts on people making homemade bullet squibs?

I don't advocate making your own squibs. People email me about their films and they are putting firecrackers on their friend and I scream back... DON'T DO IT. Professional squibs bought after you've earned a license that are controlled is what I advocate and I do not want to talk about how I used to make them. Suffice it to say there was much experimenting to find a fine-grain, high-combustible black powder and a lot of thought going into making the explosion fire away from the subject safely. Firecrackers don't do that. I remained making them safe way before I got my license.

NEAL MARSHALL STEVENS

SCREENWRITER

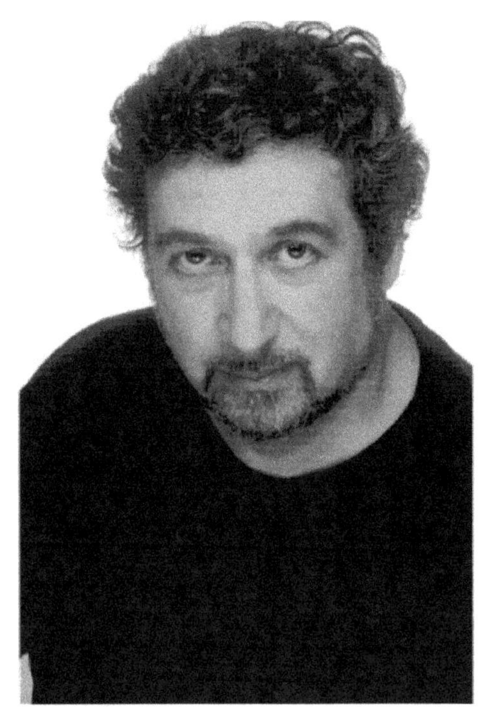

NEAL MARSHALL STEVENS

Neal Marshall Stevens has been writing for motion pictures and television for over twenty-five years. He began his career working for Laurel Entertainment starting in 1988, for which he wrote multiple episodes of the syndicated anthology series, MONSTERS, as well as serving as that show's creative consultant/story editor.

He's been extensively involved in the world of direct-to-video features for Charles Band's FULL MOON ENTERTAINMENT, where he's worked on over twenty-five projects, ranging from horror, to action, to children's fantasy, to science fiction. These DTV features include RETRO-PUPPETMASTER, HEAD OF THE FAMILY, THE CREEPS, THE WEREWOLF REBORN, TOTEM, THE SHRUNKEN CITY, MYSTERY MONSTERS, RAGDOLL, TALISMAN, and many more.

He also directed the feature, STITCHES, for FULL MOON ENTERTAINMENT in 2001, and in 2013 he wrote and directed the short thriller, THE TUB, for BFB ENTERTAINMENT.

Neal also wrote the screenplays for the theatrical feature, THIRTEEN GHOSTS, (DARK CASTLE ENTERTAINMENT – 2001), HELLRAISER:DEADER (DIMENSION PICTURES – 2005), and the science fiction thriller, SUPER HYBRID (STALLION MEDIA – 2011).

More recently, he has written a graphic novel, HAVOC BRIGADE, a science fiction thriller, released by STUDIO 407 in 2012.

You wrote such horror films as Thir13en GHOSTS (2001), HELLRAISER: Deader (2005) and SUPER HYBRID (2010) and have been prolific in a variety of other genres. What advice would you give to a filmmaker who is starting out with just an idea and is working toward making their first feature film?

The challenge for anyone, whether a screenwriter, director, or writer/director trying to break in is that there is a huge amount of material out there. There are tens of thousands of spec screenplays written every year and thousands of independent features, ranging from big budget indies with major stars to low-budget efforts shot in someone's back yard – that will simply never get bought in the former case and never find distribution in the latter.

As artists we're always told to follow our passion and we should try to tell stories that we're passionate about – but we're also creating products, either screenplays or finished films – that we want somebody to buy, that is, unless you're just looking to make movies to post for free on Youtube.

If that's the case, you have to think about that part of the process. You create art because you're trying to connect to an audience. If you don't care about connecting to an audience (if you're just "doing it to please yourself") then you shouldn't be surprised if your work fails to connect.

The whole accumulated craft of storytelling is there for the screenwriter/filmmaker to use in telling stories, not to mention everything we've learned and continue to learn about how to uniquely use the language of film to tell stories cinematically.

Yet, when I was working as a story editor at Laurel Entertainment, I read literally thousands of screenplays, many from unsold writers but also many from writers with produced credits and the overwhelming majority of them ranged from terrible to forgettable (which may be worse). If I could give a writer or filmmaker starting out just one piece of advice, it would be this. Of course, structure is important and connecting to an audience emotionally is important but the most important thing of all is to write something or direct something that is memorable.

There are scenes from movies that I saw when I was five years old that I remember as vividly as if I just saw them yesterday. Terrifying moments, funny moments, cool moments, heart-breaking moments, up-lifting moments.

Yet there are movies that I saw last year that I can barely remember even having seen at all. I've barely walked out of the theater and I've already started to forget them.

When you think of the movies that have really stuck with you, inevitably you will think of those movies in terms of a series of memorable moments – scenes, characters, lines of dialogue.

So let that be your goal. Find those memorable moments, the moments that, when a reader reads your script, or an audience member sees your script, those scenes, those characters, those exchanges of dialogue, will engrave themselves upon their memories so that fifty years from now, people will be saying – you remember that movie where that happened?

And of course they'll remember. Because everybody who saw it remembers. That's how you make a movie that endures.

When you worked on MONSTERS (1989-1991) the TV Series, what was the

creative process like coming up with stories for each episode? Did you ever run out of story and/or monster ideas?

MONSTERS had a story development process that was very different from other series, one that originated on their first series, TALES FROM THE DARKSIDE. Their original Creative Consultant for DARKSIDE was Tom Allen, a very interesting gentleman who worked as a film critic for the Village Voice and was also a Monk – he was a brother in the Franciscan Order.

So I'd first met Tom when someone I knew at NYU made an introduction and I brought him a script that I'd written and he invited me in and was very complimentary (although they didn't buy it). Later, when MONSTERS, the follow-up series to DARKSIDE came along, Tom invited me in to pitch for that show.

I pitched a bunch of ideas and then, just before I was about to leave, I tossed out one final idea that had really just struck me but which I hadn't really prepared – and that was the idea that you had this sort of folk healer who healed people by literally drawing the fever out of someone in the form of a literal monster and fighting it – and if he won, the person was cured and if not, they'd both die. And I really didn't have much more than that but that was the idea they responded to and ultimately bought.

That was my first professional sale. It was produced starring David McCallum (who I got to meet) and Dick Smith did the Make-Up (I also got to meet him) and it was the premiere episode of the series.

On a much sadder note, around half way through the first season, David Allen passed away and I got a call from Mitch Galin, the V.P., asking me if I'd be willing to step in, part time, to carry on as Creative Consultant – which, since I was running NYU's equipment room at the time, one of the worst jobs in the world, I was happy to do.

Unlike most shows, MONSTERS never had a writing staff. All of our writers were freelance. What I did as Creative Consultant (and what Tom did before me) was to have open submissions. We would read and evaluate anything from anybody, so long as they signed a release form, and we were one of the few shows that read unagented submissions and we produced a number of scripts from first-time writers.

We had interns who'd read those submissions, which were sometimes whole scripts, sometimes just treatments or outlines. They'd give me their evaluations. I'd look over the material, I'd make my recommendations and then pass them on up to Mitch Galin and Richard Rubinstein, the Boss, who'd sign of on the initial choices.

In addition, it was also my job to look for stories, both recent and also public domain stories, that could serve as the basis for adaptations and sometimes we had the authors do the adaptations (we had Gahan Wilson, for instance, adapt one of his stories) and we had a number of writers (many of them from the DARKSIDE days) also doing adaptations of short stories.

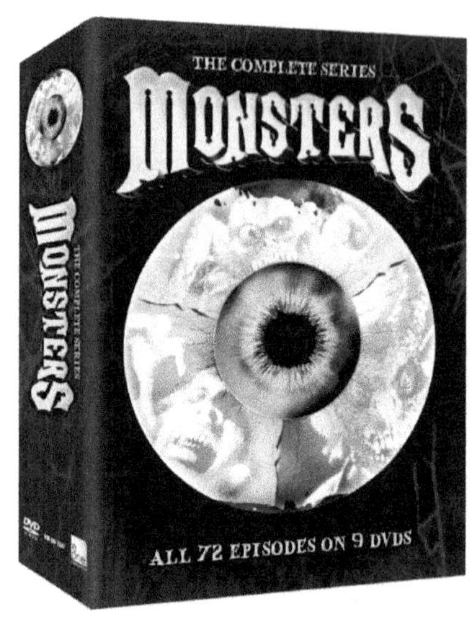

MONSTERS TV SERIES

We had two production teams running at the same time, one in New York and one in L.A., so we had to make sure that scripts for both sides of the country were up and ready for production on time – and mostly it worked.

Of course, part of the problem with MONSTERS is that we promised a monster for every episode but we were a very low-budget show with a very tight shooting schedule so there were times when we had very modest monsters.

I think that there was only one episode, HALF AS OLD AS TIME, that turned out to be a rather troubled episode and ended up with no monster. The original script was not shootable and had to be completely re-written and then, out on the west coast, the director (and I have to say, with the cooperation of the producer out there, and without really letting me know what was going on) decided to change the ending. The result was, they changed the monster from what was in the script and got a little ambitious about what the monster was going to do – and the footage turned out to be unusable.

So they ended up having to re-cut the ending – and the monster, which was a statue that was supposed to come to life (because, you see, it wasn't really a statue, it was a living thing just frozen in time) – and the bad guy was supposed to be sacrificed to him. Didn't happen. It never came to life. It's always just a statue.

But there were always more monsters and more story ideas. If there'd been a fourth season we could easily have gone on.

In your experience in the horror genre, what do you think are the key elements to a great horror story?

I think that when we look at the great horror movies they almost all have one thing in common. They all deal, in one way or another, with the violation of things that we consider normal, safe, or sacred.

There are certain fundamental things that we understand about this world – barriers that are not crossed. We should be safe in our houses, in our beds, in our bathrooms. When someone intrudes into those safe areas – the result is a feeling of horror.

We should have control over our bodies. When we lose that control – when we're paralyzed, or trapped somehow (stuck in quicksand, or trapped in a coffin) – we feel horror.

The people around us, our family, our friends – they should be as we know them. When we start to suspect that they are not, that they have changed in some inexplicable way, or maybe even have never been as we thought they were – we feel horror.

People think and feel and have hopes and dreams and souls – meat and viscera is just that stuff that we find inside the bodies of animals. The stuff that we eat (some of us, anyway). When we are reminded that we too are simply made of the same kind of stuff that we find inside animals – that we are made of meat – we feel horror.

There is an impassable barrier between the living and the dead. It is the fact that those who are dead do not come back that is, more than anything else, the defining quality of death. So whether the story you're telling is FRANKENSTEIN or NIGHT OF THE LIVING DEAD, when we experience the whole body of literary and cinematic stories that involve the dead returning to life – we feel horror.

We expect nature and the laws of nature to work. When we find ourselves confronted with a world in which the laws of nature begin to resemble the workings of a nightmare – we feel horror.

In the same way that we want to have control over our bodies, we also expect to have control over our minds and the possibility that someone or something might be controlling us, and when we begin to feel that knowingly or unknowingly, we may be acting against our own will – we feel horror.

A number of people try to work out the difference between a thriller and a horror movie and I try to make the difference clear when I talk about the sense of dread, which is present in a horror movie but not in a thriller. A car chase or being chased through the veldt by a lion involves risk of death – those scenes are part of a thriller. Finding a worm crawling under your skin or waking up in bed next to your wife – who you murdered last week and buried – those scenes are part of a horror movie.

In the horror genre, what are your favorite screen monsters, and why do they make great story characters?

There's a great challenge in terms of creating a "great" monster and "great" character. That's because you want a monster to be terrifying but in order to create a great character – any character – you have to create empathy between the character and the audience.

So we identify with Frankenstein's Monster. We identify with King Kong. And though it's a guilty pleasure, we also identify with Hannibal Lechter (I feel justified in including him since he is actually described in the movie as a "monster").

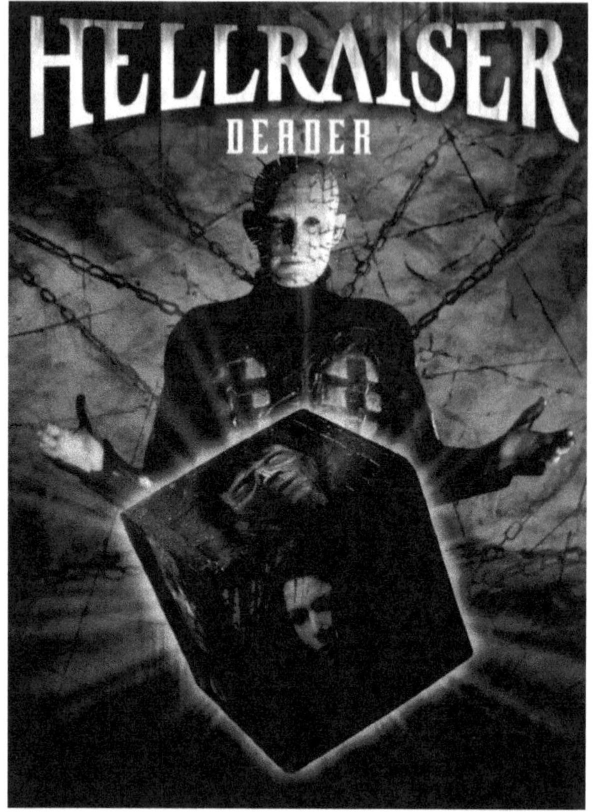

HELLRAISER: DEADER (2005), Dimension Films.

That, of course, is the challenge. These monsters embody contradictory impulses. In the latter two cases, (and maybe even in the case of Lechter) there is an aspiration toward humanity that can never be achieved because it comes into conflict with the "monster's" fundamental savage nature.

Kong reaches for the icon of civilization in the form of Ann Darrow but in the end he can never achieve it. He can only die in the end. Frankenstein's Monster can struggle toward humanity but he will never be part of it. His artificial nature dooms him to die an outcast. And Lecter even as he struggles to maintain civility, will never be civilized, but always a savage at heart. But in the absence of that conflict, monsters will always be mere forces of nature, not real personalities. That's not to say that those kinds of monsters can't be memorable in their own right. The original Terminator was just that kind of "force of nature" – he's just a machine with no conscience and no doubts and he will not stop.

Likewise the aliens in the various Aliens movies – you can't really think of them as having much in the way of personality – but they certainly work as terrifying monster/antagonists.

Godzilla, in all of his serious incarnations, is likewise, just like a force of nature. If anything, the more they tried to "humanize" Godzilla, the less interesting he became.

So a great monster can be a great character but it doesn't necessarily have to be.

The Alien is not really a great character – but it is a great monster. The same with the T-Rex in JURASSIC PARK or those nasty brain things in FIEND WITHOUT A FACE.

It's not that they don't have a kind of character. They do, but it's limited, in the way the behavior of a rat or an insect is limited. It's more a kind of behavior that allows us to relate to them as a scary, natural force – not as we would relate to a person.

If anything, for many kinds of monsters, their very lack of humanity is part of what makes them scary. That's why things like swarms of ants or rats or their giant equivalents are so terrifying – it's because we know that there is a fundamental distance between what they are and what we are

In the horror genre, what are the biggest mistakes you see filmmakers make when creating a monster on a low budget?

I think that there are usually two big mistakes. First, the tendency to become overly ambitious – and that's true not only with monsters but with effects in general, whether it's gore effects or CGI or any other kind of effect. It's better to do something that you can do really well than to do something that you're only going to be able to pull off at eighty or ninety percent – because the audience can really tell the difference.

Along the same lines, there's an almost unavoidable temptation for filmmakers, when they've spent a lot of time and money on an effect to show it off – to really "let the audience see it." So almost always they'll show it long enough to kill the illusion. There are effects that will work for twenty frames that will fall apart if you hold it for twenty-two frames and other effects that will work in shadows that will fall apart if you show them fully lit.

Just think about the scene in THE CONJURING when the girl points to the dark space behind the door. "It's right there. It's standing behind you…" And the audience just stares into that dark space, trying to see what she sees. Seriously, there's nothing that you could put in there that would have been any scarier than just that darkness and that girl's terrified face.

Few people know, that in 1895 Thomas Edison produced an 18-second film which depicts the beheading of Mary, Queen of Scots called THE EXECUTION OF MARY STUART. Arguably, that would make him one of film's earliest horror film producers! Even in 1895, an execution was chosen as the subject of a film. Do you feel as if we as a culture are desensitized to the gore and sex in horror movies and as a result the films are becoming more and more extreme? Is there a way we can fix this, or should we?

Unfortunately, there's no way that you can put that genie back in the bottle, whether you're talking about explicit sexual content, or language, or explicit gore.

When the original unrated DAWN OF THE DEAD first came out, I was one of the first people on line to see it and anyone who saw the first ten minutes of that movie back then were seeing images that had simply never been put on film before in terms of explicit gore.

I mean, you had those Herschell Gordon Lewis movies before that, but those things were so obviously unrealistic at every level that you simply couldn't take them seriously. This was completely different and while the prosthetic work might seem crude by today's standards, for those who saw it then (like me), it was incredibly shocking.

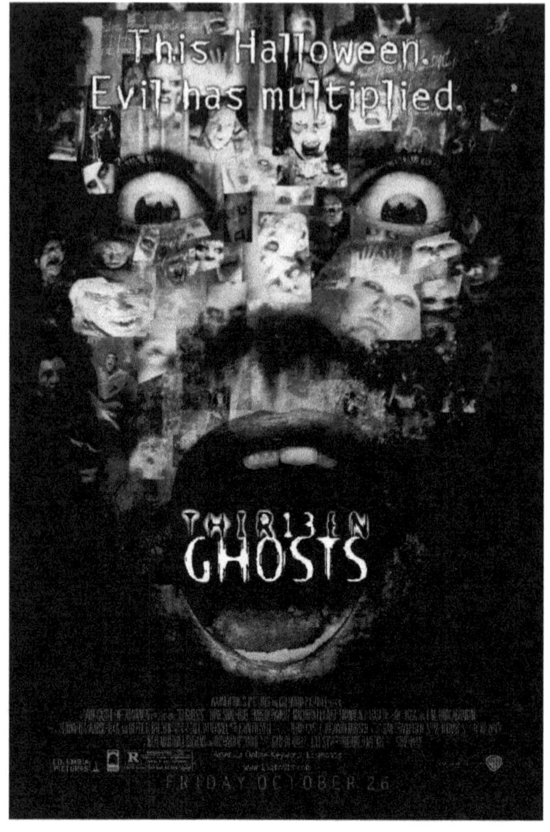

THIR13EN GHOSTS (2001), Dark Castle Entertainment.

Now today, that level of graphic violence is commonplace. GAME OF THRONES is, if anything, even more bloody and more violent than the original unrated DAWN OF THE DEAD.

So you talk to moviegoers today and try to explain what it was like watching that movie when it first came out and it just isn't possible, given the movies that they've watched growing up, for them to understand what that experience was like.

The fact is, they simply can't have a comparable experience. When you compare what the cinematic world was like before DAWN and after it – given where we are now and the extremes of gore that are routinely put on film – there isn't any place that we can go in terms of explicit violence such that audience would see it and say – My God, I've never seen anything like that before.

I mean, you always have the potential to explore material that is simply deeply offensive, like explicit rape or child-killing but if you're going to tackle subjects like that and the goal is simply to shock, then we've moved out of making horror movies and are simply entering the realm of exploitation cinema in its very worst incarnation.

What is the best way for a new director to communicate with a writer?

Well, what I would like to see (and I must confess that this has only ever happened once with any director I've ever worked with) is for the director and the writer to actually sit down and talk through the script, so that they both fully understand what the script is actually about.

I've been amazed on any number of occasions to realize, in respect to my scripts and other scripts that I've worked that have been produced, that things that seemed perfectly obvious to me, were completely missed or misunderstood by the director.

To just be able to sit down and go through the script with the writer and not talk about how it's going to shot but to just talk about what the scene is about, what's actually going on in the scene – because very often what seems to be happening isn't what's really happening. And as a writer we struggle to write those scenes in a way that make them interesting so that the characters seem to be saying one thing but really, it's obvious that they mean something else. Only to have it turn out that it wasn't quite as obvious as we thought because we come back and see the scene as the director and actors shot it, and they completely failed to convey the "something else" that the scene was supposed to be about, thus making the entire scene completely pointless or maybe even meaning the exact opposite of what it was supposed to mean. You might think that – oh, that doesn't really happen, does it? But you can watch major motion pictures and it'll pop up all the time.

For instance, you'll write a scene with a particular prop or a location in mind and the dialogue will be specific to that particular prop or that location. But for whatever reason, the prop master never bothered to read the script but simply got a list of props and didn't quite supply the correct prop, or else they changed locations but somewhere along the line, the dialogue was never corrected to fit the new prop or the new location – and it's obvious to anyone watching the movie that the line doesn't fit – but somehow it wasn't obvious to the director or the actors and any of the dozens of people on the set.

If you could chose 3 films to suggest to a new filmmaker as an example of great screenwriting in the horror genre what films would those be and why?

If I were to suggest three screenplays, I suppose they'd be to three of the great movies in the genre, THE EXORCIST, THE SHINING, and THE SILENCE OF THE LAMBS.

These movies have what any great movie in any genre has – memorable scenes and characters but also what horror movies in particular also must have – that profound sense of dread, of characters who enter into dark realms (or in term find the darkness invading their safe havens) who have those parts of their lives that think of as most inviolate and precious threatened, penetrated, contaminated, infiltrated by the forces of evil.

If pinhead and Freddy were to face off, who do you think would win?

Well, obviously Pinhead would win – he has all the forces of Hell at his command!

TIBOR TAKACS
DIRECTOR

www.tibortakacs.com

Tibor Takacs is a director of over 20 feature films and numerous episodes of network television shows. Tibor is one of the creators of the successful franchise SABRINA THE TEENAGE WITCH ABC, and is the director of the acclaimed film THE GATE, his most recent television work includes multiple episodes of the hit series MY BABYSITTER IS A VAMPIRE for the Disney Channel. His most recent feature film SPIDERS 3D produced by Millennium Entertainment/NuImage was shot in 3D and won best director at the 3DFF in 2013. Another of his TV movies BUNKS for Disney/Fresh TV was recently nominated for 2 Canadian Screen Awards 2015 Best mini series or TV movie and Best Director of a Mini Series or TV movie.

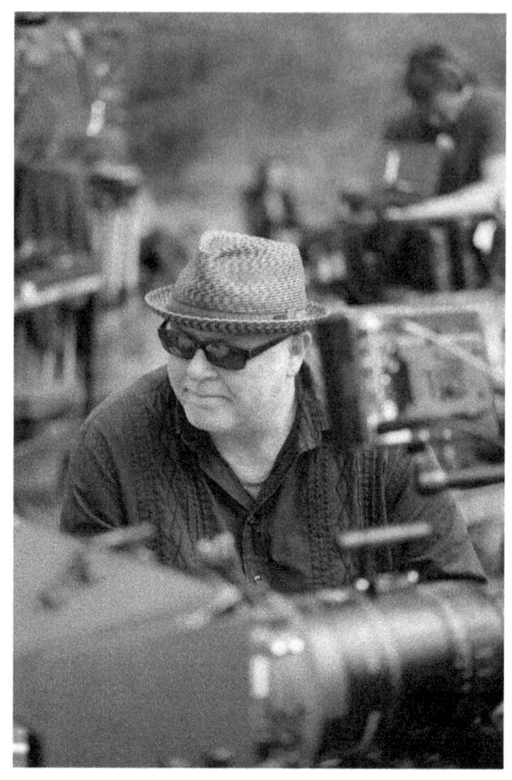

TIBOR TAKACS

Why did you want to become a director? Also, how did you get into directing horror and sci-fi films?

I was a big fan of movies from a young age, my parents took me to a lot of films mostly European fare. I read a lot as a kid and became interested in the way books were turned into movies. In high school we had a history assignment and a friend suggested we do it on film. I had access to my dad's super 8 movie camera and a hand cranked little editor. My friend and I had already shot several playful vignettes that lead us to believe we could shoot a movie. It was about pollution and the environment. After that assignment I knew I wanted to be a director. Like a lot of genre fans I watched Twilight Zone and Outer Limits on re-runs and those stories appealed to me on many levels. Sci-fi and Fantasy stories seem to be the most direct way to explore the human condition without hitting you over the head with politics.

What is your approach to working with actors on set? Also, does working with a celebrity require a different approach?

I just try to create a comfortable playful environment on set and I try very hard not to expose them to the pressures of production. The best advise I have for new directors is give your actors more attention than you ever thought they would need. Make sure they have the time and space to do their best work. Most of your work with the camera and sets and props should have been done in prep so you can focus on the actors and their performances. As for working with celebrities I suggest making their time on set as short and pleasant as possible don't waste their time by calling them to set when you are not ready to rehearse or shoot.

Do you like working in film or television better?

They all have their merits. On a TV series you have an opportunity to focus on character development so you aren't expected to constantly create spectacle. You have time to spend with actors and they already know a lot about their characters, the audience is invested and are willing to stay put without too much eye candy. TV movies want to be somewhere in the middle where focus between character and spectacle are split but you really need to worry about the audience pressing the remote and changing the channel. In a theatrical movie you have the most latitude because once people buy a ticket they have an intention to enjoy the show, it would have to be very boring to have them walk out. The same goes for VOD.

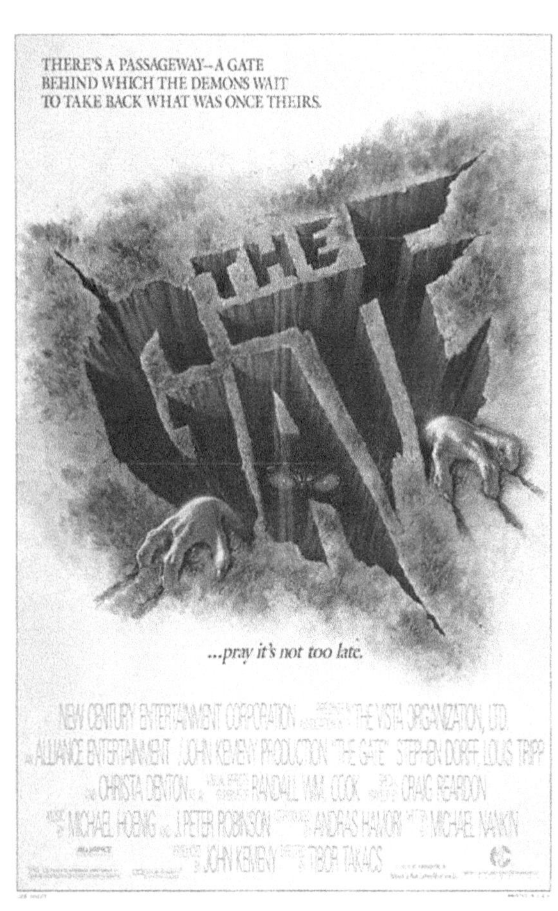

THE GATE (1987) Directed by TIBOR TAKACS.

When casting, what is the number one quality you look for in an actor?

I ask myself the question will I be able to work with this person comfortably and what extra layer will they bring to the character that I may not have thought of. Are they reacting more than acting and can they relax enough to be in the moment?

When you're on set and sitting in video village, how do you decide on what was a good performance and what isn't?

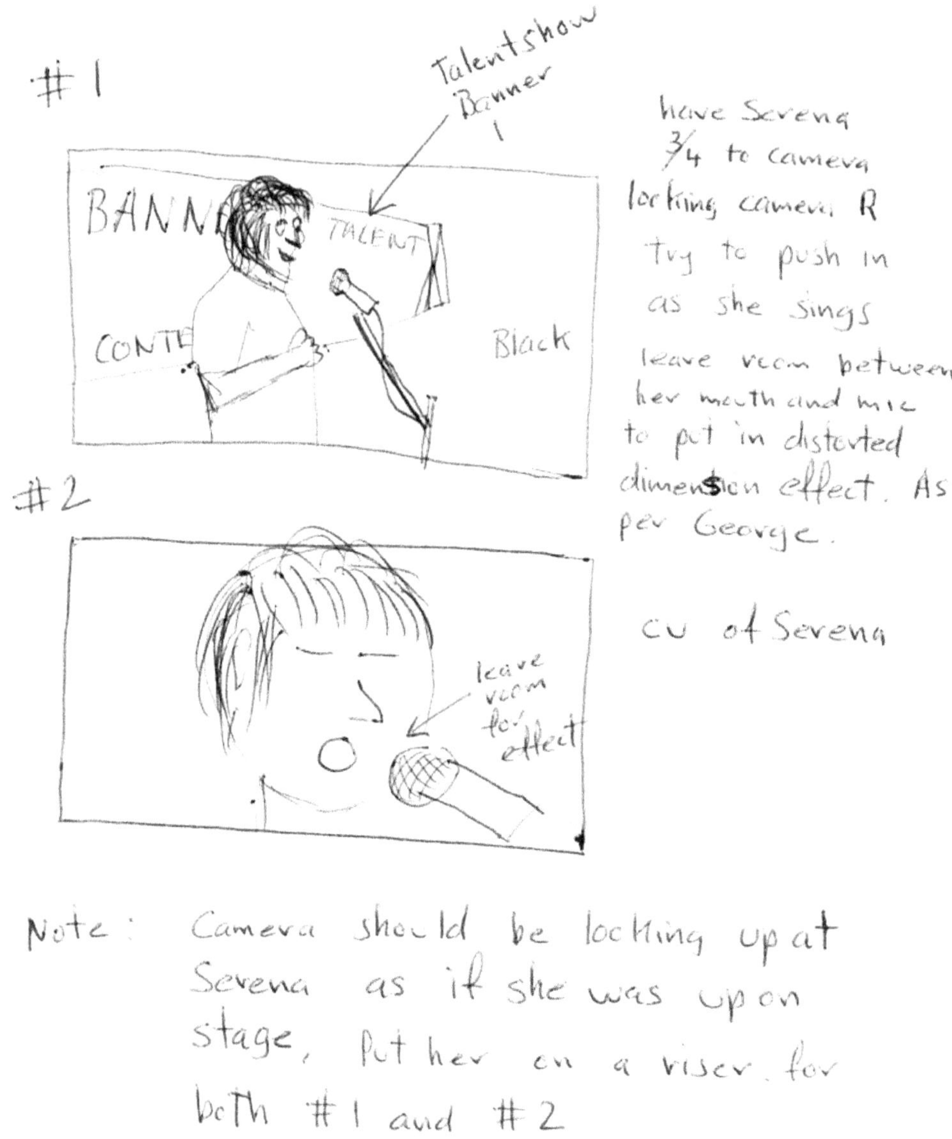

A primitive doodle done by Tibor describing inserts for a B camera on a TV show.

Maybe this sounds obvious but I need to just block out all the distractions of the set and put what I'm watching on the monitor into the context of the finished film. Is what I'm watching compelling? Once the shot is over think about what came before this shot and what is coming after, does this take fit and match with the rest of the performance and the film?

You've worked on many films that required large amounts of CGI shots and

CGI creatures. What would your advice be to a new filmmaker about to embark on a CGI heavy production? Any pitfalls they can avoid?

Prepare prepare and then prepare some more. Be efficient with CGI don't waste resources on shots that are not needed to tell the story. Storyboards are a must for the special sequences.

Do you do a lot of storyboarding? If so, why is this helpful?

Yes, it forces you to consider all the elements and aspects of the shot you are planning, then even if you change it on set you already know so much about what you need that you can improvise some improvement on what you had planned or easily shoot the board and pickup time to spend on other stuff you may not have so much control over.

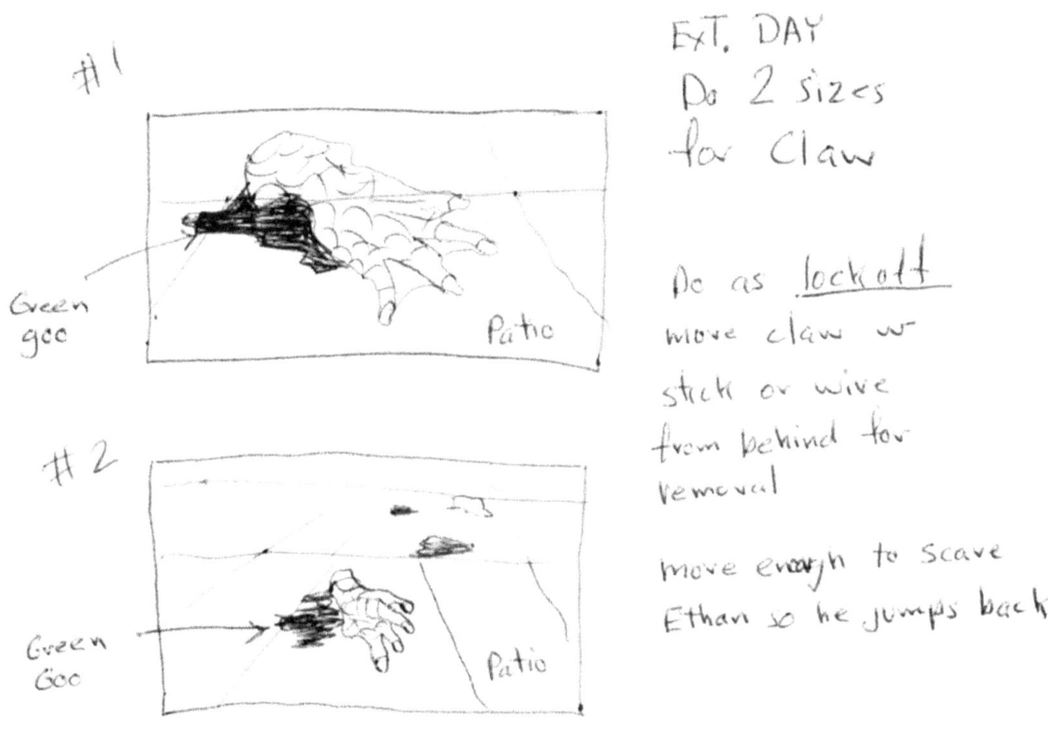

A primitive doodle done by Tibor describing inserts for a B camera on a TV show.

What were some of your biggest challenges working with 3D technology on SPIDERS 3D (2013)?

Overall the biggest challenge was trying to do a 3D film on a 2D budget.

In prep the challenge was evaluating and gathering all the off the shelf components to be able to view real time 3D on set. Luckily we had decent prep time and our DP Lorenzo Senatore was very tech savvy together we were able to track down all the equipment and software needed.

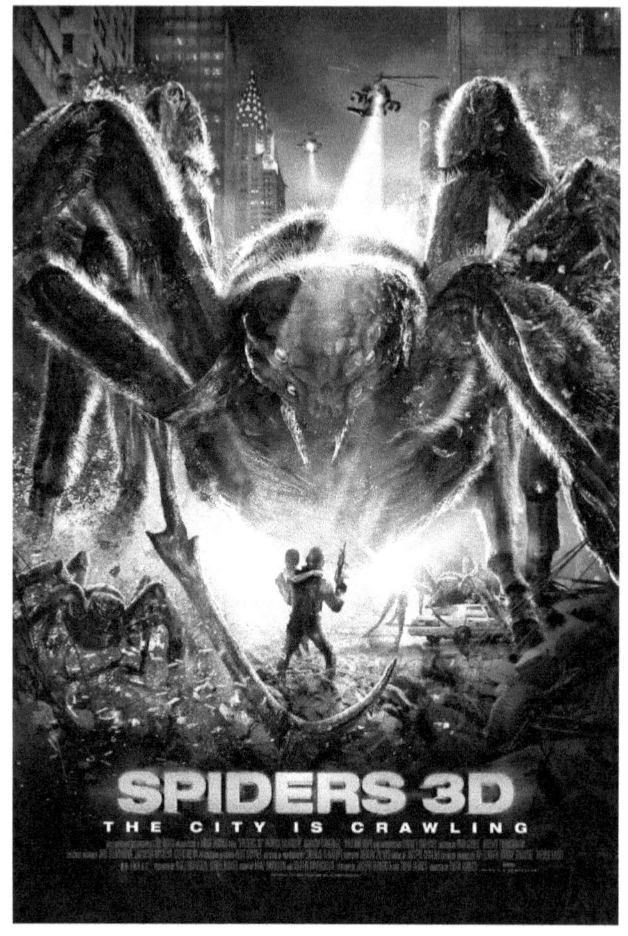

SPIDERS 3D (2013). Directed by TIBOR TAKACS.

The actual shoot went pretty smoothly, Scott Connolly our 3D systems tech kept all the complex equipment running and I carefully scheduled all lens changes which take a long time, up to 30min with alignments etc. The only thing I remember that ever slowed us down were a few overheated hard drives and a logistical problem in the first few days that prevented us from getting to evaluate our planned workflow using footage from the set. The rest of the shoot went along without major incident. As the shoot progressed the 3D aspects of the image capture faded into the background and became routine all managed very well and efficiently by our stereographer Phil Brown and our DP Lorenzo.

I've always used constantly moving cameras to reveal and exaggerate depth in a scene, this style could have been problematic in 3D. Heavier cameras, longer setup times, more light needed all make it way more difficult. But by using the latest technology incorporating lightweight cameras and portable 3D rigs I found that my regular shooting style translated very well to getting good 3D on a short schedule. With the budget we were given I needed to keep the 3D shooting process as close to the 2D shooting pace a possible. We were actually at one point getting up to 60 setups a day in 3D with near perfect alignments. Probably unheard of at the time. We were shooting a 3D movie on a 2D schedule.

I would have to say that the post production of the film was the most challenging. Since we were low budget we had to do all the 3D work (aside from the CGI) in-house so to speak using off the shelf software. None of us had any real experience delivering a full 3D feature for theatrical release to a distributor. On higher budgeted films the 3D aspects of the capture and post are contracted out to companies that specialize in this and charge a lot of money. Our 2 major tools were Final Cut

Pro and Assimilate. We did all the post 3D alignments, color correction, ghost-busting and simple compositing ourselves in a rented theater using Assimilate. We cut using Final Cut Pro our editor Joe Plenys and his assistant Tim configured a setup with the ability to watch any sequence on the timeline in 3D with the flip of a switch. As the edit progressed we settled into a pattern of mostly Joe working with a 2D monitor while I wore glasses and watched in 3D on another monitor. We had intermittent system crashes but it was workable. Our Colorist Nimrod Zalmanowitz also created our beautiful DCP that worked without a hitch. This is the final critical step in the process, the DCP is what is on the hard drive that arrives at the theater, a lot can go wrong in this step if you don't know what your doing. My biggest thrill was seeing Spiders 3D projected on a 70ft screen at the Archlight Cinema and being happy with the results. Managing the matrix of critical 3D issues like alignment, brightness , grain, and color was not easy but we had assembled a great team that pulled it off.

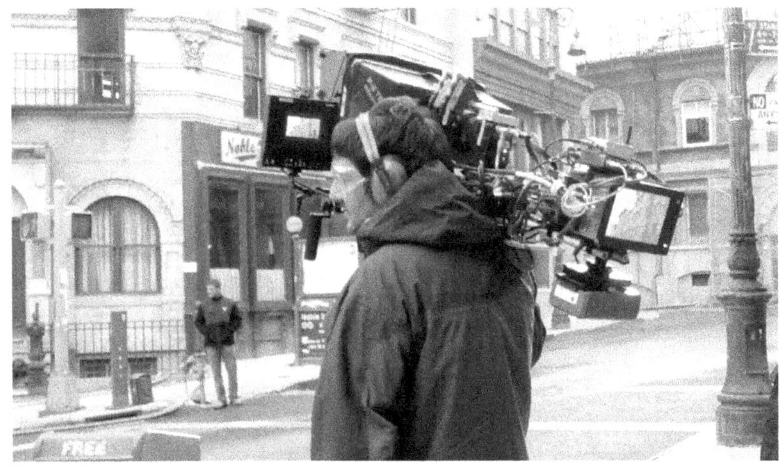
On the set of SPIDERS 3D (2013). With a special 3D camera rig.

What are some of the mistakes you see younger filmmakers make when directing for the first time?

Not focusing on the script enough, making sure that its the best it can be because if its not on the page it won't get into the film. No matter how perfect your film is technically it has to move the audience emotionally. Another suggestion is to understand that the audience's expectations rise as the film progresses so don't make the beginning more interesting than the end. Also the idea of withholding information from the audience till the last possible moment only supplying them information on a need to know basis. Its better to be intrigued than be bored in other words error on the side of confusion. Remember a big part of why they continue watching is to find out what will happen, what is coming next. I know these suggestions sound simple and obvious but you need to see and study them in other people's successful films and practice using them on your own. Years ago I heard a cool trick from a prolific successful screenwriter, when he thinks he's got a good draft he goes back into the script and removes every second line and then reads it again. Its surprising what stuff you find you don't need to tell your story.

Do you think aspiring filmmakers should go to film school or not? If not, what

is the best way to learn the trade?

At the moment I feel there is no obvious path for aspiring filmmakers to follow. The important thing is to gain discipline and develop good working habits under pressure. Get a degree in something and it doesn't have to be film. However film school can put you in touch with like minded people who can help you build a portfolio. Most importantly start making little films and videos as soon as you think you may want to be a filmmaker, the equipment doesn't matter, work on telling stories. Try writing scripts, read all you can about writing and watch a lot of movies. Try to find your style/voice this is the time to experiment and experience failure. Try to find ways to get your work seen, these days with all the latest technology its easier than ever to get a film made the trick is to find an appreciative audience. Being internet/social networking savvy is critical to getting your work out there and noticed by the right people.

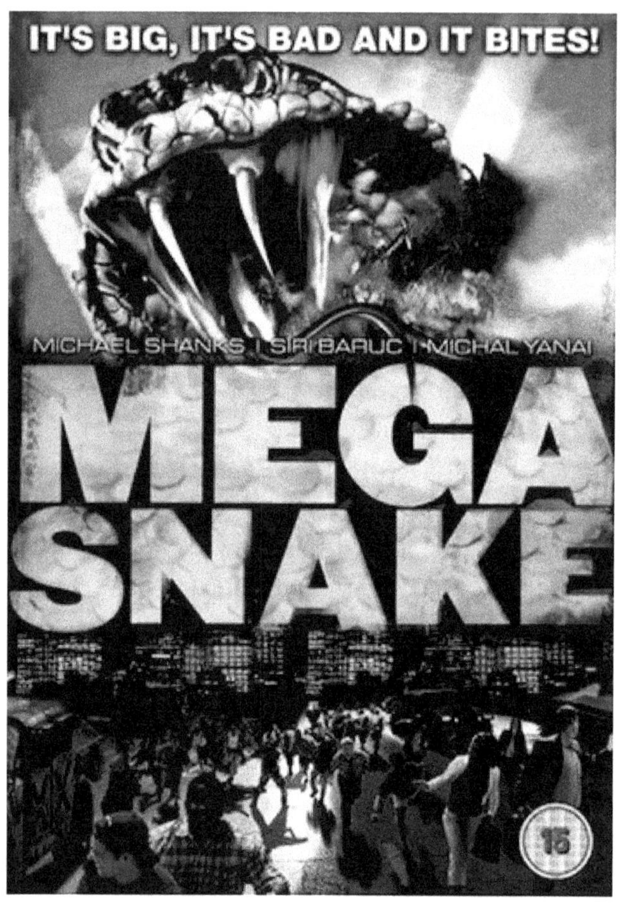

MEGASNAKE (2007). Directed by TIBOR TAKACS.

The following pages show storyboards that are directly from Tibor's film MEGASNAKE (2007) to show you an example of how some FX sequences are boarded.

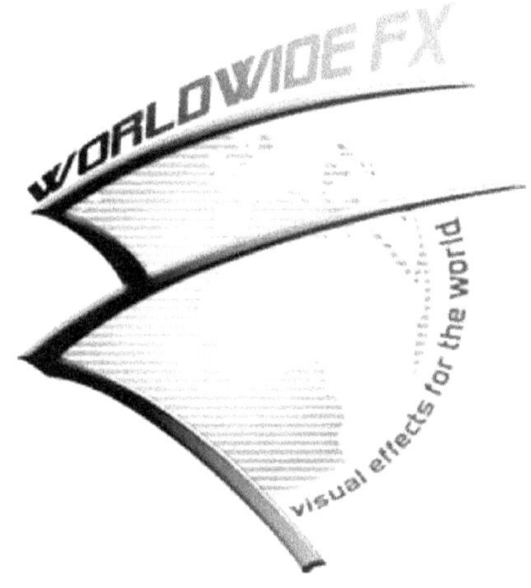

Megasnake

Sequence: Act2
Scene: Sc045

storyboard date : 2006-09-12 03:09:12
printed on : 2006-09-28 03:09:48

artists:
Victor Delchev

Megasnake / Act2 / Sc045 - 1 - Worldwide Fx 2006

PAGE 1 – MEGASNAKE STORYBOARDS

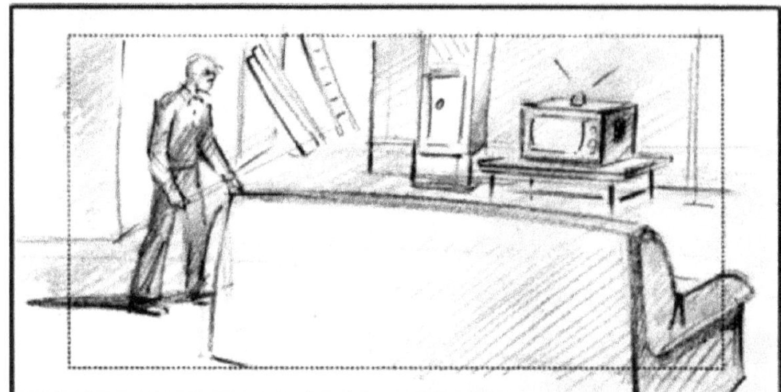

Sc045
Duff returns to the sofa....

Pg: / Night / Int

Artist: *Victor Delchev*

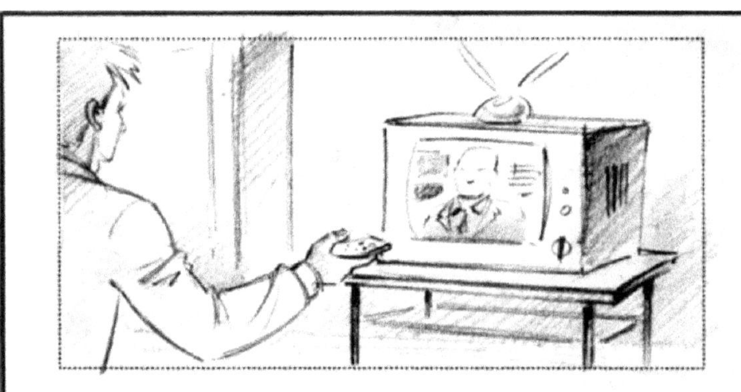

Sc045
Clicks the TV to an informercial...

Pg: / Night / Int

Artist: *Victor Delchev*

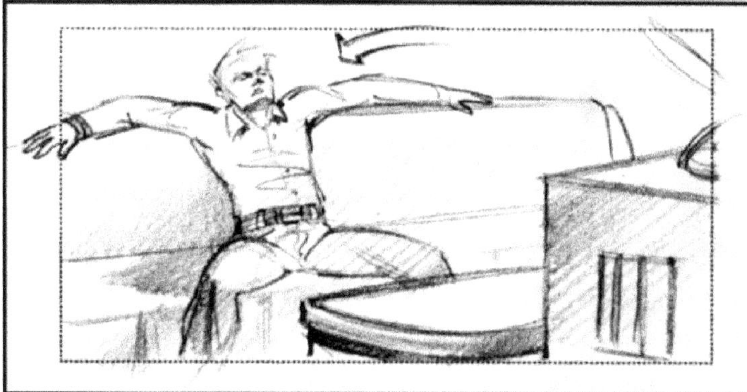

Sc045
and collapses onto the sofa with a WHOOSH....

Pg: / Night / Int

Artist: *Victor Delchev*

Megasnake / Act2 / Sc045 - 2 - Worldwide Fx 2006

PAGE 2– MEGASNAKE STORYBOARDS

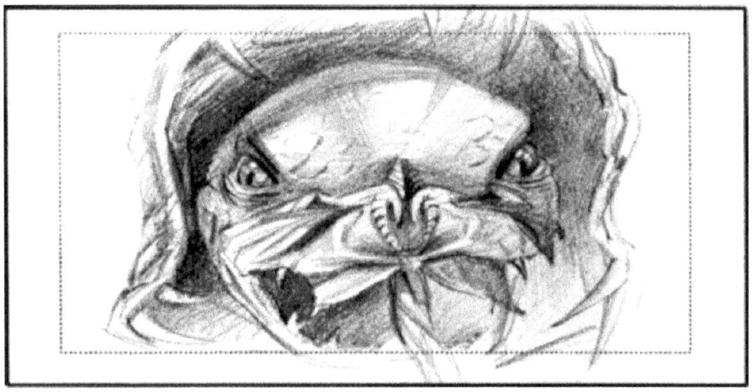

Sc045

The Untekaâs eyes pop open....

Pg: / Night / Int

Artist: *Victor Delchev*

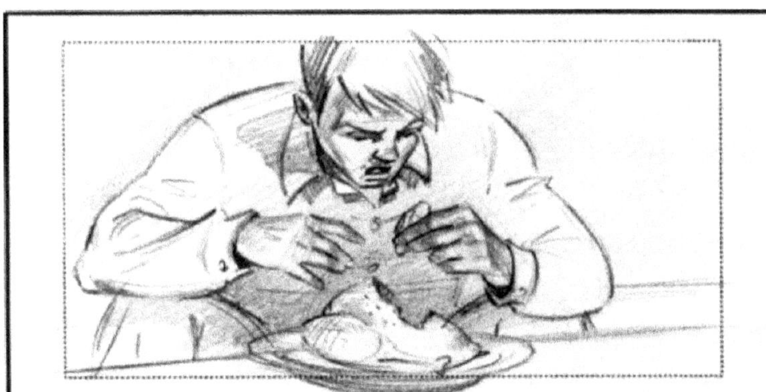

Sc045

Duff tears into chicken,...

Pg: / Night / Int

Artist: *Victor Delchev*

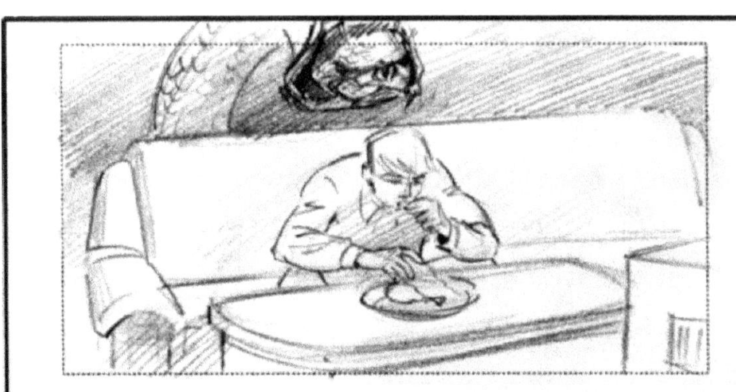

Sc045

oblivious to the red Unteka eyes cresting the sofa behind him....

Pg: / Night / Int

Artist: *Victor Delchev*

Megasnake / Act2 / Sc045 - 3 - Worldwide Fx 2006

PAGE 3– MEGASNAKE STORYBOARDS

Sc045
A sound. Duff whips his head around to check -...

Pg: / Night / Int

Artist: *Victor Delchev*

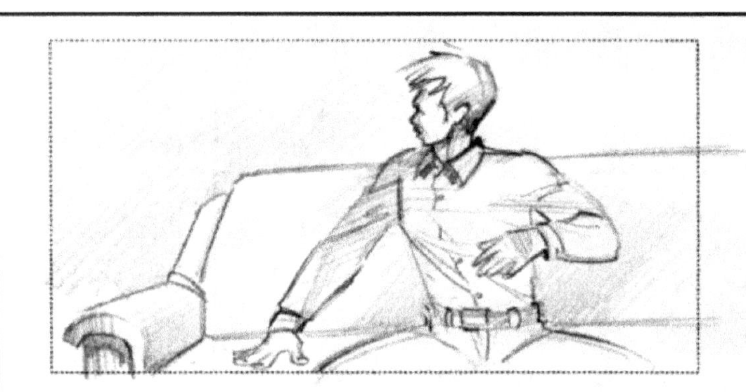

Sc045
But the Unteka moves in unison, staying just out of his sight....

Pg: / Night / Int

Artist: *Victor Delchev*

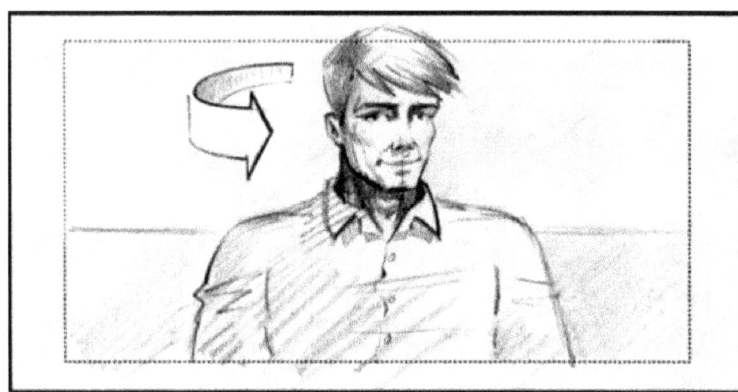

Sc045
Satisfied, Duff stretches out....

Pg: / Night / Int

Artist: *Victor Delchev*

Megasnake / Act2 / Sc045 - 4 - Worldwide Fx 2006

PAGE 4– MEGASNAKE STORYBOARDS

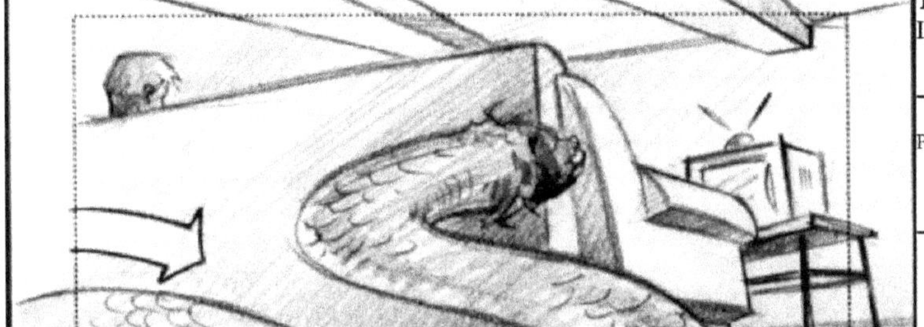

Sc045

The Untekaâs head glides around. Its body coils around the sofa....

Pg: / Night / Int

Artist: *Victor Delchev*

Sc045

ON DUFF: happily eating....

Pg: / Night / Int

Artist: *Victor Delchev*

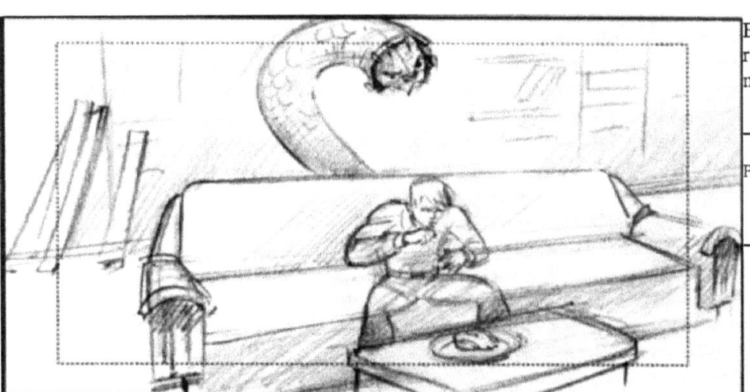

Sc045

Behind him, the Untekaâs head rises, giving us a taste of how much bigger heâs gotten....

Pg: / Night / Int

Artist: *Victor Delchev*

Megasnake / Act2 / Sc045 - 5 - Worldwide Fx 2006

PAGE 5– MEGASNAKE STORYBOARDS

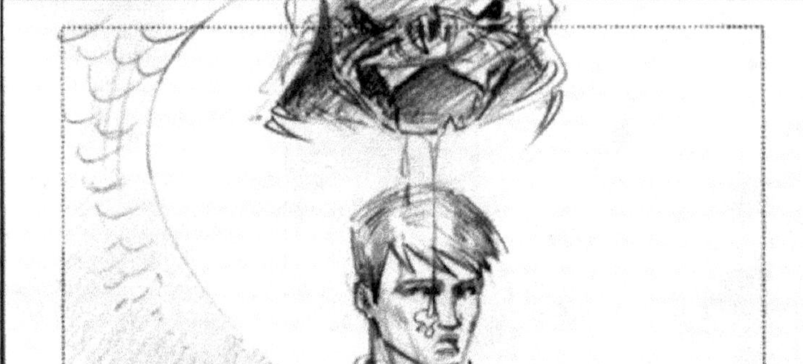

Sc045

Itâs jaw opens. A few strands of sticky saliva drip from its fangs......

Pg: / Night / Int

Artist: *Victor Delchev*

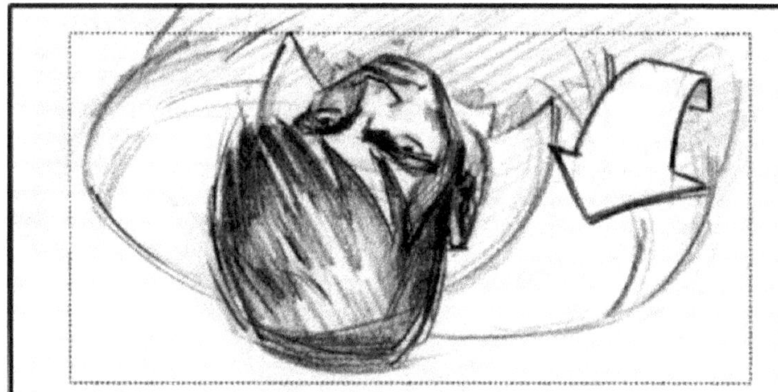

Sc045

Right onto Duffâs face. DUFF What the - He looks up ......

Pg: / Night / Int

Artist: *Victor Delchev*

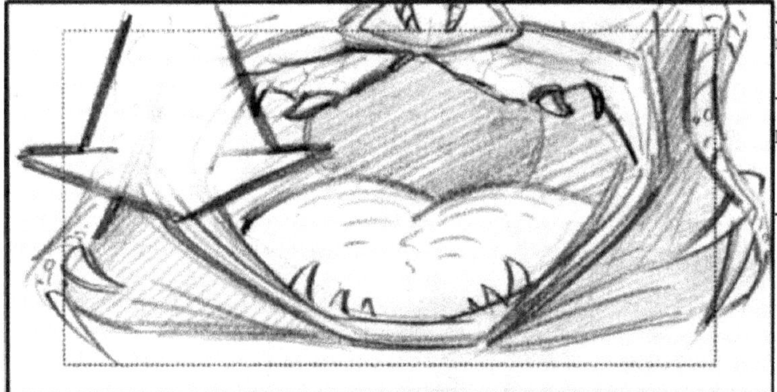

Sc045

Just in time to see the Untekaâs mouth CLAMP around his head....

Pg: / Night / Int

Artist: *Victor Delchev*

Megasnake / Act2 / Sc045 - 6 - Worldwide Fx 2006

PAGE 6– MEGASNAKE STORYBOARDS

Sc045

Duff kicks and struggles, but the Untekaâs jaws are incredibly strong....

Pg: / Night / Int

Artist: *Victor Delchev*

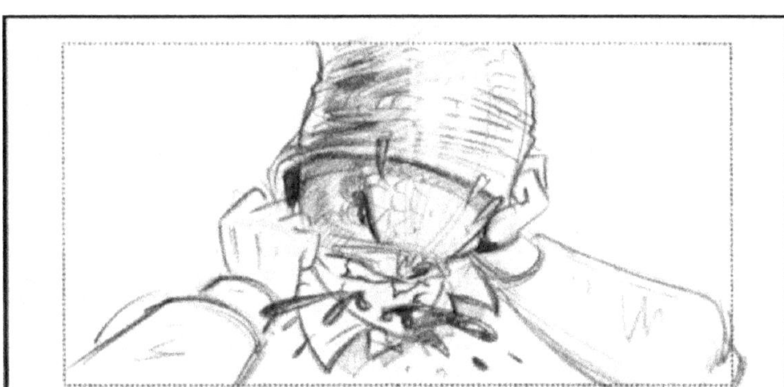

Sc045

We hear his faint cries from inside the Untekaâs head....

Pg: / Night / Int

Artist: *Victor Delchev*

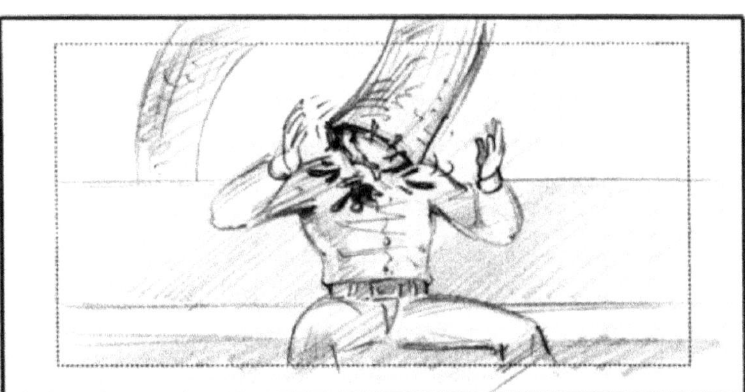

Sc045

As his screams reach a fevered crescendo - Duffâs head POPS. A juicy SQUISH. Like a grape in the Untekaâs mouth....

Pg: / Night / Int

Artist: *Victor Delchev*

Megasnake / Act2 / Sc045 - 7 - Worldwide Fx 2006

PAGE 7– MEGASNAKE STORYBOARDS

TONY TIMPONE

FORMER FANGORIA MAGAZINE, EDITOR-IN-CHIEF / AUTHOR / PRODUCER

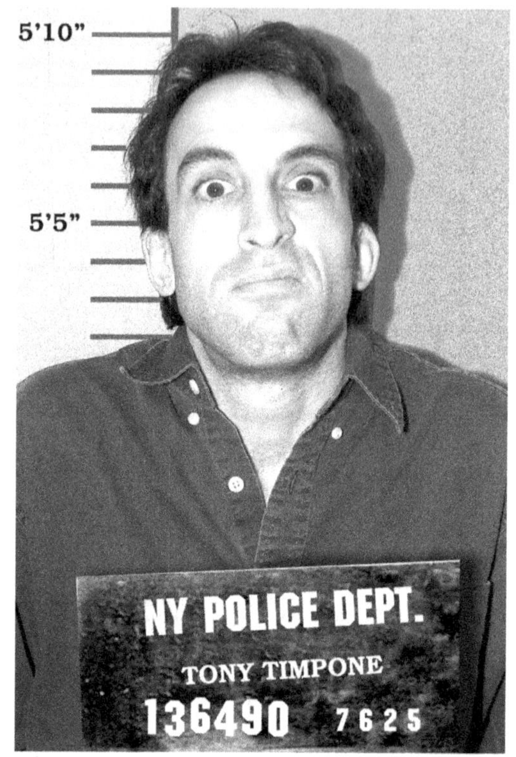

TONY TIMPONE

Tony Timpone began working with Fangoria magazine in 1985 and continued there until February 2010, when he was succeeded by Chris Alexander, a Toronto-based former writer for Rue Morgue.

In the early 1990s, Timpone helped guide the first three Fangoria movies for Columbia TriStar Home Video: Mindwarp, Children of the Night, and Severed Ties. In the early to mid-2000s, he served as an acquisitions chief for Fangoria's various video labels. In addition, he was a producer/interviewer for Fangoria TV's Screamography, a consulting producer/recurring guest on the now-defunct Fangoria Radio show with Dee Snider and Debbie Rochon, and the co-producer and long-time Master of Ceremonies of Fangoria's popular Weekend of Horrors conventions. Afterward, Timpone began running Fangoria's Video-on-Demand network.

Since 1993, Timpone has helped program international horror/fantasy festivals in Milan, Italy and Montreal, Canada. Before its closing, Timpone programmed and hosted The Two Boots Pioneer Theater's monthly "Monster Mondays" film series.

In 1996, Timpone authored the book Men, Makeup, and Monsters: Hollywood's Masters of Illusion and FX. In late 2004, he served as a producer on Bravo's five-hour documentary series The 100 Scariest Movie Moments. Timpone has been a frequent media spokesman for the horror industry, appearing on MTV, Nightline, Geraldo, Entertainment Tonight, Showbiz Today, CBS Evening News, and numerous documentaries.

Bio Source: Winkipedia

What is the current state of the horror genre? Is horror dead, or in a revival phase and why?

Horror is in better shape than ever. For example, looking at the industry trade bible Variety as a guide, seven out of the top 50 movies playing the weekend of February 13-16, 2009, were horror or dark genre films: FRIDAY THE 13TH, CORALINE, MY BLOODY VALENTINE 3D, TWILIGHT, THE UNBORN, UNDERWORLD: THE RISE OF THE LYCANS and THE UNINVITED. More people are seeing new horror films than ever before, fueled by the marketplace expansion by women turning out to see these movies in record numbers. For example, on opening weekend, 57 percent of the audience for the brutal LAST HOUSE ON THE LEFT remake was female. That's extraordinary when you consider the film's extreme subject matter and the fact that just 15 years ago, horror was a male-dominated genre.

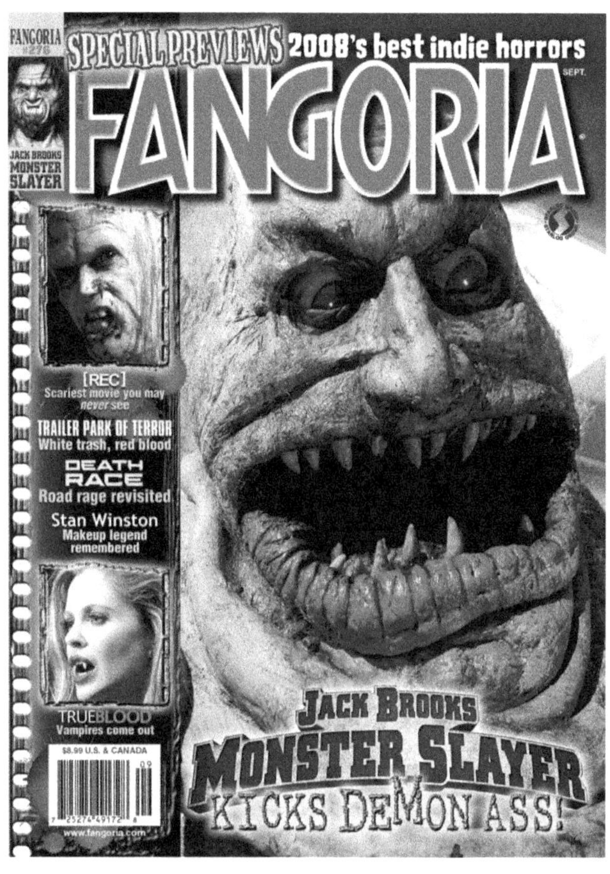

FANGORIA MAGAZINE

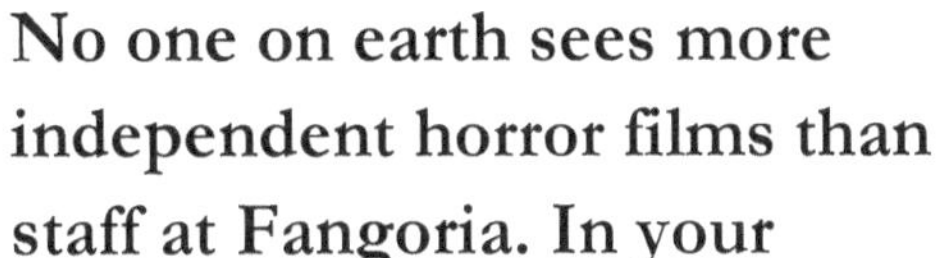

No one on earth sees more independent horror films than staff at Fangoria. In your experience at the magazine (formerly), what are the biggest pitfalls you see when reviewing horror films, both ultra low budget and studio films? Is it production quality, script, character, gore or something else, and why?

The big problem is usually story/screenplay and the inclusion of characters we care about. I want to be moved both emotionally and viscerally when I see a horror film, and not enough effort is put into those areas by filmmakers big and small. We have to identify with the characters. For me, everything else is secondary. Next, it's crucial, especially for low-budget films, that convincing/talented actors be hired to carry the film. Nothing pulls me out of a movie faster than amateur acting.

With the advent of new 3-D horror films, such as the remake of MY BLOODY VALENTINE 3-D (2009), do you think this is the new frontier for the horror film experience, and why?

Theater owners and studios have to compete with home entertainment systems that are almost as good as your average multiplex these days, so it is important for them to expand upon the movie-going experience and give the audience more bang for their buck. The 3-D systems today are much more sophisticated and "immersive" than the ones from the old days and the films less gimmicky, like the wonderful CORALINE. We will see more 3-D and Imax market penetration in the years ahead.

It seems to me that a lot of independent horror films and distributors are using B to Z level actors with a "name" value, even if that person is only in the film for a few minutes. Do you think this recycling of actors approach helps a movie in terms of fan response and sales, or is hurting the genre, and why?

For a fan, seeing a familiar genre face can make the difference in picking up a film for rental or purchase. But sometimes, hiring "low rent" actors will actually hurt the film from getting a distributor or finding their way into Blockbuster. I've heard stories from buyers who refuse to acquire C. Thomas Howell movies, for example, because he has been appearing in some many terrible Z-grade films in recent years.

As the longtime former editor and chief of Fangoria Magazine and an author, producer and horror scholar, what is it about the genre you love so much, and where do you think the future of horror will take us?

I always loved horror films because they are an escape from the mundane. I also seek an emotional engagement when I see a film, and horror movies, when done right, deliver that in spades, having viewers laughing and screaming and gasping for air.

Horror films are more popular than ever, and across many categories: from hard R slashers like FRIDAY THE 13TH to PG-13 supernatural romances like TWILIGHT. Sure, we will see a lot more remakes and TWILIGHT wannabes over the next few years, but as long as there is the occasional surprise like MARTYRS, INSIDE, CLOVERFIELD, LET THE RIGHT ONE IN, THE HOST, 28 DAYS LATER, THE ORPHANGE, SPLINTER and PAN'S LABYRINTH, the genre will continue to grow and challenge us.

JAMES WAN

DIRECTOR / PRODUCER

James Wan is the creator of the SAW series and director of SAW (2003), DEAD SILENCE (2007), DEATH SENTENCE (2007), INSIDIOUS (2010), INSIDIOUS: Chapter 2 (2013), THE CONJURING (2013), FURIOUS 7 (2015), THE CONJURING 2 (2016 and AQUAMAN (2018).

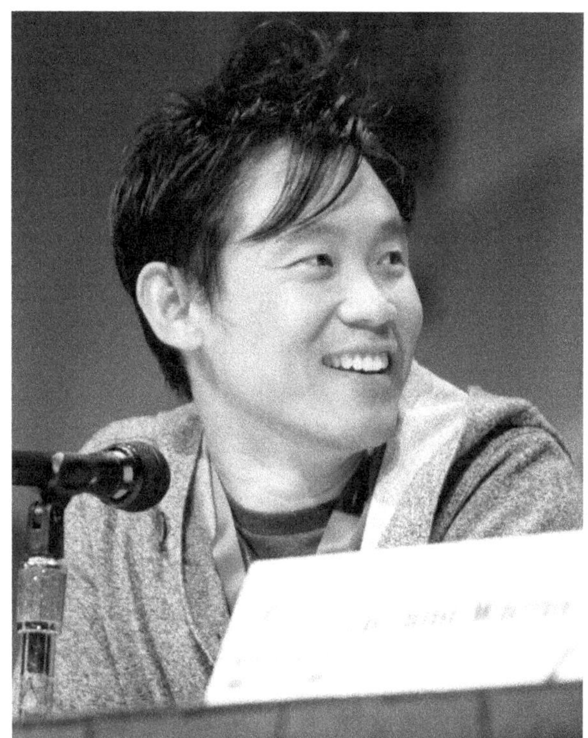

JAMES WAN
Photo Credit: Gage Skidmore (2013)

When directing a film, how do you prepare for the shoot? How do you visualize the film you want to make?

For me, it's very important to know the script inside out and have a strong vision for the film. This way, you can answer whatever questions people throw at you, and more importantly, you know which direction to improvise in when roadblocks inevitably arise.

This was the only way I could deal with the short shooting schedule for SAW, which was 18 days, and a super-low shooting budget (for a movie with a mainstream cast) of $700,000. As debilitating as it was to never get the shots you want due to budget and time constraints, at least when I was improvising by the seat of my pants, I knew that the overall picture would still be intact and therefore, I could let certain things go.

Do you use storyboards to help visualize the scenes?

Oddly enough, I'm not a big fan of storyboards even though my films tend to be very visual. Mainly, I use storyboards as a way to appease the producers/studio and to give them a peace of mind that I'm prepared for the shoot. If they feel confident in you, they'll support you more and stay off your back. But in terms of communicating with my crew, I sit down with my DP and production designer and we go through every single aspect of shots and sets, and I'll try to be as articulated as I can so that the filming can have a fighting chance at running smoothly.

What is the best way to approach directing actors in a horror film?

This is no different to directing actors in any other genre. Once again, if you know your film really well, you would know your characters too, and therefore you could guide your actors. Remember, communication is important. Your actors are like your friends, and you speak differently to one friend than you would to another. The dumb-ass joke you crack to one friend might be hilarious, while another friend might think it's totally stupid. This is the same with actors, and each actor needs to be approached differently. If you get to know them, then you'll know the best way to talk to them.

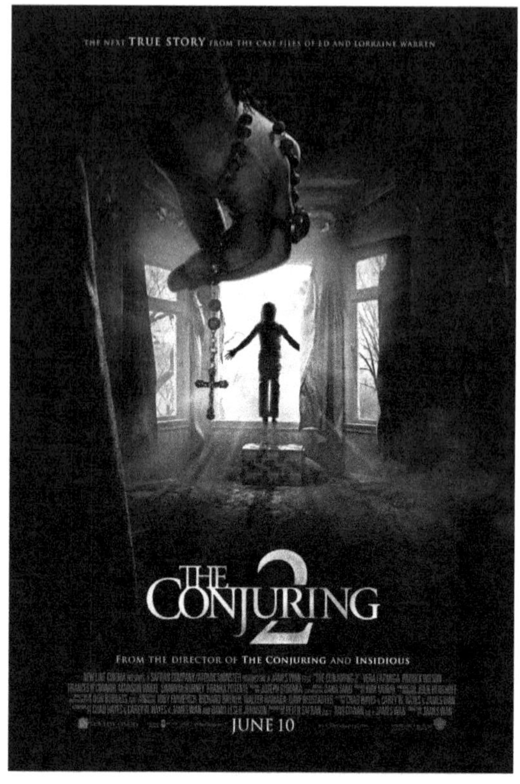

THE CONJURING 2 (2016)

What are the most important elements for a successful horror film to have, and why?

I think it's important for a successful horror movie to not be afraid to break the convention. The horror genre is so established that when a scary movie comes along and breaks some of the conventions, it is perceived as groundbreaking. I think this is what makes horror films so much fun—the unpredictability. That's why indie horror films are the best, because you're not constrained by the studio system that wants everything to be homogenized.

How is editing a horror film different from other genres?

Pacing and timing are very important. A good scare scene has the structure of telling a joke. You set up the gag, and then with the right timing, you throw in the punch line. That's how a scare works. You build up the tension (to a boiling point), and then you release the tension with a crescendo. This is usually a big "boo!" But stay away from fake scares. Nothing sucks more than the screeching cat that jumps out!

If you could pick one tip for an aspiring horror filmmaker, what would it be?

When I was in film school, I found that the best way for me to learn was to watch lots of movies that I admire and study them meticulously. And then I would just go off and put what I just learned into practice. Then over the years, from playing around making my short films, I found my own voice. Don't be afraid to just go out there and film something. And don't think it needs to be a masterpiece immediately, because ultimately, you'll learn more from your failures than your successes

CHUCK WILLIAMS

PRODUCER / ACTOR

www.chuckwilliamsfanclub.com

CHUCK WILLIAMS moved to Hollywood in 1983 to become an actor. His enthusiasm for every aspect of filmmaking quickly forced him to broaden his horizons. He has worked alongside such Hollywood heavyweights as James Cameron, Rob Cohen, Kathryn Bigelow, John Badham, Penelope Spheeris, Jonathan Kaplan, David Fincher, and Jim Kouf. Williams produced William Shatner's GROOM LAKE, Jeff Burr's Universal Studios' STRAIGHT INTO DARKNESS, Robert Englund's KILLER PAD, and the first American lucha libre film, MIL MASCARAS VS. THE AZTEC MUMMY. Most recently he produced THE TELLING with Bridget Marquardt and appeared opposite Bruce Campbell in Don Coscarelli's BUBBA HO-TEP.

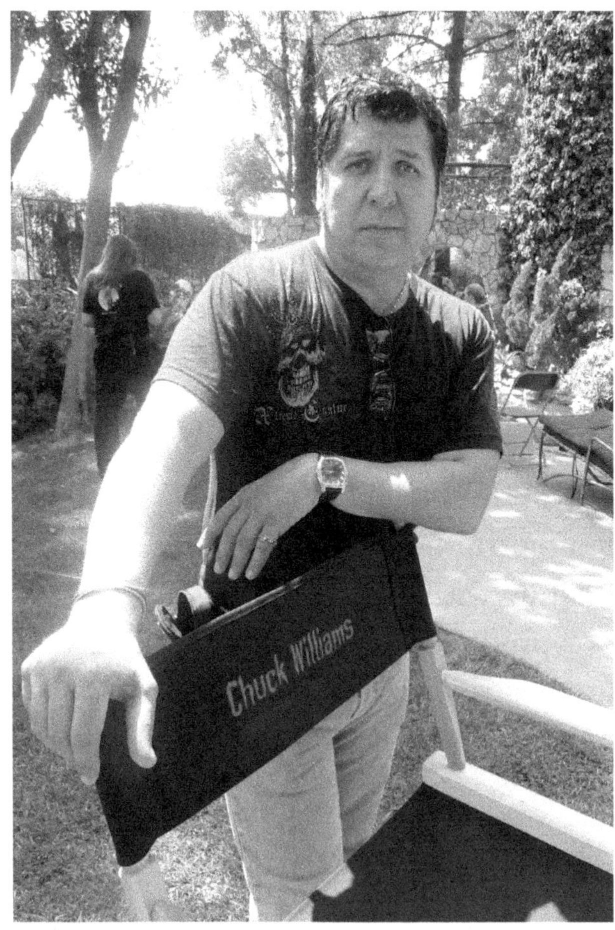

CHUCK WILLIAMS

What is the best way for a low-budget filmmaker to finance a horror film?

Rob a bank! Just kidding. Usually you first ask a family member to help get you started in the industry, and after you burn that bridge, you beg, borrow, and steal from investors, doctors, or anyone who owns a business. They'll usually take a chance on a low-budget film without getting hurt financially.

What are three of the biggest pitfalls you have encountered in making low-budget horror films?

One pitfall is having no money, which adds stress in every department. The second pitfall is that most folks think just because they own a camcorder they are ready to be filmmakers; nothing could be further from the truth. They should go spend some time on a set and get hands-on training. The third pitfall is filmmakers who hire inexperienced friends to fill important positions. This is a major pitfall. I suggest at least looking for film students in the local area to fill those unpaid, merciless jobs.

It seems to me that half the time when you hire friends you can't pay, it spells disaster for your friendship.

For a low-budget horror film, is it more beneficial to shoot in Los Angeles, or out of state, or possibly even out of the country?

I love filming outside of Los Angeles—I find most places are very accommodating with free locations, permits, crews, and there is also a general excitement that you're shooting in their town. Actors also love to shoot on location, and this is a big plus when attracting talented actors for very low pay.

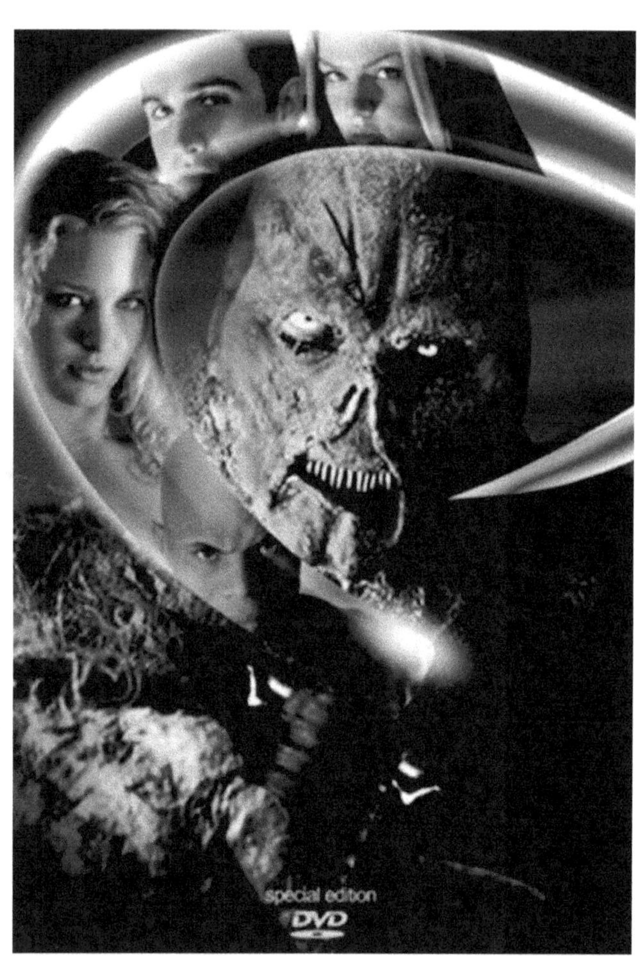

Williams as the Darkwalker!

When you're producing a low-budget horror film, what is your interaction with the director like? Does a producer's own ideas and budget restrictions often clash with the director's vision?

As a producer, you should never clash with a director. You are there to bring his vision to the screen. If not, you should have never hired him in the first place. Remember, all crew members in my book are artists. They all bring major talents to the table, and you should respect them. You should never spend time in breaking them down to feel they are not contributing. It's their film, too.

What are three tips you could share with new low-budget horror film producers to save money in the budget?

Firstly, treat everyone like family; this will help to get better communication and focus on your set, resulting in saving money and keeping everything smooth. Secondly, I used to send everyone to Costco, but now you must shop at the dollar stores for your craft service and other disposable items. You must never have a weak craft service table; your crew will start complaining, and mutiny will be right around the corner. You must feed them well with hot meals. Thirdly, you must negotiate every deal personally. Nobody is better at saving money than you. You must be hands on, not a loud-mouthed, chain-smoking, coffee-drinking producer calling the shots at arms length and completely annoying everyone.

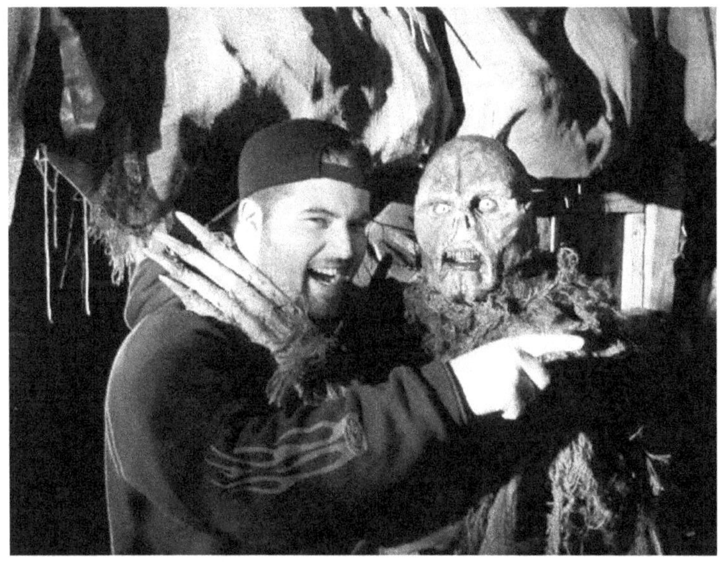

Danny Draven and Chuck Williams on the set of DARKWALKER in 2002.

What do you think are the three most important elements for a low-budget horror film to have to be sellable in the horror market?

The most important, I think, are a great story, gore, and an awesome soundtrack! A name actor is also a plus.

What is the Chuck Williams secret to dealing with day-to-day problems on set?

You should always be on set, never be cocky, and always listen to your crew. They know what is really happening, so you should treat them with respect. If you do that, I guarantee I'll be watching your movie on my HD 60-inch screen TV.

BONUS INTERVIEW:
DISCOVERY CHANNEL MAGAZINE INTERVIEW WITH DANNY DRAVEN

DISCOVERY CHANNEL MAGAZINE INTERVIEW WITH DANNY DRAVEN

Complete & Uncut Interview
Interviewed by Daniel Seifert for Discovery Channel Magazine (2014)

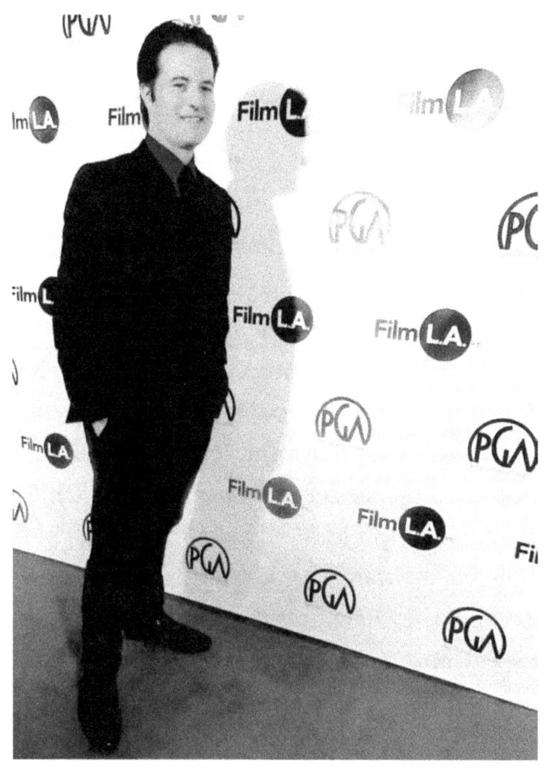

DANNY DRAVEN on the red carpet at the Producers Guild of America. He's been a member since 2009.

Excerpts of this interview were used in Discover Channel Magazine, issue 1408, for the cover story on horror called "BEHIND THE DOOR: The Science Behind Horror" written by Daniel Seifert. The following interview is the complete uncut version exclusively for the readers of TALK YOU TO DEATH.

DISCOVERY: What are you currently working on? And what's the best horror you've seen recently?

DRAVEN: I'm currently developing a TV series and writing several new genre scripts. I have also been in a mentorship with executive producer Mark Ordesky (Lord of the Rings trilogy), who's also executive producer with his Court Five partner Jane Fleming on a new series called THE QUEST on ABC. I'm learning from some amazing pros and redirecting my efforts to reach a wider audience with my work as a writer-director.

The best horror film I've seen recently was James Wan's THE CONJURING.

DISCOVERY: It seems like with the horror genre, more than any other, good editing is crucial, as you mention in your book. I'd imagine changing the timing of a scene by a second or two can completely negate the scare. Would that be fair to say (and do you have any examples)?

DRAVEN: A film starts with the writer but ends in the edit bay. In fact it often gets re-written in the edit bay in the form of cutting out scenes, repetitive dialogue, crosscuting, flashbacks, and the re-arranging of sequences. I started my career as an editor primarily in horror and sci-fi, and I can tell you first hand that an editor can make or break a scene. One misstep and an actor can look foolish or a story setup or scare can fall flat. When I edit a film I didn't direct, I actually don't look at the script until it's time to cut the scene. I cut the scene first, and then I read the scene as written, then I go back and make adjustments. I try to put my mind in the place of the audience, so when I cut a scene for the first time it stays fresh.

On a film I edited for SyFy Channel called ICE SPIDERS, I often had to retime scenes in order to make a "jump scare" work. I've found it's best to edit a scene in a way to give the audience time to let their guard down for just enough time to "scare" them back to attention. For instance, I could start a scene and show a spider hiding in the room, and build tension as characters enter the room and the spider moves around all while the characters don't know they're in danger, but the audience is aware. Or, I could edit the same scene where the characters enter the room and don't show any spider threat at all and then in a safe moment have the giant spider attack and scare the audience back to attention. Editing is like putting together a big puzzle so you just need to find the right pieces that click.

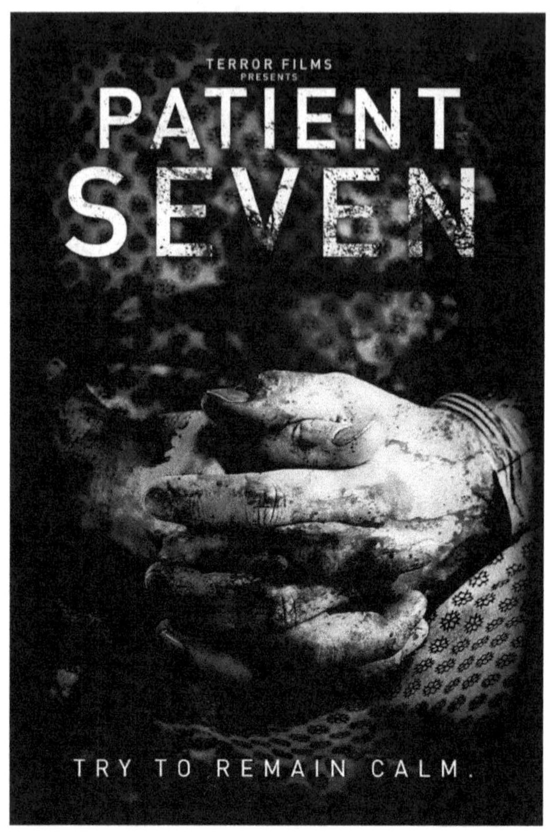

Danny Draven's latest film he directed for Terror Films called PATIENT SEVEN (2016) stars genre icon Michael Ironside (Total Recall, Scanners, Starship Troopers). Now on iTunes and Amazon!

DISCOVERY: Most audiences now think of the ol' pop-up/jump cut scare, like when a ghost jumps out of a corner, as simplistic. But I'd imagine setting up a good shock is rather complex; could you detail what it takes to create a good shocking scare?

DRAVEN: The best scares come when the audience least expects it. Part of the craft is to set this up and then pay it off. Masters of the craft sometimes pay it off more than once.

DISCOVERY: If we get into the nitty gritty, how do you use the camera to maximize fear? What angles work best/worst? Any insider tips you've picked up over your films would be great! (You mention in your Filmmakers Book of the Dead, for example, that handheld cameras should be used sparingly — is there a hard and fast rule you adhere to?

DRAVEN: Camera placement is very important and should always be decided upon by what method best facilitates the storytelling on screen. It's never a good idea to use flashy camera moves and "interesting" angles if there is no dramatic purpose to justify it. It can often have the opposite effect on the audience and quickly jar them or cause them to lose their suspension of disbelief mindset.

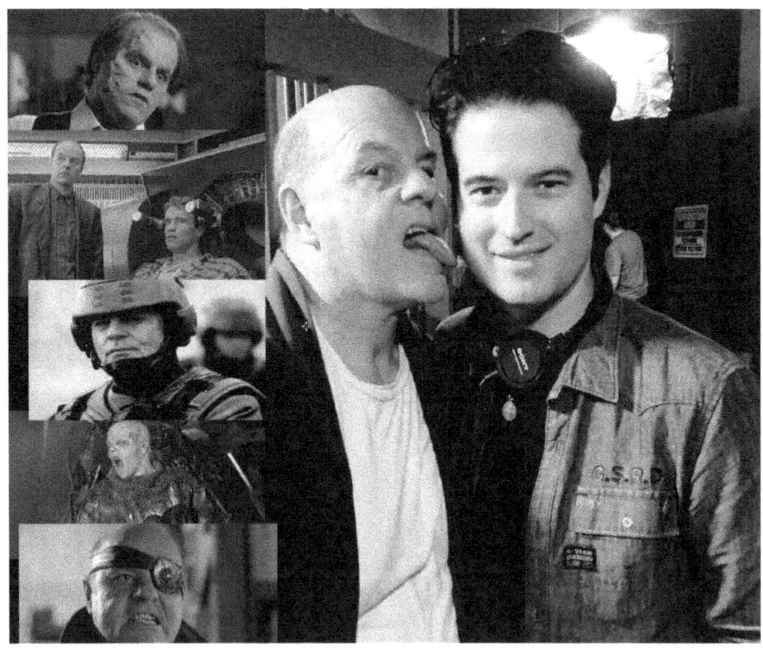

Draven on set of his new film PATIENT SEVEN (2016) with genre icon Michael Ironside (Total Recall, Scanners, Starship Troopers).

The director and the director of photography should always discuss lens choice, frame composition, camera movement, and shot coverage plans because all of these factors contribute to how an audience will experience the emotion of the scene. For instance, during a vicious fight, you may want to go handheld and keep the movement frenetic, for a solo piano performance you may want to use a camera dolly and do a slow push in to reveal the performer's face then tilt to his fingers in motion, or better yet invent a new way of doing it that is personal and unique to you as an artist. It's all very subjective and depends on the personal taste of the filmmakers, but for me, there should be no camerawork on screen that doesn't serve the story. Cool shots alone don't make cool movies.

DISCOVERY: On that note, do you have any examples when you found a scene in your films wasn't working, and you changed a small detail that suddenly made it click? It could be making an actress scream less clearly, changing the colour temperature of a shot, making a monster costume three inches shorter; whatever!

DRAVEN: It happens quite often on set. It comes with the job, but it's how you handle it that counts. The director is the captain of the ship so you must always have a solution.

I once had an actress in full monster makeup show up drunk just before the scene. The scene involved a complicated ritual, which after I blocked it with her, I could tell it wasn't going to happen. I realized that all she could do is swing her arms and go crazy in a drunken rage, so I decided to make it a fight scene instead. After talking privately with the sober actors, I called action and let them duke it out for real. I shot it. We wrapped on time. No one got hurt. The actress had a bad hangover and still doesn't remember shooting that segment. What is on the page doesn't always end up on screen.

DISCOVERY: Are you surprised at how little it takes to scare us, budget-wise?

DRAVEN: I'm not surprised at all. You can scare people with no money at all or with the biggest Hollywood budget you can find. If the story is great and the characters are compelling, the scares oftentimes invent themselves in the moment. I've found the best scares were by accident on set. I remember on one of my films, I didn't tell the lead actress the monster would jump out with the axe during the take, so she did the scene as usual then he broke though the door and chased her off the set. BEST SCARE EVER. She claims to have peed her pants after and then every scene with the monster from that point forward she was genuinely scared because she never knew when I might surprise her like that again. So each creepy set and dark corner became a possible scare for her and it translated on film very well.

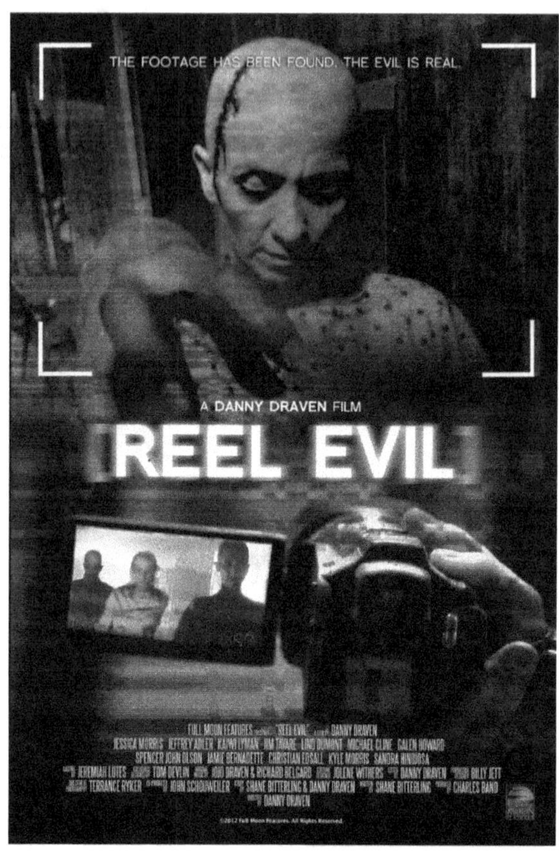

Danny Draven's found-footage indie REEL EVIL (2013) from Full Moon Features. Produced by Charles Band.

DISCOVERY: It's almost like horror is the purest form of cinema, in a way: Most films don't rely on star names, they rely on creativity, cinematography… Would you agree?

DRAVEN: There are a lot of films in all genes that don't rely on stars. What makes it work is the storytelling and characters that we root for in the film. Movies like the Evil Dead and District 9 come to mind. I think the purest form of cinema is simply a good story, well told, truthfully told, and that could be a guy in Canada making a film with just his friends or a big budget flick in LA. If you start with a "pure" script and have a strong central conflict, the rest will follow suit.

DISCOVERY: How would you describe the way you try to manipulate viewers

in a film? Do you think of it rhythmically? A five minute build up here, a slow burn scary scene there, followed by a short shock…

DRAVEN: I don't see it as manipulation but as misdirection, like a magic trick. Cinema is just one big magic trick, telling a lie to tell the truth; that is real cinema. You need to keep the audience in the seat and hopefully on the edge of it. In order to do that you need to pace the story properly and deliver the goods. In horror, the fans are rabid about the genre and are far from stupid and the conventions are already well known and established. It's very hard to give them an experience they haven't already had in another film, but if you can just do it in a new and fresh way it can be a lifesaver. Don't under estimate your audience because they're usually much smarter than you.

DISCOVERY: So many horror movies leave us with a sense that all is not well in the world — like the hand exploding from the grave in Carrie. How important is an ending in horror?

DRAVEN: The ending is crucial! Thank god monsters are hard to kill because the audience secretly wants them to strike again, just look at the Friday the 13th, Nightmare on Elm Street, and the Saw franchises. Evil can't be contained for long!

In my own projects, I always write the ending first and then work backwards. When I'm directing a film, I usually want to shoot the ending early in the shooting schedule in order to make any adjustments to other scenes leading up to the finale. All of our hard work means nothing without a satisfying ending.

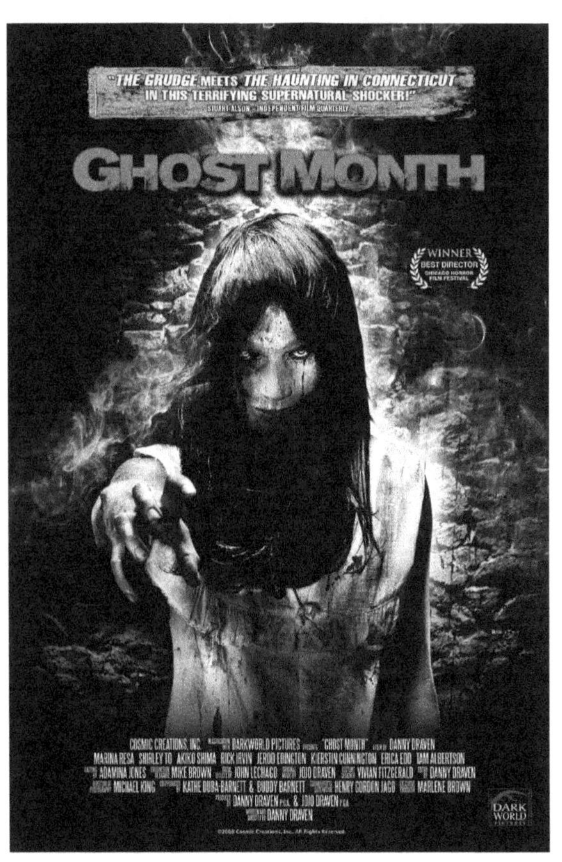

Danny Draven's supernatural indie GHOST MONTH (2009) from Lionsgate.

DISCOVERY: How do you know when you're on the right track when you're working on a film?

DRAVEN: First and foremost: Start with a great script! I'd say you know you're on the right track when an audience watches your movie and they're moved in some way and are left satisfied and hopefully with a new insight into life. In horror, maybe that could be something as simple as going

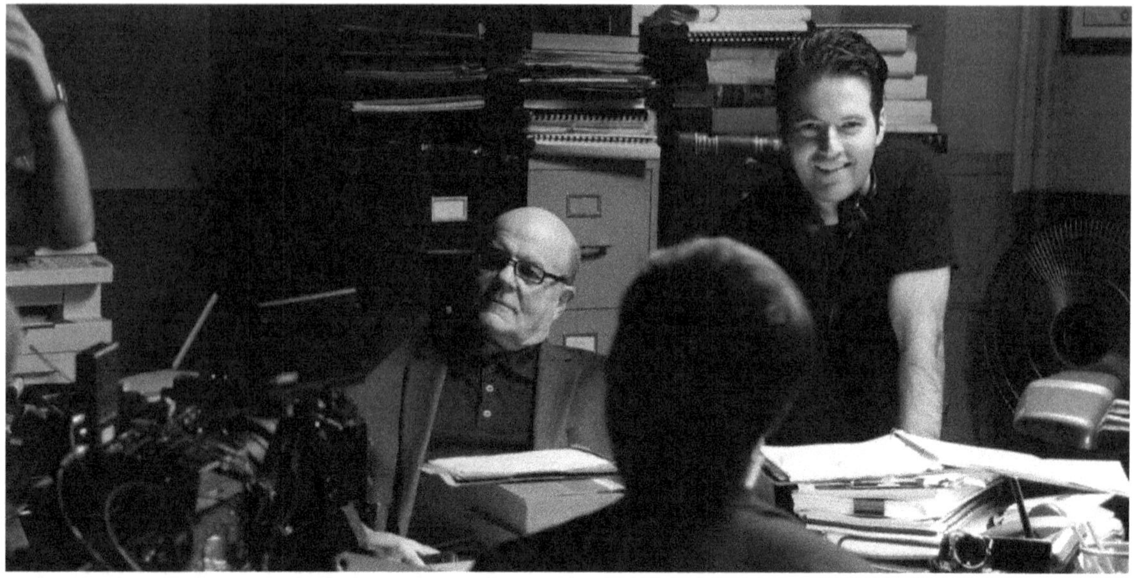

Michael Ironside (Top Gun) and director Danny Draven on the set of the horror anthology film PATIENT SEVEN (2016).

into the woods alone is not a good idea, or betraying a friend could come back to haunt you, or conjuring the devil to do your evil deeds is not worth eternal damnation!

DISCOVERY: What's your acid test for 'scary'?

DRAVEN: In 1895, the Lumiere Bros. showed a fifty-second film called Arrival of a Train to an audience. It only shows a train coming at the screen but audiences were terrified and ran from the theater hall because they thought it would run them over. Also in 1897 in Paris was The Grand Guignol theatre, which gave audiences a naturalistic and graphic on stage performance of horror entertainment and often caused patrons to faint and vomit because of the violence. It was popular, even among celebrities and royalty, until it closed in 1962. Not much has changed I think, it has just evolved with the times.

Everyone has a different tolerance level for what is scary and what isn't. Some people get scared when the music changes and they anticipate something is amiss, others laugh during a murder scene when it looks too fake, others jump at every moment they're supposed to by design and have a great time. I think the audiences in our generation are desensitized to violent images and scary moments, but if you can find a new way to scare an audience, maybe you have the next Arrival of a Train hit.

Directing horror films is a tricky business, since you're often walking on a tightrope of what is actually scary and what is laughable. For me personally, what is scary is what is behind the closed door, the unknown, my imagination creates something that is far scarier. It's deep in the subconscious, primal even. This is the most effective kind of horror.

DISCOVERY: What's the horror movie you've watched the most, and why? What lessons did it teach you about the craft?

DRAVEN: I learned the most about directing from my mentor Stuart Gordon (Re-Animator, Fortress). I produced and directed a film with him in 2002. During pre-production I went to Stuart's house with my director of photography Mac Ahlberg (Beverly Hills Cop 3, Innocent Blood) and we studied ROSEMARY'S BABY, REPULSION, and THE INNOCENTS, all favorites of mine and also landmark films that showcase masters at work. I think carefully watching and evaluating films you admire is one of the best ways to learn your craft. I spend a lot of movie time with Carpenter, Argento, Hitchcock, and Kubrick, as well as watching a lot of foreign horror films. Also Stephen King's book Danse Macabre and Clive Barker's A-Z of Horror are wonderful resources.

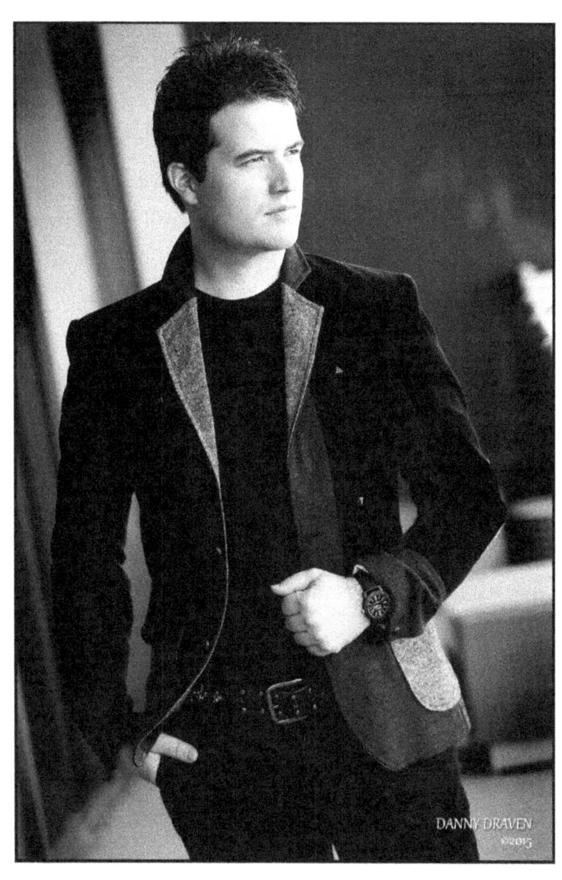

Danny Draven

DISCOVERY: You write that "if you can't find the right sound you're looking for, create it yourself [...] take a knife and stab a watermelon." What's the weirdest thing you've found yourself doing for your films?

DRAVEN: I usually do whatever it takes to get the sound desired. I had to make out with my hand once in order to replace the make-out noise needed for a kissing scene. That was awkward. I've kicked in doors, punched potato sacks, screamed bloody murder at the top of my lungs in my apartment building at the time in order to record sounds I needed. The police showed up a few times and our neighbors thought we were all crazy.

DISCOVERY: We think of people who understand comedy as "having a good sense of humour". What would you say makes for a good sense of horror?

DRAVEN: A good sense of horror could be someone who wants to experience something that is taboo. If you can open up your mind and let the filmmaker take you on a journey into the depths of hell, or into the mind of a serial killer, then I think you may have a good sense of horror. Just be open to the horror experience and don't be afraid to scream! Comedy and horror often go together. That is why you often laugh in horror movies because it relieves the tension. Everyone knows those moments when it was only a cat that jumped out, so you feel at ease again. In horror movies, laughter is the antidote to fear and when used well in the story is a great way to relax the audience until it is time to scare them again.

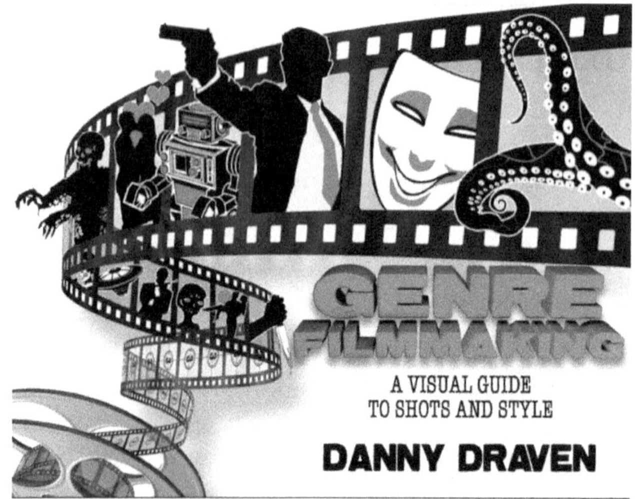

Danny Draven's 2nd book GENRE FILMMAKING: A Visual Guide to Shots and Style..

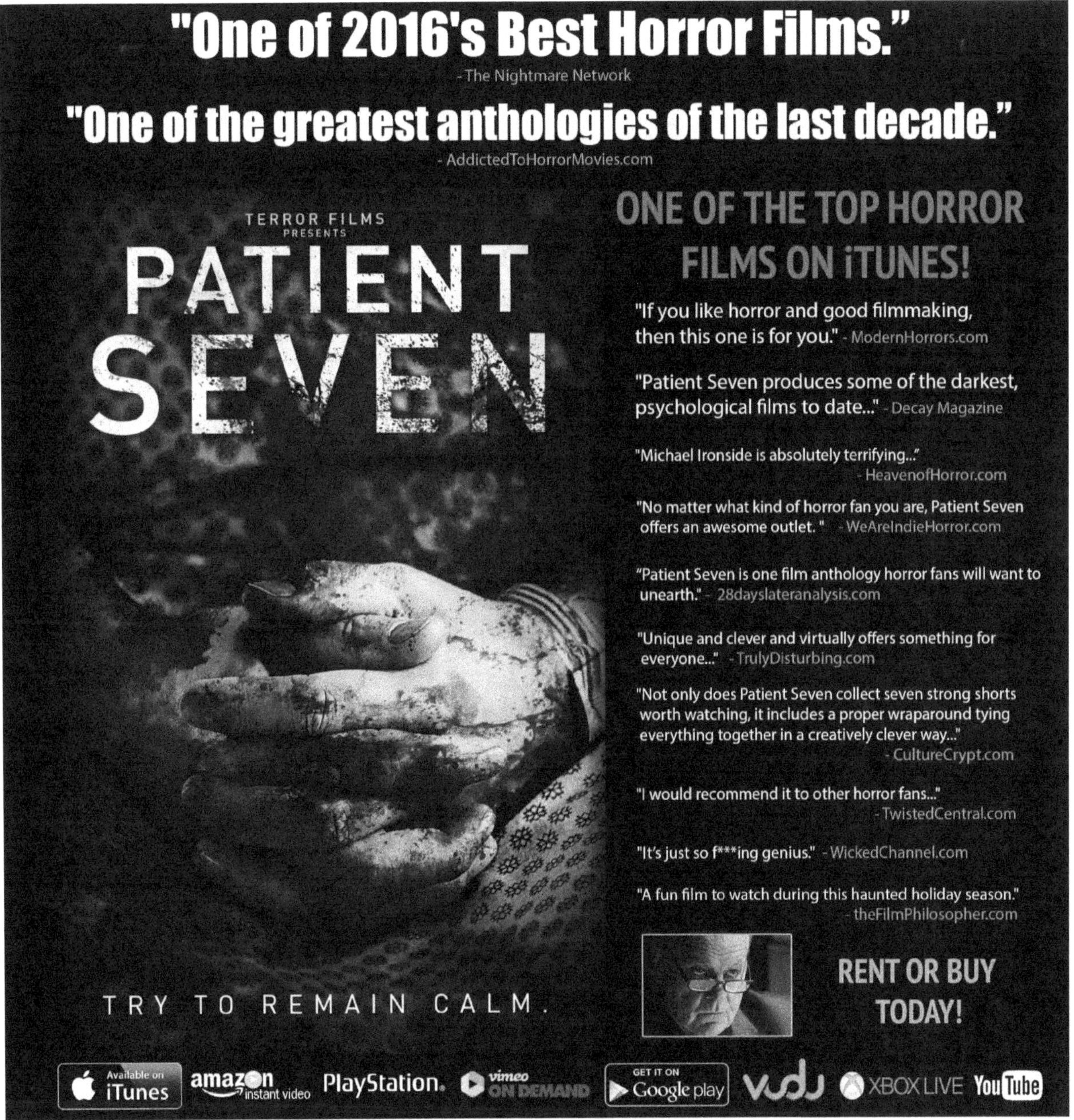
"One of 2016's Best Horror Films."
- The Nightmare Network
"One of the greatest anthologies of the last decade."
- AddictedToHorrorMovies.com
TERROR FILMS
PRESENTS
PATIENT SEVEN
ONE OF THE TOP HORROR FILMS ON iTUNES!
"If you like horror and good filmmaking, then this one is for you." - ModernHorrors.com
"Patient Seven produces some of the darkest, psychological films to date..." - Decay Magazine
"Michael Ironside is absolutely terrifying..." - HeavenofHorror.com
"No matter what kind of horror fan you are, Patient Seven offers an awesome outlet." - WeAreIndieHorror.com
"Patient Seven is one film anthology horror fans will want to unearth." - 28dayslateranalysis.com
"Unique and clever and virtually offers something for everyone..." - TrulyDisturbing.com
"Not only does Patient Seven collect seven strong shorts worth watching, it includes a proper wraparound tying everything together in a creatively clever way..." - CultureCrypt.com
"I would recommend it to other horror fans..." - TwistedCentral.com
"It's just so f***ing genius." - WickedChannel.com
"A fun film to watch during this haunted holiday season." - theFilmPhilosopher.com
TRY TO REMAIN CALM.
RENT OR BUY TODAY!
Available on iTunes
amazon instant video
PlayStation.
vimeo ON DEMAND
GET IT ON Google play
vudu
XBOX LIVE
YouTube

www.ingramcontent.com/pod-product-compliance
Lightning Source LLC
LaVergne TN
LVHW061221100826
845148LV00004B/818

* 9 7 8 0 6 9 2 8 6 9 5 1 2 *